Oscar's Favorite Actors

ALSO BY ROGER LESLIE

*Film Stars and Their Awards:
Who Won What for Movies,
Theater and Television* (McFarland, 2008)

Oscar's Favorite Actors

*The Winningest Stars
(and More Who Should Be)*

ROGER LESLIE

McFarland & Company, Inc., Publishers
Jefferson, North Carolina

ISBN (print) 978-1-4766-6956-4
ISBN (ebook) 978-1-4766-2842-4

LIBRARY OF CONGRESS CATALOGUING DATA ARE AVAILABLE

BRITISH LIBRARY CATALOGUING DATA ARE AVAILABLE

© 2017 Roger Leslie. All rights reserved

No part of this book may be reproduced or transmitted in any form or by any means, electronic or mechanical, including photocopying or recording, or by any information storage and retrieval system, without permission in writing from the publisher.

On the cover: Shelley Winters in *The Poseiden Adventure*, 1972 (Twentieth Century Fox Film Corp./Photofest); Denzel Washington in *Training Day*, 2001 (Warner Bros./Photofest)

Printed in the United States of America

*McFarland & Company, Inc., Publishers
Box 611, Jefferson, North Carolina 28640
www.mcfarlandpub.com*

Once again to Jerry,
because you "stand next to me"

Table of Contents

Preface   1

Part I. The Countdown   5

Part II. The Runners-Up: Actors Who Didn't Make the Countdown   183

1. So Close and Yet So Far   183
    Actors One Nomination from the Countdown   183
    Most Nominated Non-Winners   208

2. Legends and Trailblazers   221
    Those Who Won an Oscar   221
    Those Who Were Nominated for an Oscar   240
    Those Who Were Overlooked   251

3. Double Threat: Filmmaker-Actors   257
    Filmmakers Who Won Acting Oscars   257
    Oscar-Winning Filmmakers Nominated for Acting Oscars   262
    Non–Oscar-Winning Filmmakers Nominated for Acting Oscars   274

4. Special Acclaim   278
    Multiple Wins in a Single Category   278
    Multiple Nominations in a Single Category   279
    Record-Setting Honorary Winners   281
    Landmark Single-Year Honors   283

Countdown List   287

Bibliography   289

Index   291

Preface

The year I fell in love with movies, I also discovered award shows. Viewing movies brought one kind of excitement. Watching some of my favorites get honored at award celebrations extended my enthusiasm and added new vitality to my passion for film.

I watched my first Academy Award telecast in 1973. Angela Lansbury opened the show by singing "Make a Little Magic" and dancing across Oscar's dais, which was decorated to resemble a soundstage. During award presentations, I thrilled at hearing the theme songs of great movies boom each time they won. I was surprised to see non-movie stars like Sonny and Cher present. I wondered how *Cabaret*'s streamers hanging down over the Kit Kat Klub stage could win Best Art Direction over the innovative upside down ship in *The Poseidon Adventure*. Well past the second hour, I started counting how much sleep I would miss before getting up for school the next morning. Then I was re-engaged and as flummoxed as Roger Moore and Liv Ullmann when a young woman in Native-American dress recited with deadpan delivery a prepared rejection of Marlon Brando's Best Actor Oscar for *The Godfather* over boos echoing through the Dorothy Chandler Pavilion. The Academy Awards had all the surprises and drama of many of the most powerful movies I'd hoped would win Oscars that night.

Subsequently buying my first movie reference book, *The Academy Awards: A Pictorial History* by Paul Michael, added to the magic and mystique of the Oscars. It led to a new passion for collecting movie reference books that I reread so often I began committing facts to memory. Hungry for more knowledge, I started memorizing volumes of movie facts, beginning with every Oscar winner for Best Picture and each acting category. Over the years, I extended my body of knowledge to include every nominated performance, as well as winners in categories from Best Director to Best Song. After the first movie reference book I wrote, *Film Stars and Their Awards* was published in 2008, I became in demand as a keynote speaker relating any topic (hospital volunteers, the oil industry, garden clubs) to Oscar-nominated performances.

All those years of driving my parents to distraction with my non-stop chatter about the Academy Awards had turned into a lucrative tangent of my writing career.

While into the fourth year of researching a massive reference book about actors and the Academy Awards, I dreamed the idea for this book. Elated, I awoke in the night and composed the framework for the entire countdown before returning to bed. A year later, I have completed the final draft with the countdown supported by related sections that I hope will help readers recognize how many great and beloved actors have either been overlooked by the Academy, or earned comparatively less acknowledgment than the most honored countdown champions.

To make the countdown, actors had to meet minimal criteria: they had to win at least one Academy Award for acting and, if they won only one acting Oscar, had to have been nominated for acting at least three other times. Actors who won two or more acting Oscars did not need four nominations to make the countdown.

Initially I experimented with creating a point system to rank each actor, but discovered that that approach never proved entirely fair. For example, should a competitive award count more or less than a lifetime achievement award for acting? Should an actor who received one Oscar as a lead actor and one as a supporting actor rank higher than an actor who won two supporting Oscars that set a record only duplicated once in the entire history of the awards? How much should non-acting awards count compared to acting awards? Would winning Best Director deserve more, less, or the same value as an acting win, especially in a supporting category? Such quandaries demanded I use some subjectivity in ranking the actors.

In general, I considered several factors:

- How many Oscar wins and nominations did the actor receive?
- What Academy record(s) did the actor set?
- How close together or far apart were the actor's nominations and wins?
- How should non-acting competitive and honorary achievements factor into the ranking?
- Did some factor(s) related to the nominations or wins impact Academy history?

Being faithful to the criteria resulted in some surprising omissions. For example, twice-honored Warren Beatty has been nominated for fourteen Academy Awards, including four as Best Actor. However, neither of his wins related to his acting. He won Best Director in 1981 for *Reds* and received the 1999 Irving G. Thalberg Memorial Award, which recognized his work as a producer. Therefore, although he has far more nominations than most actors on the countdown, he did not rank because neither of his wins honored his acting. Similarly, Woody Allen has been nominated for the Oscar 24 times, including once for Best Actor (*Annie Hall*, 1977). Even though he has won four Academy Awards, every win was for directing or writing, never acting. He didn't make the countdown either.

Rosalind Russell earned four Oscar nominations, all for acting, and she did win an Oscar. Look at her list of accomplishments, and it would seem she met the criteria: four acting nominations and an Oscar win. However, that win brought Russell her only golden statuette as recipient of the Jean Hersholt Humanitarian Award for her work with the infirm, not for her acting. Thus, she too failed to make the countdown.

Because so many great actors missed the countdown, it seemed only fair to recognize them, too. Therefore, this book is divided into two parts, one of which is the countdown. The other pays tribute to the runners-up: those stars who almost made the countdown; the universally recognizable Hollywood legends and trailblazers; the doubly talented filmmaker-actors; and those whose noteworthy achievements were unique and often record-setting.

In every section of this book, actors' names are followed by their list of Oscar nominations. Every nomination in **bold print** indicates an Academy Award win. For nearly all of those victorious competitions, the winner received the familiar 13.5 inch tall solid bronze, gold-plated statuette of a naked knight holding a sword and standing on a reel of film. Officially called the Academy Award of Merit, it has been known familiarly as Oscar since 1933.

Lifetime Achievement and Jean Hersholt Humanitarian honorees receive the same statuette as competitive Academy Award winners. From 1936, when the Academy first added supporting acting categories, until 1942, Best Supporting Actor and Actress winners received plaques instead of statuettes. Intermittently between 1934 and 1960, the Academy recognized 12 child actors with a Special Honorary Academy Award known as the Juvenile Oscar. That Academy Award statuette, a scaled-down version of Oscar, stands seven inches tall. The Irving G. Thalberg Memorial Award, a rare honor given to creative producers, is a solid bronze bust of Thalberg, a film supervisor at MGM who died in 1936 at age 37. The design of that bust has gone through three transformations, with the current design used since 1966. The Academy has also created some original plaques and citations to honor their ceremonies' most frequent host, Bob Hope.

Since the Oscar statuette was first created for the 1927–1928 winners, its design has stayed the same. Only the statuette's base size has changed over the years, with the current size remaining constant since 1945.

Preface

I love movies and I love actors. My goal in writing this book was to honor as many stars, past and present, as possible. Therefore, I hope that, even if your favorite actors don't appear on the countdown, I have acknowledged them somewhere in the book with their own tribute or a mention of at least one of their performances in an Oscar-honored movie.

Part I. The Countdown

Bold entries indicate awards won, regular entries indicate nominations.

108. *Angela Lansbury*

1944 Best Supporting Actress as chambermaid Nancy Oliver in *Gaslight*
1945 Best Supporting Actress as actress Sibyl Vane in *The Picture of Dorian Gray*
1962 Best Supporting Actress as Raymond's mother in *The Manchurian Candidate*
2013 Honorary lifetime achievement award to "an entertainment icon who has created some of cinema's most memorable characters, inspiring generations of actors"

Angela Lansbury was a young British import who made it big in Hollywood during the same decade as such continental cohorts as Elizabeth Taylor and Roddy McDowall, and all three were among the few child actors of any era to become legendary adult stars. Lansbury was still a teen when she caught Oscar's attention as the saucy maid suspicious of Charles Boyer's malevolence toward young bride Ingrid Bergman in *Gaslight*. Lansbury claimed that being treated with such respect by director George Cukor, the cast and crew gave her the confidence to delve into her character and know that acting was a profession she could continue for a lifetime. That insight has helped her career thrive for seven decades. Lansbury followed her 1944 *Gaslight* performance as a very different, fresh-faced innocent unaware of the evil lurking beneath the un-altering physical perfection of Dorian Gray. Her rendition of "Goodbye Little Yellow Bird" captured her character's purity of spirit, and brought her first of six Golden Globes and a second Oscar nomination. That same year Lansbury also played Elizabeth Taylor's sister in *National Velvet*. She physically towered over the violet-eyed star and lost the 1945 Best Supporting Actress race to Anne Revere, who played their mother in the racehorse classic. Although she was only three years older than he, Lansbury played the political conspirator willing to sacrifice son Laurence Harvey's psyche, and life, in John Frankenheimer's 1962 classic Cold War thriller *The Manchurian Candidate*. The depth of psychological torture she is willing to inflict on her own child made Lansbury's character the worst Oscar-nominated mother to date, a dubious achievement only surpassed by Shelley Winters in *A Patch of Blue* and Mo'Nique in *Precious*. Lansbury's masterful characterization made Raymond's mother an indelible figure in film history. Although considered a favorite to take the Best Supporting Actress Academy Award after winning the Golden Globe, she lost Oscar to *The Miracle Worker*'s Patty Duke, who, like Lansbury in *Gaslight*, was just a teen. Oscar has overlooked many of Lansbury's great performances in Academy Award-winning movies, most notably as the lead in *Bedknobs and Broomsticks* (1971), which Disney hoped would repeat the live action/animated magic of *Mary Poppins*, and in a standout supporting role as flamboyant Salome Otterbourne in the Agatha Christie whodunit *Death on the Nile* (1978). Despite these oversights, Oscar has wooed Lansbury as a presenter and performer many times. Most notably she opened the 1972 telecast with a musical tribute to cinema, and in 1991 she introduced Best Song nominees from *Beauty and the Beast*, including the Oscar-winning title tune which she immortalized in the animated classic through her sweet interpretation as Mrs. Potts.

107. Kirk Douglas

1949 Best Actor as boxer Midge Kelly in *Champion*
1952 Best Actor as movie producer Jonathan Shields in *The Bad and the Beautiful*
1956 Best Actor as painter Vincent Van Gogh in *Lust for Life*
1995 Honorary lifetime achievement award "for fifty years as a creative and moral force in the motion picture community"

Chiseled features, a mischievous gleam and a trademark grunting line delivery distinguished Douglas from his contemporaries and made him the master of playing tough, often suave cads. He catapulted to fame as brutal boxer Midge Kelly in *Champion*. The Academy took note and, for the first time, brought Douglas into the inner circle of Oscar nominees. That same year he was in an even bigger Oscar contender, *A Letter to Three Wives*, which was up for Best Picture and won Best Director and Best Screenplay. Douglas worked steadily thereafter, and twice more captured the Academy's attention and enough votes from his contemporaries to compete for Best Actor. In 1951, he had the lead in William Wyler's *Detective Story*, but at Oscar time, only Eleanor Parker and Lee Grant were nominated for the film.

Douglas earned his second nomination the following year as the ultimate corrupt moviemaker in *The Bad and the Beautiful*. In flashback, Lana Turner, Dick Powell, and Barry Sullivan recount the cruel, sometimes criminal acts that made them loathe Douglas' character, movie producer Jonathan Shields. Douglas managed to make his character despicably fascinating, and he went into the 1952 Academy Awards with a chance to be the first male actor to win an Oscar portraying someone who wins an Academy Award in the course of his film. Gary Cooper, who earned the Golden Globe for *High Noon* that year, also won Oscar. Douglas had his role of a lifetime as anguished painter Vincent Van Gogh in Vincente Minnelli's adaptation of Irving Stone's biographical novel *Lust for Life*. It was a great year for Best Actor, with Douglas competing against Rock Hudson and James Dean in *Giant*, Laurence Olivier as *Richard III*, and that year's victor, Yul Brynner in *The King and I*. Douglas' filmography is highlighted by many Oscar-favored movies. He duped a nation as a hack reporter in *Ace in the Hole* (1951), hunted under *The Big Sky* with Best Supporting Actor nominee Arthur Hunnicutt, muscled into audiences' favor in *The Vikings* (1958) and as *Spartacus* (1960), and, along with Best Supporting Actress nominee Brenda Vaccaro, brought prestige to *Jacqueline Susann's Once is Not Enough* in 1975. Despite never taking home a competitive Oscar, Douglas made many guest appearances on the Academy's stage. Among his best loved was a comic duet with Burt Lancaster singing, "It's Great Not to Be Nominated" at the 1957 awards. Even more powerful was his appearance on Oscar's stage in January 1996. Following a near-fatal stroke, Douglas jauntily stepped out to a rousing standing ovation and, with only a pronounced slur attesting to his life-and-death struggle, accepted his lifetime achievement award. The honorary Oscar advanced his status among other contemporaries, and made him one of the Academy's favored stars.

As movie producer Jonathan Shields in *The Bad and the Beautiful* (1952), Kirk Douglas became one of the first stars to earn an Oscar nomination playing an Oscar winner.

106. Ronald Colman

1929/30 Best Actor as ex-British Army officer Hugh "Bulldog" Drummond in *Bulldog Drummond*
1929/30 Best Actor as prisoner Michel in *Condemned*
1942 Best Actor as British Officer Charles Ranier in *Random Harvest*
1947 Best Actor as actor Anthony John in *A Double Life*

Colman's dashing demeanor and debonair delivery of lines as simple as "Oh, my darling" made him the quintessential smooth British matinee idol of his era. His silent hits included *Stella Dallas*, *The Dark Angel*, and *Beau Geste*, all of which were remade as talkies without him, but for which Oscar nominated at least one cast member. In his first two sound films, Colman played both sides of the law. As bored aristocrat *Bulldog Drummond*, he helped a woman take on a corrupt hospital. *Condemned* to Devil's Island in his other movie, he risked the warden's ire by pursuing a romance with the man's daughter. Both performances brought Colman nominations during the Academy's 1929/30 season, but he lost to George Arliss as *Disraeli*. Colman was a steady and stirring presence in Oscar movies throughout the rest of the decade. He had the title role as medical hero *Arrowsmith*, which competed for four Oscars, including Best Picture. He played clever defense attorney Sydney Carton north of the English Channel in the 1935 adaptation of Dickens' *A Tale of Two Cities* (1935). Two years later, he had the lead in Frank Capra's enchanting film version of James Hilton's *Lost Horizon* (1937), which was up for multiple Oscars, including Best Picture, and won two technical awards. Also in the running for Academy Awards that year was *The Prisoner of Zenda*, in which Colman had dual roles as an English Major and a king. In 1938 Colman reunited with his *A Tale of Two Cities* co-star, Basil Rathbone for the buoyant, swashbuckling *If I Were King*, but only Rathbone got the Oscar nod. Colman was a double Oscar presence in 1942, playing down his good looks and suave appeal so that Cary Grant could be the more obvious object of Jean Arthur's affections in the Best Picture-nominated *The Talk of the Town*. Also in the running for the year's top prize was *Random Harvest*, a glittering, fairy tale romance that brought Colman back into the Best Actor fold. He returned and triumphed in the category in 1947's *A Double Life* for his harrowing portrayal of a tragic actor whose stage characterization overpowers his personality with murderous results. Arguably the most demanding role of his career, portraying *Othello*-absorbed Anthony John brought Colman the Oscar over strong competitors John Garfield in *Body and Soul*, Gregory Peck in *Gentleman's Agreement*, William Powell in *Life with Father*, and Michael Redgrave in *Mourning Becomes Electra*. Following his Oscar win, Colman made only three more feature films, one of which was a cameo as a railway official in 1956's Best Picture *Around the World in 80 Days*.

105. *Maureen Stapleton*

- 1958 Best Supporting Actress as wife Fay Doyle in *Lonelyhearts*
- 1970 Best Supporting Actress as waitress/wife Inez Guerrero in *Airport*
- 1978 Best Supporting Actress as widow Pearl in *Interiors*
- **1981 Best Supporting Actress as anarchist/writer Emma Goldman in *Reds***

Already a Tony Award-winning actress before she made her first movie, Stapleton found immediate acceptance from the Academy with a nomination for her screen debut in *Lonelyhearts*. A complex character study, the Vincent J. Donehue drama was filled with surprising characters, and Stapleton capitalized on her Actors Studio training to reveal multiple dimensions to her desperate loneliness in a handful of key scenes that are the most memorable in the film. Equally adept at playing light and dark, Stapleton was a fluffy pillow suffocating son Dick Van Dyke in the twice nominated *Bye Bye Birdie* in 1963. Stapleton so frequently excelled on stage that she only occasionally accepted film work. Her instincts were good when she agreed to join the all-star cast of *Airport*, a huge box office smash in 1970.

A *Grand Hotel* of intersecting personalities around one snowbound evening at a bustling Chicago airport, the movie gave several strong character actors a chance to shine. In the air, it was Helen Hayes as an impish stowaway. On the ground, Stapleton played the long-suffering wife of distraught Van Heflin, intent on ending his life with a concealed bomb he carries on board a Boeing 707 airliner. Stapleton's Inez Guerrero is strong and frail, a solid foundation of a relationship being pummeled by her husband's mental illness. Stapleton's final scenes are among the most moving in film history, and she and Hayes both earned well-deserved Best Supporting Actress nominations. Stapleton tied with Karen Black of *Five Easy Pieces* to win the Best Supporting Actress Golden Globe, but Hayes took the category on Oscar night. The next year Stapleton was up for another Golden Globe for *Plaza Suite*, a film that the Academy ignored. Later that decade, she worked with Woody Allen to play the love interest of newly separated E. G. Marshall. The scene where Stapleton attempts to dance at a party amid Marshall and his depressive family members serves as the moral touchstone of the film, the moment that reveals just how shrouded in darkness are those *Interiors*. Stapleton was victorious with both the New York and LA Film Critics in 1978, but she lost her third Oscar competition to the biting comic performance of Maggie Smith in *California Suite*. But in 1981, the Best Supporting Actress award had Stapleton's

10 Part I. The Countdown

Amid a gathering crowd of strangers, Inez Guerrero (Maureen Stapleton) faced the fallout of her husband's deadly decision in *Airport* (1970).

name etched into it from the beginning of the Oscar season. As revolutionary author Emma Goldman, Stapleton was able to reveal her astounding range as an actress. She won more awards for that film performance than any other, and on her last time competing for Oscar, she took him home, too.

104. Lee Grant

    1951 Best Supporting Actress as A Shoplifter in *Detective Story*
    1970 Best Supporting Actress as wealthy mother Mrs. Enders in *The Landlord*
    1975 Best Supporting Actress as wife/mistress Felicia Karpf in *Shampoo*
    1976 Best Supporting Actress as wife/mother Lili Rosen in *Voyage of the Damned*

    Grant is an ideal supporting player who can take very little time on screen to create indelible characterizations. She originated the role of the shoplifter languishing at New York City's 21st police precinct in the stage version of *Detective Story*. For the film adaption she made her screen debut, won Best Actress at the Cannes Film Festival, and earned her first Oscar nomination. Though the film was a strong contender at the 1951 Academy Awards, *Detective Story* couldn't overcome the bulldozing power of *A Streetcar Named Desire*, which rode off with three of the four acting victories, including Kim Hunter as Best Supporting Actress. Getting blacklisted soon after curtailed Grant's chances to make movies for many years, but in the 1960s Grant's performances in works by Jean Genet earned her an Obie for *The Maids* and brought her back into Academy range with a role in the Oscar-nominated film *The Balcony*. Grant reconnected with Oscar in a big way as the murder victim's widow demanding that Sidney Poitier stay on the case in 1967's Best Picture *In the Heat of the Night*. Grant and Poitier gave Oscar-worthy performances, but when the 1967 nominations were announced, only Rod Steiger, who went all the way to a Best Actor victory, was nominated from *In the Heat of the Night*'s cast. The '70s was Grant's Oscar decade, beginning with *The Landlord* in which she played a rich and comically overbearing mother who tries to impose not-so-funny racist limitations on her grown son's relationships. In 1975, Grant and the other Best Supporting Actress nominees went into the Oscars with eyes on Ronee Blakley and Lily Tomlin from *Nashville* as potential winners. But it was Grant, as an unfaithful wife and one of Warren Beatty's many stylist clients and lovers in *Shampoo* that made her the victor. Often a win can quell Oscar's enthusiasm for future performances, but Grant was nominated again in the same category the following year for *Voyage of the Damned*. Among one of the largest all-star casts of that era, Grant's performance was singled out for the film's only Oscar nod. As a wife, mother, and victim of anti–Semitism focused on her family's traumatic reaction to their plight, Grant wrung from audiences compassion for the personal, interpersonal, and global impact of being stranded on a ship of Jews that no country would let dock. Ten years after her last acting nomination, Grant directed the documentary feature *Down and Out in America*, which won the Oscar for its producers, Milton Justice and Grant's husband, Joseph Feury.

103. *Ethel Barrymore*

- **1944 Best Supporting Actress** as mother Ma Mott in *None But the Lonely Heart*
- 1946 Best Supporting Actress as widowed invalid Mrs. Warren in *The Spiral Staircase*
- 1947 Best Supporting Actress as judge's wife Lady Sophie Horfield in *The Paradine Case*
- 1949 Best Supporting Actress as sickly neighbor Miss Em in *Pinky*

When theatre grand dame Ethel Barrymore won Best Supporting Actress in 1944, she and her brother Lionel, Best Actor in 1930/31 for *A Free Soul*, became the first siblings to both earn acting Academy Awards. Ethel and her brothers, Lionel and John, were the core of the Barrymore acting dynasty that included their parents, Maurice Barrymore and Giorgiana Drew, and has trickled down generations to include Ethel's grandniece, popular actress Drew Barrymore who first gained fame in the Oscar-winning *E.T. The Extra-terrestrial* in 1982. On stage, Ethel excelled in every type of role, and repeated the success in movies, usually as a supporting player. She had key roles in two silent films that shared the title of Best Actress Oscar competing talkies. In 1919 she was *The Divorcee*, but in a different plot than the one that won Norma Shearer Best Actress in 1929/30. In a 1926 short, Barrymore played Camille, a role that Greta Garbo reprised to an Oscar nomination in a lavish 1937 full-length production. The 1940s was Barrymore's movie heyday, as she earned more supporting acting nominations than anyone else that decade. Although she claimed to have thought little of her performance as Cary Grant's dying mother in *None But the Lonely Heart*, she impressed the Academy, who bestowed upon her a Best Supporting Actress Oscar in her first competition. She was up again in 1946 in a showier role as a gruff, bedridden invalid with a murderer slinking up *The Spiral Staircase* in pursuit of her mute caregiver, Dorothy Maguire. The hit thriller, directed by Robert Siodmak, was as suspenseful as any film by Hitchcock, who directed Barrymore to her next nomination for *The Paradine Case*. As testimony to her powerful presence, Barrymore had sparse screen time in a role that required little emoting, but the Academy loved her and gave her the film's only nomination. That same year, Barrymore also had the pivotal role of a political power broker who inspired maid Loretta Young to pursue a congressional seat in *The Farmer's Daughter*. Barrymore ended the decade competing once more for Best Supporting Actress against *Pinky* co-star Ethel Waters. Elia Kazan's social conscious piece on racism had Barrymore and Waters as neighbors whose enmeshed lives turned the tide of a local conflict that led Pinky (Jeanne Crain) to stark realizations about her worth and heritage. Once again playing a tough woman felled by poor health, Barrymore embodied the strength and determination of older women in 1940s cinema. Barrymore also broke gender barriers for Oscar when she became the first female to present Best Picture, giving *Hamlet* the top prize of 1948. Besides Agnes Moorehead, who remained Oscarless, Barrymore, Lee Grant, and Maureen Stapleton are the only actors with four Academy Award nominations exclusively in the Best Supporting Actress category. Grant won in her third competition, Stapleton in her last. Only Barrymore earned her win the first time she was recognized by the Academy.

102. Tommy Lee Jones

1991 Best Supporting Actor as accused conspirator Clay Shaw in *JFK*
1993 Best Supporting Actor as deputy Samuel Gerard in *The Fugitive*
2007 Best Actor as veteran Hank Deerfield in *In the Valley of Elah*
2012 Best Supporting Actor as congressman Thaddeus Stevens in *Lincoln*

Gruff, pockmarked and baggy-eyed, Tommy Lee Jones can wrest multiple emotions from a single line, and has impressed the Academy with roles that range from creepy to exalting. Jones started in movies as an Oscar A-lister, making his film debut as Ryan O'Neal's college buddy, Hank Simpson in *Love Story*, which garnered seven nominations, including Best Picture, and a single win. He earned his first Golden Globe nomination as Doolittle Lynn in *Coal Miner's Daughter*, but Sissy Spacek's Oscar-winning performance so dazzled the Academy that she was the only cast member they nominated. In 1991 Jones achieved the same feat as Clay Shaw in *JFK*. He stood out among an extensive all-star cast by accentuating the dark underpinnings of Shaw's gay alter ego, Clay Bertrand. Jones was considered a likely winner for that year's Oscar, but Academy sentiment favored established character actor Jack Palance in *City Slickers*. Jones returned to Oscar's inner circle an almost certain Best Supporting Actor winner as the U.S. Marshall in relentless pursuit of *The Fugitive*, Harrison Ford. By most accounts, Jones' toughest competition was Ralph Fiennes as homicidal S.S. commandant Amon Goeth in that year's big winner, *Schindler's List*. Jones bit into his savory role with gusto, added heft to the already exciting premise, and vaulted his way to Best Supporting Actor victory. The following year Jones sparred with two Best Actress contenders. He played opportunistic federal prosecutor "Reverend" Roy Foltrigg fighting a high-profile case against Susan Sarandon in *The Client*, and the loving but frustrated husband of mentally unbalanced Best Actress winner Jessica Lange in *Blue Sky*. 2007 was a milestone year for Jones. Not only did he star in the year's Best Picture, *No Country for Old Men*, but he also moved up the ranks to lead actor nominee as the quietly seething father and former MPO unraveling the disquieting details of his soldier son's disappearance in *In the Valley of Elah*. Jones' performance brought the generally well-reviewed movie its only Oscar nomination. After winning the 2012 SAG Award for Best Supporting Actor, Jones once again led the pack heading into Oscar's showdown with his inspiring interpretation of Thaddeus Stevens, the impassioned Radical Republican congressman from Pennsylvania instrumental in helping *Lincoln* secure freedom for African Americans. His category was the closest of that year, as five former winners seemed almost equally likely to take home their second or (in the case of *Silver Linings Playbook*'s Robert De Niro) third statuette. Though Jones lost to *Django Unchained*'s Christoph

Waltz, both his and Daniel Day-Lewis's historic and historical portrayals seem destined to remain classics.

101. Alan Arkin

    1966 Best Actor as Russian lieutenant Yuri Rozanov in *The Russians Are Coming! The Russians Are Coming!*
    1968 Best Actor as deaf-mute confidant Singer in *The Heart Is a Lonely Hunter*
    2006 Best Supporting Actor as veteran Grandpa in *Little Miss Sunshine*
    2012 Best Supporting Actor as movie producer Lester Siegel in *Argo*

With prodigious talent and an uncanny flair for blending comedy and poignancy, sometimes in the delivery of a single line of dialog, Arkin wowed the Hollywood Foreign Press and the Academy in his debut film, *The Russians Are Coming! The Russians Are Coming!*. As a zampolit Lieutenant from a Russian submarine grounded off the coast of New England, Arkin was alternately menacing and hilarious, wringing so many laughs he won the Best Actor, Musical or Comedy Golden Globe and helped the groundbreaking Cold War comedy warrant four Oscar nominations, including Best Actor for him and Best Picture for the movie. The staggering range of his talent shone through the following year when he portrayed one of movie history's most menacing villains. As Roat in *Wait until Dark*, he stalked a blind innocent (Best Actress nominee Audrey Hepburn) to retrieve a doll laced with heroin that he thinks she's hiding. His range stretched in yet another direction the following year with his tender portrayal of the compassionate mute who becomes confidant to many townspeople in the moving adaptation of Carson McCullers' *The Heart Is a Lonely Hunter*. His second Best Actor nomination kept him a front runner amid a stellar group of competitors that included Alan Bates in *The Fixer*, Ron Moody in *Oliver!*, favored candidate Peter O'Toole in *The Lion in Winter*, and the year's dark horse winner, Cliff Robertson in *Charly*. Despite steady work, Arkin did not return to Oscar-nominated films until the 1990s with roles in *Edward Scissorhands* and *Glengarry Glen Ross*. Both of those performances had him competing for awards other than Oscar. Although *Thirteen Conversations about One Thing* brought him several awards, the film appeared nowhere on the 2001 Academy Awards ballot. Five years later, Arkin garnered his third Oscar nomination, this time as a supporting player. Though his performance as a cursing grandfather with a heroin addiction was short, his piquant yet compassionate advice to his granddaughter inspired her irreverent *Little Miss Sunshine* pageant routine in the movie's climax, keeping his character a focal point even after his screen time ended. With so small a role, Arkin did not enter the 2006 ceremony as a sure winner: eyes instead were on Eddie Murphy in *Dreamgirls* and Jackie Earle Haley in *Little Children*. But Arkin, beloved by generations of his contemporaries, proved a popular victor. In 2012, Best Picture winner *Argo* showcased many fine performances, but only Arkin was singled out for a nomination. It was Arkin whose "*Argo* f*** yourself" line became an instant catchphrase. In one of the only races in Oscar history where every nominee was a former winner, Arkin, like Tommy Lee Jones, Robert De Niro, and Philip Seymour Hoffman, lost to Christoph Waltz in *Django Unchained*. Arkin's four nominations span nearly half a century, making him a perennial favorite who earned his slot in the Oscar countdown.

100. Walter Huston

1936 Best Actor as motor company executive Sam Dodsworth in *Dodsworth*
1941 Best Actor as the devil, Mr. Scratch in *The Devil and Daniel Webster* (AKA *All That Money Can Buy*)
1942 Best Supporting Actor as father Jerry Cohan in *Yankee Doodle Dandy*
1948 Best Supporting Actor as prospector Howard in *The Treasure of the Sierra Madre*

Walter Huston is the father and first generation of an acting dynasty that has more total award nominations and wins than the Barrymores, the Redgraves, or the Fondas. One of the few actors of his generation to alternate between supporting character and lead actor roles, Huston played *Abraham Lincoln* long before Henry Fonda in *Young Mr. Lincoln,* Raymond Massey in *Abe Lincoln in Illinois,* and Daniel Day-Lewis in *Lincoln*. Huston first impressed his Academy cohorts by reprising his stage success as Sam Dodsworth, the title character introduced in Sinclair Lewis' 1934 novel. Although some of today's movie historians consider his acting style in the movie far ahead of its time, the Academy clearly saw its greatness and filed Huston among its five Best Actor performances of 1936. As Dodsworth, the self-made automobile magnate, Huston won the New York Film Critics Circle's Best Actor laurels, but on Oscar night, he lost to Paul Muni in *The Story of Louis Pasteur*. In 1938, he played a small town preacher in *Of Human Hearts*, but it was Beulah Bondi as his wife that earned the film's only Oscar nomination. Able to conquer the most eccentric character challenges, Huston received his only other Best Actor nomination playing the devil in *All That Money Can Buy*. Originally called *The Devil and Daniel Webster* after the Stephen Vincent Benét short story on which it was based, the film was retitled so it wouldn't be confused with another Oscar contender of 1941, *The Devil and Miss Jones*. Huston played entertainer Jerry Cohan enthusiastically to earn his first Best

Supporting Actor nomination for *Yankee Doodle Dandy* in 1942, but it was James Cagney as his son George who danced away with the Academy Award for that film, in the lead actor category. Back in 1941, Walter Huston played Captain Jacobi in *The Maltese Falcon*, the first film directed by his son John to be embraced by Oscar. Seven years later, Walter and John made Oscar history. In 1948, John wrote and directed *The Treasure of the Sierra Madre*, then cast Walter as Howard, the grizzled old prospector. Accepting his Best Supporting Actor prize, Walter Huston beamed, "Many, many years ago, I brought up a boy, and I said to him, 'If you ever become a writer, try to write a good part for your old man sometime.' Well, by cracky, that's what he did." When John also won Oscars that night for his screenplay and direction, they became the first Oscar-winning father and son, and among the few family members to both win Oscars on the same night.

99. Robin Williams

 1987 Best Actor as armed forces disc jockey Adrian Cronauer in *Good Morning, Vietnam*
 1989 Best Actor as English teacher John Keating in *Dead Poets Society*
 1991 Best Actor as former college professor/mystical vagrant Parry in *The Fisher King*
 1997 Best Supporting Actor as psychologist Sean McGuire in *Good Will Hunting*

Thanks to television's *Mork and Mindy* and his raucous stand-up routines, Williams was already a superstar before entering movies. For his first leading role, Williams gamely recreated the animated energy of *Popeye*, but public and Academy reaction to the film was tepid. Two years later, Williams toned down his trademark short-circuitry with dreamlike precision as the title character in *The World According to Garp*. But TV actors and comics have an especially difficult time impressing Oscar, and at the 1982 Academy Awards, *The World According to Garp* earned only two nominations, for supporting players Glenn Close and John Lithgow. Then the electric comedian found an ideal outlet for channeling his spastic energy when Barry Levinson let him improvise many of his comic announcements as military radio DJ Adrian Cronauer in *Good Morning, Vietnam*. Many moviegoers found it exciting to see the popular standup and television icon amid the nominees, but the 1987 Best Actor race seemed preordained for Michael Douglas in *Wall Street*.

Two years later, Williams muted his frenetic sparks to offer a deep, textured performance as uniquely inspiring teacher John Keating in the hugely popular *Dead Poets Society*. Williams calibrated every note of the Oscar-winning screenplay with perfect pitch, and turned in a performance that confirmed to any doubters that he was a first-rate dramatic actor. His string of hits continued with *Awakenings*, where he played the doctor who helped bring once catatonic patients like Robert De Niro back to vibrancy. The movie competed for Best Picture, but De Niro, not Williams, earned that film's acting nod. The following year he played tragedy most convincingly in *The Fisher King* as quixotic homeless man Parry. Williams' fantasy scene set in Grand Central Station is among the most mesmerizing sequences on celluloid. In 1997, Williams was nominated for the first time in the supporting category. As Matt Damon's wise therapist forced to face some troubling inconsistencies in his own personality, Williams was a gloriously grounding force in the inspiring film. Following a tight Oscar race against early favorite Burt Reynolds in *Boogie Nights*, Williams earned the award.

As John Keating, a teacher who inspired his students to "seize the day" in *Dead Poets Society* (1989), Robin Williams impressed Academy members with his depth and range.

Overtly moved by the accolade, Williams did not sidestep into familiar frantic shtick, but offered a heartfelt acceptance speech that resonated as one of the most sincere in Oscar history. Williams shone in other Oscar winners, including *Aladdin* (1992) and *Mrs. Doubtfire* (1993), and nominees such as *The Birdcage* (1996), but his next closest chance at another Oscar nod came when he played a stoic psychopath in *One Hour Photo* (2002), a performance ranked in intensity with Gene Hackman's in *The Conversation* and Robert De Niro's in *Taxi Driver*. High and worthy praise indeed.

98. *Philip Seymour Hoffman*

2005 Best Actor as author Truman Capote in *Capote*
2007 Best Supporting Actor as CIA operative Gust Avrakotos in *Charlie Wilson's War*

2008 Best Supporting Actor as school principal Father Brendan Flynn in *Doubt*
2012 Best Supporting Actor as philosophical leader Lancaster Dodd in *The Master*

The film industry mourned the untimely death of Philip Seymour Hoffman in 2014, noting how much future greatness would not be captured on film. But just as many mourners acknowledged that Hoffman's body of work burgeoned with enough implosive, indelible performances to teach aspiring actors mastery of their craft for generations to come. Hoffman credited his movie breakthrough to *Scent of a Woman*, which was up for Best Picture of 1992 and won Al Pacino his long-awaited Best Actor prize. Two years later, Hoffman was the deputy slugged by Best Actor nominee Paul Newman in *Nobody's Fool*. Hoffman's star soared in 1996 when he played storm chaser Dustin Davis in the Oscar-nominated box office hit, *Twister* and then began his collaborations with writer/director Paul Thomas Anderson in *Hard Eight*. The two men worked together again the following year in *Boogie Nights*, in which Hoffman made shy, disheveled boom operator Scotty J. so sadly appealing that his attempt to reach out to sex idol Dirk Diggler was a poignant and shattering highlight of the film. In 1999 he played an angelic nurse in *Magnolia* and a devilish bully in *The Talented Mr. Ripley*. Though a worthy candidate for a supporting nod for either film, Hoffman instead saw Tom Cruise and Jude Law receive Best Supporting Actor nominations for the respective films. In 2005's *Capote*, Hoffman so permeated the mannerisms and psyche of the effete author that he swept every major Best Actor prize. By Oscar night, the Best Actor statuette was already primed to have his name etched onto the pedestal. Monitoring the worth of a part by its depth and challenge rather than length, Hoffman subsequently accepted an amalgam of lead and supporting roles, and earned three more Oscar nominations all in the Best Supporting Actor category. His performance as disheveled, brilliant CIA agent Gust Avrakotos gave *Charlie Wilson's War* its only Academy Award recognition. He followed that searing portrayal with an even more hauntingly enigmatic one as Father Flynn, the boys' school principal whose relationship with some students leaves everyone in *Doubt* except a driven Meryl Streep. In both years, the Best Supporting Actor race was a lock for the ultimate winners, Javier Bardem in 2007's *No Country for Old Men*, and Heath Ledger in 2008's *The Dark Knight*. Hoffman went into the 2012 competition evenly matched with the other nominees, all of whom, like Hoffman, were former winners. As psycho-dramatic bon vivant Lancaster Dodd, Hoffman preached and persuaded with the flair of a Charles Foster Kane. Larger than life on screen, Hoffman culled four Oscar nominations and one win in only seven years. Once his career built momentum, nothing but his tragic demise could stop it.

97. Frances McDormand

1988 Best Supporting Actress as wife Mrs. Pell in *Mississippi Burning*
1996 Best Actress as police chief Marge Gunderson in *Fargo*
2000 Best Supporting Actress as teacher Elaine Miller in *Almost Famous*
2005 Best Supporting Actress as miner Glory in *North Country*

McDormand's alliance with the Coen brothers has given Hollywood some of its most tense and comic moments in film history. After marrying director/writer Joel Coen in 1984, she made her film debut in the Coens' first hit, *Blood Simple*. Although the movie garnered recognition from other film organizations, even winning Independent Spirit Awards in the first year of its existence, the Academy bypassed it. Three years later, McDormand earned her first nomination in Alan Parker's historical drama *Mississippi Burning*. As the abused wife of racist Deputy Brad Dourif, McDormand had one of the toughest assignments for an actor: give the hit-the-audience-between-the-eyes moral message speech that adroit viewers already knew. She performed the monologue with such sincerity that it became a highpoint of the movie. She lent her voice to *Barton Fink*, which earned Michael Lerner a Best Supporting Actor nod in 1991, and shared multiple Best Cast prizes with the large ensemble of *Short Cuts*, which brought Robert Altman a 1993 Best Director Oscar nod. In 1996, McDormand gave her landmark performance as pregnant police chief Marge Gunderson, fumbling her way to solving a gruesome kidnapping gone tragically bad in *Fargo*. McDormand hit every line with perfect pitch, capitalizing on the Midwestern accent ("Yah?") and priceless lines ("No, I just think I'm going to barf") to draw humor and make Marge an endearing movie icon, not a regional caricature. McDormand had a series of acceptance speeches to give before she reached Oscar's podium as Best Actress. 2000 was also a huge year for McDormand. She won multiple Best Supporting Actress prizes as a university chancellor having an affair with Michael Douglas in the Oscar-winning *Wonder Boys*. But the Academy favored her in *Almost Famous*, for which she was nominated against co-star Kate Hudson. McDormand syphoned laughs as a mother consumed with worry after she allowed her teenage son to travel unchaperoned with a rock band. Both favored to win Best Supporting Actress, McDormand and Hudson may have canceled each other's votes, leaving room for dark horse Marcia Gay Harden to take the category for *Pollock*. McDormand supported Best Actress nominee Diane Keaton in *Something's Gotta Give* in 2003, and then returned to her dramatic roots in *North Country*. Serving a similar function in *North Country* as she did in *Mississippi Burning*, McDormand this time let her body, deteriorating from ALS, give the social conscious message. A character actress with enough talent and appeal to carry a film as its star, McDormand delivers a top notch performance with every new movie, and her lead actress win and supporting nominations put her in the final tier of the Oscar countdown.

96. *Julia Roberts*

1989 Best Supporting Actress as daughter/wife/mother Shelby Eatenton Latcherie in *Steel Magnolias*
1990 Best Actress as prostitute Vivian Ward in *Pretty Woman*
2000 Best Actress as law office file clerk Erin Brockovich in *Erin Brockovich*
2013 Best Supporting Actress as daughter Barbara Weston-Fordham in *August: Osage County*

From her earliest movie performances, Roberts had the same ethereal screen presence that made the likes of Marilyn Monroe and Audrey Hepburn legends. In 1988, she was nominated for an Independent Spirit Award for *Mystic Pizza*, bringing her to the attention of Herbert Ross as he adapted *Steel Magnolias* for the big screen.

With Robert Harling's beautifully modulated tragicomic script, it would

In *Steel Magnolias* (1989), diabetic Shelby (Julia Roberts) risked her life for "30 minutes of wonderful" despite concerns from her mom, M'Lynn (Sally Field).

seem that any actor could excel as one of its Southern blossoms. But of the powerhouse cast that included Oscar winners Sally Field, Shirley MacLaine, and Olympia Dukakis, only Roberts, the youngest, least known of the cast, won Oscar's heart, and nomination. As Shelby, whose signature color is pink and who would "rather have 30 minutes of wonderful than a lifetime of nothing special," Roberts emanated the unmistakable beams of star power that have cast shadows up the Hollywood hills ever since. With her 1989 nomination, she and brother Eric, a 1985 nominee for *Runaway Train*, joined a handful of siblings to each have Oscar nods. As loveably romantic hooker Vivian in *Pretty Woman*, Roberts proved a box office champion and Oscar's Cinderella, coming to the ball with a second consecutive nomination, this time as Best Actress. The 1990 Best Actress race belonged to Kathy Bates in *Misery*, but moneymaking momentum that reached new heights for Roberts in the 1990s in such Oscar-nominated hits as *Hook* (1991), *Michael Collins* (1996), and *My Best Friend's Wedding* (1997) led to the role of a lifetime: the low class, high minded, vulgar dressing, compassion driven *Erin Brockovich*. No one doubted that Oscar would make his move to honor Roberts with a well-deserved victory. Roberts came to the ceremony the belle of the ball, and left one of its most popular winners. With her Academy Award victory Roberts became the first female actor (and second overall after Geoffrey Rush in 1996) to win the BAFTA, Golden Globe, SAG, Critic's Choice Award, and Oscar all for the same movie. Roles in multiple genres and of varying demands helped balance the respect for her talents with her invincible appeal, leading ultimately to yet another acknowledgment from Oscar in 2013. The anticipated film version of Tracy Letts' Pulitzer Prize drama *August: Osage County* owed much of its praise to its cast. The performances were universally revered, and Oscar singled out Roberts and Meryl Streep for their acidic scenes as a daughter and mother truth-tellin' in the aftermath of tragic circumstances. Roberts' broad smile and inviting gaze have always registered with film fans, but her acting power, which illuminates the screen just as brightly, has inspired the Academy, registering her among their favorites as well.

95. Nicole Kidman

2001 Best Actress as prostitute/singer Satine in *Moulin Rouge!*
2002 Best Actress as author Virginia Woolf in *The Hours*
2010 Best Actress as mother/wife Becca Corbett in *Rabbit Hole*
2016 Best Supporting Actress as adoptive mother Sue Brierley in *Lion*

Porcelain-lovely Australian actress Nicole Kidman had always been held in high regard by her peers, but a broadly publicized split from Tom Cruise coincided with a career surge, and finally the Academy took note. In 1991,

Kidman received her first Golden Globe nomination playing opposite Dustin Hoffman in *Billy Bathgate*. Although the Academy ignored the movie, it added to Kidman's international fan base that exploded when she starred in the 1995 box office hit, *Batman Forever*. That same year, she seemed a sure bet to garner her first Oscar nomination after winning the very first Empire Award as lead actress, a Critic's Choice Award and Golden Globe playing comically crazed news anchor Suzanne Stone in *To Die For*. That wasn't the stone the Academy went for in 1995, as they rounded out their Best Actress category with Sharon Stone in *Casino*. Kidman played lead character Isabel Archer in Jane Campion's adaptation of the 1881 Henry James classic *The Portrait of a Lady*, but Barbara Hershey's standout supporting role earned the film its only acting Oscar nomination of 1996. While married to Tom Cruise, Kidman costarred with him in three movies: *Days of Thunder* (1990), *Far and Away* (1992), and director Stanley Kubrick's final film, *Eyes Wide Shut* (1999). Of these movies, the Academy cited only *Days of Thunder* for a single technical award. With the new millennium came a flourish of great roles and adulation enough to secure Kidman's reputation as one of the most revered A-list actors of her generation. Kidman bedazzled as courtesan Satine in *Moulin Rouge!* and earned her first Academy Award nomination. Through the following award season, she kept jostling for Best Actress domination with Julianne Moore from *Far from Heaven* and Renée Zellweger in *Chicago*, ultimately triumphing at the Academy Awards as suicidal author Virginia Woolf whose time ran out in *The Hours*. She was expected to receive a third consecutive Best Actress nomination for her 2003 performance in *Cold Mountain*, but the Academy only acknowledged her main costars, Best Actor nominee Jude Law and Best Supporting Actress winner Renée Zellweger. Cast recognition for *Nine* in 2009 gave Kidman's career new award momentum, and the following year she was up for Oscar again struggling with Aaron Eckhart to emerge from the *Rabbit Hole* of grief after the death of their young son. That Best Actress race belonged to Natalie Portman as the emotionally unraveling ballerina in *Black Swan*. Six years later, Kidman was again short-listed by Oscar, for the first time in the supporting category. Though praise for her performance as an understanding adoptive mother was abundant, Viola Davis' work in *Fences* dominated the Best Supporting Actress category the entire 2016 award season. Nevertheless *Lion* once again proved that any role, small or large, could showcase Kidman's talent and warrant respect from her Academy peers.

94. Geoffrey Rush

1996 Best Actor as pianist David Helfgott in *Shine*
1998 Best Supporting Actor as theater manager Philip Henslowe in *Shakespeare in Love*

2000 Best Actor as writer The Marquis de Sade in *Quills*
2010 Best Supporting Actor as speech therapist Lionel Logue in *The King's Speech*

One of Australia's most beloved stars, Rush has conquered every acting medium, earning three BAFTAs (for *Shine*, *Elizabeth*, and *The King's Speech*), a Tony for *Exit the King*, an Emmy for turning Peter Sellers' demons into pathos in *The Life and Death of Peter Sellers*, and the Academy Award for *Shine*. Nearly 20 years into his career, Rush was relatively unknown to Academy members when he stuttered and sputtered and squinted his way into Oscar history by winning Best Actor as real-life David Helfgott, the abused prodigy whose triumph as a pianist is waylaid by his schizoaffective disorder. Initially 1996 was not expected to be the year he won Oscar, for his competitors all revealed dynamic winning potential. Leading the pack were Tom Cruise at his most appealing as *Jerry Maguire* and Billy Bob Thornton playing *Sling Blade*'s Karl Childers in a role Oscar loves to reward—a mentally handicapped hero. Woody Harrelson was physically disabled in *The People vs. Larry Flynt*, and Ralph Fiennes opened hearts in the year's Oscar powerhouse, *The English Patient*. That award season Rush quickly dominated the Best Actor competitions and became the first actor in history to win a BAFTA, Golden Globe, SAG, Critic's Choice and Academy Award for a single performance. Since then, 25 more stars from Julia Roberts in 2000 to Leonardo DiCaprio and Brie Larson in 2015 have duplicated his achievement. Throughout the past three decades Rush has stayed in demand. Following his Oscar victory he continued to *Shine* with three award-winning performances. He seethed with sinister intensity as Inspector Javert in *Les Misérables* (1998), one of the few movie versions of Victor Hugo's classic not up for Oscars, and added markedly to two vastly different Elizabethan hits that contended for Best Picture. In *Elizabeth*, he was the queen's zesty secretary and spymaster, Francis Walsingham, and in *Shakespeare in Love* he provided grimy comic relief as theatrical impresario Philip Henslowe. It was for that performance that the Academy gave Rush his second nomination. In 2000, he was the longshot for Best Actor as The Marquis de Sade in the often challenging *Quills*. But ten years later, Rush was infectiously endearing as Lionel Logue, the Australian language therapist who empowered King George VI to win over his people with a stammer-free address in the inspiring Best Picture winner, *The King's Speech*. Rush's relationship with Oscar started at the top with a Best Actor victory. Since then, tackling roles of various lengths has put him on the list of both lead and supporting rosters, keeping him on Academy members' minds, and in their favor, for twenty years.

93. Helen Mirren

1994 Best Supporting Actress as British monarch Queen Charlotte in *The Madness of King George*
2001 Best Supporting Actress as maid Mrs. Wilson in *Gosford Park*
2006 Best Actress as British monarch Queen Elizabeth II in *The Queen*
2009 Best Actress as wife Sofya Tolstoy in *The Last Station*

Helen Mirren was twice named Best Actress at Cannes Film Festivals before Oscar took note of her riveting talent. In 1984, she won at Cannes for her touching portrayal of grieving widow Marcella in *Cal*. The hit brought Mirren a BAFTA nomination, but despite U.S. distribution, failed to be recognized by the Academy. She was Cannes' Best Actress again in 1994 as Queen Charlotte in *The Madness of King George*, and this time the Academy took note, placing Mirren in the supporting competition. That year, Dianne Wiest won virtually every supporting actress trophy for *Bullets over Broadway*, a streak that sustained through Oscar night. In 2001 Mirren seemed primed to win Best Supporting Actress as housekeeper Mrs. Wilson in Robert Altman's lush, nostalgic murder mystery set at *Gosford Park*. Mirren and Jennifer Connelly of *A Beautiful Mind* took turns winning most of the Best Supporting Actress trophies leading to Academy Award's night, but Mirren enjoyed a late season boost when she won two SAGs just before the Oscars, one an individual acknowledgment of her supporting performance, and the other as a member of the ensemble. But *A Beautiful Mind* turned out to be Oscar's favorite of 2001, and Connelly took the supporting trophy. Mid-decade came Mirren's career-topping performances as Elizabeth I and Elizabeth II. A month before *The Queen* premiered in theaters with Mirren embodying every nuance of Elizabeth II, Mirren made awards news by winning an Emmy for the HBO series *Elizabeth I*. While still riding the wave of enthusiasm for her portrayal of the first monarch, Mirren caught the crest of universal enthusiasm for a performance of the second that was almost unprecedented in the history of motion pictures. From the film's release in September until the Oscars' February 25 telecast, fans and critics trailed Mirren like Buckingham Palace corgis, and award organizers etched Mirren's name into their trophies like crown jewels. Again Mirren took home two SAG awards in one night, this time as Best Female Actor in a Television Movie for *Elizabeth I* and Best Female Actor for the motion picture *The Queen*. Despite respected work from 2006 Oscar nominees Penélope Cruz in *Volver*, Judi Dench in *Notes on a Scandal*, Meryl Streep in *The Devil Wears Prada*, and Kate Winslet in *Little Children*, no one doubted that the Best Actress Academy Award awaited Mirren's nameplate, too. In 2009 Mirren won Best Actress at the Rome International

Film Festival as Leo Tolstoy's frustrated, combative wife Sofya in *The Last Station*. The performance brought her back to Oscar for another Best Actress race that Sandra Bullock won for *The Blind Side*. In 2014, Mirren was up for a Golden Globe for *The Hundred-Foot Journey*, but lost to Amy Adams in *Big Eyes*. Surprisingly, Oscar overlooked both performances.

92. Ben Kingsley

1982 Best Actor as barrister/political and spiritual leader Mahatma Gandhi in *Gandhi*
1991 Best Supporting Actor as head mobster Meyer Lansky in *Bugsy*
2001 Best Supporting Actor as underworld recruiter Don Logan in *Sexy Beast*
2003 Best Actor as former Iranian colonel/common laborer Massoud Amir Behrani in *House of Sand and Fog*

Britain-born Kingsley had been in movies ten years before Richard Attenborough saw the potential for an uncanny physical transformation into Mahatma Gandhi as the title character in his 1982 epic biography. Kingsley's evolution from the idealistic lawyer to the social revolutionary whose nonviolent protest embodied the conscience of the free world made Kingsley an international star, helped bring the film global acclaim, and positioned Kingsley and the movie as top contenders for that year's Academy Awards. Kingsley's victory as Best Actor would be no small feat. Besides Jack Lemmon's stirring performance as a father looking for his *Missing* son in South America, Kingsley would have to outshine three actors either at the top of their skills, or long overdue an Oscar win. Dustin Hoffman was a potential winner for his most appealing performance to date as *Tootsie*. But he had won Best Actor for *Kramer vs. Kramer* just three years earlier. More momentum seemed to go to Peter O'Toole for his comic tour de force in *My Favorite Year*. This marked O'Toole's seventh nomination, tying him with Richard Burton for most nominations without a win. Surely this might have been his time if not for an equally deserving Paul Newman, up for his seventh nomination (sixth as an actor) for *The Verdict*, considered by many to be his finest performance. So many equally deserving actors seemed to level the competitive field. As Oscar night evolved and *Gandhi* began taking the lion's share of awards, it was clear that Kingsley's portrayal, which in a biography of this depth and magnitude carried the weight of the entire film, brought him a deserved Oscar. Subsequent supporting parts kept Kingsley a vibrant presence in movies, and earned him his next two Academy Award nominations. In *Bugsy* he excelled as infamous Mob's Accountant Meyer Lansky, but some of his momentum may have been interrupted by the fact that his co-star, Harvey

Keitel, was up in the same category. *Schindler's List* seemed primed to fill double Best Supporting Oscar slots in 1993. At Oscar time, Kingsley as compassionate Itzhak Stern was not on the ballot, but Ralph Fiennes as sinister Amon Goeth was. Kingsley took a huge risk and tackled a character far from his dignified persona in *Sexy Beast*, in which he played sociopath Don Logan. The Academy connected with his unsympathetic character, but gave that year's Best Supporting Actor Oscar to Jim Broadbent as the long-suffering husband in *Iris*. In 2003, Kingsley again found a leading role worthy of his talents in *House of Sand and Fog*, a shattering account of lives colliding toward destruction during a dispute over property ownership. The multifaceted role made Kingsley a lead contender with Johnny Depp for *Pirates of the Caribbean: The Curse of the Black Pearl* and winner Sean Penn in *Mystic River*. Kingsley's balance of supporting and leading nominations confirms that he excels in roles from minor to epic.

91. *George C. Scott*

1959 Best Supporting Actor as Assistant State Attorney General Claude Dancer in *Anatomy of a Murder*
1961 Best Supporting Actor as professional gambler Bert Gordon in *The Hustler*
1970 Best Actor as U.S. Army General George S. Patton, Jr., in *Patton*
1971 Best Actor as chief of medicine Dr. Herbert Bock in *The Hospital*

Scott allegedly loathed the Academy Awards and frequently made disparaging remarks about the "meat parade" of having actors compete for a prize for works he considered incomparable. Although it may seem that Scott always hated the Oscars, some reports suggest that he actually wanted to win his 1959 competition, and was so disappointed by his loss that it soured him on the Academy. Whether or not that's how his relationship with Oscar originated, his was one of the most cantankerous yet revered Academy-honored careers. In *Anatomy of a Murder* he was a shrewd, relentless prosecuting attorney. Scott shared that year's Best Supporting Oscar ballot with Arthur O'Connell playing a lawyer for the defense in the case, and both lost the Academy Award to Hugh Griffith in one of *Ben-Hur*'s record-breaking eleven wins. If Scott had issues with the Academy that first time in competition, he didn't voice them. But his second time, when nominated for *The Hustler*, he did. Again up for Best Supporting Actor, and once more competing against a co-star (this time, Jackie Gleason), Scott declined his nomination, presumably because he disliked Oscar competitions and campaigns. His efforts caused little stir in 1961, and George Chakiris won the category for *West Side Story*. Scott garnered equally impressive reviews as jingoist General Buck

Turgidson in *Dr. Strangelove*, but the Academy was so enamored of Peter Sellers' three characterizations, Sellers earned the film's only acting Oscar nod. Always a perfectionist, Scott researched extensively to become George S. Patton, and frequently fought with the film's producer, Frank McCarthy, to interpret the military giant his own way. Effusive praise for his performance led to talk of Oscar. When nominated, Scott refused his acknowledgment, to which Academy President Daniel Taradash responded, "A person responsible for the achievement cannot decline the nomination after it is voted. Actually, Mr. Scott is not involved. It is his performance in *Patton* which is involved." Ironically, Scott's disdain for Oscar campaigning gave him one of the most effective campaigns in Oscar history. His vocal disapproval of the awards made consistent front page news, kept his performance in the forefront of Academy voters' minds, and led to his win. The following year, Scott was nominated once more, again in the lead actor category, as an unraveling doctor in *The Hospital*. This time, Scott made no public statement about the nomination, and as easily as that, the controversy he stirred faded into Oscar history. The fact that the Academy gave him his fourth nomination after he summarily dismissed the awards and the organization speaks to the impact his work had on his voting colleagues. Uncompromisingly committed to his craft, Scott won the unwelcome favor of the Academy with four nominations and a lead actor win, placing him in the countdown for a statuette he never accepted, but recommended to the Academy they donate to the Patton Museum in Fort Knox, Kentucky. Instead, it ended up at the Virginia Military Institute Museum in Lexington, Virginia.

90. Holly Hunter

1987 Best Actress as television news producer Jane Craig in *Broadcast News*
1993 Best Actress as wife/mother Ada in *The Piano*
1993 Best Supporting Actress as secretary Tammy Hemphill in *The Firm*
2003 Best Supporting Actress as hair stylist Melanie in *Thirteen*

Georgia-born spitfire Hunter first caught the Academy's eye as obsessively ambitious Jane Craig in *Broadcast News*. Despite being released within the last weeks of 1987, the movie caught such immediate Oscar buzz that it began the season as the favored top contender of the year. Garnering effusive praise were all members of the cast, from broadcast anchors William Hurt and Albert Brooks to self-professed neurotic news producer Holly Hunter. In a quintessential example of a film that piques too early in award's season, by the time the nominations were announced, *Broadcast News* had lost much of its edge, evident especially by the omission of James L. Brooks from the

Best Director roll. While nearly everyone else remained a longshot, Hunter sustained some hope for still winning Best Actress. Edging ahead of her, however, were Cher as an unlucky-in-love widow in *Moonstruck* and Glenn Close, whose crazed jilted lover in *Fatal Attraction* became fodder for punchlines and visual jokes from all the major talk show comics. Ultimately, it was Cher who carried Oscar home that night. At Hunter's next competition, nothing interrupted her beeline to victory. Hunter played a mute heroine in *The Piano* whose terse expressions and taut, jolting mannerisms conveyed her contained fury at the injustice of women in nineteenth century New Zealand. Her voiceover narration infused the tense drama with sparks of insight and revelations that served to convey director Jane Campion's complex themes. Hunter embodied it all, and on Oscar night, no one doubted that the Best Actress statuette seemed destined for Hunter. It was. The fact that Hunter was also nominated for Best Supporting Actress that year for a very different role in *The Firm* only seemed to further confirm her winning fate. As Gary Busey's smoking (both literally and figuratively) secretary, Hunter's scenes were among the highlights of the legal thriller. Her 1993 Best Actress victory made Hunter the first female nominated for both lead and supporting acting awards in a single year to win the lead, not the supporting, prize. The year before, Al Pacino became the first to achieve the same among male actors. Ten years after accepting her Academy Award, Hunter was among the nominated again. For her difficult role as a flawed mother struggling to rein in a once good daughter gone astray at age *Thirteen*, Hunter gave the movie prominence, brought in an adult audience, and earned the film its only Academy recognition. Like Julia Roberts, Geoffrey Rush, Ben Kingsley, and George C. Scott, Hunter snagged nominations evenly split between lead and supporting performances. But of these stars, only Hunter doubled her power with two competitions in a single year.

89. *Jennifer Lawrence*

2010 Best Actress as daughter Ree Dolly in *Winter's Bone*
2012 Best Actress as widow Tiffany Maxwell in *Silver Linings Playbook*
2013 Best Supporting Actress as wife Rosalyn Rosenfeld in *American Hustle*
2015 Best Actress as inventor entrepreneur Joy Mangano in *Joy*

Talk about a girl on fire! Before she rose to top box office draw as Katniss Everdeen, Panem's defiant teen in *The Hunger Games*, Lawrence awed the Academy as a similarly altruistic daughter in search of her father while chilled through *Winter's Bone*. Her powerful performance anchored the intense drama, made her the Chicago Film Critics' Most Promising Performer, and endeared the indie mystery to the Academy. As a result, the sleeper hit saw its way through the Ozark ice to net four major nominations, including Best Picture of 2010. By Oscar night, Lawrence, Annette Bening, Nicole Kidman, and Michelle Williams had to sidestep Natalie Portman's *Black Swan* steamroll to Best Actress victory. Between 2012 and 2015 *The Hunger Games* franchise escalated Lawrence to Hollywood powerhouse for both talent and ticket revenue. Despite fine performances, inventive costumes and makeup, and enrapturing set designs, none of the four movies garnered attention from the Academy. But Lawrence continued to be Oscar's darling of the 2010s. At age 22, she became the second youngest Best Actress winner, after Marlee Matlin in *Children of a Lesser God* (1986), for her portrayal of sad yet comic young widow Tiffany, Bradley Cooper's hesitant hookup and thriving dance partner in *Silver Linings Playbook*. The next year Lawrence reteamed with Bradley Cooper and director David O. Russell to play Christian Bale's sassy wife Rosalyn in *American Hustle*. Early in the 2013 award season Lawrence dominated supporting actress competitions. *American Hustle* brought her a Best Supporting Actress Golden Globe to go along with her Best Actress, Musical or Comedy statue for *Silver Linings Playbook*. Then she won her first and so far only BAFTA and added a third notch to her Oscar headboard. But her star soared so quickly that some reports suggested Lawrence's marketing team worried that winning a second Academy Award so fast might negatively impact her career, much like Oscar's first double acting winner, Luise Rainer. On Oscar night Lawrence lost the supporting competition to Lupita Nyong'o in the night's big winner, *12 Years a Slave*. The following year, Lawrence's name was not on an Academy acting ballot, but another franchise film, *X-Men: Days of Future Past* competed for Best Visual Effects. With *Joy*, Lawrence proved that her appeal can not only carry a film, but also overshadow tepid reviews to impress her Academy peers. Now embraced as a woman in charge of her career and her unbridled talent, Lawrence earned her third consecutive Oscar nomination under the direction of David O. Russell, and broke Academy records as the only actor with so many nominations by age 25. Witty, insightful, determined, crass, unflinching—Lawrence can express any emotion with rapturous results. With so many years ahead of Lawrence, the Academy might expect their young peer to continue dominating her Oscar categories for decades.

88. *Anthony Hopkins*

1991 Best Actor as psychiatrist/serial killer Dr. Hannibal Lecter in ***The Silence of the Lambs***

1993 Best Actor as head butler Mr. James Stevens in *The Remains of the Day*

1995 Best Actor as U.S. President Richard Nixon in *Nixon*
1997 Best Supporting Actor as former U.S. President John Quincy Adams in *Amistad*

A dynamic presence since his earliest days in film, Hopkins got his introduction to Oscar as Richard the Lionhearted, the son that Best Actress winner Katharine Hepburn fought to take the throne from husband and king, Henry II when *The Lion in Winter* ended his reign. Although Hopkins competed for his first BAFTA for the movie, he was not recognized with an Oscar nomination for the 1968 classic. He was also overlooked in 1980 as compassionate Dr. Frederick Treves, who treated Best Actor nominee John Hurt as *The Elephant Man*. Instead Hopkins built his stellar film reputation by perfecting characterizations as some of the most diabolical real and fictional villains in history. He earned lead actor Emmys as accused kidnapper and baby killer Bruno Hauptmann on trial in *The Lindbergh Kidnapping Case* in 1976 and then was a startling Adolf Hitler in *The Bunker* in 1981. Ten years later, Hopkins was even more shocking as caged and cagy Hannibal the Cannibal Lecter in *The Silence of the Lambs*. When Hopkins' 16 minute, 10 second performance took the 1991 Best Actor Academy Award over solid competitors Warren Beatty as *Bugsy*, Robert De Niro in *Cape Fear*, Robin Williams in *The Fisher King*, and Golden Globe winner Nick Nolte in *The Prince of Tides*, he set an Academy record for the shortest performance to win a lead acting Oscar. For alternating odd-numbered years throughout the 1990s, Hopkins remained a vibrant presence at the Academy Awards. His repressed butler, Mr. Stevens in *The Remains of the Day* was a smoldering tour de force. Chances of a potential second Best Actor win in only three years were escalated by his BAFTA-winning performance that same year as heart-touched then heart-shattered academic and author C.S. Lewis in *Shadowlands*, which brought Debra Winger her third Best Actress Oscar nomination as the woman he loves and loses to cancer. Hopkins lost the 1993 Best Actor prize to Tom Hanks in *Philadelphia*. Hopkins added splashes of pathos and sympathy as another often vilified historic figure, Richard Nixon, but throughout the 1995 award season Best Actor belonged to Nicholas Cage in *Leaving Las Vegas*. Hopkins set another Academy record in 1997 by becoming the only actor to date nominated for playing two U.S. Presidents when he followed his *Nixon* nod with a supporting-nominated depiction of John Quincy Adams in *Amistad*. After six unsuccessful bids for Golden Globes—for *Magic* in 1978, *The Tenth Man* in 1988, and for the four performances acknowledged by Oscar—Hopkins received the Hollywood Foreign Press' 2003 Cecil B. DeMille Award for lifelong contribution to acting. Chances seem promising that Hopkins will follow in the footsteps of other British actors such as Alec Guinness and Laurence Olivier by one day adding to his competitive lead actor Oscar a matching statuette for Lifetime Achievement.

87. William Hurt

1985 Best Actor as rapist/prisoner Luis Molina in *Kiss of the Spider Woman*
1986 Best Actor as speech teacher James Leeds in *Children of a Lesser God*
1987 Best Actor as television news anchorman Tom Grunick in *Broadcast News*
2005 Best Supporting Actor as mobster Richie Cusack in *A History of Violence*

Hurt, a Julliard-trained actor, was nominated for the Golden Globe's New Star of 1980 for *Altered States*, which was up for two Oscars. The following year he ignited the screen with Kathleen Turner in *Body Heat*. Their scintillating sexuality rivaled John Garfield and Lana Turner in *The Postman Always Rings Twice*. Like the 1946 noir classic, *Body Heat* enraptured audiences but was ignored by the Academy. Hurt was a comically beefy slug hiding a painful secret in *The Big Chill*. While any member of the ensemble could have been up for Oscar, that honor was reserved solely for Glenn Close. In 1985 Hurt and Raúl Juliá went before the cameras to film *Kiss of the Spider Woman*. Originally cast as imprisoned activist Valentin Arregui, Hurt switched characters with Juliá and took on the showier role of effeminate, fantasy-spinning accused child molester Luis Molina. Hurt's towering stature proved a captivating contrast to his character's softness. The indelible impression rippled across the globe with award wins from Cannes, Italy, London, L.A., and on to the Academy Awards. Despite international victories, Hurt had to overcome many hurdles to hear his name called on Oscar night. As the first independent film to garner nominations in four major categories, *Kiss of the Spider Woman* was not expected to achieve much beyond that milestone. In an era when playing a homosexual could be career suicide, Hurt unabashedly embodied the dazed revelries and calculated machinations revealed late in the film. Instead of alienating voters, it inspired them. Further, Hurt's competition had advantages he didn't. Harrison Ford, nominated for the first time for *Witness*, was the biggest box office star of all time thanks to the *Star Wars* and *Indiana Jones* franchises. Sentiment for beloved James Garner might have inspired votes for him in *Murphy's Romance*. Former winners Jack Nicholson and Jon Voight reached new acting heights for their respective work in *Prizzi's Honor* and *Runaway Train*. But Hurt won the Oscar, then secured subsequent Best Actor nominations for *Children of a Lesser God* the next year, and *Broadcast News* the year after that. In 1988, Hurt was expected to rank among the most consecutively nominated lead actors with a fourth nomination for *The Accidental Tourist*. Surprisingly, the Best Picture nominee only earned an acting nomination for Geena Davis, leaving Hurt's Best Actor streak at three. Hurt was a welcome addition to the Best Supporting Actor roster of 2005 for his small but significant appearance as Viggo Mortensen's vengeful brother at the end of *A History of Violence*. As an actor, Hurt has always taken risks that resulted in some of the most varied performances to capture the Academy's imagination, and votes.

86. Jon Voight

1969 Best Actor as hustler Joe Buck in *Midnight Cowboy*
1978 Best Actor as Vietnam veteran Luke Martin in *Coming Home*
1985 Best Actor as convicted bank robber Manny in *Runaway Train*
2001 Best Supporting Actor as sports commentator Howard Cosell in *Ali*

Voight owes his career to his breakthrough role as a naïve hustler in John Schlesinger's *Midnight Cowboy*. So good was Voight as cherubic Joe Buck that he was never once overshadowed by Dustin Hoffman in the much showier role of tubercular thief Ratzo Rizzo. Critics lavished praise on both actors, and when their names appeared on the 1969 Best Actor ballot, the Academy had one of those rare years when two competing co-stars' chances seemed equally bright. Peter O'Toole, though delightful in a musical remake of *Goodbye, Mr. Chips*, was only a threat if the Academy wanted to make up for bypassing his Oscar-worthy performance in *The Lion in Winter* the previous year. Richard Burton could also cause an upset, as his towering performance in *Anne of the Thousand Days* would be his sixth to go unrewarded. But sentiment and a grand characterization by still unacknowledged Hollywood legend John Wayne in *True Grit* would prove the spoiler, and The Duke accepted his Academy Award and the adulation of generations of contemporaries. In 1972 Voight was expected to be up for *Deliverance*, which ended up with a Best Picture, but no acting, nominations. Solid work in projects of varying genres led to his being cast opposite Jane Fonda in her passion project, a look at the aftermath of war that hoped to be to Vietnam what *The Best Years of Our Lives* was to World War II. *Coming Home* was generously embraced, and at Oscar time it was up for all the major awards, and was one of the rare films to earn Oscar nominations in all four acting categories. Voight was favored to win from the start. Although Robert De Niro gave a wrenching performance in the year's Best Picture, *The Deer Hunter*, and Warren Beatty co-directed (along with Buck Henry) himself to a delightful comic performance in *Heaven Can Wait*, Voight's name was called on Oscar night. In 1985 he embodied the angst that made *Runaway Train* a runaway hit, and was shortlisted again for Oscar. The international suspense thriller cast him as an escaped convict in a Best Actor list in which every nominee except James Garner as a pharmacist in *Murphy's Romance* found themselves on one side of the law or the other. Harrison Ford was a detective in *Witness,* Jack Nicholson was a hit man in *Prizzi's Honor,* and winner William Hurt was a convict imprisoned in Brazil in *Kiss of the Spider Woman.* The Academy didn't see much of Voight for several years, but they honored him with his first nomination as Best Supporting Actor in *Ali.* As Ali's verbal sparring opponent, Howard Cosell, Voight so immersed himself in the character that he was virtually unrecognizable. In a comeback performance praised by the Academy, Voight proved once again his versatility and success.

85. *Julie Christie*

1965 Best Actress as fashion model/actress Diana Scott in *Darling*
1971 Best Actress as prostitute Mrs. Constance Miller in *McCabe & Mrs. Miller*
1997 Best Actress as former actress Phyllis Mann in *Afterglow*
2007 Best Actress as wife/Alzheimer's patient Fiona in *Away from Her*

Lovely young Julie Christie burst into world cinema in two roles so diverse she captured the affections of fans of traditional movies and of contemporary pictures focused on Swingin' London in 1965. David Lean cast her as Lara, love interest of both revolutionary Tom Courtenay and dedicated physician Omar Sharif in the sweeping epic *Doctor Zhivago.* Meantime, young filmmaker John Schlesinger cast Christie in place of original choice Shirley MacLaine in *Darling,* an innovative black and white drama that followed the exploits of an immoral model. As powerfully alluring as she was in *Doctor Zhivago,* it was the meatier, more demanding role as Diana Scott in *Darling* that registered with Academy voters. They declared 1965 The Year of Julie Christie, and she proved an ebullient Oscar recipient when she won Best Actress over fellow Brits Julie Andrews in *The Sound of Music* and Samantha Eggar in *The Collector,* French former winner Simone Signoret in *Ship of Fools,* and new American star Elizabeth Hartman in *A Patch of Blue.* Although neither won Best Picture, which went to *The Sound of Music,* both of Christie's hits dominated the awards, taking both the color (*Doctor Zhivago*) and black and white (*Darling*) costume prizes, as well as Best Adapted (*Zhivago*) and original (*Darling*) screenplay.

Always in control of her own career, Christie has made both British and American hits for the past six decades, earning Oscar nominations in four of them. In Robert Altman's "anti-western," *McCabe & Mrs. Miller,* Christie played an opium addict who opened a successful brothel with Warren Beatty. The film earned Christie, but not Beatty, an Oscar nod. A couple for part of

Lee Marvin, Julie Christie, Shelley Winters and Martin Balsam took home Oscars in 1965, but only Christie started the evening a clear front-runner to win her competition.

the 1970s, Christie and Beatty starred in *Shampoo*, for which neither was up for an Oscar, then *Heaven Can Wait*, which brought Beatty but not Christie a lead acting nod. It wasn't until 1997 that Christie again found herself among the nominated for Alan Rudolph's ensemble piece, *Afterglow*. In it, Christie shone as an unhappily married, faded actress. Although Christie won multiple awards for the performance, she was one of four British actresses who seemed to cancel each other out in favor of Oscar's winner, American actress Helen Hunt in *As Good As It Gets*. If ever Christie had a shot at her second Academy Award, it was for her delicate, shattering performance as a vibrant woman whose mind, and wonderful marriage, are crushed by her Alzheimer's disease. In 2007, Christie won nearly every Best Actress prize imaginable. But the tide gradually shifted. At the Golden Globes, Marion Cotillard won Best Actress, Musical or Comedy for *La Vie en Rose* while Christie won Best Actress, Drama. At the BAFTAs, which understandably most often goes to a British actress, Cotillard bested Christie. Suddenly Christie's lock on Oscar was no longer secure. In the end, the Academy chose Cotillard. Though her greatest Oscar glory so far came at the beginning of her international career, Christie has remained a dominant acting force, and a favorite of Oscar for more than forty years.

84. Diane Keaton

1977 Best Actress as aspiring singer/girlfriend Annie Hall in *Annie Hall*
1981 Best Actress as journalist/writer Louise Bryant in *Reds*
1996 Best Actress as daughter/sister Bessie in *Marvin's Room*
2003 Best Actress as playwright Erica Barry in *Something's Gotta Give*

Keaton's perennial appeal comes as much from her diverse acting talents as her joyfully quirky, self-effacing persona. From the beginning of her movie career in the 1970s, she has always balanced dramatic roles with her trademark comic gems. In 1972, she played Kay Adams in *The Godfather* and also reprised for film her Tony-nominated stage performance in *Play It Again, Sam*, the work that began her lifelong collaboration with Woody Allen. In 1977, Allen based his character, Annie Hall, on Keaton and cast her to essentially play herself during their romantic relationship. In April of 1977 *Annie Hall* opened to instantaneous praise that sustained its power up to Oscar nomination time. In October of 1977, Keaton won equally enthusiastic reviews in the much darker *Looking for Mr. Goodbar*. Her performances in both films were so highly touted that the question leading into the announcement of that year's Oscar nominees was not *if* Keaton would be up for Best Actress, but for which movie would the Academy recognize her? Tuesday Weld's name was called out for the Best Supporting Actress short list for *Looking for Mr. Goodbar*, while Keaton and Allen were up for the leads in *Annie Hall*. In one of the strongest years for women, Keaton competed against Jane Fonda in *Julia*, and three actress directed by Herbert Ross: Marsha Mason in *The Goodbye Girl*, and Anne Bancroft and Shirley MacLaine in *The Turning Point*. "Yeah, well, la-di-da, la-di-da," when Keaton was named Best Actress on Oscar's golden anniversary she became the first star to win an Academy Award playing a character based on herself. In 1981, Keaton was again a front runner for Best Actress as *Reds* seemed likely to sweep the major awards. Keaton's director and co-star Warren Beatty won Best Director, but subsequent major awards went to *Chariots of Fire*, the surprise Best Picture winner, and *On Golden Pond*, for which Henry Fonda beat Beatty for Best Actor and Katharine Hepburn bested Keaton for Best Actress. Keaton was both surprised and delighted in 1996 when her performance was singled out from the cast of *Marvin's Room* for the film's only nomination. Every other actor in the movie—Meryl Streep, Leonardo DiCaprio, Hume Cronyn, and Gwen Verdon—was considered a potential nominee. But Keaton, as the sister who sacrificed her independence to care for her ailing parents, delivered a performance that shot right through Academy voters' hearts. Despite all around great reviews, *Something's Gotta Give* also earned only one nomination in 2003: Diane Keaton for Best Actress. Keaton dominated that race until Charlize Theron's toweringly terrifying portrayal of serial killer Aileen Wuornos in *Monster* carried her to victory. Keaton's relationship with Oscar started at the top. She was integral to *The Godfather* dynasty that brought 28 nominations and two Best Picture wins, and then won the Oscar as Annie Hall, one of film's most endearing comic icons. Equal nominations for comic and dramatic performances in movies spanning four decades warranted Keaton's place as one of Oscar's favorite leading ladies.

83. *Joanne Woodward*

1957 Best Actress as wife/dissociative identity disorder sufferer Eve White/Eve Black/Jane in *The Three Faces of Eve*
1968 Best Actress as schoolteacher Rachel Cameron in *Rachel, Rachel*
1973 Best Actress as wife Rita Walden in *Summer Wishes, Winter Dreams*
1990 Best Actress as wife/mother India Bridge in *Mr. & Mrs. Bridge*

The year 1958 was a very good year for Joanne Woodward. In January, she was nominated for her first Academy Award. In February she married Paul Newman, a union that lasted until Newman's death 50 years later. In March, she won the Best Actress Oscar for her compelling portrayal of a meek woman suffering from multiple personality disorder. Despite excelling in a complex role, Woodward was no shoo-in to win that year. For the first time in their careers, glamorous Elizabeth Taylor (*Raintree County*) and Lana Turner (*Peyton Place*) were competing for Oscar, and both gladly campaigned to solicit votes. Lower profile nominees were Deborah Kerr, up for her fourth Oscar for *Heaven Knows, Mr. Allison*, and former winner Anna Magnani for *Wild Is the Wind*. Woodward's less than enthusiastic remarks about the peers who voted for her stunned some Academy members, but others were impressed that she had the courage to vocalize what was already common knowledge: winning an Oscar was as much a marketing as an acting achievement. Also in 1958, Woodward and Newman made *The Long, Hot Summer*, the first of ten movies in which they both starred. The Academy was more impressed with their collaborations as actor and director when, in 1968, Newman directed Woodward in *Rachel, Rachel*, a unique character study of a lonely spinster traumatized into emerging from lifelong isolation and delusion.

At the Oscars, Woodward and Newman became one of the few married couples both nominated for an Academy Award for a single project: Woodward was up for Best Actress; as the producer, Newman was a contender for Best Picture. That year's Best Actress race ended in a tie between Katharine Hepburn and Barbra Streisand, and *Rachel, Rachel* lost Best Picture to *Oliver!* In 1972, Woodward won Best Actress at Cannes for *The Effect of Gamma Rays on Man-in-the-Moon Marigolds*, but the Academy didn't take to Paul Newman's adaptation of Paul Zindel's Pulitzer Prize play. The following year, Woodward expressed concern that the producers who changed the title of *Death of a Snow Queen* to *Summer Wishes, Winter Dreams* might lose its potential audience. The small movie about Woodward's gradual thaw toward becoming a more compassionate woman put her in contention for the 1973 Oscar against two box office champions, Ellen Burstyn in *The Exorcist* and Barbra Streisand in *The Way We Were*, as well as newcomer Marsha Mason in *Cinderella Liberty* and ultimate winner Glenda Jackson in *A Touch of Class*. Woodward earned her only nomination playing opposite Paul Newman in their last starring vehicle as *Mr. & Mrs. Bridge*. The James Ivory drama took a slow, downbeat look at a lifelong relationship between two loving but very disconnected people. Both stars were expected to compete for a 1990 Oscar, but only Woodward made the final cut. She lost to Kathy Bates in *Misery*. Outspoken, strong-willed, and very public about the fact that her private life always superseded her professional aspirations, Woodward's marriage to Paul Newman kept her in the spotlight, but her talent and boldness made her an independent figure respected by the Academy.

82. Jane Wyman

1946 Best Actress as pioneer farm wife Ora Baxter in *The Yearling*
1948 Best Actress as farm girl Belinda McDonald in *Johnny Belinda*
1951 Best Actress as nanny Louise "LouLou" Mason in *The Blue Veil*
1954 Best Actress as doctor's widow Helen Phillips in *Magnificent Obsession*

Always the dependable supporting player and more often the staunch leading lady, Wyman broke into Oscar's sphere in 1943 playing Jack Carson's wife in *Princess O'Rourke*, an Olivia de Havilland vehicle that won the Best Original Screenplay Academy Award. Two years later Wyman played Ray Milland's girlfriend in 1945's Best Picture *The Lost Weekend*. That performance brought her to the attention of Clarence Brown, who directed her the following year in *The Yearling*. As the earthy pioneer mother prickling from the deaths of several of her children, she withheld affection for her one surviving son for fear of losing him, too. As courage gradually thawed her reticence,

Wyman glowed on screen. The transformation had the Academy checking her name as one of the five Best Actress nominees of 1946. She lost to Olivia de Havilland for her work in *To Each His Own*. Following Wyman's initial competition, roles grew more plentiful and varied. Playing a deaf mute in a film that centered on her character's rape was a grand risk at the time. Expressing a rainbow of emotions without uttering a word, and being the focal point of a sensitive subject rarely covered overtly in mainstream movies could either dampen or catapult her career. The 1948 Oscars confirmed the stratospheric results. It was a year when every Best Actress performance was bold and complex. Ingrid Bergman was zealous warrior *Joan of Arc*. Olivia de Havilland faced insanity in *The Snake Pit*. Bed-ridden hypochondriac Barbara Stanwyck had only the phone to connect her to the outside world in the thriller *Sorry, Wrong Number*. Irene Dunne, in her fifth unsuccessful bid for Oscar, was the compassionate Swedish matriarch in George Stevens' heartwarming *I Remember Mama*. With twelve nominations, *Johnny Belinda* was the highest profile movie of the 1948 Academy Awards. Voters recognized how Wyman's performance imbued the film with a textured pathos that made it a classic by honoring her with the film's only win. As the first actor since the silent film era to win an Academy Award for a non-speaking performance, Wyman accepted her award by saying, "I accept this, very gratefully, for keeping my mouth shut once. I think I'll do it again." Wyman earned two subsequent nominations for performances under the direction of Curtis Bernhardt and Douglas Sirk, both experts at showcasing females in what were known in their day as traditional women's pictures. Like Ma Baxter in *The Yearling*, LouLou Mason in *The Blue Veil* was at first defined by the death of her infant. A new life included unexpected career and relationship developments. In 1954, the fine performances of Wyman and Rock Hudson tempered the melodrama of multiple plot calamities in *Magnificent Obsession*, bringing Wyman one last chance at Oscar. In a category expected to belong to Judy Garland in *A Star Is Born*, the statuette instead went to future Princess of Monaco, Grace Kelly in *The Country Girl*.

81. Burt Lancaster

    1953 Best Actor as U.S. Army 1st Sergeant Milton Warden in *From Here to Eternity*

    1960 Best Actor as traveling salesman/con artist/evangelist Elmer Gantry in *Elmer Gantry*

    1962 Best Actor as convicted murderer Robert Stroud in *Birdman of Alcatraz*

    1981 Best Actor as mobster Lou in *Atlantic City*

A tough taskmaster whose background as an acrobat gave his screen appearances an energized athleticism, Lancaster valued independence, selecting roles and even co-founding with Harold Hecht and James Hill the Hecht Hill Lancaster production company which brought to the screen multiple hits during the 1950s and 1960s, including Oscar's 1955 Best Picture *Marty*. Melding a dark attractiveness with a beaming smile he labeled "the grin," Lancaster made his first impression in movies in the Best Director-nominated noir classic, *The Killers* in 1946. Two years later he was the young husband of invalid Barbara Stanwyck, a Best Actress nominee, in the suspense thriller *Sorry, Wrong Number*, the first of several movies he made opposite women who were nominated for or won Best Actress. In *Come Back, Little Sheba* Lancaster tried to drink away his disappointment for marrying Shirley Booth. In *The Rose Tattoo*, he was Anna Magnani's imposing, impetuous lover, and in *The Rainmaker*, he conned late bloomer Katharine Hepburn into seeing hope for love that had, until his arrival, eluded her. Lancaster was among the five cast members up for acting honors for the biggest Oscar winner of 1953, *From Here to Eternity*. Lancaster competed for Best Actor against co-star Montgomery Clift; two young actors in costume dramas, Marlon Brando in *Julius Caesar* and Richard Burton in *The Robe*, and William Holden, who took the prize for *Stalag 17*. Oscar didn't call upon Lancaster again until he blazed across the screen as Sinclair Lewis' evangelical charlatan, the electric *Elmer Gantry*. It would have been a showcase role for any actor, but hulking, wavy-haired Lancaster ignited the screen during impassioned preaching soliloquies, contrasting with more contemplative moments of awaking conscience with faith healer Jean Simmons and jilted prostitute Shirley Jones. Lancaster, Supporting Actress Jones, and screenwriter Richard Brooks all won 1960 Academy Awards for the Brooks-directed feature.

Two years later, Lancaster won multiple awards and an Oscar nomination as a reclusive, seemingly unreformable prisoner in *Birdman of Alcatraz*. Every Best Actor nominee that year gave performances that maintain classic status, with Peter O'Toole as *Lawrence of Arabia*, Jack Lemmon as an alcoholic detoxing from *Days of Wine and Roses*, and Marcello Mastroianni plotting murder in *Divorce Italian Style*. But none impressed the Academy as much as Gregory Peck in *To Kill a Mockingbird*. Lancaster's career resurged in 1981 when he swept many of the critical honors as a smalltime bookie in *Atlantic City*. Despite rave reviews for his performance, Lancaster and his fellow nominees knew that the Academy would give revered actor Henry Fonda his first competitive prize for *On Golden Pond*. Lancaster ended the decade as mythically grand Doc Graham in the inspiring Best Picture nominee *Field of Dreams*. His further contributions to other great Oscar winners such as *Separate Tables* and *Judgment at Nuremberg*, and nominees like *Gunfight at O.K. Corral* and *Seven Days in May* make it easy to see why the lusty actor so easily charmed his Academy peers.

With Peter Ustinov (left), his *Elmer Gantry* co-star Shirley Jones, and Elizabeth Taylor, Burt Lancaster basked in his 1960 Oscar victory.

80. Barbara Stanwyck

1937 Best Actress as mother Stella Dallas in *Stella Dallas*
1941 Best Actress as burlesque dancer Sugarpuss O'Shea in *Ball of Fire*
1944 Best Actress as wife Phyllis Dietrichson in *Double Indemnity*
1948 Best Actress as wife Leona Stevenson in *Sorry, Wrong Number*
1981 Honorary lifetime achievement award "for superlative creativity and unique contribution to the art of screen acting"

Ask movie experts to name the ultimate tear jerking scene, and they'll likely mention rain-soaked Barbara Stanwyck watching her daughter's wedding at the end of *Stella Dallas*. Ask them to identify moviedom's quintessential femme fatale, and expect them to begin with Stanwyck's double-crossing lover protected by *Double Indemnity*. Such classic performances make it all the more confounding that one of the most respected legends of film never won a competitive Academy Award. The range of just her four nominated performances reveals the scope and depth she could convey as a motion picture actress. Her first nomination came for one of her most indelible and defining roles. As *Stella Dallas*, Stanwyck embodied the conflicts and compassion of a devoted mother who recognized that the only way to give her child the life she dreams was to sacrifice the bond which had become, for her, a beloved lifeline. Stanwyck's expression, in close-up, in the final scene is as moving as any ever filmed. As the deliciously named Sugarpuss O'Shea, Stanwyck was indeed a *Ball of Fire* in Howard Hawks' endearing comedy about a slatternly dance hall girl in hiding with a house full of intellectual, and virginal, academicians. With her painted face, baubled costumes, and base dialect, Stanwyck was the ideal subject for the professors' linguistic study, and an enchanting teacher who ignited the passions that Gary Cooper and his colleagues had no idea what to do with—until Stanwyck set them straight. In mink, sunglasses, and platinum blonde wig, Stanwyck embodied the cool, cruel, and cutting essence of film noir as murderous Phyllis Dietrichson in *Double Indemnity*. Never speaking much higher than a whisper, Stanwyck enticed Fred MacMurray, legions of intrigued moviegoers, and her Academy colleagues to a third Oscar nomination. Ingrid Bergman, as the victim in *Gaslight* rather than the villainess, won that year's Best Actress trophy. *Sorry, Wrong Number*, a popular radio thriller, became a movie vehicle for Stanwyck, who had the audience terrified and rooting for her survival from a potential killer even though her character was a spoiled hypochondriac. Bedridden throughout the movie, Stanwyck had to convey all the nuances of her character with vocal inflection and facial expression. She handled it so expertly, the movie became one of the most chilling entertainments of the decade. At the 1948 Academy Awards, Stanwyck's performance brought the Anatole Litvak thriller its only nomination. Despite the Academy's fondness for her, and their awareness that it was time she joined the ranks of Oscar-winning actors, they voted instead for Jane Wyman in *Johnny Belinda*. Stanwyck's movie career stayed strong throughout the 1950s, with lead roles in *Titanic*, which won the 1953 Oscar for Best Story and Screenplay, and *Executive Suite*, which earned the cast a special citation at the 1954 Venice Film Festival, but resulted in an acting Oscar nomination only for supporting player Nina Foch. Finally in 1981 the Academy made up for their omissions by giving Stanwyck an honorary "Golden Boy," as she called it, in recognition of her enduring legacy.

79. *Greta Garbo*

1929/30 Best Actress as prostitute Anna Christie in *Anna Christie*
1929/30 Best Actress as fallen woman Madame Rita Cavallini in *Romance*

1937 Best Actress as Dame Marguerite Gautier (Camille) in *Camille*
1939 Best Actress as Soviet envoy Lena Yakushova (Ninotchka) in *Ninotchka*
1954 Honorary Award "for her unforgettable screen performances"

In 1924 Garbo mesmerized Sweden on celluloid as a duchess who helped a fallen priest redeem himself in *The Saga of Gösta Berling*. In 1927 she radiated internationally when Hollywood fell in love with her in the silent classic *Flesh and the Devil* from director Clarence Brown, an alliance that brought Garbo most of her Oscar attention. In 1929 the world gasped as Garbo talked. In 1932, as disillusioned Russian ballerina Grusinskaya seeking asylum at *Grand Hotel*, Garbo uttered the prophetic words, "I want to be alone." In 1939, the world roared when Garbo laughed as *Ninotchka*. And in 1948, seven years after her last commercially released motion picture, Garbo disappeared from movies. Although she intended just the opposite, the more inaccessible and then aloof Garbo became, the stronger her hold on the world that savored her beauty, marveled at her talent, and could never release the enchanting grip she sustained on anyone who saw her movies. Her first two talking pictures in Hollywood earned her Best Actress nominations at the 1929/30 Academy Awards. *Romance* was a success, but merely asserting "Garbo talks!" on the poster of *Anna Christie* ensured a hit. Garbo's trembling, gothic sadness amid Clarence Brown's dreary port setting elevated her performance to legendary. Although a likely winner for *Anna Christie*, Garbo lost to *The Divorcee* Norma Shearer. For *Camille*, Garbo again seemed the strongest contender for Oscar after winning awards from both the New York Film Critics and the National Board of Review. Her 1937 Oscar film presence was enhanced by also having starred in *Conquest* opposite Best Actor nominee Charles Boyer. A stunning performance and multiple competing films didn't bring Garbo the Oscar. Instead, *The Good Earth*'s Luise Rainer enjoyed her second consecutive Best Actress victory. In another year, Garbo's name might have been inside the Best Actress envelope for *Ninotchka*. But in 1939 neither Garbo's comic charm nor Bette Davis' courage in *Dark Victory* could topple Vivien Leigh's Tara-saving efforts in *Gone with the Wind*. Garbo set two New York Film Critics Circle records, taking home their first ever Best Actress prize in 1935 for *Anna Karenina*, and becoming their first multiple winner two years later for *Camille*. Grateful to the Big Apple critics, Garbo made her only effort to attend an award ceremony by heading to their 1940 banquet. En route, she was swarmed by such zealous fans that she slipped back into her hotel room, and soon receded from the public eye altogether. Despite two more National Board of Review wins, for *Ninotchka* and for her last film, *Two-Faced Woman* in 1941, the Academy didn't honor Garbo until six years after she disappeared from Hollywood. Charles Brackett ended the 1954 Academy Award ceremony by presenting her an honorary Oscar. Predictably, Garbo was not there. In her stead, future Best Actress nominee Nancy Kelly accepted by confirming what still holds true, "There's only one Garbo."

78. Morgan Freeman

1987 Best Supporting Actor as pimp Fast Black in *Street Smart*
1989 Best Actor as chauffeur Hoke Colburn in *Driving Miss Daisy*
1994 Best Actor as prison inmate Red in *The Shawshank Redemption*
2004 Best Supporting Actor as retired boxer/gym employee Eddie "Scrap-Iron" Dupris in *Million Dollar Baby*
2009 Best Actor as South African President Nelson Mandela in *Invictus*

It may now take a stretch of the imagination to envision Morgan Freeman as anyone but the stately baritone persona for which he is now indelibly known, but Oscar first took note of Freeman in a role the antithesis of the one that inspired producers to cast him as God in *Bruce Almighty*. After building a career over decades in theater and daytime television, Freeman expanded his résumé with stellar supporting performances in sometimes offbeat projects. One such movie was Jerry Schatzberg's *Street Smart*, in which Freeman played a pimp who abused his prostitutes and menaced reporter Christopher Reeve. Despite the film's tame box office, the Academy couldn't overlook Freeman, and put him in contention for Best Supporting Actor against front-runners Denzel Washington in *Cry Freedom* and the winner, Sean Connery in *The Untouchables*. Two years later, Freeman moved up to Best Actor competitor when he reprised his Off-Broadway role of an unflappable chauffeur to a cantankerous old Southerner in *Driving Miss Daisy*. After winning the Golden Globe for Best Actor, Musical or Comedy as Hoke, he joined *Born on the Fourth of July*'s Tom Cruise and *Dead Poets Society*'s Robin Williams as potential winners for the Best Actor Academy Award. But Oscar's surprise win of 1989 came for Best Actor as Daniel Day-Lewis pulled an upset for *My Left Foot*. Like *Street Smart* seven years earlier, *The Shawshank Redemption* barely made a box office ripple in its initial release, but impressed critics and award committees, including the Academy, which recognized it with nominations in seven categories, including Best Picture, and Best Actor for Freeman. It lost every major prize to *Forrest Gump*. The 2004 Oscar season took a few dramatic turns. Early on, it appeared that *The Aviator* would finally bring director Martin Scorsese his long-overdue Oscar, and seemed primed to join the Best Picture winners as well. In the Best Supporting Actor category, Thomas Hayden Church was an early favorite to win for *Sideways*, with Clive Owen fogging the mix by winning the Golden Globe for *Closer*. But a little engine with plenty of gusto called *Million Dollar Baby* found traction with audiences, critics, and Academy voters, and Clint Eastwood's underdog movie held new promise for a TKO. The movie's late-season attention, and divided enthusiasm for the Church and Owen performances opened voters' eyes to the power of Morgan Freeman's work as the narrator and supporting foundation of *Million Dollar Baby*. Although some Academy voters might have wanted to wait to honor Freeman in a lead acting role, more capitalized on the opportunity to reward him for what turned into the year's big winner.

Freeman returned to the Best Actor competition in 2009 for *Invictus*, another hit helmed by Clint Eastwood. Ideal as unifying South African leader Nelson Mandela, Freeman earned his first nomination in a biographical performance befitting his regal stature in Hollywood.

77. Julianne Moore

1997 Best Supporting Actress as porn actress Maggie "Amber Waves" in *Boogie Nights*
1999 Best Actress as wife/mistress Sarah Miles in *The End of the Affair*
2002 Best Actress as wife/mother Cathy Whitaker in *Far from Heaven*

Morgan Freeman, Cate Blanchett, Hilary Swank and Jamie Foxx all earned Oscars in 2004, with Freeman and Swank winning for the year's Best Picture, *Million Dollar Baby*.

2002 Best Supporting Actress as wife/mother Laura Brown in *The Hours*
2014 Best Actress as linguistics professor Alice Howland in *Still Alice*

In 1993, Julianne Moore made her first big entrée into Oscar contenders as part of the large ensemble of Robert Altman's *Short Cuts*. Praised by critics, the movie built momentum en route to the Oscars by winning Independent Spirit Awards as Best Feature and Best Director. Of the entire cast, only Moore was singled out for a Spirit nomination. The Academy was less enthusiastic, nominating *Short Cuts* only for Best Director. In Moore's most famous scene, she argues with husband Matthew Modine while standing naked from the waist down. Her monologue was so powerful it quelled any misgivings expressed by detractors off put by the nudity. She culled even more positive reviews, and her first Oscar nomination, in 1997 for Paul Thomas Anderson's *Boogie Nights* as an aging porn star who mothers the inexperienced industry upstarts while struggling to regain custody of a child she lost because of her profession and her cocaine addiction. Moore's wordless few seconds in response to a court decision proved why she is considered one of the greatest actresses of her generation. She was next nominated for Neil Jordan's adaptation of Graham Greene's *The End of the Affair*, but 1999's Best Actress race belonged to Hilary Swank in *Boys Don't Cry*. Following multiple Best Actress wins for *Far from Heaven*, Moore went into the 2002 Best Actress Oscar race a close frontrunner with Renée Zellweger from *Chicago* and gradual momentum-building Nicole Kidman of *The Hours*. Moore's delicate performance as a depressed housewife in *The Hours* also put her in contention for Best Supporting Actress, making Moore the ninth of currently eleven actors in Oscar history to compete in both acting categories in a single year. Unfortunately, her Oscar results repeated Signourney Weaver's (1988) and Emma Thompson's (1993), sending Moore home empty-handed. Her consistent Oscar presence, such as appearing in *I'm Not There*, which earned Cate Blanchett a 2007 Oscar nod, and nurturing Best Actor nominee Colin Firth as *A Single Man* in 2009, left many baffled that Moore was overlooked in 2010 for Best Picture nominee *The Kids are All Right*, while Annette Bening and Mark Ruffalo vied for acting honors. Moore's bristling performance as Sarah Palin in *Game Change* netted her most every 2012 TV award and added a Primetime Emmy to a trophy shelf already glistening with prizes from the Cannes, Berlin, and Venice Film Festivals; from the Golden Globes, SAG, and critics circles across the nation. A dozen years without Oscar consideration made Moore's reemergence in the Best Actress Oscar race of 2014 seem long overdue. In 2007 Julie Christie had competed for Best Actress for *Away from Her* as an Alzheimer's patient seen from the viewpoint of her devoted husband. In *Still Alice*, Moore faced the same disease from the perspective of the patient, a bright linguistics professor frazzled and frightened, but fighting against the dimming of her own mind. After winning virtually every Best Actress award, Moore radiated raw emotion throughout Oscar night, and glowed as bright as the statuette she could finally call her own.

76. *Jennifer Jones*

1943 Best Actress as saint Bernadette Soubirous in *The Song of Bernadette*
1944 Best Supporting Actress as daughter Jane Hilton in *Since You Went Away*
1945 Best Actress as amnesiac Singleton in *Love Letters*
1946 Best Actress as orphan Pearl Chavez in *Duel in the Sun*
1955 Best Actress as doctor Han Suyin in *Love is a Many-Splendored Thing*

Young Jennifer Jones so impressed filmmaker David O. Selznick that he called her back after what she thought was a botched screen test for a little movie called *Claudia*. Although she lost the part to another future starlet, Dorothy McGuire, the screen test was life-altering for two reasons. First, it brought Jones into Selznick's sphere, where she entranced him, becoming his muse, his love, and his wife. Second, it brought the unknown actress to the attention of director Henry King, who thought her ethereal innocence could convey the sincerity of faith befitting a saint. As the title character in *The Song of Bernadette*, Jones' awe at seeing a vision of the Virgin Mary seemed enshrouded in a halo, setting the perfect tone for the religious epic that inspired an impressive twelve nominations at the 1943 Academy Awards. The Best Actress race included two former winners, Joan Fontaine in *The Constant Nymph* and Greer Garson as *Madame Curie*, but three Oscar newcomers led the competition. Jean Arthur was as appealing as ever in *The More the Merrier*, but eyes, veering occasionally toward Jones as a potential spoiler, were focused on expected victor Ingrid Bergman in *For Whom the Bell Tolls*. Jones was a surprising but deserving winner and celebrated not only her win, but also her 25th birthday. The following year she switched to the supporting category helping mother Claudette Colbert keep the home fires burning in *Since You Went Away*. But more meaningful to Jones at that Oscar ceremony was her presentation of the Best Actress award to Bergman for *Gaslight*. As friends, Jones felt bad for beating out Bergman for her expected win the previous year, so announcing her as the next year's winner was particularly satisfying. To avoid being typecast as only loveable characters, Jones stretched her skills to play Singleton, a murderer unaware of her crime because of amnesia in *Love Letters*. David O. Selznick cast his beloved Jones as the lead in *Duel in the Sun*, an epic Western he intended to be the next *Gone with the Wind*. Although it didn't reach that status, it was a box office success, and it brought Jones, and supporting actress Lillian Gish, the movie's only two Oscar nominations. Jones was at her most enchanting as a Eurasian doctor who discovered that *Love is a Many-Splendored Thing* despite opposition to her interracial romance with war correspondent William Holden. Always selective about her roles, Jones made only eight movies after her last nominated hit. She found a new generation of fans thanks to the box office power of the disaster film genre of the 1970s. Earning a Golden Globe nomination for her sympathetic role as Lisolette Mueller in *The Towering Inferno* boded well for yet another Oscar competition, but in the end the only cast member of the movie nominated was Fred Astaire, who played her love interest.

75. Susan Sarandon

    1981 Best Actress as clam bar waitress/aspiring croupier Sally in *Atlantic City*
    1991 Best Actress as waitress Louise in *Thelma & Louise*
    1992 Best Actress as mother/wife Michaela Odone in *Lorenzo's Oil*
    1994 Best Actress as lawyer Reggie Love in *The Client*
    1995 Best Actress as nun Sister Helen Prejean in *Dead Man Walking*

Fresh and pretty, and equally intelligent and headstrong, Sarandon has sculpted a career out of bold choices and varied roles. In 1975, many movie fans first loved her as naïve newlywed Janet in *The Rocky Horror Picture Show*, while Academy members met her when she attended the Oscars with her husband at the time, Chris Sarandon, a nominee for *Dog Day Afternoon*. Two years after they divorced, she was cast by Louis Malle as a down-on-her-luck waitress determined to make good in the crime drama *Atlantic City*. Once the movie won the Golden Lion at the Venice Film Festival, it gradually built an audience and gained increasingly enthusiastic critical acclaim until the Academy nominated it for the five major awards of 1981: Best Picture, Best Director, Best Original Screenplay, Best Actor for Burt Lancaster, and Best Actress for Sarandon. For her debut Oscar competition, Sarandon lost to Katharine Hepburn in *On Golden Pond*. Sarandon expressed her disappointment when her name didn't make the 1988 Best Actress ballot as expected for her lusty, comic performance as a baseball groupie in *Bull Durham*. But three years later Sarandon and Geena Davis were the center of Oscar attention for their rollicking performances as fugitives *Thelma & Louise*. The road movie captured the imagination of filmgoers to make it an instant classic, and its box office only increased when feminist debates stirred social commentary about the movie's message. At the center of the film were the writing and the lead performances, all of which were up for Oscars. Odds-makers gave Sarandon a slight edge toward victory over Davis, who had won a 1988 supporting Oscar, but did not rule out Jodie Foster's chances for *The Silence of the Lambs*. That film swept all the major categories, including Best Actress. From then on, however, Sarandon remained the primary presence in nearly every Best Actress race of the 1990s. She had a great chance to win in 1992 as a mother desperate to find a cure for her critically ill son in the biographical drama *Lorenzo's Oil*. Sarandon was particularly unforgettable in the scene where she cradled her suffering child and encouraged him to run to Baby Jesus if he was ready to die. Sarandon's main competition in 1992 was Emma Thompson, who won the award for *Howards End*. As *The Client*'s only Oscar nominee, Sarandon may not have been a lead contender for her 1994 competition, but she had built up such momentum that an Oscar victory seemed eminent. It came the following year when Tim Robbins, her spouse at that time, directed her in *Dead Man Walking*.

As befitting their social and political enthusiasm, the adaptation of Sister Helen Prejean's memoir about death row was a harrowing and multidimensional exploration of the issue. At the heart of it was Sarandon as the compassionate nun who sought grace over vengeance. Despite solid

Death row inmate Matthew Poncelet (Sean Penn) finally responded to the impassioned efforts of Helen Prejean (Susan Sarandon) to prevent his execution in *Dead Man Walking* (1995).

performances from all her competitors, especially Elisabeth Shue in *Leaving Las Vegas* and Meryl Streep in *The Bridges of Madison County*, the 1995 Best Actress race belonged to Sarandon.

74. Anne Bancroft

1962 Best Actress as teacher Annie Sullivan in *The Miracle Worker*
1964 Best Actress as wife/mother Jo Armitage in *The Pumpkin Eater*
1967 Best Actress as wife/mistress Mrs. Robinson in *The Graduate*
1977 Best Actress as prima ballerina Emma Jacklin in *The Turning Point*
1985 Best Actress as mother superior Sister Miriam Ruth in *Agnes of God*

Anne Bancroft always remained an enigma. While she originally sculpted her career with serious, dramatic stage and screen performances, she married and occasionally excelled in comic roles with zany Mel Brooks. Throughout her career, her characterizations stood out no matter the genre, and her broad Italian grin could convey triumph (*The Miracle Worker*), seduction (*The Graduate*), resignation (*The Turning Point*), and skepticism (*Agnes of God*). Bancroft won a Tony as Annie Sullivan in *The Miracle Worker*, and she repeated the triumph with an Oscar in 1962. On Broadway in *Mother Courage and Her Children* on Academy Awards night, Bancroft honored Joan Crawford's request to accept the Best Actress prize on her behalf. Still in full costume and makeup for her stage role, Bancroft was beaming in photos of Crawford eventually presenting her the statuette. It was Bancroft who announced Sidney Poitier as Best Actor of 1963, at which time she whispered to him, "Enjoy it. It doesn't last long." Bancroft's second nomination came for a somber character analysis of a fertile woman in a troubled marriage in writer Harold Pinter's *The Pumpkin Eater*. Except for Bancroft's performance, the small black and white movie was outdazzled by lush color productions of *My Fair Lady*, the night's big winner, and *Mary Poppins*, for which Julie Andrews won Best Actress. In 1966, a year when Bancroft was not even nominated, she finally experienced ascending the stairs onto the Santa Monica Civic Auditorium stage to accept a Best Actress award when she proxied for Elizabeth Taylor, the winner for *Who's Afraid of Virginia Woolf?*. Not cracking a smile until she neared the podium, she offered thanks barely above a whisper. Bancroft's touchstone role that, to her bemusement, remained in the forefront of moviegoers' minds through a lifetime of inspired performances was her portrayal of lusty Mrs. Robinson in *The Graduate*. Perhaps because Bancroft let the character's sexual allure seep through more ardent expressions of cynicism, amusement, even ire, Mrs. Robinson embodied a timeless sexiness forever stroking the psyche of film fans. In a Best Actress race that could have gone in any of five directions, Bancroft lost to Katharine Hepburn in *Guess Who's Coming to Dinner*. Like Bette Davis over Anne Baxter in *All About Eve*, Bancroft was said to have been given a more fully drawn character to play in *The Turning Point* than her Best Actress competitor, Shirley MacLaine. Her fading ballerina had the pivotal lines ("It wouldn't matter worth a damn"), yet because MacLaine had yet to win in her fourth acting race, both women seemed equally matched as potential winners. The Oscar went to Diane Keaton in *Annie Hall*. Although her role was smaller than Jane Fonda's in *Agnes of God*, Bancroft got the Best Actress nomination in 1985. As that year's roster of Best Actress nominees was announced, Bancroft beamed, fully enjoying the moment. Never one to suffer bombast, she rolled her eyes when presenter F. Murray Abraham delayed announcing Geraldine Page the winner to editorialize about her. Sincere, sexy, silly, Bancroft could do it all, and always seemed to relish the experience.

73. *Susan Hayward*

1947 Best Actress as singer Angie in *Smash-Up—The Story of a Woman*
1949 Best Actress as unwed mother Eloise Winters in *My Foolish Heart*
1952 Best Actress as actress/singer Jane Froman in *With a Song in My Heart*
1955 Best Actress as Broadway actress Lillian Roth in *I'll Cry Tomorrow*
1958 Best Actress as death row inmate Barbara Graham in *I Want to Live!*

Allegedly without a single acting lesson her entire life, Susan Hayward was a steady presence in the Best Actress category from the late 1940s to the late 1950s. Like many other aspiring actresses of her generation, she ventured to Hollywood to screen test to play Scarlett O'Hara in *Gone with the Wind*. Instead, she was one of the few women cast in *Beau Geste*, for which the Academy cited Brian Donlevy for a Supporting Actor nomination in 1939. Steady work eventually brought her to Oscar in a juicy starring role playing the types of characters for which she would be most remembered, and most often nominated. By today's standards, Hayward's vehicles may seem drunk with melodrama, but in their day, they were cutting edge, sometimes scandalous social commentaries. In 1945 watching Ray Milland struggle against wall-crawling hallucinations in *The Lost Weekend* was startling. Seeing Hayward, a woman, facing the same demons just two years later bordered on shocking. Her skill at conveying compassion and complexity from her characterizations gave her dramas heft, and the Academy marveled at her skills. In the 1930s and early '40s, audiences found one level of grit from a Bette Davis film. Susan Hayward took them even deeper. In *Smash-Up—The Story of a Woman*, Hayward retraced the descent that left her bandaged and clinging to a life soaked in alcohol. A reversal of *A Star Is Born*'s plot, and indirectly based on the sad downfall of one of Bing Crosby's wives, Hayward's character faced real problems based on a real person, as Hayward would in all her nominated performances, except for *My Foolish Heart*. In the 1950s, Hayward's biographical performances were even more polished. Without histrionics, Hayward depicted the tragic lives of fallen entertainer Jane Froman in *With a Song in My Heart*, and Lillian Roth in *I'll Cry Tomorrow* with a bit lower lip but an erect backbone. Fans and the Academy saw and loved the personal strength she gave women who sometimes lacked it. Always tipping the scale just a bit further toward hopeless ends, Hayward found the vehicle-of-a-lifetime as death row inmate Barbara Graham in *I Want to Live!* Like the title of her other nominated works, this one felt shaded in yellow journalism. But this time both Hayward as the star and Robert Wise as director worked with such sincerity to avoid highlighting the natural sensationalism of a film based on an actual woman sent to the electric chair that both were up for Oscars. For Hayward's fifth nomination, the Academy was fully behind her work, and she earned more votes than competitors Deborah Kerr in *Separate Tables*, Shirley MacLaine in *Some Came Running*, Rosalind Russell as *Auntie Mame*, and Elizabeth Taylor in *Cat on a Hot Tin Roof*. It took an actress of Hayward's stature to temper the inherent melodramatics of her films with characterizations where hard-luck, hardboiled heartbreak felt real and compelling.

72. *Paul Muni*

- 1928/29 Best Actor as murderer awaiting execution James Dyke in *The Valiant*
- 1932/33 Best Actor as fugitive James Allen in *I Am a Fugitive from a Chain Gang*
- **1936 Best Actor as chemist/microbiologist Louis Pasteur in *The Story of Louis Pasteur***
- 1937 Best Actor as writer Emile Zola in *The Life of Emile Zola*
- 1959 Best Actor as family physician Dr. Sam Abelman in *The Last Angry Man*

Born into a family of actors, Muni enjoyed early stage success and instant movie stardom when the Academy singled him out for a Best Actor nomination for his first movie, *The Valiant*. The part-silent, part-sound movie, released during Oscar's second season, revealed Muni's ability to draw from audiences sympathy for and identification with complex characters. As James Dyke, he was a convicted killer who compassionately strove to persuade two women that he was not their son and brother so they could continue with their lives after his execution. Early films rarely showed such extremes in a single character, and the compelling portrayal rested squarely on Muni's capable shoulders. His next nomination again came for playing a prisoner, this time an unfairly incarcerated everyman who resorts to criminal means in order to escape. Mervyn LeRoy's groundbreaking drama still packs a wallop, as Muni's piercing gaze pulled viewers deeply into his favor. Thereafter, he became *the* actor's actor of the 1930s. His portrayal of coal miner Joe Radek in *Black Fury* so impressed the Academy that, when he was overlooked for a nomination, his peers made him a write-in candidate in one of only two years the Academy allowed the alternative voting strategy. This rare feat concurred with another Oscar anomaly, the announcement of how each candidate ranked. According to Academy records, Muni earned more write-in tallies than all three actors from *Mutiny on the Bounty*, leaving Muni only votes behind the year's winner, *The Informer*'s Victor McLaglen. A focused, dedicated thespian, Muni immersed himself in his characterizations, especially in the biographies for which he was so revered. He prepared for roles doing research so thorough that, once cameras rolled, he had already become the men he portrayed. A lively Louis Pasteur, Muni bowled over audiences and the Academy, and won Best Actor over such beloved performances as Gary Cooper in *Mr. Deeds Goes to Town*, Walter Huston as *Dodsworth*, William Powell in *My Man Godfrey*, and Spencer Tracy in *San Francisco*. The following year he seemed likely to repeat his Best Actor victory when *The Life of Emile Zola* went into Oscar night favored as the potential big winner. His chances seemed even better because he was also praised for his performance as Chinese farmer Wang Lung in another top 1937 Best Picture nominee, *The Good Earth*. However, Spencer Tracy turned the tables and beat Muni as lead actor. Personally reserved and iconoclastic, Muni withdrew from Hollywood by the late 1930s, returning for only rare characterizations that intrigued him. The last such role earned him his fifth and final Oscar nomination. As a dedicated doctor whose down-home approach to medicine squeezed him out of a modernizing profession, Muni impressed the Academy as *The Last Angry Man*. His nomination served as a gracious tip of the hat to Muni, who retired soon after.

71. Shirley MacLaine

   1958   Best Actress as good-time girl Ginny Moorehead in *Some Came Running*
   1960   Best Actress as elevator operator Fran Kubelik in *The Apartment*
   1963   Best Actress as prostitute Irma La Douce in *Irma La Douce*
   1975   Best Documentary Feature for *The Other Half of the Sky: A China Memoir*

Part I. The Countdown 53

1977 Best Actress as ballet studio cofounder Deedee Rodgers in *The Turning Point*
1983 Best Actress as mother Aurora Greenway in *Terms of Endearment*

A high-kicking pixie with bobbed red hair and freckles, MacLaine bounded onto the big screen with a life-relishing energy that made her a magnetic screen presence. Hitchcock launched her film career when casting her in the delightful black comedy *The Trouble with Harry*. Though the film had no trouble impressing moviegoers or critics, Oscar paid it no mind. In an era of astounding beauties like Elizabeth Taylor and Marilyn Monroe, MacLaine ushered in a new Oscar-worthy leading lady, an Everywoman whose foibles and eccentricities charmed. In 1958 *Some Came Running* graced three acting categories. Its only lead player up was Academy newcomer MacLaine. The pinnacle of her performance as too-often dismissed Ginny came when she visited the woman whom she suspects will win the heart of the man she loves. Bristling with a hopelessness she's reticent to embrace, MacLaine was an acting wonder to behold. But in 1958, Academy voters were more focused on fifth-time nominee Susan Hayward in *I Want to Live!* In 1960, *The Apartment* was the film to beat, and the early award season spotlight was on MacLaine as suicidal elevator operator Fran Kubelik. Elizabeth Taylor's miraculous recovery from her brush with death shifted the spotlight and brought Taylor the Oscar. "I lost to a tracheotomy," MacLaine quipped. MacLaine reteamed with *The Apartment* star Jack Lemmon and director Billy Wilder for *Irma La Douce*, and of the three, this time only she was picked up by Oscar's radar. In a wide-open race where previous nominees MacLaine, Leslie Caron, and Natalie Wood competed against Oscar newcomers Rachel Roberts and Patricia Neal, it was Neal who took the award for her short but intense performance in *Hud*. Bob Fosse gave MacLaine the chance to show movie audiences her electric musical talents in *Sweet Charity* in 1969. The Academy nominated it for three awards, but none for acting. MacLaine next branched out as a filmmaker and became one of the first actresses to earn a nomination for work behind the camera with a Best Documentary Feature nod in 1975. With 11 nominations, *The Turning Point* could have been Oscar's favorite in 1977. Instead, it suffered the Academy's biggest shut-out, sending MacLaine and fellow Best Actress nominee Anne Bancroft home empty-handed. Six years later, the spotlight was focused only on MacLaine. Few actors have gone into an Oscar night more poised to win than MacLaine in 1983, even though her *Terms of Endearment* co-star Debra Winger competed in the same category, which sometimes proves a vote-splitting results shifter. MacLaine's self-absorbed Aurora Greenway's metamorphosis when facing her grown daughter's cancer embodied the fear, fury, and fateful resignation of life's toughest changes. In her acceptance speech, MacLaine drew gales of laughter by noting that the endless Oscar telecast felt as long as her career. Then she asserted, "I deserve this." Indeed, she did.

70. Deborah Kerr

1949 Best Actress as mother Evelyn Boult in *Edward, My Son*
1953 Best Actress as adulterous wife Karen Holmes in *From Here to Eternity*
1956 Best Actress as teacher Anna in *The King and I*
1957 Best Actress as novice Sister Angela in *Heaven Knows, Mr. Allison*
1958 Best Actress as spinster Sybil Railton-Bell in *Separate Tables*
1960 Best Actress as wife Ida Carmody in *The Sundowners*
1993 Honorary lifetime achievement award "in appreciation for a full career's worth of elegant and beautifully crafted performances"

One of Hollywood's luckiest breaks was catching the imagination of a pretty, refined Scottish stage and film actress in the 1940s known as Deborah Kerr. She quickly rose to top box office stardom in England, and repeated the achievement after her first movies in the U.S. Even though *Black Narcissus* earned Kerr a Best Actress citation from the New York Film Critics, and the Academy favored the movie with two technical wins, most famously for Jack Cardiff's color cinematography, Kerr and her castmates were overlooked by Oscar in 1947. But two years later the Academy embraced her moving portrayal of a grieving mother in *Edward, My Son*, and Kerr was an Oscar nominee. Her elegant demeanor and eloquent diction would have typecast her as British snobs or spinsters if Kerr had not been bold about tackling diverse roles. Her lusty portrayal of an unfaithful officer's wife in *From Here to Eternity* put her at the forefront of the 1953 Best Actress race where the three delightful British imports, Kerr, Leslie Caron as *Lili*, and Audrey Hepburn taking a *Roman Holiday* muscled attention from American actresses Ava Gardner in *Mogambo* and Maggie McNamara in the controversial *The Moon is Blue*. Enchanting Hepburn took the Academy Award. Undaunted, Kerr again led the 1956 Best Actress competition as the likely winner, as it seemed she and Yul Brynner's electrifying chemistry in *The King and I* could earn them both Oscars. Brynner won, but Kerr lost to *Anastasia*'s Ingrid Bergman for what is considered a conciliatory gesture by the Academy for Hollywood's ostracizing Bergman after her affair with Roberto Rossellini. 1957's Best Actress race evenly matched five talented actresses, yet some thought Kerr finally winning as a nun in *Heaven Knows, Mr. Allison* would punctuate the many fine performances since she played Sister Clodagh in *Black Narcissus*. She lost again, this time to Oscar newcomer Joanne Woodward in *The Three Faces of Eve*. Kerr's third nomination in a row came for *Separate Tables*, directed by Delbert Mann and produced by cast member Burt Lancaster. As had happened in 1956, her co-star, David Niven, won Best Actor, but Kerr lost Best Actress, this time to Susan Hayward in *I Want to Live!* Mann speculated that Kerr lost because Lancaster, wanting to show up sooner in the film, had many of Kerr's early, and best scenes cut. At her sixth nomination for *The Sundowners*, Kerr was ready to finally win, as she was on the brink of becoming one of Oscar's most overlooked talents. Her chances seemed strong, as *The Sundowners* came into the awards with five nominations, all in major categories. Alas, Elizabeth Taylor's brush with death took all the headlines, and the Oscar, making Kerr the most nominated actor without a win. Her record was eventually tied by Thelma Ritter and Glenn Close, and surpassed by Richard Burton and Peter O'Toole. The Academy made amends to Kerr who, still lovely though somewhat frail by her early seventies, accepted her lifetime achievement award in 1993 for nearly 50 years of enchanting performances.

69. *Vanessa Redgrave*

1966 Best Actress as wife Leonie Delt in *Morgan!*
1968 Best Actress as dancer Isadora Duncan in *Isadora*
1971 Best Actress as Scottish monarch Mary, Queen of Scots in *Mary, Queen of Scots*
1977 Best Supporting Actress as Nazi resister Julia in *Julia*
1984 Best Actress as feminist Olive Chancellor in *The Bostonians*
1992 Best Supporting Actress as mother Ruth Wilcox in *Howards End*

To take nothing from other talented members of the five-generation Redgrave acting dynasty—including her Oscar-nominated father Michael Redgrave, sister Lynn Redgrave, and son-in-law Liam Neeson—Vanessa almost singlehandedly deserves credit for the Redgraves' status as one of the most award-honored acting families in movie history. Statuesque, glint-eyed Vanessa first hit her stride as part of Europe's new wave of cinema that dazzled Hollywood in the mid–1960s. She made her initial international mark in 1966 in *Blowup*, which earned director Michelangelo Antonioni Best Director as well as Best Story and Screenplay nominations, as Anne Boleyn in the Best Picture-winning *A Man for All Seasons*, and in *Morgan!*, for which she earned her first Academy Award nomination. That year's Best Actress race was the most attention-getting of the night, as every star was foreign born, and two of those actresses, Vanessa and Lynn Redgrave, were sisters. The distinguished Redgraves seamlessly avoided the sibling rivalry angle played up by the press, which sustained great mileage from a similar competition in 1941 between much less congenial sisters Olivia de Havilland and Joan Fontaine. Both

Redgraves attended, but the winner, fellow Brit Elizabeth Taylor, did not. From then on, Vanessa Redgrave found a succession of vehicles that conveyed both her acting prowess and her desire to stretch beyond the confines of mainstream comfort. She reteamed with *Morgan!* director Karel Reisz to play innovative dancer Isadora Duncan in *Isadora* and earned her second Best Actress nod. As she had in *A Man for All Seasons*, she played British royalty again in 1971, this time as *Mary, Queen of Scots*. In another competition dominated by British thespians, Redgrave and the other English actresses, Julie Christie, Glenda Jackson, and Janet Suzman, lost to American star Jane Fonda in *Klute*. In 1977 Redgrave and Fonda teamed as the central figures in *Julia*, Fred Zinnemann's artistic masterpiece based on Lillian Hellman's short story in *Pentimento* about how The Resistance of World War II impacted a lifelong friendship. Though they played equally important figures in the story, Fonda was up for Best Actress but Redgrave landed in the supporting category. Her alternately lush and understated performance immediately resonated with the Academy, and only fear of what her political activism might lead her to say in her acceptance speech left any room to doubt Redgrave would win that award. When she did, she became the first actor to win a supporting award playing a title character. She did make political comments during her acceptance speech, but tied them into the themes of *Julia*. The next decade, Redgrave returned to lead acting competition for *The Bostonians*, the first movie directed by James Ivory to earn an actor an Oscar nod. In 1992 Redgrave enchanted with an ethereal, languid performance in Ivory's *Howards End*, but it was Emma Thompson in the lead role that won for that movie. Fifty years into her career, Redgrave is still captivating audiences and her peers, leaving open the possibility that other Oscar fare might still be on the horizon.

68. *Norman Shearer*

1929/30 Best Actress as wife Jerry in *The Divorcee*
1929/30 Best Actress as daughter Lucia "Lally" Marlett in *Their Own Desire*
1930/31 Best Actress as daughter Jan Ashe in *A Free Soul*
1934 Best Actress as poet Elizabeth Barrett in *The Barretts of Wimpole Street*
1936 Best Actress as lover Juliet Capulet in *Romeo and Juliet*
1938 Best Actress as French monarch Marie Antoinette in *Marie Antoinette*

After becoming a star playing familiar, often wholesome young women, Norma Shearer trailblazed into film history as one of the first actors to portray independent-thinking and -living women in Hollywood's pre-code era. She capitalized on new opportunities afforded by her personal alliance with producer Irving Thalberg, after whom the Academy named its Irving G. Thalberg Memorial Award in 1937, and the Academy quickly recognized her talent with Oscar nominations. In 1929/30, Academy rules allowed single nominations for multiple performances, and Shearer was nominated for two roles. In *Their Own Desire*, she portrayed a wholesome young woman upset by her parents' impending divorce. Fearing that her portrayal of yet another nondescript righteous young woman would begin to bore audiences, she tackled the role of *The Divorcee* in the envelope-pushing melodrama. Although no records indicate why, both she and Best Actor winner George Arliss received nominations for two movies, but have gone down in Oscar history as having won for one of the two. For Shearer, the racier role took the prize. With *A Free Soul* in 1930/31, Shearer became the first Oscar-winning actor to compete for another Academy Award the following season. The Academy's interest in her work persisted throughout the 1930s. When the pre-code film era ended in 1934, Shearer segued into roles in more lavish costume dramas, and her fan base only grew.

Robert Browning (Fredric March) was enchanted by Elizabeth (Oscar nominee Norma Shearer), one of *The Barretts of Wimpole Street* (1934).

Because the biographical storyline implied that Elizabeth Barrett Browning had to fight for independence from an incestuously protective father, *The Barretts of Wimpole Street* almost wasn't made. But with Shearer in the lead and able support from respected British actor Charles Laughton as her father, *The Barretts of Wimpole Street* became a hit, and Shearer earned another nomination. It was the last year the Academy nominated just three Best Actresses, and Shearer and Grace Moore of *One Night of Love* lost to Claudette Colbert in *It Happened One Night*. Testimony to Shearer's prodigious talent was the fact that she earned a nomination as Juliet Capulet when she was 34 years old. The lavish and expensive production took liberties with Shakespeare, downplaying the fact that the lovers were supposed to be in their teens. An audience and Academy favorite, the movie kept Shearer the most nominated actress of the decade. The trend expanded two years later thanks to an equally elaborate production of *Marie Antoinette*, with Shearer up for Best Actress as the French monarch and Robert Morley up for Best Supporting Actor as a pitiable Louis XVI. Earlier that year Shearer won Best Actress for the role at the Venice Film Festival in only its fourth year, but the Oscar went to Bette Davis for *Jezebel*. In retrospect that competition was a passing of the torch to Davis, whose reign as most-nominated actress was just beginning as Shearer's came to an end. A recent resurgence in Shearer's contribution to moviemaking helped drop the suggestion that she was Hollywood's "forgotten star." Instead, she remains one of its most revered.

67. *Leonardo DiCaprio*

1993 Best Supporting Actor as brother/son Arnie Grape in *What's Eating Gilbert Grape*
2004 Best Actor as aviator/producer/mogul Howard Hughes in *The Aviator*
2006 Best Actor as Rhodesian mercenary Danny Archer in *Blood Diamond*
2013 Best Actor as stockbroker Jordan Belfort in *The Wolf of Wall Street*
2013 Best Picture as co-producer (with Joey McFarland, Martin Scorsese and Emma Tillinger Koskoff) of *The Wolf of Wall Street*
2015 Best Actor as fur trapper Hugh Glass in *The Revenant*

What's Eating Gilbert Grape owed much to the squinting elation of DiCaprio as Johnny Depp's developmentally challenged brother, Arnie. In fact, some of director Lasse Hallström's most indelible images in the movie focus on DiCaprio's innocent, bewildered face. Playing much younger than his 19 years, DiCaprio won multiple awards for his performance, but lost the Oscar to Tommy Lee Jones in *The Fugitive*. After bursting onto Oscar's radar,

DiCaprio has remained a central illumination in Academy range, often with multiple blips in a single year. In 1996, he confronted mother Meryl Streep and brought brief elation to Best Actress nominee Diane Keaton amid the tender turmoil of *Marvin's Room*. That same year, he played tragic ruffian Romeo in Baz Luhrmann's *William Shakespeare's Romeo + Juliet*. The Academy cited the film with a single nomination, for Art Direction, and DiCaprio's performance proved to everyone, including director James Cameron, that he could keep audiences enraptured by his magnetic presence even amid titanic special effects. In 1997 DiCaprio became a megastar as lead in moviedom's highest grossing blockbuster by stowing away on the *Titanic*. Despite DiCaprio's visceral portrayal that continued to electrify the onboard romance even through the capsizing suspense, the Academy recognized Kate Winslet and Gloria Stuart for the only acting nods amid that film's fourteen Oscar nominations. In 2002, he played opposite Oscar contenders Daniel Day-Lewis in *Gangs of New York* and Christopher Walken in *Catch Me If You Can*, but DiCaprio didn't have his second flight with Oscar until he starred in *The Aviator* to become the second actor, after Jason Robards, Jr., of *Melvin and Howard*, to be nominated for playing eccentric billionaire Howard Hughes ("It's the wave of the future, the wave of the future"). Robards lost to Timothy Hutton in *Ordinary People*, and DiCaprio to Jamie Foxx in *Ray*. DiCaprio was expected to be up for Best Actor in 2006 for *The Departed*, but that year's Best Actor surprise was not an omission, but a nomination for *Blood Diamond* instead. He reteamed with Kate Winslet for Sam Mendes' *Revolutionary Road* in 2008, but the Academy gave supporting player Michael Shannon the movie's only acting nomina-

After six nominations in three different categories, Leonardo DiCaprio fulfilled everyone's expectations by winning Best Actor as *The Revenant* (2015).

tion. *Inception* was up for Best Picture in 2010, and *Django Unchained* in 2012, but DiCaprio's next nomination did not come until 2013 when he reteamed with frequent collaborator, director Martin Scorsese, for *The Wolf of Wall Street*. By not only starring as but also co-producing the biographical story of stockbroker and scam artist Jordan Belfort, DiCaprio earned two nominations in 2013. That film went home without an Oscar, but during that same ceremony, *The Great Gatsby*, with DiCaprio charming and deluded in the title role, earned Oscars in two artistic categories.

By 2015, no one in or outside the Academy doubted that DiCaprio's time to win had finally come for his seminal performance as *The Revenant*. As the brightest blip on Oscar's screen, he went into the ceremony the only sure winner from any of the top categories. Through little dialogue and a startlingly realistic fight with a bear, environmentally conscious DiCaprio weathered the cold as frontiersman Hugh Glass with such pointed intensity that he cut a path straight to Oscar's stage where he thanked his peers and continued campaigning to restore balance to the Earth's ecosystem.

66. *Ellen Burstyn*

> 1971 Best Supporting Actress as mother Lois Farrow in *The Last Picture Show*
> 1973 Best Actress as actress/mother Chris MacNeil in *The Exorcist*
> **1974 Best Actress as waitress/aspiring singer Alice Hyatt in *Alice Doesn't Live Here Anymore***
> 1978 Best Actress as adulterous housewife Doris in *Same Time, Next Year*
> 1980 Best Actress as healer Edna Mae McCauley in *Resurrection*
> 2000 Best Actress as widow Sara Goldfarb in *Requiem for a Dream*

At her core, Ellen Burstyn has always conveyed a toughness that has enthralled Oscar no matter what the genre or the role. Along with the other supporting players from *The Last Picture Show*, Burstyn captivated the Academy. As earthy Lois Farrow, one of many local women who forever lost their heart to earthy cowboy Sam the Lion (Ben Johnson in his Oscar-winning role), Burstyn lost her only Best Supporting Actress race to co-star Cloris Leachman. From its inception, high-concept horror movie *The Exorcist* was destined to be a crowd-pleaser, but Oscar rarely embraced the genre. But 1973 changed all that, and *The Exorcist* went into the awards in a head-to-head race with *The Sting* to be the big winner of the night. Whereas *The Sting* garnered only one acting nomination, for Robert Redford as Best Actor, *The Exorcist* competed in three acting categories, with Burstyn the only one up for the lead. In her first foray as a Best Actress contender, Burstyn had as good a chance as any playing an actress and terrified mother determined to free her daughter from the demons that took possession of her. That year Glenda Jackson in *A Touch of Class* won her second Best Actress prize in only four years. Burstyn owned the next year on stage and screen, winning the Best Actress Tony for *Same Time, Next Year* and the Oscar for *Alice Doesn't Live Here Anymore*, a feat only previously achieved by José Ferrer in 1950 and Shirley Booth in 1952. Burstyn's Oscar profile was elevated that year by not only starring in the movie that won her Best Actress, but also appearing in *Harry and Tonto*, for which Art Carney won Best Actor. The movie adaptation of *Same Time, Next Year* likely would not have materialized without Burstyn reprising her performance as Doris, the warmest and most comical character for which the Academy ever recognized her. In 1980, Burstyn understandably voiced her frustration with distributors of *Resurrection*. She awed critics, but the movie did not find the audience it deserved because of poor marketing. Raising the bar on her career and showing depth and power rarely demanded of her in previous roles, her tour de force as a woman whose near-death experience gives her a healing touch is a wonder to behold. Despite getting lost in box office oblivion, *Resurrection* made such an impact with industry insiders that the Academy acknowledged Burstyn and supporting actress Eva Le Gallienne with nominations. In a great year for Best Actress, mesmerizing Burstyn, tough Gena Rowlands as *Gloria*, delightful Goldie Hawn as *Private Benjamin*, and stone cold Mary Tyler Moore in *Ordinary People* lost to Sissy Spacek's spot-on interpretation as *Coal Miner's Daughter* Loretta Lynn. Burstyn's decade-long reign as an Academy favorite came to a close, but at the onset of the new century she re-emerged with another indelible performance in Darren Aronofsky's *Requiem for a Dream*. Playing most of her scenes alone, Burstyn singlehandedly grabbed audiences and held them through the relentless tension of seeing her descent into addiction. With six nominations and a win, her grip on Oscar has been equally firm.

65. *Sissy Spacek*

1976 Best Actress as high school student Carrie White in *Carrie*
1980 Best Actress as singer Loretta Lynn in *Coal Miner's Daughter*
1982 Best Actress as wife Beth Horman in *Missing*
1984 Best Actress as farmer Mae Garvey in *The River*
1986 Best Actress as wife Babe Magrath in *Crimes of the Heart*
2001 Best Actress as choral teacher Ruth Fowler in *In the Bedroom*

Of all film genres, horror is the most overlooked by the Academy. Considering age ranges of most nominated performances, teens are among the least represented. Thus, Sissy Spacek's Best Actress nomination for the teen horror film, *Carrie*, adapted from Stephen King's first hit novel, testifies to the grasp her performance had on audiences and the Academy. Spacek was spellbinding as a telekinetic teen who took bloody revenge at her prom, and then used her power to finally even the score with her sadistic mother, played by Supporting Actress nominee Piper Laurie. Although Spacek lost Best Actress to Faye Dunaway in *Network*, it set her career on solid ground. The following year, the New York Film Critics named her Best Supporting Actress for *3 Women*, but Robert Altman's character study proved too esoteric for Academy tastes, and Oscar ignored the movie altogether. As the film adaptation of Loretta Lynn's life story prepared for casting, the country legend herself picked Spacek from a headshot, and declared her the film's *Coal Miner's Daughter*. At age 29, Spacek convincingly played Lynn from age 14 to her 30s and did her own singing of all the superstar's country western hits. In a strong year for Best Actress, Spacek won over former winners Ellen Burstyn (*Resurrection*) and Goldie Hawn (*Private Benjamin*), and her strongest competitors, Gena Rowlands in *Gloria*, and Mary Tyler Moore in the year's Best Picture, *Ordinary People*. Every other year throughout most of the 1980s, Spacek's name appeared on the Best Actress ballot. She and Jack Lemmon shared shock and dismay in the political eye-opener, *Missing*, and both were Oscar nominated. In 1984, a glut of farm movies filled the Best Actress race, with Spacek in *The River*, Jessica Lange in *Country*, and Sally Field winning for *Places in the Heart*.

Spacek's most exciting post-victory competition came in 1986, when the Best Actress race was virtually unpredictable. Spacek was hilarious as Babe, the youngest Magrath sister in the adaptation of Beth Henley's Pulitzer Prize comedy *Crimes of the Heart*. Perhaps the most innocent would-be murderer on celluloid, Spacek added many fine touches (the popcorn on the gas oven is one of multiple gems), and her Southern inflection made funny lines so hysterical ("I'm not liberal, I'm a Democratic") that Spacek won multiple critics awards and shared lead potential for the Oscar with Kathleen Turner of *Peggy Sue Got Married* and ultimate winner Marlee Matlin in *Children of a Lesser God*. A committed actress who never indulged in stardom, Spacek remained selective about her roles, and found a plum part of a mother whose grief detonated with anger at the death of her grown son in Todd Field's indie hit *In the Bedroom*. Spacek, newcomer-to-Oscar Tom Wilkinson as her husband, and former Supporting Actress winner Marisa Tomei as their son's girlfriend all earned Oscar nominations in 2001. The movie's nominations were rounded out with a Best Picture and Best Screenplay nod. Although the movie won none of its competitions, it brought Spacek back to Hollywood to attend the awards, and gave a new generation of filmgoers a chance to see her master craftsmanship fully engaged. Horror, biography, political thriller, comedy, drama: Spacek has done it all with Oscar-worthy excellence.

In *Crimes of the Heart* (1986) sisters Meg (Jessica Lange), Babe (Sissy Spacek) and Lenny (Diane Keaton) reminisced about Mama and that old cat.

64. *Jeff Bridges*

1971 Best Supporting Actor as high school athlete Duane Jackson in *The Last Picture Show*
1974 Best Supporting Actor as car thief Lightfoot in *Thunderbolt and Lightfoot*
1984 Best Actor as alien Starman in *Starman*
2000 Best Supporting Actor as U.S. President Jackson Evans in *The Contender*
2009 Best Actor as singer Otis "Bad" Blake in *Crazy Heart*
2010 Best Actor as U.S. Marshall Rooster Cogburn in *True Grit*
2016 Best Supporting Actor as Texas Ranger Marcus Hamilton in *Hell or High Water*

Like Vanessa Redgrave, Jeff Bridges came from a family of actors. Unlike Redgrave, Bridges is still the only member of his clan to be recognized by the Academy with acting nominations. He was only 22 when Peter Bogdanovich hired him as a central character in his adaptation of Larry McMurtry's *The Last Picture Show*. The ensemble piece so balanced the amount of screen time among every actor that it became the only movie in

Oscar history to earn four acting nominations only in supporting categories. Despite fine reviews for playing an athletic high school senior, Bridges lacked the momentum of co-star Ben Johnson, who won the award. As a young accomplice, Bridges seemed to be having such fun in Michael Cimino's comic caper, *Thunderbolt and Lightfoot*, that he generated the film's comic relief and earned another Oscar nomination. Oscar odds were against him but favored either *The Towering Inferno*'s Fred Astaire in his only Oscar competition, or three cast members from *The Godfather Part II*, which fulfilled its promise to outrank *The Godfather* in Oscar wins. Bridges lost to newcomer Robert De Niro as young Vito Corleone. Like Walter Huston, who was nominated as the devil in *All That Money Can Buy* in 1941, and Cecil Kellaway who was up as a leprechaun in *The Luck of the Irish* in 1948, Bridges was an otherworldly character in *Starman*, and became the first star to compete for an Oscar playing an alien. Again, Bridges impressed the Academy, but as the only nominee for *Starman* and the only actor ever nominated for a movie directed by John Carpenter, Bridges did not go into the awards expecting to win. 1984's *Amadeus* took most of the major awards, including Best Actor for F. Murray Abraham. Because the 2000 Best Supporting Actor competition belonged to *Traffic*'s Benicio Del Toro throughout the award season, Bridges' nomination as fictional President Jackson Evans in *The Contender* was perceived as a welcome comeback into the Academy's inner circle. That continual long shot status made his front-running momentum for Best Actor in 2009 for *Crazy Heart* a glorious joy. Although fellow nominees George Clooney in *Up in the Air* and Colin Firth in *A Single Man* kept Bridges' victory from being inevitable, his win was rousingly acknowledged when Kate Winslet announced him the victor. Bridges' Academy momentum was so strong that he earned a nomination the very next year for reprising an already iconic Oscar role that earned John Wayne Best Actor in 1969. As Rooster Cogburn, Bridges took an equally gritty and engaging approach to the character, and the Academy loved it. In five of his seven Oscar-nominated performances, Los Angeles-born Bridges was most often nominated playing Southerners, but the range of his talent was exemplified by the fact that his nominated characters extend all the way to outer space. That's an Oscar star.

63. *Kate Winslet*

1995 Best Supporting Actress as sister Marianne Dashwood in *Sense and Sensibility*
1997 Best Actress as fiancée Rose DeWitt Bukater in *Titanic*
2001 Best Supporting Actress as author Young Iris Murdoch in *Iris*
2004 Best Actress as girlfriend Clementine Kruczynski in *Eternal Sunshine of the Spotless Mind*

2006 Best Actress as wife/mother Sarah Pierce in *Little Children*
2008 Best Actress as tram conductor/Auschwitz SS guard Hanna Schmitz in *The Reader*
2015 Best Supporting Actress as marketing executive Joanna Hoffman in *Steve Jobs*

Of all of Oscar's favorite stars, Kate Winslet may have a history that best exemplifies the impact and suspense that make the Academy Awards ceremony such a fulfilling thrill. Like many talented ingénues, Winslet made a stunning impact in her first worldwide success as a murderous teen in *Heavenly Creatures*. The movie earned only a glimpse of Oscar attention with a single writing nomination, but Winslet's work was now in the Academy's range. Like other traditional Oscar courtships, 20-year-old Winslet received her first Academy Award nomination in the supporting category playing Best Actress nominee Emma Thompson's younger sister in *Sense and Sensibility*. 1995 was a great year for women in film. Although Thompson lost Best Actress to Susan Sarandon in *Dead Man Walking*, she won Best Adapted Screenplay for the Jane Austen period romance. Winslet's bold and charming performance earned her a SAG and BAFTA, but she lost the Oscar to Mira Sorvino in *Mighty Aphrodite*. Two years later, Winslet starred in the biggest box office champion of all time, playing an abused fiancée who spread her wings thanks to a shipboard romance in *Titanic*. The movie went into the Academy Awards an easy front runner, and Winslet graduated from supporting nominee to lead actress contender. For this film, Winslet set her first Oscar record for being the youngest person nominated for two academy awards, a record she would best with every subsequent nomination. Playing the younger Rose in the *Titanic* flashbacks while Best Supporting Actress nominee Gloria Stuart played her in current time made them the first actors to both be nominated for playing the same character in the same movie. Winslet duplicated that record in 2001 when she and Judi Dench portrayed author Iris Murdoch in different stages of her life in *Iris*. Winslet's fourth nomination in the intriguing mind-erasing romance *Eternal Sunshine of the Spotless Mind* once again put her in a Best Screenplay-winning movie, and had Oscar now pressing to see her finally win. Despite Winslet's extra momentum that year for also starring in the Best Picture nominated *Finding Neverland*, 2004 was a *Million Dollar Baby* year, and Hilary Swank won instead. Two years later, Winslet played the envelope-pushing unfaithful housewife in Todd Field's *Little Children*, but, as expected, the Best Actress envelop contained Helen Mirren's name for *The Queen*. By 2008, 33-year-old Winslet's sixth nomination made her Best Actress race the seeming now-or-never nail-biter which previously brought disappointment to Deborah Kerr as a lead actress and Thelma Ritter as a supporting star. Momentum built throughout the 2008 award season. At the Golden Globes, Winslet won twice, as Best Supporting Actress for *The Reader* and as Best Actress, Drama for *Revolutionary Road*. In an ideal scenario where Oscar seals the romance in the final act, Winslet was up for Best Actress for *The Reader* and won for her complex portrayal of a woman caught between individual conscience and blinding mob mentality. This time, the thrill belonged to Winslet.

62. Angelina Jolie

1999 Best Supporting Actress as mental ward patient Lisa Rowe in *Girl, Interrupted*
2008 Best Actress as telephone switchboard supervisor Christine Collins in *Changeling*
2013 Jean Hersholt Humanitarian Award

Unlike other actors such as Jane Fonda, Vanessa Redgrave, and Michael Douglas who have followed in a parent's footsteps, become an actor, and then won an Oscar first, Angelina Jolie did not beat her father, Jon Voight, to the Academy Award podium. Twenty-one years before Jolie won an Oscar, Voight was named Best Actor of 1978 for *Coming Home*. But Jolie's rise to stardom was meteoric, going from near obscurity in the mid–1990s to conquering television for her stunning work as troubled model, *Gia* and as Cornelia Wallace, wife of Alabama governor *George Wallace*. Before the blaze of television awards dimmed, Jolie conquered the big screen with a troublingly complex and altogether enrapturing portrayal of a dangerous game-playing and ego-shattering psyche patient in *Girl, Interrupted*, one of the first film adaptations of a YA novel to win over the Academy. In 1999, the Best Supporting Actress category highlighted an array of actresses, all new suitors of Oscar. Toni Collette was Best Supporting Actor nominee Haley Joel Osment's stalwart mother in *The Sixth Sense*, Catherine Keener went brain traveling through *Being John Malkovich*, Samantha Morton was a deaf mute smitten with Best Actor nominee Sean Penn in *Sweet and Lowdown*, and Chloë Sevigny was Best Actress winner Hilary Swank's understanding, gender neutral girlfriend in *Boys Don't Cry*. In her younger days, some of Jolie's off-set eccentricities might have been off-putting to some older Academy members, but her talent was undeniable, and the voting members saw clear to honoring Jolie for her supporting work. Jolie quickly soared to box office queen of the hill in hi-tech blockbusters, but Jolie continued to hone her skills by tackling complex dramatic roles that kept her under Oscar consideration radar. Yet it took nearly ten years before the Academy nominated her again. In 2007, other award organizations, including SAG, nominated her for *A Mighty Heart*, but the Academy waited until the following year to recognize her for the first time as a lead actress in Clint Eastwood's 1920s period piece, *Changeling*. In an infuriating demonstration of injustice, Jolie was the grieving mother of a lost son arrogantly dismissed by authorities when she tried to insist that the boy they returned to her was not her son. It was a showcase role ideally suited to Jolie's stature and prowess. Jolie was in the middle of the pack of 2008 contenders, with *Frozen River*'s Melissa Leo and *Rachel Getting Married*'s Anne Hathaway enjoying their introduction to Oscar, but with odds favoring Meryl Streep in her fifteenth nomination for *Doubt* and six-time nominee and first-time winner Kate Winslet in *The Reader*. While nothing diminished Jolie's power as a filmmaker, her world renowned humanitarian efforts as a Special Envoy for United Nations High Commissioner for Refugees transformed press attention from tabloid vixen to revered altruist. Although her honorary Oscar recognition came much younger than such previous winners as Rosalind Russell and Audrey Hepburn, who were both dying of cancer when the Academy singled them out, Jolie became one of the few female actors to win the Jean Hersholt Humanitarian award, and she did so when she was only 38. Bone china features and stellar conditioning make her one of Hollywood's exquisite beauties, but Jolie earned her accolades with hard work before the camera, and philanthropy coupled with determination that has made her a leading inspiration of her generation.

61. *Frank Sinatra*

1945 Special Award to *The House I Live In* starring Frank Sinatra, for a short subject film promoting tolerance
1953 Best Supporting Actor as U.S. Army private Angelo Maggio in *From Here to Eternity*
1955 Best Actor as drummer/poker player Frankie "Dealer" Machine in *The Man with the Golden Arm*
1970 Jean Hersholt Humanitarian Award

Mention show business legends, and Frank Sinatra will always appear near the top of any list. A crooner who made fans swoon and who inspired generations of singers with his ability to extract fresh marrow from any song, Sinatra had already left a full lifetime legacy before he made his show business comeback by venturing into movies. Whenever Sinatra embarked on any project, he was sure to do it in a big way. In 1945, he came to the Academy Awards as one of the honorary winners of *The House I Live In*, a ten-minute film against anti–Semitism and racial prejudice directed by Mervyn LeRoy and starring Sinatra. Also at that year's Oscar ceremony, Sinatra enjoyed a more extensive profile because *Anchors Aweigh*, in which Sinatra shared star billing with Gene Kelly and Kathryn Grayson, was up for five awards including

Best Picture, Best Score, which it won, and Best Song for "I Fall in Love Too Easily." Not only did Sinatra introduce the song in the film, but he also sang it at the Academy Awards during the first year the nominated songs were all performed on Oscar's stage. His next musical to hit the right notes with Oscar was *On the Town*, which won Best Score in 1949. For individual Academy Award recognition, Sinatra first competed for an Oscar in a non-musical role. He played headstrong Army Private Angelo Maggio, who makes the mistake of inciting the ire of sadistic staff sergeant Fatso Judson, played by Ernest Borgnine, in *From Here to Eternity*. The Fred Zinnemann potboiler found quick favor with the Academy, becoming one of only a handful of movies to earn five acting nominations, and headed into Oscar night vying with *Roman Holiday* as the film to take most of the major prizes. *From Here to Eternity* realized its full potential, winning eight of its thirteen nominations, including Best Picture, Best Director for Zinnemann, and both Best Supporting Acting prizes, for Donna Reed and for Sinatra. Four Sinatra movies blanketed the Oscars with nominations in multiple categories in 1955. He had been nominated for a Best Foreign Actor BAFTA for the hospital drama *Not as a Stranger*, up for a technical Academy Award. Sinatra and Debbie Reynolds introduced the title song from their comedy *The Tender Trap*, which competed for Best Song. Sinatra played Nathan Detroit to Marlon Brando's Sky Masterson in *Guys and Dolls*, a jubilant musical that competed in four categories. But his stirring portrayal of a heroin addict in Otto Preminger's *The Man with the Golden Arm*, red-flagged by the Hays Code for its hard-hitting content, brought Sinatra his only lead actor bid for Oscar. This performance once again connected Sinatra with fellow Italian Ernest Borgnine, whose performance as *Marty* beat Sinatra's for Best Actor. Although he was never nominated again, Sinatra remained a consistent Oscar presence. In the late 1950s, two of his biggest hits, "All the Way" from *The Joker is Wild* and "High Hopes" from *A Hole in the Head* won Best Song. A popular Oscar participant, Sinatra hosted the Academy Awards solo in 1962, co-hosted in 1974, and over the years presented competitive awards to winners such as Eva Marie Saint for *On the Waterfront* and Jack Albertson for *The Subject was Roses*, as well as honorary Oscars to Cary Grant and Rosalind Russell. Among the wealthiest entertainers in history, Sinatra consistently used his money and influence to advance causes he loved. The Academy, always enamored of Sinatra's talents and influence, honored those humanitarian efforts with the Jean Hersholt award in 1970. Although that year the competitive awards were stirred by months of disparaging remarks about the Academy from George C. Scott and then Goldie Hawn's shocked announcement of Scott as Best Actor for *Patton*, the ceremony was balanced by a proliferation of honorary awards to actors. Warm tributes impacted the lifetime achievement accolades for Orson Welles and especially Lillian Gish, and were capped off by the Academy's honoring Sinatra, who seemed moved and grateful for the peer acknowledgment.

60. *Charlton Heston*

**1959 Best Actor as merchant Judah Ben-Hur in *Ben-Hur*
1977 Jean Hersholt Humanitarian Award**

Heston's introduction to Oscar started at the very top when director Cecil B. DeMille cast him in the lead as the circus manager in his 1952 big top spectacle, *The Greatest Show on Earth*. It earned high-flying box office receipts and generous award consideration from other organizations, including supporting nods for James Stewart and for Gloria Grahame, who instead was nominated for and won the Best Supporting Actress Oscar for that year's *The Bad and the Beautiful*. As the leads, Heston and Betty Hutton generated some interest from the Academy. Although Oscar's affection for the movie did not extend to any performances, it did culminate in a Best Picture win over powerhouses such as *High Noon* and *The Quiet Man*. Heston made a strong impression on DeMille, who next cast him as Moses in his multi-million dollar VistaVision extravaganza *The Ten Commandments*. The 1956 movie gave Heston another box office smash in a Best Picture contender, but again all the performances were overlooked. But *The Ten Commandments*, and *Ben-Hur* three years later, not only made Heston one of the biggest box office champs of the decade, but also forever connected him with biblical spectacles that remain perennial favorites among movie lovers. *Ben-Hur* was already a maverick movie character thanks to the 1925 silent starring Ramón Novarro, which was the most expensive, and one of the most successful movies to come from the silent screen era. Remaking the epic was a gargantuan feat, but William Wyler entrusted the beloved title character to chiseled, teeth-clenching matinee idol Heston, who interpreted the role with a seamless blend of honor and gusto. *Ben-Hur* went into the 1959 Oscars the expected winner, but the Best Actor race could have followed innumerable turns. If Oscar wanted to honor a foreign import, he might choose Laurence Harvey from *Room at the Top*. If he were feeling lighthearted, he could honor maraca-shaking, sax-playing, cross-dressing Jack Lemmon from the comic classic *Some Like It Hot*. Should the Academy feel sentimental, they could mark ballots for Paul Muni, whose *The Last Angry Man* nomination was his first in over twenty years, or James Stewart, whose small town lawyer in *Anatomy of a Murder* was hailed by some as the best performance of his career. But Heston, like his movie, dominated the awards, and in his only competition, Heston won Best Actor, one of a record-setting eleven wins for Oscar champ *Ben-Hur*. Throughout Heston's career, the Academy was always most impressed by his big-budget spectaculars, including Oscar nominated *El Cid* in 1961 and *The Agony and the Ecstasy* in 1965, or Oscar winners *Planet of the Apes* in 1968 and *Earthquake* in 1974. Heston presented at or co-hosted many Oscar telecasts, most famously in 1972 when he was to start the show but was detained by a flat tire on the Santa Monica freeway. Tight-lipped Clint Eastwood struggled to fill in with opening comments when Heston flew across the stage to save Eastwood and the moment. Five years later Heston was a featured player on Oscar's stage, this time accepting his Jean Hersholt humanitarian award from Bette Davis. By impressing the Academy twice and contributing to ceremonies during multiple decades, rugged activist Heston muscled his way into Oscar favor with talent and charity.

59. Mary Pickford

**1928/29 Best Actress as socialite Norma Besant in *Coquette*
1975 Honorary lifetime achievement award "in recognition of her unique contributions to the film industry and the development of film as an artistic medium"**

As the only female founding member of the Academy besides screenwriter Jeanie MacPherson, Pickford seemed an obvious choice to warrant a prominent spot on Oscar's countdown. Although deserved, her status is not without the kind of controversy that makes for enticing Academy lore. After reigning as America's first movie sweetheart in the silent film era, the wholesome Pickford had retired by the time she, husband Douglas Fairbanks, Sr., and 34 other actors, directors, screenwriters, producers, technicians, and lawyers founded the Academy in 1927 and hosted its first awards banquet on May 16, 1929. But her involvement with the Academy reignited a new interest in returning to work before the camera, and Pickford risked her ironclad reputation by daring to star in a sound picture, bobbing her famous cascading locks, and playing a flirtatious good-time girl in *Coquette*. The gamble paid off. Her movie was a hit, and her new image added to rather than destroyed the beloved relationship she had formed with most pre–Jazz Age moviegoers. With the second Oscar nominations looming, Pickford took another risk by inviting the Academy board, who selected all nominees and winners in the first years of Oscar, to the famous Pickfair estate she shared with Fairbanks for tea and some personal promotion. Her efforts raised eyebrows but generated the results she sought. Although the popular *Coquette* earned only mixed reviews, the Academy nominated her for the Oscar, making Pickford the first actor to successfully campaign for an Academy Award. While some applauded her proactive approach, others questioned the credibility of an organization where a founding member could influence her colleagues through self-promotion. Thus, her efforts were not just the first successful campaign for Oscar. They also led to the first Oscar reform, ultimately shifting voting power from a small, elite board to the Academy members at large. Pickford holds the record for winning Best Actress over the most nominees, as that year six different women were nominated. Her competition included Ruth Chatterton as *Madame X*; Betty Compson in *The Barker*; Oscar's first posthumous nominee, Jeanne Eagels of *The Letter*; Corrine Griffith as *The Divine Lady* under the Oscar-winning direction of Frank Lloyd; and energetic Bessie Love in that season's Best Picture, *The Broadway Melody*. The pique of Pickford's comeback rested almost exclusively on her Oscar-winning performance in *Coquette*, but the Academy always remembered her as a founding member. In 1939 they honored fellow co-founder, Douglas Fairbanks, by then her ex-husband, and in 1975 they saw fit to single out Pickford for her contribution to film history and her initial efforts to create an Academy of Motion Picture Arts and Sciences with a generous tribute by Gene Kelly. By then Pickford was 83 years old and too ill to attend the ceremony. But she did appear on the telecast in a pre-taped segment that began with a brief tour of her beloved Pickfair, then concluded with Pickford, dressed in fur-lined satin, accepting her second Oscar, which she assured she would always cherish. Once and always, Pickford was indeed America's sweetheart.

58. *Sidney Poitier*

1958 Best Actor as escaped prisoner Noah Cullen in *The Defiant Ones*
1963 Best Actor as itinerant worker Homer Smith in *Lilies of the Field*
2001 Honorary lifetime achievement award "in recognition of his remarkable accomplishments as an artist and as a human being"

Twenty-four years after Hattie McDaniel first shattered racial barriers with a Best Supporting Actress Oscar victory for *Gone with the Wind*, Sidney Poitier achieved an even greater feat by breaking the color barrier as a lead performer. Inclusion of Black actors made gradual progress in Oscar's early decades. Ten years after Hattie McDaniel won Best Supporting Actress, Ethel Waters was nominated in the same category for *Pinky*. Director Otto Premigner loved to challenge traditional mores, and so his directing, while also dating, Dorothy Dandridge to a Best Actress nomination for *Carmen Jones* proved a huge leap for the very White Academy. But in 1958, opinions clearly began to change thanks to Poitier's reputation as an engrossing actor who refused to portray Black stereotypes, and as a man of stellar personal integrity. He and Tony Curtis were both nominated as escaped prisoners chained together in Stanley Kramer's *The Defiant Ones*. Competing against a co-star often suggests that the actors will split votes, which may have happened in 1958. Although both Curtis and Poitier were first-time nominees, scales tilted toward more votes for Poitier in a showier role. Also a front-runner was Paul Newman in his first nomination as Brick in *Cat on a Hot Tin Roof*, with some longshot consideration illuminating the works of previous two-time winner Spencer Tracy in *The Old Man and the Sea*, and David Niven in *Separate Tables*, a respected drama and one of the most nominated films of the year. In one of the Academy's biggest surprises, Niven took the Best Actor trophy, but Poitier was now a contender. When he returned to the Best Actor race five years later, his biggest competition came again from Paul Newman. Poitier was in a small but beloved drama about a drifting handyman whose fate brings him into the lives of some determined nuns in *Lilies of the Field*, while Newman continued to solidify his antihero persona as self-centered cowboy *Hud*. Worked into the mix was first-time nominee Albert Finney whose comically randy turn as *Tom Jones* was one of the main reasons the film was the year's big winner. On Oscar night, Anne Bancroft announced Poitier as Best Actor. Amid the audience's cacophonous applause, Bancroft whispered, "Enjoy it. It doesn't last long."

At the 1963 Oscars, ebullient winner Sidney Poitier took presenter Anne Bancroft's advice to enjoy the brief peak of adulation.

Poitier was a dominant force throughout the racially turbulent 1960s. In *A Patch of Blue,* his touching portrayal of the compassionate stranger who rescues a blind woman (Best Actress nominee Elizabeth Hartman) from her abusive mother (Best Supporting Actress winner Shelley Winters) was a surprise oversight in 1965. Two years later, Poitier was overlooked again probably because he gave such great performances in three of Oscar's favorites: he was the beloved teacher in *To Sir, with Love,* the surprise guest who tested racial understanding and the impact of genuine love in *Guess Who's Coming to Dinner,* and the Philadelphia detective who faced more adversity from the Mississippi police than the murder suspects in the Best Picture winner, *In the Heat of the Night.* For the next four decades, Poitier continued to represent the most indomitable aspects of the human spirit, and in 2001, the Academy acknowledged a lifetime of achievements that extended far beyond his profound impact on equalizing opportunities for people of all ethnicities.

57. Sophia Loren

1961 Best Actress as widowed shopkeeper Cesira in *Two Women*
1964 Best Actress as mistress/wife Filumena Marturano in *Marriage Italian Style*
1990 Honorary lifetime achievement award to "one of the genuine treasures of world cinema who, in a career rich with memorable performances, has added permanent luster to our art form"

Few international movie stars have ever been more physically sumptuous on screen than Italy's most revered acting treasure, Sophia Loren. Today, when female actors of staggering beauty deglamorize for dramatic roles, as did Halle Berry in *Monster's Ball* and Charlize Theron in *Monster,* Academy votes seem almost inevitable. But in the 1960s, being a daunting beauty and international superstar in the second foreign language performance to compete for an Academy Award (one year before Loren's nomination, Greek actress Melina Mercouri was up for *Never on Sunday*) were setbacks that Loren could only overcome with an enthralling performance as a mother fighting the ravages of war against herself and her daughter in *Two Women.* The 1961 Best Actress competition was among the most varied in history. Oscar newcomer Piper Laurie added resonance to Robert Rossen's *The Hustler,* and versatile Geraldine Page was up for *Summer and Smoke,* a less enthusiastically received adaptation of a Tennessee Williams work than *A Streetcar Named Desire, Cat on a Hot Tin Roof,* or *Suddenly, Last Summer.* More attention was focused on Audrey Hepburn in *Breakfast at Tiffany's* and frontrunner Natalie Wood, now an A-list star and darling of two of that year's top Oscar contenders, *Splendor in the Grass* and *West Side Story.* Winning more than twenty international awards, including Best Actress as Cannes, built enthusiasm for Loren's performance as Oscar night approached. Like *Mildred Pierce* nominee Joan Crawford in 1945, Loren couldn't face the pressure of competing in person on Oscar night. Instead of claiming to be ill as Crawford did, Loren admitted that imagining a live international audience seeing her raw reaction to either winning or losing filled her with such terror that she found every excuse not to attend the ceremony. When Burt Lancaster announced her name, a roar of approval rippled across the globe and Greer Garson accepted on behalf of the "wildly beautiful and talented" star. Loren did grace Oscar's stage the following year to name Gregory Peck Best Actor. In 1964, Loren's second nomination came for another collaboration with director Vittorio De Sica, this time for her feisty comic entanglement with frequent collaborator Marcello Mastroianni, a partnership that kept them two of the biggest world box office draws of the decade. In 1990, the Academy extended another laurel to the still-striking Loren by giving her a lifetime achievement award for being a cinema treasure. This time Gregory Peck presented to her, and she tearfully embraced the Oscar and the Academy's praise. Loren had her next momentous date with Oscar when she announced *Life is Beautiful* as the 1998 Foreign Language Film winner by saying only, "The Oscar goes to … Roberto!" and fellow Italian Roberto Benigni catapulted up and teetered his way toward the stage on the backs of Dorothy Chandler Pavilion seats. Throughout her life, dark, exotic, gracious and beloved Loren handled her relationship with Oscar as adroitly as her career and her marriage to producer Carlo Ponti. Her captivating looks drew favorable attention, but her talent, elegance, and steadfastness made her an enduring film icon.

56. *Henry Fonda*

1940 Best Actor as ex-convict migrant worker Tom Joad in *The Grapes of Wrath*
1957 Best Picture as co-producer (with Reginald Rose) of *12 Angry Men*
1980 Honorary lifetime achievement award to "the consummate actor, in recognition of his brilliant accomplishments and enduring contribution to the art of motion pictures"
1981 Best Actor as retired college professor Norman Thayer, Jr., in *On Golden Pond*

Of all the Hollywood icons of the 20th century, Henry Fonda was among the least honored by Oscar for most of his career. An expected nomination for *Young Mister Lincoln* never materialized in 1939, most likely because the greatest year of American cinema was top heavy with outstanding performances, leaving several performances that would have garnered recognition most other years just missing the final nomination list. The following year, however, the Academy more than compensated for the oversight by making him a lead contender for his classic performance as Okie Tom Joad in John Ford's adaptation of John Steinbeck's *The Grapes of Wrath*. Ironically, one of his competitors was Raymond Massey, who, unlike Fonda the year before, was nominated for playing the sixteenth President in *Abe Lincoln in Illinois*. Though beloved for his stage work, neither Massey, nor *The Great Dictator*'s Charles Chaplin, who had already earned an honorary award in the Academy's premiere year, led going into Oscar night. Instead, eyes were on Fonda, Laurence Olivier in the year's Best Picture, *Rebecca*, and *The Philadelphia Story*'s James Stewart, who many thought should have won the year before for *Mr. Smith Goes to Washington*. Apparently Fonda and his *The Grapes of Wrath* director John Ford didn't share the press's optimism about their chances to win, for they skipped the Oscars to take a fishing trip. Ford won, and Fonda lost to his buddy James Stewart. For decades, Fonda gave thoughtful, top-notch performances in movies such as *Jezebel* (1938), *Mister Roberts* (1955), *The Best Man* (1964), and *Sometimes a Great Notion* (1971) that brought Oscar recognition only to his co-stars. Even his inspired performance as Juror #8, the moral compass of Sidney Lumet's *12 Angry Men*, did not bring him a Best Actor nod, but did put him in contention for Best Picture as one of the film's producers. At age 75 and in poor health, Fonda's lifetime achievement honor seemed to close the parentheses on his recognitions from Oscar. Humbly accepting the award, Fonda focused on the privilege he felt working with great filmmakers and stars for nearly fifty years as an actor. But thanks to his daughter Jane, already Best Actress winner twice, neither Henry Fonda's career, nor his greatest Oscar glory, was over. Jane optioned the film rights to *On Golden Pond* as a vehicle for the two of them to finally work together. The heartwarming tone of the family drama was made more poignant by the authentic effort of the two Fondas to find an emotional connection like their estranged characters. In Oscar history, the results of no acting race were more surefire than Fonda's Best Actor win as cantankerous octogenarian Norman Thayer. On Oscar day, articles featured full-page photos of Fonda with headlines such as, "Does anyone think Henry Fonda will *not* win?" Though too ill to attend the ceremony, Fonda watched at home with his wife as the Academy made an exception and permitted Jane to accept on his behalf. Near the very end of his life, Fonda went from overlooked legend to one of Oscar's most honored stars.

55. *Christoph Waltz*

2009 Best Supporting Actor as SS Colonel Hans Landa in *Inglourious Basterds*

2012 Best Supporting Actor as ex-dentist/bounty hunter Dr. King Schultz in *Django Unchained*

When Austria-born actor Christoph Waltz won his second Best Supporting Actor prize at the 82nd Academy Awards, he became the ninth member of the exclusive and rare group of two-time supporting Oscar winners. By Oscar night of the 2009 awards, his first victory was a foregone conclusion. Quentin Tarantino's *Inglourious Basterds* opened to almost universal acclaim, and most film review text focused on Waltz in the role of menacing, charming, idiomatically funny ("If the shoe fits, you wear it"), and startlingly vicious Nazi "Jew Hunter" SS-Standartenführer Hans Landa. Screenwriter Tarantino considered Landa one of his best characters, and he claimed only Austrian/German actor Waltz's impeccable interpretation could have made *Inglourious Basterds* worth filming. Waltz's lock on Oscar began when he won Best Actor at Cannes, then summarily nabbed Best Supporting Actor from the likes of the New York and LA film critics, BAFTA, the Golden Globes, and then took home two SAGs, for Best Supporting Actor and as a member of the Best Cast. At the Oscars, glaring praise for Waltz's performance outshone other well-reviewed work, particularly Woody Harrelson in *The Messenger* and finally-nominated Christopher Plummer for *The Last Station*. When Waltz won, his became the first Oscar-winning performance spoken in multiple languages: English, French, German, and Italian. The *Inglourious* movie made Waltz a glorious star and a favorite collaborator of director Quentin Tarantino. While the press extensively covered the competitive verve that went into casting the other characters of *Django Unchained*, Waltz was an obvious choice to play crafty, opportunistic bounty hunter Dr. King Schultz. At awards time, Waltz racked up another BAFTA and Golden Globe, but the Oscar race was anyone's to win. In one of the few times in Academy history, every Best Supporting Actor nominee was a former winner: Alan Arkin had the best lines ("Argo f*** yourself") and most magnetic role in the night's Best Picture winner, *Argo*. Robert De Niro's chances seemed strong for becoming a three-time Oscar winner as Bradley Cooper's dad in *Silver Linings Playbook*. Philip Seymour Hoffman mesmerized as *The Master*. Tommy Lee Jones seemed to go into the competition a frontrunner as abolitionist Thaddeus Stevens in *Lincoln*. But as he had just three years earlier, Waltz took the category, and followed Walter Brennan, Anthony Quinn, Peter Ustinov, Shelley Winters, Jason Robards, Jr., Melvyn Douglas, Dianne Wiest, and Michael Caine in securing two supporting acting Academy Awards. Waltz follows Brennan and Wiest and Jack Nicholson as the only winners to earn multiple Oscars collaborating with the same director. Brennan was directed by William Wyler in *Come and Get It* (co-directed by Howard Hawks) and *The Westerner*, Wiest worked for Woody Allen in *Hannah and Her Sisters* and *Bullets over Broadway*, and Nicholson won Best Supporting Actor for *Terms of Endearment* and Best Actor for *As Good As It Gets* for James L. Brooks. Because Waltz's achievement is so recent, he is also the only two-time supporting winner with no other nominations. He joins Luise Rainer, Helen Hayes, Vivien Leigh, Kevin Spacey, and Hilary Swank as the only actors to win twice with exactly two career nominations, and is the only one with both wins as a supporting player.

54. *Kevin Spacey*

1995 Best Supporting Actor as con artist Roger "Verbal" Kint in *The Usual Suspects*
1999 Best Actor as advertising executive Lester Burnham in *American Beauty*

Like the surprise ending of *The Usual Suspects*, Spacey sneaked up on his first Academy Award victory with the stealth and command of a true artist of his craft. The 1995 Oscars brought both Spacey and his former high school classmate, Mare Winningham as the title character in *Georgia*, their first nominations, both as supporting players. Award pundits placed their chances of winning among the middle of their respective competitors. The Best Supporting Actor race began with a level playing field, as all five actors were first-time nominees. Early front-runners Ed Harris of *Apollo 13* and James Cromwell of *Babe* had the added advantage of being in movies up for Best Picture, while Brad Pitt of *12 Monkeys* and Tim Roth of *Rob Roy* earned positive reviews for their stark characterizations. But Spacey, like the quiet but knowing character he played, limped confidently toward a victory confirmed when Dianne Wiest announced him one of the first winners of the night. Spacey reserved most of his thank yous for *The Usual Suspect*'s director, Bryan Singer, and for his mother, who accompanied him to the ceremony. She was at his side again for the 1999 Oscars, and this time Spacey had the advantage over his Best Actor competitors by starring in the movie that had all the late-season momentum to take the big prizes. Despite *American Beauty*'s allure, Spacey had especially formidable competition. Denzel Washington's performance in *The Hurricane* was pegged as a highlight of his entire career, with the film's director, Norman Jewison, claiming Washington's performance was the most powerful acting he'd ever seen. Sometime during award season, first-time nominee Russell Crowe was considered the likely winner for *The Insider*. Sean Penn was in his second Best Actor race for Woody Allen's *Sweet and Lowdown*, and Richard Farnsworth had sentiment on his side for giving his poignant performance in *The Straight Story* while battling the cancer that would soon take his life. But in Spacey's acceptance speech, he pinpointed his character's appeal by sharing how he revealed all

Lester Burnham's worst qualities in such a way that the audience could grow to love him. That slight-of-hand was trademark Spacey, who can sculpt something mesmerizing from every character nuance. Spacey dedicated his performance to his friend, mentor, and father figure Jack Lemmon, and cited Lemmon's work in *The Apartment* as one of the finest that cinema had ever had. Interestingly, Spacey's double win paralleled Lemmon's, who was the first actor to win Oscars first for a supporting role, and then a leading one. Spacey set a new Oscar record by becoming the first actor to win in both acting categories in the same decade. Victories for every other star to achieve that feat (Helen Hayes, Jack Lemmon, Ingrid Bergman, Maggie Smith, Meryl Streep, Jack Nicholson, Gene Hackman, Jessica Lange, Denzel Washington and Cate Blanchett) came over multiple decades. His victories occurred only four years apart, putting him just one year from the record, as Meryl Streep won Best Actress in 1982, just three years after taking the supporting prize. At the beginning of his Best Actor acceptance speech, Spacey questioned whether his career would be all downhill from there. He shouldn't have worried. Although he has yet to receive another Academy Award nomination, Spacey maintains his status as one of the most prolific and insightful actors of his generation.

53. *Hilary Swank*

1999 Best Actress as boyfriend Brandon Teena/Teena Brandon in *Boys Don't Cry*
2004 Best Actress as boxer/waitress Maggie Fitzgerald in *Million Dollar Baby*

Ten years after Noriyuki "Pat" Morita was an Oscar nominee for the original box office hit, *The Karate Kid*, he reprised his role of Mr. Miyagi for *The Next Karate Kid*. Already the fourth film of the franchise, *The Next Karate Kid* kept the material fresh by serving up a gender-bending twist, as Miyagi mentors his first young female, played by Hilary Swank. The film launched Swank's career, and led to another gender-bender, *Boys Don't Cry* in which she played Teena Brandon, a transgender man who hides his female anatomy and history by living as male Brandon Teena. Only the strength of Swank's textured performance could overcome the limitations that would seem to have kept it from ever garnering Oscar's highest acting honor. With the exception of 1996, when four of the five Best Picture nominees were independent features, small, especially low budget, niche films like *Boys Don't Cry* are generally Oscar oversights. But massive critical praise for the movie, and especially Swank's immersion into the character, made the movie a box office hit, and started momentum toward Swank bulldozing victoriously through over twenty critics and film festival Best Actress competitions. At Oscar time, Swank was still not a shoe-in to win. Her greatest competition was Annette Bening, hailed as the early frontrunner for *American Beauty*, the movie snowballing with the most momentum toward Oscar victories. But Swank prevailed, and she ended her Academy Award acceptance speech with a tribute to Brandon Teena's legacy for encouraging independence and diversity. Most post–Oscar print about Swank concentrated on the fact that she forgot to thank her husband Chad Lowe. Another chance came five years later when Oscar started eying Swank again for another physically transforming role, this time as boxer Maggie Fitzgerald in Clint Eastwood's *Million Dollar Baby*. The opposite of *Boys Don't Cry*, this mainstream movie with a healthy budget and A-list cast built late season momentum over early favorites *The Aviator* and *Sideways* to take most of the top Oscars, including Swank for Best Actress. Once again, Swank usurped Annette Bening, this time of *Being Julia*, as Best Actress favorite. Swank remedied her last oversight by first acknowledging husband Lowe, then expressing ample gratitude to director, producer, and star Eastwood. Because her lead acting Oscar wins came only five years apart, Swank ranks behind Luise Rainer (consecutive wins), Bette Davis and Olivia de Havilland (three years apart), as a star who became a double Best Actress winner within so brief a timeframe. Swank remains a role model for dreamers. In both Oscar acceptance speeches, she referred to her humble beginnings, describing how she grew up in a trailer park and confessing that she and her mom once lived in their car. She is also the embodiment of physical transformation for her art, as both the role of the transgender male and as a champion boxer required months of conditioning and lasered commitment to training for and living as her characters. That dedication has thus far given Swank two unforgettable roles which she polished into Oscar gems.

52. Vivien Leigh

1939 Best Actress as Southern belle Scarlett O'Hara in *Gone with the Wind*
1951 Best Actress as Southern belle Blanche DuBois in *A Streetcar Named Desire*

For all those who balked at the thought of a British actress being able to embody the courage, charm, and grandiose delusions of great American Southern belles, Scarlett O'Hara would have chirped, "Fiddle-dee-dee!" while Blanche DuBois would have turned a mirror on Leigh's career and exclaimed, "Oh look, we have created enchantment." No single role in Hollywood history drew more media attention than the quest for the perfect Scarlett O'Hara, Margaret Mitchell's fiery heroine of her Civil War saga *Gone with the Wind*.

Producer David O. Selznick even used his search for a $100,000 pre-production marketing strategy, attracting nearly 2,000 interested applicants that included former Oscar winners Norma Shearer, Katharine Hepburn, and Bette Davis, all of whom pursued the part with ferocity. It couldn't have hurt that lovely young British actress Vivien Leigh's agent worked for Selznick's brother, who arranged a screen test that ultimately brought her the role over final-stretch possibilities Jean Arthur, Joan Bennett, Paulette Goddard, and Miriam Hopkins. Leigh was everything the public could have imagined of O'Hara, and at Oscar time, *Gone with the Wind* seemed destined to match its record-setting box office receipts with unprecedented Academy Award wins.

Leigh had formidable Best Actress competition. Bette Davis gave the performance of her career in *Dark Victory*, but she had already won two Best Actress prizes, including one just the previous year, playing a Southern belle in *Jezebel*, a role allegedly given Davis as consolation for not getting to play Scarlett O'Hara. Two legends, Irene Dunne in *Love Affair* and Greta Garbo

Bedraggled but undeterred, Mammy (Hattie McDaniel), Melanie (Olivia de Havilland) and Scarlett (Vivien Leigh) faced the ravaging Civil War in *Gone with the Wind* (1939).

in *Ninotchka*, were still Oscarless in their fourth film roles to bring them into competition, and newcomer Greer Garson was just starting her record-setting run of Best Actress races with *Goodbye, Mr. Chips*. Leigh prevailed. On screen in *Gone with the Wind* for 2 hours, 23 minutes and 32 seconds, she set and still holds the record for longest screen time of any Oscar-winning performance. Leigh encapsulated her thank yous with a general tribute to *Gone with the Wind* producer, "Mr. David Selznick." By the time 20th Century Fox agreed to a film version of the then-controversial *A Streetcar Named Desire*, Leigh had played Blanche DuBois in a London stage production and Jessica Tandy originated the role on Broadway. Because of her star quality, Leigh was the only major player in the movie not from the original New York cast. As she had with Scarlett O'Hara, Leigh captured every nuance of the withering Southern belle, and Oscar blared its trumpets of praise and brought Leigh her second nomination. Unable to attend because she and husband Laurence Olivier were performing Shakespeare on Broadway, Leigh listened to the Oscar broadcast on a backstage radio, expecting Katharine Hepburn to win for *The African Queen*. When Ronald Colman announced Leigh the winner, Greer Garson, one of Leigh's 1939 Best Actress competitors, accepted the award on her behalf. Of all the actors to go two-for-two in their Oscar legacy, Leigh stands out for creating Academy Award gold from performances based on two of the most iconic characters from literature. While others have portrayed both Scarlett O'Hara and Blanche DuBois in various productions or sequels, wildly energetic Leigh stamped such an indelible mark on them that they will forever be connected to the strikingly beautiful and fiercely talented actress.

51. Helen Hayes

1931/32 Best Actress as mother Madelon Claudet in *The Sin of Madelon Claudet*
1970 Best Supporting Actress as airplane stowaway Ada Quonsett in *Airport*

If great gifts come in small packages, then petite Helen Hayes's gargantuan talent was a fitting treasure for the acting profession. She was already a revered stage actress when she made her sound film debut in *The Sin of Madelon Claudet*. For the lush tale of unwed motherhood, false imprisonment, and secret sacrifice, the Academy singled out Hayes as their fifth Best Actress. Hayes commanded the 3-contender category that year, winning over the previous year's victor, Marie Dressler in *Emma*, and another stage icon, Lynn Fontanne in *The Guardsman*. The victory made Hayes the first stage actress to become an Academy Award winner. Hayes accepted her Best Actress award from presenter Lionel Barrymore, and claimed she hadn't felt such excitement since the birth of her daughter. Three years later, Hayes and screenwriter husband Charles MacArthur became the first Oscar-winning married couple when he shared with Ben Hecht a Best Original Story prize for *The Scoundrel*. Despite Hollywood success, Hayes returned to the New York, Chicago, and Washington, D.C., stage, and accepted only rare movie projects. She was up for a Golden Globe for *Anastasia* in 1956, but no Academy Award nomination followed. Then in 1970, compelling suspense and a glittering cast made *Airport* a massive hit, and the Academy recognized it with ten nominations. Two nods came in the Best Supporting Actress category, where Hayes, in the comic role of crafty stowaway Ada Quonsett, and Maureen Stapleton as downtrodden wife Inez Guerrero, provided one of the tightest Oscar races between two actors from the same movie. Duel settings—a bustling airport and a claustrophobic airplane with a bomb-toting passenger seated beside Hayes—put characters in either locale except Hayes, who dominated in both. When Gig Young announced Hayes the winner and Rosalind Russell accepted for her friend, Hayes became the first person to win acting Oscars in both lead and supporting categories. With victories 39 years apart, she also became the star with the longest span between Academy Award victories. Although she missed that Oscar ceremony, she did attend the following year. Instead of presenting the Best Supporting Actor prize, she co-hosted the ceremony with Sammy Davis, Jr., Alan King, and Jack Lemmon, who would join her two years later as the first stars to win acting Oscars in both lead and supporting categories. To date, Hayes remains the only female to win Oscars in both categories for her only nominations. Among male actors, only Kevin Spacey has exactly two nominations and two wins, each in a different acting category. In 1977, Hayes became the first actor (and second person, after composer Richard Rodgers) to win an Oscar, Tony, Emmy, and Grammy. She has been immortalized with the Helen Hayes Theatre on Broadway and the Helen Hayes Award, given for excellence in all categories of stage production in Washington, D.C. Helen Hayes Award recipients include Oscar winners Jason Robards, Jr., Mercedes Ruehl, and Cate Blanchett. A tiny titan in movies, television, and especially on stage, Helen Hayes, known worldwide as The First Lady of the American Theatre, also deserved her status as one of the Academy's first Grande Dames.

50. Luise Rainer

1936 Best Actress as actress Anna Held *The Great Ziegfeld*
1937 Best Actress as servant O-Lan in *The Good Earth*

Luise Rainer's relationship with Oscar is a study in contrasts, epitomizing the heights and valleys that span international stardom. The German actress so dazzled in her early Austrian film roles that Hollywood took note, and MGM brought her to American on a three-year contract. In the shortest amount of time, she would end up the longest reigning Oscar-winning actor. Production of the romantic comedy *Escapade*, a remake of a successful Luise Rainer German hit, was already half completed when Myrna Loy dropped out of the project. Louis B. Mayer reluctantly replaced her with Rainer, whose scenes were squeezed into existing footage. Upon seeing herself on a Hollywood screen, Rainer ran from the cinema horrified by how big and "full of face" she appeared. Filmgoers' responses were just the opposite. The movie made Rainer an instant studio starlet. In her next film, *The Great Ziegfeld*, she would work on only the earlier half of production, as her character, Anna Held, is the first wife of Flo Ziegfeld, whom he replaces with his second wife, played, coincidentally, by Myrna Loy. Initially Louis B. Mayer balked at Rainer taking the part, as he thought it too small for his new star. The public was also skeptical, thinking she did not resemble actress Anna Held enough to play her convincingly. Despite the brevity of her performance, Rainer enraptured audiences and the Academy, especially in a single scene where during a telephone conversation she bravely hides her heartbreak while congratulating her ex-husband on his new marriage. Rainer did not attend the 1936 Academy Awards because she thought she had no chance of winning, but win she did, for what at the time was the shortest performance to earn an Oscar. Like Claudette Colbert two years earlier, Rainer was whisked to the ceremony in time to receive her statuette and pose for photos with the year's Best Actor, Paul Muni. Both stars next appeared in *The Good Earth*. Despite Rainer's being the year's current Best Actress, Louis B. Mayer thought that role of O-Lan, a silent, subservient peasant, would be too small and shadowy a part after her emotional tour de force as Anna Held. The role's stark contrast to her last performance, however, was the very reason she was so stunning, and the Academy nominated her for another Oscar. Despite competition from the likes of Irene Dunne in *The Awful Truth*, Janet Gaynor in *A Star Is Born*, Barbara Stanwyck in *Stella Dallas*, and expected winner Greta Garbo in *Camille*, Rainer won again, becoming the first actor to win Academy Awards in consecutive years. Age 28 at the time of her second victory, she remains the youngest actor to win two Oscars. This avalanche of accolades, later claimed Rainer, destroyed her career. She followed *The Good Earth* with *The Great Waltz*, which earned Miliza Korjus a Best Supporting Actress nomination, but no project good or great ever followed. While still the Academy's double Best Actress champ, a disenchanted Rainer left Hollywood. Despite having the shortest career of almost any Oscar winner in history, Rainer's longevity extended her reign as not only the oldest Oscar winner, but also the person who lived as an Oscar winner the longest. By age 104, the woman whose Hollywood career was clustered in a scant three years, was united with Oscar for nearly 80.

49. Dianne Wiest

1986 Best Supporting Actress as actress/caterer/writer Holly in *Hannah and Her Sisters*
1989 Best Supporting Actress as divorced mother Helen Buckman in *Parenthood*
1994 Best Supporting Actress as actress Helen Sinclair in *Bullets over Broadway*

"Gee," lovably unassuming Dianne Wiest began her first Academy Award acceptance speech, "This isn't like I imagined what it would be in the bathtub." As she does with every performance, Wiest won over her audience with a revealing genuineness that makes her a magnetic, and magnanimous actor. She spent the rest of her acceptance speech saying that she was currently working on her fourth movie for director Woody Allen, and thus was spending time with the same artistic and technical crews with whom she had worked on all previous Woody Allen projects. In *Hannah and Her Sisters*, Wiest played the scattered sibling who struggled to create a professional identity with forays into acting and catering and writing. The ensemble project was a huge box office success, and headed into the 1986 Oscars as a potential big winner of the night. Wiest and co-star Michael Caine won both supporting Academy Awards. At the end of the decade, Wiest returned to Oscar's red carpet for another indelibly insightful comic portrayal, this time as frazzled single mom to Martha Plimpton and Joaquin Phoenix in *Parenthood*. The following year, she was considered a strong candidate for another Supporting Actress nomination as the compassionate Avon lady who takes in misfit *Edward Scissorhands*, but the film garnered only one Oscar nod, for Best Makeup. After further collaborations with Woody Allen that included *The Purple Rose of Cairo* (1985), *Radio Days* and *September* (respectively released at the beginning and end of 1987), Wiest worked with him again in *Bullets over Broadway*. The movie was an instant hit, and the Academy matched *Hannah and Her Sisters* with the same number of nominations. Allen was again up for Best Director and Best Original Screenplay, and Wiest returned with another Best Supporting Actress nod, this time against co-star Jennifer Tilly. Every few years, after sweeping the critical and film festival awards, one actor heads to the Academy Awards nearly assured of accepting Oscar, too. 1994 was just such a year for Wiest. She charmed as a histrionic, vain, aging actress, and introduced "Don't speak" into movie lore as one of the most memorable comic lines in film history. When Tommy Lee Jones announced Wiest the winner, she once again won over the audience in the first words of her acceptance speech. "Oh gosh, just let me put on my glasses. This is as surprising and marvelous as it was the first time. Although this time I need glasses!" This win is especially unique because of the rarity of an actor winning two Best Supporting Actress Oscars. In the history of the Academy Awards, only Shelley Winters had achieved the feat (in 1959 and 1965). Three decades later, Wiest joined Winters as the only actors to duplicate a victory in this category. To date, no one else has matched their achievement. Wiest also is the first actor to win exactly two Academy Awards directed by the same director. Walter Brennan and Jack Nicholson had two of their three Oscar-winning performances under the same director. In 2012, Christoph Waltz tied Wiest's record with two Best Supporting Actor Academy Awards under the direction of Quentin Tarantino. Winsome, poignant, and instinctively funny, Wiest earned her Oscars and respect to become a most delightful Academy record-setter.

48. Melvyn Douglas

1963 Best Supporting Actor as rancher Homer Bannon in *Hud*
1970 Best Actor as former mayor Tom Garrison in *I Never Sang for My Father*
1979 Best Supporting Actor as business mogul Benjamin Rand in *Being There*

From his earliest training in a Shakespearean repertory company that traveled in the Midwest, Douglas took his career and craft as an actor very seriously. With his thin mustache and lips that alternated between pert and pouting, Douglas had the same matinee idol looks that made his contemporaries of early sound pictures headline stars. Despite fine performances in prestigious movies, Douglas' popularity did not manifest quickly. In 1936 he had roles in two movies that earned acting Oscar nominations, playing Virginia senator John Randolph to Best Supporting Actress nominee Beulah Bondi's Rachel Jackson in *The Gorgeous Hussy* and wooing Best Actress nominee Irene Dunne in *Theodora Goes Wild*. The following year, he was the dismissive father whose son comes of age thanks to the guidance of Best Actor winner Spencer Tracy in *Captains Courageous*. 1939 finally seemed to give Douglas the role that could have attracted Oscar, as he was the suitor who made Greta Garbo laugh in the romantic comedy *Ninotchka*. The film generated four major Oscar nominations, including Garbo's last for Best Actress, but Douglas was barely acknowledged as a potential Best Actor. Too dedicated to squander his talent, Douglas sought other venues for acting, eventually winning a lead acting Tony Award in 1960 for *The Best Man*, for which he was replaced by Henry Fonda in the movie adaptation, and a 1967 Emmy for *Do Not Go Gentle into That Good Night*. But the decade his star glimmered in other media, he returned to movies as a seasoned character actor in roles as weary professionals and aging fathers. As the Dansker in 1962's *Billy Budd*, Douglas shared screen time with Best Supporting Actor nominee Terence Stamp in the title role. The next year, Douglas was himself nominated in that category as cattle rancher Homer Bannon in *Hud*. The tense drama owed much to Douglas' frustration with arrogant rebel son Paul Newman, and both men, as well as Best Actress nominee Patricia Neal, all seemed among the lead contenders for their respective acting categories. Newman lost to Sidney Poitier, but Neal won, as did Douglas, who sent Brandon deWilde, who played his grandson in *Hud*, to accept on his behalf. Aging seemed to strengthen Douglas' skills and put him in even greater demand, and in 1970 he earned his only lead acting Oscar nomination for *I Never Sang for My Father*. Unlike *Hud*, where audiences identified more with the parent, *I Never Sang for My Father* told the struggle between a grown son striving for a connection to his rigid, cold dad. The somber drama won kudos for Douglas and Gene Hackman as the father and son, and both earned Academy Award nominations. Douglas lost to George C. Scott, but was featured on stage that night to present an honorary award to Lillian Gish. At the end of the decade, Douglas was again up for Best Supporting Actor as business mogul and Presidential advisor Ben Rand in *Being There*. As he had for *Hud*, Douglas missed that year's ceremony. When he won, he joined Katharine Hepburn as the only multiple acting Oscar winner who never showed up at the awards for any victory. In poor health, Douglas lived only one more year. Thus, his second Oscar ended his career on the highest of notes, ensuring that his later career success exemplified the stature and integrity he gave to his profession.

47. *Jason Robards, Jr.*

1976 **Best Supporting Actor as newspaper editor Ben Bradlee in *All the President's Men***
1977 **Best Supporting Actor as author Dashiell Hammett in *Julia***
1980 Best Supporting Actor as tycoon Howard Hughes in *Melvin and Howard*

Referred to by fellow double Oscar winner Kevin Spacey as "the elder statesman of the American theater," Robards' greatest acting contributions came on stage, where he brought to life characters created by iconic playwrights such as Harold Pinter, Arthur Miller, Clifford Odets, Eugene O'Neill, and Lillian Hellman. His later connection with O'Neill and Hellman highlighted his film career. After playing disillusioned son Jamie Tyrone on stage in O'Neill's masterpiece, *Long Day's Journey into Night*, Robards illuminated cinema screens in one of his first film performances. Despite the movie's universally glowing reviews, Katharine Hepburn earned its only Oscar nomination. But his performance put Robards on movie radar. In 1965 he reprised his Broadway role as misfit Murray Burns in the hit comedy *A Thousand Clowns*, but only supporting player Martin Balsam was cited, and then won, for acting. Both Robards and Stella Stevens were considered for 1970 nominations for Sam Peckinpah's *The Ballad of Cable Hogue*, but not until Robards made three biographical figures larger than life on film did the Academy note Robards' commanding resonance. With eight nominations, *All the President's Men* was right up there with *Rocky* and *Network* as the potential big winner at the 1976 Oscars. It won half of it categories, including Best Supporting Actor for Robards as wary but bold *Washington Post* editor Ben Bradlee, whom Robards acknowledged in his acceptance speech for letting him "come out and play with him." Robards was not a guaranteed winner in 1976, as Burgess Meredith as *Rocky*'s trainer and Laurence Olivier as a sadistic Nazi dentist in *Marathon Man* had, like Robards, won multiple awards leading up to Oscar night. The following year, Robards was drawn to the role of author Dashiell Hammett in part because of the detective novelist's relationship with playwright Lillian Hellman, whose works Robards had brought to life on stage. At the 1977 Academy Awards, so little suggested Robards would win that he didn't even attend. Robards' role was relatively short; in the same category was *Julia* co-star Maximilian Schell; the press favored Alec Guinness as Obi-Wan Kenobi in the megahit *Star Wars*; and as the Best Supporting Actor of the previous year, Robards would have to make history by becoming the first to win supporting acting Oscars in consecutive years. When Michael Caine and Maggie Smith announced Robards the winner, he did set that record, which to date has never been duplicated. The only other actors with consecutive wins— Luise Rainer, Spencer Tracy, Katharine Hepburn, and Tom Hanks—all won for leading roles. In 1980's *Melvin and Howard*, Robards' entrancing opening sequence performance as recluse Howard Hughes brought him his third nomination. When Leonardo DiCaprio was up for Best Actor as Hughes in *The Aviator* in 2004, Robards also joined the short list of pairs of actors who both earned Academy Award nominations playing the same character. Even rarer for the Robards/DiCaprio coup: they are among the few pairs nominated as a biographical character that was not a U.S. President or British royalty. His sandy, bass voice and languishing delivery made Robards the thinking actor's mentor. The stage may still claim him, but his Academy records make his contributions to film just as indelible.

46. Peter Ustinov

1951 Best Supporting Actor as Roman emperor Nero in *Quo Vadis*
1960 Best Supporting Actor as slave dealer Lentulus Batiatus in *Spartacus*

1964 Best Supporting Actor as small-time crook Arthur Simpson in *Topkapi*
1968 Best Story and Screenplay as co-author (with Ira Wallach) of *Hot Millions*

Urbane intellectual Peter Ustinov may have concentrated his efforts exclusively on acting less than any other star that made Oscar's countdown. The litany of professions in which he excelled included author, screenwriter, playwright, and columnist; comedian and humorist; movie, opera, and stage play director; radio broadcaster and television presenter; academician and diplomat. Yet most people who know Ustinov remember him best for his contribution to movie acting. Although he worked in British movies throughout the 1940s as an actor, screenwriter, director, and producer, Oscar first acknowledged Ustinov for his robust portrayal of Nero in Mervyn LeRoy's *Quo Vadis*. Thanks to zealous campaigning by producer Dore Schary, the Biblical epic earned eight nominations, with most of the attention going to Ustinov and Leo Genn for filling two Best Supporting Actor slots in a competition that included Kevin McCarthy in *Death of a Salesman*, Gig Young in *Come Fill the Cup*, and winner Karl Malden in *A Streetcar Named Desire*. Ustinov donned another toga for *Spartacus* in 1960 and beguiled the Academy as crafty slave trader Batiatus. In a solid race that included Peter Falk, Jack Kruschen, Sal Mineo, and Chill Wills, Ustinov's odds were likely increased by his also giving a fine performance in another big Oscar contender that year, *The Sundowners*. When Eva Marie Saint announced Ustinov the winner, he became the first and would remain the only actor to win an Academy Award in a film directed by Stanley Kubrick. Ustinov stayed on a roll during the 1960s. In 1962, he directed Terence Stamp to a Best Supporting Actor nomination for *Billy Budd*, then in 1964 was a nominee himself in the same category for Jules Dassin's delicious caper, *Topkapi*. His was the movie's only nomination, and in a film teeming with sharp writing and slick performances, Ustinov stole the show as a seemingly vapid con artist fumbling his way through a heist in which his feeble shystering might be genuine or could be the cleverest trick of them all. His comic bumbling so impressed the Academy that just four years after winning his first Best Supporting Actor trophy, he received a matching one. Ustinov was overseas directing Sophia Loren in *Lady L* during the 1964 ceremony, so fellow comic and friend Jonathan Winters picked up his award from presenter Angela Lansbury. In 1968, Ustinov starred in and co-wrote *Hot Millions*, one of the first movies about computer hacking which turned out to be a sleeper hit. Like *Topkapi*, Ustinov's *Hot Millions* earned a single Oscar nomination, but the writing award went to Mel Brooks for *The Producers*. When Agatha Christie adaptations resurged in the 1970s, Ustinov played Hercule Poirot in several installments, including

Death on the Nile, which won a Best Costume Oscar. Perhaps if the Academy had not already honored Ustinov with two competitive prizes, they might also have honored him with a Jean Hersholt Humanitarian Award for his work with UNICEF, much as they did Audrey Hepburn in 1992. Instead, the Academy streamlined their acknowledgment of Ustinov's hearty and heady contributions to film with two Supporting Actor awards, making him the first actor to win two Oscars in the 1960s.

45. Judi Dench

    1997 Best Actress as British monarch Queen Victoria in *Mrs. Brown*
    1998 Best Supporting Actress as British monarch Queen Elizabeth in *Shakespeare in Love*
    2000 Best Supporting Actress as village elder Armande Voizin in *Chocolat*
    2001 Best Actress as author Iris Murdoch in *Iris*
    2005 Best Actress as theater owner Laura Henderson in *Mrs. Henderson Presents*
    2006 Best Actress as teacher Barbara Covett in *Notes on a Scandal*
    2013 Best Actress as unwed mother Philomena Lee in *Philomena*

In early cinema history, Marie Dressler exemplified the quintessential late-in-life rise to stardom. Then in the late 1990s, after nearly half a century of solid work, a bevy of BAFTAs, and a record number of Laurence Olivier awards for her British stage work, Dench replaced Dressler as the ultimate model of a star that glimmers steadily for decades, then ignites with meteoric fervor. In 1966 she won her first BAFTA as Most Promising Newcomer to Leading Film Roles for *Four in the Morning*, a British drama released around Europe which never made it to the U.S. Despite small roles in Oscar shaded hits such as *A Room with a View* (1986), *Henry V* (1989), and *Hamlet* (1990), Dench insisted she had no film career until John Madden cast her as *Mrs. Brown*. Dench crackled with impassioned fervor as Victoria, the reclusive widowed monarch who blossomed thanks to a possibly platonic liaison with a Scottish servant that generated royal scandal and public criticism. Oscar season began with Helena Bonham Carter the lead Best Actress contender for *The Wings of the Dove*. But she was quickly usurped by Dench, who seemed a sure bet to win until an old Oscar pattern re-emerged. Usually when one American actor is competing against all foreign stars, the American wins. In 1997, four Brits—Dench, Bonham Carter, *Afterglow*'s Julie Christie, and Kate Winslet of *Titanic*—vied for the top prize against Helen Hunt in *As Good As It Gets*. If anyone could break the old tradition, it seemed Dench's performance could. Alas, Hunt won. But the disappointment didn't last long.

The following year, the Academy was so determined to make up for the oversight that Dench's 8-minute, 4-scene comic gem of a performance as bemused Elizabeth I in *Shakespeare in Love* brought her an Oscar for the second shortest Best Supporting Actress performance in history. Dench was on screen two minutes longer than record-holder Beatrice Straight in *Network*. With her *Shakespeare in Love* role, Dench joined a handful of actors in Academy history nominated for portraying the same character that earned another actor a nod the same year. In 1998, she was up as Elizabeth I in *Shakespeare in Love*, while Cate Blanchett competed for Best Actress in *Elizabeth*. In 2001, Dench vied for lead actress while Kate Winslet competed for Best Supporting Actress both portraying author Iris Murdoch at different stages of her life in *Iris*. Since Dench's popular win, few years pass when she is not an Oscar contender. She was up in the supporting category once more, for *Chocolat*, and since has vied for Best Actress four more times. In *Iris* she was shattering, in *Mrs. Henderson Presents*, enchanting. *Notes on a Scandal* brought out both pathos and contempt for a lonely lesbian who manipulates her way toward a relationship with a fragile young teacher.

In 2013 Dench returned to the Best Actress roster in an illustrious, compassionate performance as *Philomena*, a woman seeking reconciliation with

Philomena Lee (Judi Dench) reflected on the son she was forced to abandon in *Philomena* (2013), the movie that brought Dench her seventh nomination in only 16 years.

her son and her scarred past. Oscar has never seen a delayed burgeoning of a career like Dench's. She earned all of her seven nominations after the age of sixty. That record, which keeps growing as she continues working, gives her more than twice as many as the three post–60-year-old nods earned by Spencer Tracy, Edith Evans, Laurence Olivier, Melvyn Douglas, Katharine Hepburn, and Paul Newman. Although she finds the label "national treasure" too dusty, Dench nevertheless is a beloved Brit whose Oscar-winning expressions at The Globe have since given her career an indelible impression across the globe.

44. Robert Duvall

1972 Best Supporting Actor as lawyer/consigliere Tom Hagen in *The Godfather*
1979 Best Supporting Actor as U.S. Army Lieutenant Colonel William "Bill" Kilgore in *Apocalypse Now*
1980 Best Actor as U.S. Marine Lieutenant Colonel Bull Meechum in *The Great Santini*
1983 Best Actor as singer Mac Sledge in *Tender Mercies*
1997 Best Actor as preacher Euliss F. "Sonny" Dewey—The Apostle E. F. in *The Apostle*
1998 Best Supporting Actor as lawyer Jerome Facher in *A Civil Action*
2014 Best Supporting Actor as judge Joseph Palmer in *The Judge*

Although he is one of the most independent talents in film history, Duvall's career usually clustered him with different groups of actors. Rugged, prickly, and intense, Duvall was an unlikely leading man like contemporaries and friends, Gene Hackman and Dustin Hoffman. Duvall first caught Oscar's attention before Hackman and Hoffman by making his film debut in the small but unforgettable role as reclusive Boo Radley in 1962's *To Kill a Mockingbird*, but he gained fame after them. Following hits where other actors received Oscar nominations, including *Captain Newman, M.D.*, *True Grit*, and *M*A*S*H*, Duvall earned his first Academy Award recognition as the don's adoptive son Tom Hagen in the 1972 megahit, *The Godfather*. Duvall shared the spotlight and the Supporting Actor category with fellow Oscar newcomers James Caan and Al Pacino. All three had a shot at a win, with Duvall's biggest push coming after the New York Film Critics named him their Best Supporting Actor. On Oscar night, one early indication that *The Godfather* would bow to *Cabaret* in most categories came when Joel Grey topped all three of Don Corleone's sons for the Supporting Actor prize. In 1974 Duvall appeared in two Best Picture contenders directed by Francis Ford Coppola, *The Godfather Part II* and *The Conversation*, then reteamed with

Coppola in 1979 for *Apocalypse Now*, where he was unforgettable as Lieutenant Kilgore, who loved the smell of napalm in the morning. Being the only member of the deserving cast nominated for the grueling, groundbreaking film intensified his chances for an Oscar win. The Golden Globes gave their Best Supporting Actor prize to both Duvall and to Melvyn Douglas for *Being There*, a strong indication that one of them would win the Academy Award. The fact that Duvall had yet to win and Douglas already had a Best Supporting Oscar for *Hud* tilted hopes in Duvall's favor. On Oscar night, absent Douglas won. As a militant, competitive but occasionally vulnerable father in *The Great Santini*, Duvall would have had a great shot at a Best Actor win had Robert De Niro's portrayal of *Raging Bull* Jake LaMotta not immediately been hailed as one of cinema's most iconic performances. But in 1983 Duvall's gentle depiction of an alcoholic country singer reaching toward redemption in *Tender Mercies* was universally lauded. Although he enjoyed home court advantage as the only American competing against all Brits, his category did generate suspense because all his competitors—*Educating Rita*'s Michael Caine, *Reuben, Reuben*'s Tom Conti, and *The Dresser*'s Albert Finney and Tom Courtenay—earned critics or festival awards. When Duvall prevailed, he joined a rare cluster of actors like John Wayne and Gary Cooper who won Best Actor for playing cowboys. Directing himself to a Best Actor nomination in 1997 for *The Apostle* gave Duvall membership to the prestigious network of actor/directors that included Charles Chaplin, Orson Welles, Laurence Olivier, Woody Allen, and Warren Beatty. Despite such honorable company in so many groups, powerhouse Duvall has always stood alone in his film choices, and as a confident, independent actor.

43. *Greer Garson*

> 1939 Best Actress as wife Katherine Chipping in *Goodbye, Mr. Chips*
> 1941 Best Actress as orphanage founder Edna Kahly Gladney in *Blossoms in the Dust*
> **1942 Best Actress as wife Kay Miniver in *Mrs. Miniver***
> 1943 Best Actress as scientist Marie Curie in *Madame Curie*
> 1944 Best Actress as socialite wife Susie Parkington in *Mrs. Parkington*
> 1945 Best Actress as Irish maid Mary Rafferty in *The Valley of Decision*
> 1960 Best Actress as First Lady Eleanor Roosevelt in *Sunrise at Campobello*

With porcelain elegance and harp string intonations, Greer Garson almost overtook Sweden's Greta Garbo as the Hollywood import that could have been identified solely as GG. An invitation from MGM inspired Garson to leave her bourgeoning London stage career to try American moviemaking.

Her first performance, as the glowing muse and eventual wife of aging schoolteacher Charles Edward Chipping (played by Robert Donat) in *Goodbye, Mr. Chips*, instantly made her a movie star and Oscar nominee. The film ranked as one of the ten nominated for the Academy's Best Picture from among the grandest lot of Hollywood classics in history. Donat, the centerpiece of the movie, won Best Actor, and rose petal beauty Garson competed for Best Actress against winner Vivien Leigh in *Gone with the Wind*. Thereafter, the Academy loved everything Garson did. Nothing could stall the momentum Garson built throughout the 1940s as film after film, year after year she was named a Best Actress contender. While Bette Davis was setting a record as the first actor to earn Oscar nominations in five consecutive years (1938–1942), Greer Garson registered nominations that would tie that record starting in 1941 with her showcase role as children's rights champion Edna Gladney in *Blossoms in the Dust*. The part had everything: extensive range, screen time in almost every scene, and a rousing climactic speech before the Texas legislature, yet Garson lost to Joan Fontaine in *Suspicion*. The next year, Garson got the role of a lifetime as *Mrs. Miniver*, the courageous wife who stoked the home fires while facing tragedy and keeping her family brave and together amid London air raids. While the Academy kept honoring Bette Davis with nods for roles as jealous killers, mendacious wives, and slow-blooming wallflowers, Garson competed against her annually playing groundbreaking heroines for which audiences cheered. Her towering performance as Mrs. Miniver swept her to a 1942 Oscar victory, endeared her to world audiences, and solidified her position as a symbol of female strength and stability amid the chaos of World War II. Her 5½ minute acceptance speech has gone down in Oscar history as one of the longest. The following year she reteamed with Walter Pidgeon, her husband in both *Blossoms in the Dust* and *Mrs. Miniver*, as pioneering chemist *Madame Curie*. The last year Garson and Bette Davis competed against each other was in 1944 with Davis in *Mr. Skeffington* and Garson rising from maid to society matron as *Mrs. Parkington*, her fourth consecutive Oscar-nominated performance opposite Walter Pidgeon. Next Garson teamed with handsome newcomer Gregory Peck in *The Valley of Decision*, in which she rose from maid to civil conscience of a steel mill town. The hit movie gave Garson her sixth acting nomination, the most of anyone to date except for Norma Shearer (if her two 1929/1930 nominations are counted separately) and Bette Davis, whom Garson had just tied as the only actors with five nominations in consecutive years. That record still remains theirs exclusively. In the 1960s, Garson led rather than followed Davis with one final Best Actress nomination. Two years before Davis was in *What Ever Happened to Baby Jane?*, Garson enjoyed another career spike playing Eleanor Roosevelt in *Sunrise at Campobello*. Although she didn't win in 1960, frequent presenter Garson appeared on stage that year to give Burt Lancaster his Best Actor statuette.

The following year, Garson accepted the Best Actress honors for absent Sophia Loren. Although her nominations spanned four decades, Garson's angelic, courageous screen presence as Mrs. Miniver forever symbolizes the hope never lost among the rubble of the Second World War.

42. Sally Field

1979 Best Actress as cotton mill factory worker Norma Rae Webster in *Norma Rae*
1984 Best Actress as widow/farmer Edna Spalding in *Places in the Heart*
2012 Best Supporting Actress as First Lady Mary Todd Lincoln in *Lincoln*

Few other actors in Oscar history overcame more obstacles against Academy credibility than spitfire Sally Field. In the 1960s, the motion picture industry kept television at bay, leaving little room for a TV star to break into film. Teens were still rarely nominated for Oscars, and while Patty Duke managed to become a teenage television sitcom star after winning her Academy Award, a teen sensation on the small screen had little chance of transforming her popularity into big screen respect. Further, of the new genres of film that gained popularity that decade, beach movies were among the most readily discounted by the Academy. Thus, when Field first gained fame as beachcombing sitcom teen *Gidget*, few could have expected her to become an Academy favorite in subsequent decades. The road to Oscar's heart was further delayed by other hits, playing an airborne acolyte in *The Flying Nun*, and joining box office champ Burt Reynolds in the featherweight *Smokey and the Bandit* movies. But in 1976, Field gave one of television's most staggering performances as *Sybil*, an abuse victim whose multiple personality disorder required Field to drift in and out of 16 personalities, both female and male. The astounding achievement earned Field her first Emmy, and availed her to better career opportunities. She proved her movie mettle as determined Southern textile worker and Union advocate *Norma Rae*, a performance she nailed so precisely that, starting at the Cannes Film Festival, a domino trail of 1979 Best Actress honors tumbled in her direction. At the Golden Globes, Field won Best Actress, Drama, and Bette Midler won Best Actress, Musical or Comedy for *The Rose*. On Oscar night, Midler provided the only hiccup of suspense as a possible upset, but Field triumphed. Carefully selected roles led to another towering performance as a Depression era widow determined to save her farm and family in Robert Benton's nostalgic *Places in the Heart*. 1984 filmgoers flocked to a rash of rural dramas that brought Field, Jessica Lange in *Country*, and Sissy Spacek in *The River* to the Best Actress race. Setting dominated the entire category, as Field's other competitors were Vanessa

Redgrave in *The Bostonians* and Judy Davis, her closest rival for the prize, in *A Passage to India*. Only five years after winning Best Actress for her first nomination, Field joined Luise Rainer and Vivien Leigh as the only stars to go two-for-two in the Best Actress category. Bette Davis had as well, if one doesn't count her write-in votes for *Of Human Bondage*; since Field, Hilary Swank has joined the exclusive group. Unlike Rainer, Leigh, and Swank (so far), Field eventually earned another nomination. She was considered for *Absence of Malice*, *Murphy's Romance*, *Steel Magnolias*, and *Forrest Gump*, all of which brought other actors nominations, but not until she played mentally fragile, emotionally unraveling Mary Todd Lincoln did the Academy add her to the ballot, this time for Best Supporting Actress of 2012. The category put her in a taut race against favorite Anne Hathaway in *Les Misérables*, Amy Adams of *The Master*, Jacki Weaver in *Silver Linings Playbook*, and potential spoiler Helen Hunt in *The Sessions*. When Hathaway won, she stopped to hug Field before proceeding to the stage. No one knows better than Field how magnanimous a career feat she achieved by rising from her small screen beginnings to her status as a revered motion picture actress and producer. Both her Oscar acceptance speeches attest to it. In her first, she began with, "They said this couldn't be done." In her second, Field opened her heart to the Academy by acknowledging, "I haven't had an orthodox career and I've wanted more than anything to have your respect." Two lead acting Oscars within five years confirmed that she earned it.

41. Mickey Rooney

1938 Honorary award for his "significant contribution in bringing to the screen the spirit and personification of youth, and as [a] juvenile [player] setting a high standard of ability and achievement"
1939 Best Actor as student Mickey Moran in *Babes in Arms*
1943 Best Actor as student/delivery boy Homer Macauley in *The Human Comedy*
1956 Best Supporting Actor as World War II infantryman Dooley in *The Bold and the Brave*
1979 Best Supporting Actor as retired racehorse jockey Henry Dailey in *The Black Stallion*
1982 Honorary lifetime achievement award "in recognition of his 60 years of versatility in a variety of memorable film performances"

Compact as a moonstone, yet with talent the size of the Milky Way, Rooney was a successful entertainer from the age of seven. At 15, he cast a spell on audiences and enchanted the Academy as Puck in *A Midsummer*

Night's Dream, which was up for the 1935 Best Picture but left every member of the illustrious cast off the ballot. With galactic speed, the teenaged Rooney rose to the heights of the profession in roles that showcased his diverse skills. MGM cranked out thirteen Andy Hardy vehicles, with Rooney playing the indomitable optimist who could solve any youthful problem by putting on a show so energetic that sparks alternately shot from his gleaming smile and dancing shoes. Despite the grueling schedule demanded for generating so many consecutive hits, Rooney varied his onscreen persona by concurrently playing bullies in dramatic projects. He proved a good luck charm for Spencer Tracy, who won consecutive Best Actor Oscars with Rooney's support, briefly in *Captains Courageous* (1937) and throughout *Boys Town* (1938). Rooney's depth and diversity certainly helped the Academy select him as their first male recipient of the honorary juvenile award. Shirley Temple had won it before him; Deanna Durbin won with him in 1938. Of the ten child actors who won the special juvenile honor between 1934 and 1960, Rooney and Judy Garland were the only stars to progress to competitive Oscar contenders. The year after he won his miniature statuette, he vied for Best Actor against Clark Gable in *Gone with the Wind*, Laurence Olivier in *Wuthering Heights*, James Stewart in *Mr. Smith Goes to Washington*, and winner Robert Donat in *Goodbye, Mr. Chips*. Rooney earned his place among those legends because *Babes in Arms* gave him a forum to showcase his talents for a spectrum of emotions, musical talents, and even impersonations of fellow actors whom he usurped to become the most popular international male star of the late 1930s and early 1940s. World War II inspired more somber Americana fare, and Rooney traded in his tap shoes for a newspaper delivery boy's bicycle in Clarence Brown's *The Human Comedy*. The film's rich texture and sincerity emanated from Rooney's performance, and the Academy once again nominated him for Best Actor. Although he was 23 at the time, Rooney became the first and still only star to be nominated for multiple Oscars portraying teenagers. In 1956, Rooney was tapped by the Academy for his first supporting nomination as a World War II infantry man in *The Bold and the Brave*. Though he arrived that night the heavy favorite to win, he lost to Anthony Quinn's brief performance in *Lust for Life*. Around age 60, Rooney's supernova career reignited. In homage to his role in the 1945 hit *National Velvet*, director Carroll Ballard cast Rooney as a jockey trainer in *The Black Stallion*. While the opening sequences of the movie showcased entrancing cinematography and score, Rooney's performance carried the plot throughout the rest of the film and brought him one last time into Oscar contention. Though sentiment was on his side, Rooney lost to another senior actor, Melvyn Douglas in *Being There*. On a roll, Rooney followed this Oscar nomination with a 1980 Tony nod for *Sugar Babies*, 1981 Golden Globe and Emmy wins for *Bill*, and the Academy's lifetime achievement in 1982. Because none of Bob Hope's five honorary citations from the Academy came exclusively for acting, and both of Laurence Olivier's honorary Oscars recognized his work before and behind the camera, Rooney remains the only person to win two special Academy Awards expressly for acting. Ultimately, Rooney's star flickered for ninety years, giving him one of the longest and brightest careers in movie history.

40. Emma Thompson

1992 Best Actress as sister Margaret Schlegel in *Howards End*
1993 Best Actress as housekeeper Miss Kenton in *The Remains of the Day*
1993 Best Supporting Actress as barrister Gareth Peirce in *In the Name of the Father*
1995 Best Actress as sister Elinor Dashwood in *Sense and Sensibility*
1995 Best Adapted Screenplay as screenwriter of *Sense and Sensibility*

Emma Thompson's masterful talent might have seemed daunting to the everyday moviegoer, perhaps even critics, if not for her malleable humor. The combination gives her inspiring characterizations a deceptive dollop of ease that makes her onscreen presence magnetic. Thompson's early alliance with then-husband Kenneth Branagh gave her the role of Catherine of Valois in her first Oscar film, *Henry V*. Three years later, she imbued *Howards End*, Merchant-Ivory's study of stifling class and manners, with enveloping warmth. Even initial reviews hinted that Thompson had charmed everyone, likely even Oscar. The theme for the 1992 Academy Awards paid homage to women, and appropriately the Best Actress category was varied and international. Respected French superstar Catherine Deneuve made a stunning comeback in *Indochine*. Mary McDonnell rose to ranks of lead actress nominee as a bitter paraplegic in *Passion Fish*. Michelle Pfeiffer slipped in for her third nomination in the small but satisfying *Love Field*. Susan Sarandon had the most touching performance of her career as a mother desperate to save her dying young son in *Lorenzo's Oil*. Thompson and Supporting Actress nominee Vanessa Redgrave earned the only acting nominations for *Howards End*, and both seemed likely to take their respective categories. Earlier in the telecast, Redgrave lost to Marisa Tomei in *My Cousin Vinny*, but Thompson triumphed, and humbly shared her vantage point from stage looking out at the many faces that "entertained, influenced, and thrilled" her. The next year Thompson made two movies: in *The Remains of the Day* she reteamed with director James Ivory to play a reserved maid aching for the love of her coworker, Anthony Hopkins, and in Jim Sheridan's *In the Name of the Father* she played British solicitor Gareth Peirce. The Academy embraced both performances, and Thompson and Holly Hunter became the first two actors in history to both compete in two acting categories in the same year. Thompson lost both competitions to stars of *The Piano*, with Hunter the expected victor for Best Actress and young Anna Paquin the surprise upset in the supporting category. Soon after, Thompson ventured into screenwriting by adapting Jane Austen's *Sense and Sensibility*.

She captured Austen's deft humor and romance so well the film was a box office hit and then lead contender for the 1995 Oscars. When awarded the Best Adapted Screenplay honors, Thompson followed Barbra Streisand, who won Best Actress for *Funny Girl* in 1968 and Best Song for "Evergreen" from *A Star Is Born* in 1976, as the only Oscar-winning actress to win a second Academy Award in a non-acting category. Because Streisand shared her Best Song win with lyricist Paul Williams, Thompson set the record as the only Best Actress winner to independently earn another Oscar in a non-acting category. With characteristic humor, Thompson began that acceptance speech by admitting she'd just visited with Jane Austen to tell her about the grosses. In subsequent decades, the Academy has shockingly failed to nominate Thompson for two performances that were considered locks. In 2003's *Love Actually*, Thompson's heartbreaking silent realization to the strands of Joni

The Dashwoods (Emma Thompson, Kate Winslet and Gemma Jones) navigated the comic labyrinth of pre-Victorian romance in Thompson's Oscar-winning adaptation of *Sense and Sensibility* (1995).

Mitchell gave cinema one of its most indelible scenes. In 2013, by culling humanity and even humor from an implacable depiction of author P.L. Travers in *Saving Mr. Banks*, she made most every critic's short list of definite Best Actress nominees, but wasn't amid the final five at Oscar time. Plucky, confident, and sometimes brimming with silliness, Thompson endears herself to award audiences. But on screen, her sincerity and depth stun them to silence, as there is no doubt she is master of her craft.

39. Anthony Quinn

1952 Best Supporting Actor as revolutionary's brother Eufemio Zapata in *Viva Zapata!*
1956 Best Supporting Actor as painter Paul Gauguin in *Lust for Life*
1957 Best Actor as rancher Gino in *Wild Is the Wind*
1964 Best Actor as musician peasant Alexis Zorba in *Zorba the Greek*

A pugilist background and dark physical hues thanks to a part Mexican-American heritage helped Quinn literally fight his way into film, becoming the favorite supporting player for ethnic ruffians who spiked the conflict in any drama or adventure by physically antagonizing the hero. With curled fists and a snarl, he menaced as a Chinese, Eskimo, Filipino, Italian, and Sioux. Tall and imposing, he could also enhance group shots, as he did in *Waikiki Wedding*, for which "Sweet Leilani" won the 1937 Best Song Oscar. Before he was a noted actor that the Academy began honoring, Quinn had roles in other Oscar-nominated dramas. He was a henchman for gambler Brian Donlevy in *Union Pacific* (1941), matador Manolo de Palma in *Blood and Sand* (1941), and one of the suspected cattle thieves set to die by an impetuous posse in the 1943 Best Picture nominee, *The Ox-Bow Incident*. After following Marlon Brando as Stanley Kowalski in *A Streetcar Named Desire* on Broadway, Quinn played brother Eufemio to Brando's Emilio in *Viva Zapata!* While Best Actor nominee Brando was seemingly the one with the best potential to earn the film an Oscar, mostly for the Academy to make amends for not giving him the prize the previous year for the film version of *A Streetcar Named Desire*, Quinn instead took the Best Supporting Actor prize over fellow Oscar newcomers Richard Burton in *My Cousin Rachel*, Jack Palance in *Sudden Fear*, Arthur Hunnicutt in *The Big Sky*, and previous Best Actor winner Victor McLaglan of *The Quiet Man*. Although Quinn was not on hand to accept from presenter Greer Garson, the victory brought him international notice, and soon Quinn was in Spain filming *La Strada*, one of the landmark roles of his career. The centerpiece of Federico Fellini's mythical film, Quinn's interpretation of the Goliath circus strong man showed his true mettle as an actor. Had the Academy been more open to nominating foreign language performances back then, Quinn would surely have been a contender. Instead, *La Strada* went down in Oscar history as the first movie to win in the new Best Foreign Language Film category. Throughout the rest of his career, Quinn accepted any role, lead or supporting, that appealed to him. He may have been drawn to the small role of Paul Gauguin in *Lust for Life* because he was a painter himself. Though on screen only about eight minutes, his intoxicated and intoxicating presence reverberated throughout the movie, and became one of filmdom's brief gems. On Oscar night Mickey Rooney was expected to win for *The Bold and the Brave*, but Anthony Quinn's name was in the envelope. This time, Quinn was on hand to accept from presenter Nancy Kelly. His speech downplayed competition among actors. Instead he suggested that with each role he only competed with himself, and this Oscar was acknowledgment that he'd won this fight. After two consecutive supporting victories, Quinn's subsequent nominations came for Best Actor, making him the only actor with two supporting wins to earn subsequent nominations in lead roles. Besides Shelley Winters, who started as a lead actress nominee and then earned the rest of her nominations as a supporting player, every other double supporting acting winner was, to the Academy, always a supporting contender. Ironically, Quinn's Oscar-winning performances were not his most revered. Instead, he will forever be remembered as *Zorba the Greek*. Thanks to Quinn's performance that crescendoed with a lusty dance in celebration of life, the movie became an instant classic. The Academy nominated the international hit in seven categories, including Best Picture, Best Adapted Screenplay, Best Supporting Actress for Lila Kedrova (who won), and Best Actor for Quinn. Had Quinn not already won twice and Rex Harrison not perfected his Henry Higgins in *My Fair Lady* with over 1,000 stage performances, Quinn might not have lost to Harrison. Having represented so many ethnicities, it is no surprise that Quinn's most indelible lead performances came as an Italian strongman and a Greek peasant, and that his Oscars came for playing a Mexican revolutionary and a French painter. In Oscar history, he is the second actor, behind Walter Brennan, to win multiple Best Supporting Actor Academy Awards. Because Brennan won a third, Quinn reigns as the first person in history to win exactly two supporting Oscars.

38. *Shelley Winters*

1951 Best Actress as clothing factory worker Alice Tripp in *A Place in the Sun*
1959 Best Supporting Actress as Jewish wife/mother in hiding Petronella Van Daan in *The Diary of Anne Frank*
1965 Best Supporting Actress as mother Rose-Ann D'Arcey in *A Patch of Blue*

1972 Best Supporting Actress as shipwrecked passenger Belle Rosen in *The Poseidon Adventure*

Shelley Winters overcame bombshell stereotyping by steamrolling her way into the role of drab factory worker Alice Tripp in *A Place in the Sun*. Dubious about the abilities of an actress known for flamboyant scene stealing both on and off camera, director George Stevens only relented to give Winters a brief screen test at the Hollywood Athletic Club. For several minutes, he saw no one but a dowdy young woman crumpled in a corner chair as he waited for the blond sexpot to arrive. When he realized that mousy waif was Winters already in character, she got the part, new respectability as a dramatic actress, and her only lead acting Oscar nomination. *A Place in the Sun* and Winters were so well received that she, Katharine Hepburn of *The African Queen*, and Vivian Leigh in *A Streetcar Named Desire* were all touted as the likely Best Actress of 1951. When Ronald Colman, whom Winters supported in his Oscared performance in *A Double Life*, stepped on stage to present her category, Winters thought, *How sweet. The Academy selected Ronny to present me the Oscar*. When Colman announced Vivien Leigh the winner, Winters swore she heard Colman call her name, and headed up the aisle toward the stage until husband Vittorio Gassman stopped her. At the end of that decade, George Stevens, whom Winters called her favorite director, cast her as petrified pessimist Mrs. Van Daan in *The Diary of Anne Frank*. When the real Otto Frank visited the set and suggested that Winters could win the Oscar, she promised to donate it to the Anne Frank Museum in Amsterdam if his prediction was accurate. Edmond O'Brien did announce Winters the victor that year. She began expressing thanks by recognizing "that wonderful little girl, Miss Anne Frank, who wrote with such depth and perception about human beings" and later kept her promise to donate her Oscar to Anne's museum. During the 1960s, Winters received accolades from other award organizations for characterizations Oscar overlooked. Among the most impressive were *Lolita*'s love-starved mother Charlotte in 1962 and *Alfie*'s older American lover Ruby in 1966. An avid civil rights advocate, Winters won her second Oscar as deplorable Rose-Ann D'Arcey, a racist, abusive mother who blinded her daughter in *A Patch of Blue*, which Winters described in her acceptance speech as a "sensitive, beautiful picture about integration." She further thanked director Guy Green, "who truly understood the role I played better than I did." With this victory, Winters became the first person to win Best Supporting Actress twice. Throughout Oscar history, this award traditionally goes to talented (usually young) Academy newcomers or legendary international stars. Winters' achievement is even more impressive because every acting category except Best Supporting Actress has multiple repeat winners, and because she alone held the record for 29 years. Only

Dianne Wiest has joined Winters as a double supporting actress winner. Like whiney Mrs. Van Daan or slatternly Rose-Ann D'Arcey, Winters' matronly characters were intentionally shrill and unappealing.

But for *The Poseidon Adventure*, she gained 35 pounds to play Belle Rosen, a lovable grandmother climbing toward safety in a capsized ocean liner. Funny ("Mrs. Peter Pan I'm not") and courageous, Winters was so winning in her struggle that during her heroic swim to save Gene Hackman when he was trapped underwater, audiences often chanted, "Go! Shelley, go!" and movie critics identified the role as her most appealing in perhaps her last forty films. *The Poseidon Adventure* broke box office records, earned Oscar's first Special Academy Award for its visual effects, and anchored eight competitive nominations, including Winters as Best Supporting Actress. Always a wisecracking interview, Winters guested on nearly every talk show to promote the movie and campaign for a third Oscar. Winning the Golden Globe boded well for another record-breaking victory, but she lost the Academy Award to Eileen Heckart in *Butterflies are Free*. A bawdy, blowsy Actors Studio

Cruisers James Martin (Red Buttons) and Belle and Manny Rosen (Shelley Winters and Jack Albertson) rang in the New Year as a tidal wave of tragedy approached in *The Poseidon Adventure* (1972).

alumnus, Winters was a trailblazing character actress whose Best Supporting victories solidified her place in the pantheon of Oscar's favorite stars.

37. Jodie Foster

1976 Best Supporting Actress as child prostitute Iris "Easy" Steensma in *Taxi Driver*
1988 Best Actress as waitress Sarah Tobias in *The Accused*
1991 Best Actress as FBI trainee Clarice Starling in *The Silence of the Lambs*
1994 Best Actress as isolated woods dweller Nell Kellty in *Nell*

Whether guided by her manager/mother as a child, or independently as an adult, Foster has always had a strong command of her craft and career. In 1976, she was in a plethora of movies—five in all—an abundance of work not seen regularly since the old studios cranked out vehicles for Shirley Temple or Margaret O'Brien. The 1976 performance that intrigued Oscar was her fiercest: for most of *Taxi Driver*, Foster was barely more than a glimpsed figure that captivated Robert De Niro's Travis Bickle. But she became the focus of Act III, finally igniting Martin Scorsese's simmering study of a descent into madness. Despite being only 14 at the time, Foster was a formidable contender in a Best Supporting Actress race that could have gone any direction. She was a favorite, but so was Piper Laurie as a crazed religious zealot in *Carrie*. No one was counting out impressive Jane Alexander for her cautiously retaliatory role in helping reveal *All the President's Men*, or even Lee Grant for *Voyage of the Damned*, although Grant had just won in that category the previous year. In the smallest role of the five, Beatrice Straight came up the surprise victor for her few intense scenes opposite unfaithful husband William Holden in *Network*. Foster kept a low profile to earn a degree from Yale and contend with prompting an assassination attempt on President Ronald Reagan that mirrored the plot of *Taxi Driver*. But Foster returned to moviemaking in 1988 with what many fellow actors considered one of the toughest roles an actor could tackle. Foster played Sarah Tobias, a loose and provocative young woman who survived a gang rape and then the public humiliation of having to relive it during a trial to convict the rapists. 1988's Best Actress race was supposed to belong to either Glenn Close, up for her fifth Oscar of the 1980s in the diabolical *Dangerous Liaisons*, or Sigourney Weaver, who was up against Foster for *Gorillas in the Mist*, as well as for Supporting Actress in *Working Girl*. A first in Oscar history, Weaver lost both competitions, first to Geena Davis in *The Accidental Tourist* and then to Foster in *The Accused*. Three years later, Foster was evenly marked for potential victory with Geena Davis and Susan Sarandon as *Thelma & Louise*. Because Davis and Foster had won before (both in 1988), Sarandon had a slight edge. But 1991 belonged to *The Silence of the Lambs*, and for the first time since 1975's *One Flew Over the Cuckoo's Nest*, a single film swept all five major awards, including another Best Actress win for Foster.

In a quid pro quo battle of wills, Foster made Clarice Starling every bit as intriguing as Anthony Hopkins' Hannibal Lecter, and they have continued to be regarded as excellent lead acting Oscar choices. She won rave reviews as a feral woman left to survive in the wild since childhood in *Nell*, the 1994 hit that had movie fans flailing their arms and impersonating Foster's delivery of the line,

Hannibal Lecter (Anthony Hopkins) invaded the psyche of FBI agent Clarice Starling (Jodie Foster) in *The Silence of the Lambs* (1991).

"T'ee in the way" [tree in the wind]. An actor since she was barely more than an infant, Foster has kept a watchful eye on her privacy, and has selected movie roles that challenge and intrigue. The same year Foster won her second Oscar, she expanded her power and influence in the profession as director of the hit *Little Man Tate*. Though all her Academy recognition has remained with her work as an actor, Oscar respects an artist of Foster's caliber, which helps confirm why two Best Actress victories so close in years were well-deserved.

36. *Glenda Jackson*

1970 Best Actress as artist Gudrun Brangwen in *Women in Love*
1971 Best Actress as recruitment consultant Alex Greville in *Sunday Bloody Sunday*
1973 Best Actress as divorced mother Vicki Allessio in *A Touch of Class*
1975 Best Actress as wife Hedda Gabler in *Hedda*

For a brief spell in the 1970s, Glenda Jackson's relationship with Oscar mirrored Katharine Hepburn's. It was one-sided admiration, with the Academy honoring Jackson time after time, and Jackson responding to the praise with Hepburnesque detachment. The major difference in their careers, thanks mostly to the state of art in her decade of nominations, was that Jackson consistently accepted roles in films that reconsidered the role of sexuality and gender in intimate relationships. Following a brief uphill climb to stardom in the 1960s that included an uncredited role in 1963's *This Sporting Life*, which earned Richard Harris and Rachel Roberts lead acting Oscar nominations, Jackson blazed onto the international landscape thanks in part to writer/producer Larry Kramer. After seeing Jackson on the London stage, he allayed United Artist executives' trepidations about her unconventional looks and cast her as mercurial artist Gudrun in *Women in Love* under the direction of Ken Russell. Her nuanced performance rocked Oscar's Richter scale. In a rare Best Actress race where everyone was up for the first time, Jackson shared the ballot with Jane Alexander in *The Great White Hope*, Ali MacGraw in *Love Story*, Sarah Miles in *Ryan's Daughter*, and Carrie Snodgress in *Diary of a Mad Housewife*. Jackson won *Women in Love*'s only Academy Award, but, like Hepburn, ignored the Oscars and allowed friend Juliet Mills to accept the award for her. The next year, Jackson again contributed to a movie that explored sexual relationships as layered, complex phenomena. Like *Women in Love*, *Sunday Bloody Sunday* was nominated for Best Actress and Best Director, but not Best Picture. This time under the direction of John Schlesinger, Jackson was not the artist, but a recruitment officer sharing the love of a young male artist with Best Actor nominee Peter Finch. More detached but no less fascinating than Gudrun, the character of Alex Greville showcased new facets of Jackson's talents, and the Academy nominated her again. This time, Jackson and three other British thespians (Julie Christie, Vanessa Redgrave, and Janet Suzman) lost to American actress Jane Fonda in *Klute*. Still examining sexual relations, but this time with comic intentions, Jackson was a gloriously unfettered free spirit having a fling that became more emotionally meaningful than she expected with American businessman George Segal in *A Touch of Class*. Wise, witty, and guileless, Jackson delivered comic slashes and, with a shift in inflection and a tilt of her chin, eased their sting with lines audiences could chew on for days. Like Jackson herself, it was a smartly unconventional romantic comedy, and Jackson won Oscar's favor once more. Despite her indifference to the awards, the Academy this time chose her over two favored actresses in box office citadels, Ellen Burstyn in *The Exorcist* and Barbra Streisand in *The Way We Were*. Uninterested in the Oscar ceremony, Jackson let *A Touch of Class* director Melvin Frank accept her statuette. In 1975 Jackson tackled the part of many actresses' dreams, Hedda Gabler in Trevor Nunn's film version called *Hedda*. This time, Jackson was not expected to take home Oscar, as Golden Globe winners Ann-Margret of *Tommy* and Louise Fletcher of *One Flew Over the Cuckoo's Nest* were favored, and Fletcher won. Hope ran high with rave reviews for both Jackson and Mona Washbourne for the biopic of Stevie Smith in Robert Enders' *Stevie*. Although Jackson won Best Actress from the National Board of Review in 1981 and Washbourne won a supporting citation from the New York Film Critics, both women, and the film, were ignored by the Academy, likely because of distribution troubles that delayed its general release for three years. With four nominations and two wins in six short years, Jackson was Oscar's favored actress of the early 1970s. Though she never basked in the glory, her work has kept her an admired talent of her generation.

35. Alec Guinness

1952 Best Actor as bank clerk Henry Holland in *The Lavender Hill Mob*
1957 Best Actor as British commanding officer Colonel Nicholson in *The Bridge on the River Kwai*
1958 Best Adapted Screenplay as screenwriter of *The Horse's Mouth*
1977 Best Supporting Actor as Jedi knight Ben "Obi-Wan" Kenobi in *Star Wars*
1979 Honorary lifetime achievement award "for advancing the art of screen acting through a host of memorable and distinguished performances"
1988 Best Supporting Actor as father William Dorrit in *Little Dorrit*

Guinness admitted what many actors know but few verbalize: he loved, and sometimes even needed, the occasional ego stroke that came from recognition of his work. Fortunately, his characterizations were often classic, and so the praise was always deserved. In 1946, he played pale young gentleman Herbert Pocket in the Oscar-winning, Best Picture-nominated adaptation of *Great Expectations*, directed by David Lean. Their professional alliance created some of history's greatest cinema classics. One of his first movie hits as lead actor was in an eccentric little British comedy from director Charles Crichton called *The Lavender Hill Mob*. As mild-mannered banker Henry Holland whose interview about a bank heist is traced through flashbacks, Guinness is a wonder: so droll audiences would laugh until their stomachs spasmed, yet so gentle they rooted for him regardless of the outcome of the investigation. New to Oscar, Guinness lost the Best Actor race to Gary Cooper in *High Noon*. But during his next Academy venture, Guinness could have started preparing an acceptance speech midway through the filming of David Lean's *The Bridge on the River Kwai*. No one but Guinness could have ridden the fine line between commitment and obsession as he did as Colonel Nicholson, the POW building a bridge to raise morale of his imprisoned troops in the epic hit. After Guinness pocketed Best Actor prizes from BAFTA, the

National Board of Review, the New York Film Critics, and the Hollywood Foreign Press, he and the movie went into Oscar night the anticipated big winners. Against former winners (Marlon Brando, Charles Laughton, Anthony Quinn) and newcomer Anthony Franciosa, Guinness seemed to take his category easily. Not in attendance in 1957, Guinness let Jean Simmons accept his Oscar. The following year, he wrote and starred in another British hit comedy, *The Horse's Mouth* for frequent film collaborator, director Ronald Neame. Guinness won the Volpi Cup for Best Actor at the Venice Film Festival, then became one of the only actors to also compete for a writing Oscar when the Academy overlooked his acting, but nominated him for Best Adapted Screenplay. Guinness's keen eye for successful movies inspired him to accept occasional supporting roles, as he did when playing Prince Faisal in 1962's Best Picture *Lawrence of Arabia* and General Yevgraf Zhivago in the lush Oscar-winning *Doctor Zhivago* in 1965, both under the direction of David Lean.

One of his most beloved roles was as wise warrior, mentor and Jedi leader Obi-Wan Kenobi in the 1977 intergalactic blockbuster *Star Wars*. As the character who did not believe in luck, but trusted that the Force would be with them, Guinness was an accessible and courageous sage. The science fiction megahit introduced Guinness to a new generation of adoring fans and

Thanks to his Oscar nomination as Obi-Wan Kenobi in *Star Wars* (1977), Alec Guinness is the only actor nominated from any of the top four highest-grossing box office film franchises in history.

brought him back to Oscar for his first supporting competition. Although expectations of a win were dashed when Jason Robards, Jr., won as Dashiell Hammett in *Julia*, Guinness returned to the forefront of the Academy's awareness. Close analysis of his long and varied contribution to movies inspired the honorary award in 1979. This time, Guinness was present at the ceremony and accepted the award himself. Nearly a decade later, he was nominated a final time for one of the longest supporting performances in history. In Christine Edzard's 360-minute adaptation of Charles Dickens' *Little Dorrit*, Guinness awed as the title character's selfish, pretentious father, William. Throughout the movie, Guinness was concurrently proud and bedraggled, pompous and pitiable. His final nod uniformly rounded out his relationship with Oscar, as he lost to Kevin Kline for *A Fish Called Wanda* in a performance directed by Charles Crichton, who directed Guinness to his first nomination.

34. Peter O'Toole

1962 Best Actor as British lieutenant colonel T. E. Lawrence in *Lawrence of Arabia*
1964 Best Actor as British monarch King Henry II in *Becket*
1968 Best Actor as British monarch King Henry II in *The Lion in Winter*
1969 Best Actor as schoolmaster Arthur Chipping in *Goodbye, Mr. Chips*
1972 Best Actor as 14th Earl of Gurney Jack in *The Ruling Class*
1980 Best Actor as film director Eli Cross in *The Stunt Man*
1982 Best Actor as actor Alan Swann in *My Favorite Year*
2002 Honorary lifetime achievement award "to Peter O'Toole, whose remarkable talents have provided cinema history with some of its most memorable characters"
2006 Best Actor as actor Maurice in *Venus*

More than 50 years before Oscar host Ellen Degeneres referred to Best Supporting Actor winner Jared Leto as the prettiest person at the 2013 Oscars, Peter O'Toole was among the first male actors consistently called physically beautiful as he raced across the sandy landscapes in his first starring role as *Lawrence of Arabia*. His statuesque physique and those mesmeric eyes shining through chiseled features made him a joy to behold, but his prodigious talent demanded ever greater attention. O'Toole's emergence as a leading actor in the David Lean epic rivaled any that came before or since. If that were the only role O'Toole had ever taken, he would still have been a superstar. But O'Toole continued to impress his peers time and again, as the acting branch lauded him with eight nominations, but the general Academy never followed through with a much deserved competitive win. O'Toole's nemesis was not his skill, but his timing. Every great performance—and there were many that could have earned Oscars—came in a year when someone else in his category was longer due the prize, or had an exceptional circumstance that dropped their name into the ballot box.

O'Toole's first nomination as T. E. Lawrence was bested by five-time nominee Gregory Peck as Atticus Finch in *To Kill a Mockingbird*. In 1964, O'Toole was on equal footing with *Becket* co-star Richard Burton, but both were outshone by Rex Harrison as Henry Higgins in *My Fair Lady*, a role he'd played on Broadway more than 2,200 times. Although it missed the opportunity to honor O'Toole as Henry II in *Becket*, the Academy had another chance when he played the monarch again in a more caustic battle of wills against Best Actress winner Katharine Hepburn in *The Lion in Winter*. He was favored to win, and many still considered the Academy's failure to honor him with the Best Actor prize of 1968 one of the most egregious oversights in Oscar history. But Cliff Robertson had overcome a long personal struggle to bring *Charly* to the big screen. Couple the valiant effort with an impassioned

Peter O'Toole (here as T. E. Lawrence with Anthony Quinn as Auda Abu Tayi in *Lawrence of Arabia*, 1962) broke his streak as one of the most nominated non-winners by receiving a lifetime achievement Oscar in 2002.

performance as a mentally challenged, sympathetic character (often Oscar's favorite), and O'Toole lost again. He could have been the first actor to win an Oscar playing the same character (Arthur Chipping) that already brought another actor (Robert Donat) the Oscar when he was up for the musical remake of *Goodbye, Mr. Chips*. But in 1969, John Wayne donned an eyepatch and the entire world—especially the Academy—knew it was time to honor one of Hollywood's biggest legends with an Oscar. Only someone of O'Toole's power could earn an Oscar as a loopy earl with thinks he's Jesus Christ in *The Ruling Class*, but could the Academy possibly honor him in that small film over Marlon Brando as *The Godfather*? Despite grand turns as a bombastic director in *The Stunt Man* and an uproarious lush of a fading star in *My Favorite Year*, O'Toole did not appear on Oscar's stage to accept an Academy Award until Meryl Streep handed him a lifetime achievement award in 2002. To indicate how much O'Toole still wanted to win Best Actor, he inquired if accepting the honorary Oscar would destroy his chances of ever winning a competitive one. Early consideration in 2006 suggested that O'Toole would finally reach the Academy acknowledgment he craved, but praise for his performance in *Venus* was overshadowed by Forest Whitaker's sweep that season of every Best Actor award, including Oscar, as *The Last King of Scotland*. Towering in both stature and talent, O'Toole was one of Oscar's great champions. Securing eight nominations without a competitive win was an Academy record, but his legacy is not for tippling near the edge of victory, but for a body of work that the Academy kept recognizing, and loving, for almost 50 years.

33. Al Pacino

- 1972 Best Supporting Actor as former soldier/mafia boss Michael Corleone in *The Godfather*
- 1973 Best Actor as policeman Frank Serpico in *Serpico*
- 1974 Best Actor as mafia don Michael Corleone in *The Godfather Part II*
- 1975 Best Actor as bank robber Sonny Wortzik in *Dog Day Afternoon*
- 1979 Best Actor as defense attorney Arthur Kirkland in *… And Justice for All*
- 1990 Best Supporting Actor as crime boss Big Boy Caprice in *Dick Tracy*
- **1992 Best Actor as retired U.S. Army Lieutenant Colonel Frank Slade in *Scent of a Woman***
- 1992 Best Supporting Actor as real estate salesperson Ricky Roma in *Glengarry Glen Ross*

Part I. The Countdown

Pacino has the uncanny skill of creeping into a role, mounting an emotional assault to captivate audiences and leave them rapturously in his grasp. In 1972, he played militant, honorable Michael Corleone in *The Godfather*. At awards time, different organizations alternately considered him a lead and supporting player. The National Society of Film Critics named Pacino their Best Actor of the year, while the National Board of Review picked both Pacino and *Cabaret*'s Joey Grey as their Best Supporting Actors. The Golden Globes nominated him for Best Actor, which he lost to co-star Marlon Brando, but the Oscars dropped him to the supporting category with fellow Corleone brothers James Caan and Robert Duvall. Pacino may have lost that race to Joel Grey simply because the Academy was equally torn about the category in which he really belonged. Regardless, *The Godfather* made him an instant star. Pacino followed that performance with a critically acclaimed turn as a heartbroken drifter in *Scarecrow*, and as antiestablishment cop *Serpico*. The Academy nominated him for the latter, and that year he and Jack Nicholson competed in the first of three consecutive Best Actor races, making them the pivotal Oscar contenders of the 1970s. They both lost in an upset to Jack Lemmon in *Save the Tiger*, but returned to compete the following year in the two movies that wrestled for top honors on Oscar night, Nicholson's *Chinatown* and Pacino's *The Godfather Part II*. Any Academy members who felt Pacino should have already won an Oscar as Michael Corleone had even more reason to vote for him here. As Michael's responsibilities and moral judgments shaded with more nuances than the younger Michael had to grapple with, Pacino gave a tour de force that stood alone as Oscar-worthy. He became the first actor nominated in both acting categories for playing the same character in two different movies. But equally loved that year was Nicholson as J.J. Gittes in *Chinatown*. Although *The Godfather Part II* triumphed as the big winner of the 1974 Oscars, both men were again usurped by a longshot—Art Carney in *Harry and Tonto*. The following year they were again equal frontrunners for Best Actor, with Nicholson as the antihero of *One Flew Over the Cuckoo's Nest* and Pacino shooting frenetic sparks as a jittery bank robber in *Dog Day Afternoon*. His "Attica! Attica!" chant became legendary, and no one could guess which of the decade's two most nominated stars would take home Oscar. It was Nicholson. Pacino ran one more Best Actor race in the 1970s, ending the decade in ... *And Justice for All*, where he introduced another classic movie line, "You're out of order! You're out of order! The whole trial is out of order!" With stiff competition from Dustin Hoffman in *Kramer vs. Kramer* and Peter Sellers in *Being There*, Pacino ended up losing to Hoffman. Nominated in half of the years over a single decade, Pacino was still without an Oscar. He started the 1990s with the only acting nomination from *Dick Tracy*'s array of colorful villains. By now Academy whispers suggested he should win for something, anything already, but he lost that supporting bid to Joe Pesci in *Goodfellas*. Then in 1992, Pacino risked becoming Oscar's biggest loser when he earned his seventh and eighth nominations for *Scent of a Woman* and *Glengarry Glen Ross*. With these two nominations, he surpassed by one nomination both Richard Burton and Peter O'Toole as the most nominated actor who never won. When the Best Supporting Actor prize went to Gene Hackman in *Unforgiven*, it seemed that Oscar would finally come to Pacino as lead actor. The Academy delivered as expected, and the crowd at the Dorothy Chandler Pavilion rose to its feet before Pacino made them laugh with, "You broke my streak." He also broke a new Academy record. Only five actors before Pacino had been nominated in both lead and supporting categories the same year. In the first four instances, the actor always won the supporting prize. The fifth time, Sigourney Weaver lost in both categories. With his *Scent of a Woman* victory, Pacino became the first star to be nominated in both acting categories in a single year and win in the lead actor category. In his acceptance speech, Pacino called his role as blind, embittered, but wiser for the pain Frank "Hoo-uh!" Slade "any actor's dream part." With signature aplomb, he made it his own, and finally won an Academy Award.

32. *Geraldine Page*

1953 Best Supporting Actress as rancher's wife Angie Lowe in *Hondo*
1961 Best Actress as minister's spinster daughter Alma Winemiller in *Summer and Smoke*
1962 Best Actress as actress Alexandra Del Lago in *Sweet Bird of Youth*
1966 Best Supporting Actress as mother Margery Chanticleer in *You're a Big Boy Now*
1972 Best Supporting Actress as friend Gertrude in *Pete 'n' Tillie*
1978 Best Actress as interior decorator Eve in *Interiors*
1984 Best Supporting Actress as mother Mrs. Ritter in *The Pope of Greenwich Village*
1985 Best Actress as mother Carrie Watts in *The Trip to Bountiful*

Before F. Murray Abraham announced the Best Actress of 1985, he read the winning name in the envelope and gasped, "Uh, I consider this woman the greatest actress in the English language ... Geraldine Page." Actors of many generations shared his sentiment and studied her subtle craft of culling various shades of personality to flesh out her characters. While Helen Hayes was Broadway royalty, Page was queen of Off-Broadway, as her performance as Alma in the 1952 revival of Tennessee Williams' *Summer and Smoke* gave Off-Broadway its first megahit. For her performance, Page won the first Drama Desk Award ever presented to an actor in a non–Broadway production.

More Tennessee Williams alliances earned Page her first of four Tony nominations as aging actress Alexandra Del Lago in *Sweet Bird of Youth*. Though the stage was her first love, Page tried movies in the 1950s, and was Oscar nominated for her film debut opposite John Wayne in *Hondo*. When Hollywood didn't deliver quality scripts, she resumed her stage work until she began reprising her live creations on celluloid. Instantly beloved by the Hollywood Foreign Press, Page was nominated for four consecutive Best Actress, Drama Golden Globes, winning for *Summer and Smoke* and *Sweet Bird of Youth*, and nominated for *Toys in the Attic* (1963) and *Dear Heart* (1964). The first two performances also found her competing for Oscar, losing first to Sophia Loren in *Two Women* and then Anne Bancroft in *The Miracle Worker*. She was up for both the Golden Globe and Oscar for her supporting role in Francis Ford Coppola's *You're a Big Boy Now*. As a comically smothering mom, Page seems to be relishing the pure joy of moviemaking in every scene. She was less pivotal but just as memorable in 1972's *Pete 'n' Tillie* as Carol Burnett's eccentric friend. Although it was her fifth nomination without a win, she was not favored to take Best Supporting Actress, which went to Eileen Heckart of *Butterflies are Free*. In 1975 she was hauntingly zealous as faith-healing evangelist Big Sister in *The Day of the Locust*, but only Burgess Meredith was cited by Oscar with an acting nomination from the film. Just three actresses have earned lead acting Academy Award nominations under Woody Allen's direction. Page's delicately crumbling dismissed wife in *Interiors* is the only of those actresses not to win the Oscar: Diane Keaton won for *Annie Hall* the previous year, and Cate Blanchett swept the Best Actress category throughout the 2013 award season. Yet Page in *Interiors* gave among the most profoundly realized characterizations of any Allen film. She had a shot at Best Actress of 1978, but leading the race were Jill Clayburgh as *An Unmarried Woman* and winner Jane Fonda of *Coming Home*. By the time Page was nominated for her two-scene performance in *The Pope of Greenwich Village*, she was already considered a legend that the Academy inexcusably had failed to honor with a golden boy. Colleges could use her few minutes on screen as a grieving mother to teach an entire acting class, but Page, at age 61, lost to the only other nominee her senior, Peggy Ashcroft of *A Passage to India*.

In 1985, Page had two Oscar-winning hits, *White Nights* and a sleeper sensation adapted from a 1953 Horton Foote play called *The Trip to Bountiful*. Although it was a small production compared to *Out of Africa* starring Meryl Streep and *The Color Purple* with Whoopi Goldberg, Page's heart-rending struggle out of her oppressive domestic situation via a bus journey to her childhood home had Page reaching new cinematic heights. Page, Streep, and Goldberg competed for the Oscar with *Sweet Dreams'* Jessica Lange and *Agnes of God's* Anne Bancroft in a role Page had originated on stage. Shy Page

At the 1985 Oscars, first-time nominees William Hurt and Anjelica Huston stood with Best Actress Geraldine Page, a winner after eight nominations, and producer/director Sydney Pollack.

revealed how well she took in stride her unsuccessful bids for Oscar. When told that if she didn't win for *The Trip to Bountiful* she would be the most nominated actor never to win, she smiled, "I would love to be champion!" As F. Murray Abraham announced Page's victory, Streep led the standing ovation that lasted nearly an entire minute. On stage, Page thanked her director and her company, but mostly writer Horton Foote. It was a moment of glory that came in the nick of time. A little more than a year later, Page died, but left a legacy as deep, broad, and quiet as the bluebonnet landscape of her deserted Bountiful.

31. *Audrey Hepburn*

> 1953 Best Actress as princess Anya "Smitty" Smith/Princess Ann in *Roman Holiday*
>
> 1954 Best Actress as chauffeur's daughter Sabrina Fairchild in *Sabrina*

Part I. The Countdown

1959 Best Actress as nurse Sister Luke in *The Nun's Story*
1961 Best Actress as escort Holly Golightly in *Breakfast at Tiffany's*
1967 Best Actress as housewife Susy Hendrix in *Wait until Dark*
1992 Jean Hersholt Humanitarian Award

Audrey Hepburn made such an auspicious American movie debut as *Roman Holiday*'s runaway royalty that many forget her film résumé began in England, and included the Academy Award-winning *The Lavender Hill Mob*. The Belgian import's elegance and sinewy body were ideal pallets for redefining beauty with assured intelligence. Blossoming on Broadway as *Gigi* brought her to Hollywood and *Roman Holiday*. Hepburn was a regal swan who never lost the duckling sensibilities that would forever make her approachable to audiences. In her first awards season, she won Best Actress from the New York Film Critics and the Hollywood Foreign Press, and was among the few Hollywood newcomers in history who seemed a sure bet to win a lead acting Oscar in her first starring role. Although Leslie Caron charmed as *Lili*, Ava

Irving Radovich (Eddie Albert) didn't notice romance blossoming between Princess Ann (Audrey Hepburn) and journalist Joe Bradley (Gregory Peck) during their *Roman Holiday* (1953).

Gardner showed her acting mettle in *Mogambo*, Deborah Kerr simmered with sexual allure in *From Here to Eternity*, and Maggie McNamara overcame the controversy of *The Moon is Blue*'s adult content, Hepburn's was the expected name Donald O'Connor announced for Best Actress.

That same year she balanced her trophy case with a Tony for *Ondine*, then made the perfect choice for an onscreen follow-up to *Roman Holiday* by playing *Sabrina*. This time, instead of running away from privileged status as a princess, she pined for it as a chauffeur's daughter. Equally enchanting in this role, she represented the other side of the lucky coin that made her an instantly beloved movie star, and her appeal intensified. Again she was up for the Oscar, this time with Judy Garland in *A Star Is Born* and Grace Kelly in *The Country Girl* receiving all the Best Actress prizes leading up to the Academy Awards. In an era when Hollywood was mesmerized by European royalty, they awarded Kelly the prize before she left acting to reign in Monaco. In 1956, Hepburn earned Globe and BAFTA nominations as Russian royalty in *War and Peace*, but none of the film's three Oscar nominations was for acting. Her two hits in 1957, *Love in the Afternoon* opposite Gary Cooper and *Funny Face* with Fred Astaire, cemented her screen persona of a fashionista whose maturity attracted older men. In *Roman Holiday* it was Gregory Peck; in *Sabrina*, Humphrey Bogart and William Holden; in 1957, she charmed Coop and Astaire. *Love in the Afternoon* brought her another Golden Globe nomination, but the movie was not up for Oscars. *Funny Face* was nominated for four, but none for its cast. When she reached age 30, Hepburn broadened the scope of her characterizations and won new respect for the range of her acting as an intelligent, morally conflicted missionary nurse and sister in *The Nun's Story*. BAFTA and the New York Film Critics again named her their Best Actress, and she entered her third Oscar race a favorite to win. Equal consideration was given to Elizabeth Taylor, Golden Globe winner for *Suddenly, Last Summer*, and National Board of Review honoree Simone Signoret in *Room at the Top*. Signoret took the Oscar, but Hepburn's reign as Hollywood's favorite import continued. *Breakfast at Tiffany's* heightened her status as a fashion trend-setter, and revealed a bohemianism that kept her relevant in the new era of the 1960s. Throughout the decade, her Oscar-nominated filmography covered various genres: social dramas (*The Children's Hour*), mysteries (*Charade*), musicals (*My Fair Lady*), and thrillers (*Wait until Dark*), the last of which brought her another Best Actress nomination. A welcome and frequent Oscar presenter, Hepburn is the female who has given out the most Best Picture Oscars: in 1955 to *Marty*, 1960 to *The Apartment*, 1966 to *A Man for All Seasons*, and 1975 to *One Flew Over the Cuckoo's Nest*. Besides Helen Hayes, Hepburn is the only star on the countdown with EGOT. Her wins bookmarked her career: she began with Oscar and Tony, and ended with an Emmy for Outstanding Individual Achievement, Information Programming in *Gardens of the World with Audrey Hepburn*, then a posthumous Best Spoken Word Album for Children Grammy for *Audrey Hepburn's Enchanted Tales*. In her final stage of life, she also earned the Cecil B. DeMille lifetime achievement award from the Hollywood Foreign Press and the Humanitarian Award from the Academy. Ranked by the American Film Institute (AFI) behind only Marilyn Monroe and Katharine Hepburn as the greatest female legend of the 20th century, Audrey Hepburn imbued every character with the iconic style and humanitarian warmth with which she lived her life.

30. Gregory Peck

    1945 Best Actor as missionary priest Father Francis Chisholm in *The Keys of the Kingdom*
    1946 Best Actor as pioneer farmer Ezra "Penny" Baxter in *The Yearling*
    1947 Best Actor as journalist Phil Green in *Gentleman's Agreement*
    1949 Best Actor as U.S. Army Brigadier General Frank Savage in *Twelve O'Clock High*
    1962 Best Actor as lawyer Atticus Finch in *To Kill a Mockingbird*
    1967 Jean Hersholt Humanitarian Award

The first native Californian to win an acting Oscar, Peck will always be remembered for his most indelible role. As *To Kill a Mockingbird*'s widowed father and small town lawyer standing up to racial prejudice in Depression-era Alabama, he was such an indestructible tower of integrity that AFI singled out his interpretation of Atticus Finch as the most heroic character in film history. But this role came two decades after his alliance with Oscar built such massive momentum that Peck became the most nominated male actor of the 1940s, outranking even Laurence Olivier and Gary Cooper. He so dominated the last half of the decade that his multiple movies every year between 1945 and 1949 filled Oscar ballots. In 1945, besides starring with Best Actress nominee Greer Garson in *The Valley of Decision* and Best Supporting Actor Michael Chekhov in *Spellbound*, he registered his first nomination for *The Keys of the Kingdom* playing a missionary priest in China. Often the sole figure in the epic story, Peck's personal integrity and selflessness seeped into his characterization, creating a screen persona for which he was forever admired. His earthy kindliness as a pioneer father in *The Yearling* earned him the Golden Globe and had him competing for the Best Actor Oscar against James Stewart in *It's a Wonderful Life*, Larry Parks in *The Jolson Story*, Laurence Olivier as *Henry V*, and Fredric March, who won for *The Best Years of Our Lives*. That same year Peck had a *Duel in the Sun* with Best Actress nominee Jennifer Jones. In 1947, besides starring with Best Supporting Actress

Ethel Barrymore in *The Paradine Case*, Peck played a reporter challenging anti–Semitism by masquerading as a Jew in Elia Kazan's *Gentleman's Agreement*. In a race where most contenders won a single Best Actor award leading up to the Academy Awards, Peck's chances to take home Oscar were enhanced because his film seemed primed to win the big prizes. It did win three of its eight categories, including Best Picture, but Peck lost to Ronald Colman in *A Double Life*. In 1949 he gave what some critics considered his best performance to date as a cold Brigadier General who gradually thaws in *Twelve O'Clock High*. Winning the New York Film Critics Award buoyed his chances for Oscar, but 1949 belonged to *All the King's Men*, including its star, Broderick Crawford. Until Peck was again nominated and won in 1962, he starred in movies consistently represented at the Oscars. In 1953 Audrey Hepburn won Best Actress for *Roman Holiday*, *Designing Woman* took Best Story and Screenplay in 1957, Burl Ives was named the 1958 Best Supporting Actor for *The Big Country*, and in 1961 *The Guns of Navarone*'s seven nominations included a nod for Best Picture and a win for Best Special Effects. Then came *To Kill a Mockingbird*. Author Harper Lee was so taken by Peck's compassionate rendering of the character based on her father that she gave Peck her late father's treasured pocket watch. At the Golden Globes, Peck won Best Actor, Drama and Marcello Mastroianni won in the Musical or Comedy category for *Divorce Italian Style*. Come Oscar night, even Peter O'Toole's dazzling debut as *Lawrence of Arabia* couldn't outshine Peck, who finally won on his fifth chance at Best Actor. Movies that appeared on both Peck's vitae and Oscar ballots included *Captain Newman, M.D.* (1963), *Marooned* (1969), *The Omen* (1976), *The Boys from Brazil* (1978), and the 1991 *Cape Fear* remake of the original 1962 hit in which he had starred. Before he ranked twelfth on AFI's list of most legendary stars of the 20th century and received lifetime achievement honors and film festival tributes, Peck was honored by the Academy for his humanitarian efforts supporting Martin Luther King, Jr.'s nonviolent approach to racial equality. He received the Hersholt during his 1967–1970 reign as president of the Academy. The only other actors to serve as president were Bette Davis, who preceded him but only kept the job for two months in 1941, Jean Hersholt (1945–1949), and Karl Malden (1989–1992). Poignantly accepting the Hersholt the year that the Oscars were postponed because of MLK's assassination, Peck used his acceptance speech to encourage others to send contributions to King's fund in Atlanta, Georgia. Such altruism reinforced why Peck was the perfect actor to play Atticus Finch.

29. *Gene Hackman*

1967 Best Supporting Actor as bank robber Buck Barrow in *Bonnie and Clyde*

1970 Best Supporting Actor as college professor/writer Gene Garrison in *I Never Sang for My Father*
1971 Best Actor as narcotics detective Jimmy "Popeye" Doyle in *The French Connection*
1988 Best Actor as FBI agent Rupert Anderson in *Mississippi Burning*
1992 Best Supporting Actor as sheriff Little Bill Daggett in *Unforgiven*

Until Gene Hackman and contemporaries like Dustin Hoffman, Robert Duvall, and Al Pacino changed the landscape for headline stars, most Hollywood leading men had matinee idol features. While the gangster genre and film noir made room for the Bogarts and Cagneys, Hollywood courted generations of dashing stars from Rudolph Valentino to Cary Grant to Warren Beatty. Cagney movies inspired Hackman to act and Beatty movies launched his career. After casting Hackman in *Lilith* (1964), Beatty remembered him for *Bonnie and Clyde*, which the Academy nominated in every major category. While beautiful Beatty and Faye Dunaway made bank robbers sexy, Hackman, as Clyde's comically daft ("Don't sell that cow!") older brother, made them fun. Hackman and Michael J. Pollard, as the Barrow Gang's driver, competed against each other for the Oscar, but after Hackman was named the National Society of Film Critics' first ever Best Supporting Actor, he had an edge for the Academy Award. They both lost to George Kennedy in *Cool Hand Luke*. Thanks to his Oscar nomination, Hackman's career skyrocketed, and he began his workhorse tradition of completing multiple movies in a single year. For example, in the ten years of filmmaking after *Bonnie and Clyde*, Hackman starred in 28 motion pictures, including critically acclaimed *Downhill Racer* and Oscar winner *Marooned* (both 1969), Cannes Film Festival favorite *Scarecrow* (1973), and Oscar nominee *Bite the Bullet* (1975). At the beginning of the 1970s he eased toward lead actor status playing Gene Garrison, the complex son striving to connect with an insatiably disgruntled Melvyn Douglas in *I Never Sang for My Father*. As the central character, Hackman could have competed against Douglas for Best Actor of 1970. But when the Academy placed him in a supporting slot, his chances to win seemed strong. By the time he lost to John Mills in *Ryan's Daughter*, Hackman was already playing a role he found initially so intimidating that *The French Connection*'s director William Friedkin had to talk him out of abandoning the project.

With a volatile temper and an impulsive zeal for catching drug smugglers that jeopardized his squad, Hackman rocked on the balls of his feet and flailed his fists with an intensity that seemed to show his very nerves on end. *The French Connection* was a groundbreaking hit, and the Academy honored it with most of 1971's biggest prizes, including Best Actor. By following his Oscar-winning turn in *The French Connection* with the lead in the box office record breaker *The Poseidon Adventure*, Hackman became a critically admired and commercially viable leading man. Capitalizing on his freedom to choose diverse projects, Hackman showed his range with a hilarious cameo in *Young Frankenstein* the same year he simmered toward implosion in *The Conversation*. Almost unrecognizable as a mustached, bespeckled surveillance expert morally frying beneath a stoic gaze, Hackman was considered a certain Best Actor nominee. *The Conversation* was up for Best Picture, but Hackman was left off the ballot. Many critics consider the mid-1970s the zenith of Hackman's career. While some cite *The Conversation*'s Harry Caul as his most brilliant performance, others argue that it came the next year as private detective Harry Moseby in the less-successful *Night Moves*. Both performances earned him other critical award recognition, but no Oscar nod. Following hits with *Superman* (1978) and epic Oscar favorite *Reds* (1981), Hackman again competed for Best Actor in 1988 when he muscled his way through *Mississippi Burning*, this time as a sympathetic law enforcer. He and the film had early Oscar momentum that shifted to Dustin Hoffman and *Rain Man* when historians railed about how *Mississippi Burning* minimized the contributions of African Americans in the civil rights saga it depicted. In 1992, Hackman won prize after prize as one of the Western genre's nastiest villains, Sheriff "Little Bill" Daggett. Crass, impudent, and arrogant, Daggett was the kind of villain audiences love to hate. On Oscar night, Hackman had Jack Nicholson of *A Few Good Men* closest to him near the finish line. But as anticipated, Hackman won, making him one of an elite group of stars (that already included Nicholson) to win acting Oscars in both lead and supporting categories. Besides his famous cameo as the blind hermit in *Young Frankenstein*, Hackman showed his greatest flair for comedy as the churlish patriarch of *The Royal Tenenbaums*. Wes Anderson wrote the role for Hackman, whose

Detective Popeye Doyle (Gene Hackman) raced after a speeding subway in the classic car chase from *The French Connection* (1971).

performance barely missed earning him another Best Actor nomination in 2001. An unconventional hero with features more recognizable on a friendly neighbor than a big screen heartthrob, Hackman diversified the image of a Hollywood leading man by becoming the first of his unglamorous peers to win the respect of, and statuettes from, his Academy peers.

28. Olivia de Havilland

1939 Best Supporting Actress as wife Melanie Hamilton Wilkes in *Gone with the Wind*
1941 Best Actress as American traveler Emmy Brown in *Hold Back the Dawn*
1946 Best Actress as mother Josephine "Jody" Norris in *To Each His Own*
1948 Best Actress as mental patient Virginia Stuart Cunningham in *The Snake Pit*
1949 Best Actress as heiress Catherine Sloper in *The Heiress*

After an impressive 1935 film debut as Hermia in Max Reinhardt's multiple Oscar winner *A Midsummer Night's Dream*, pure-complexioned, lullaby-voiced Olivia de Havilland made the first of a series of romantic adventures opposite Errol Flynn in *Captain Blood*, which competed against *A Midsummer Night's Dream* for Best Picture. From then on she was frequently featured in Best Picture nominees such as *Anthony Adverse* (1936) and, playing Maid Marion to Errol Flynn's gallant thief, *The Adventures of Robin Hood* (1938). While she was filming those hits, nearly every other female was beating a path to Selznick International Pictures/MGM for a chance to audition to play Scarlett O'Hara in *Gone with the Wind*. de Havilland effortlessly slipped into the role of the more appealing Southern belle, Melanie. The movie lived up to all its grandiose expectations, and at Oscar time it garnered the lion's share of nominations, including two for Best Supporting Actress: Hattie McDaniel as Mammy, and de Havilland as Scarlett's unsuspecting rival. McDaniel burst into tears of joy after accepting the award and returning to her table; de Havilland burst into tears of disappointment after congratulating her co-star. Two years later, de Havilland would need to stiffen her upper lip even more when she ended up competing for Best Actress against her sister, *Suspicion*'s Joan Fontaine. Unlike future rivalries that were only created by the media to build suspense, such as Julie Andrews and Audrey Hepburn in 1964 or Lynn and Vanessa Redgrave in 1966, de Havilland and her younger sister genuinely did not get along. Their 1941 Oscar competition would render their rift irreparable. Older, more ambitious, and more competitive than Fontaine, de Havilland may have liked her chances of winning Best Actress for a charmingly unpredictable romance, *Hold Back the Dawn*. Yet Fontaine was evenly matched with her, as both were up for their second Academy Award in movies nominated for Best Picture, but not for Best Director. When Ginger Rogers announced Fontaine the winner, Fontaine allegedly dismissed de Havilland's attempted congratulatory gesture, and their relationship steadily deteriorated thereafter. In 1946 de Havilland reteamed with *Hold Back the Dawn* director Mitchell Leisen in a small film that showcased her range. In the tradition of films like *Madame X* and *The Sin of Madelon Claudet*, *To Each His Own* featured de Havilland as a mother who must hide her identity from her beloved son. The soap opera would not have been primed for Oscar picking had de Havilland not been so good at playing a woman who aged, withdrew, yet strengthened over thirty years. She won her first Oscar, and she and Fontaine became the first siblings in Academy history to both win lead acting prizes. Among the greatest reviews of de Havilland's career came as a psychiatric patient in the startling drama *The Snake Pit*. Although the showcase role brought her Best Actress honors from the National Board of Review and the New York Film Critics Circle, she lost the Oscar to Jane Wyman in *Johnny Belinda*. But de Havilland was back the next year with even better odds at winning a second Best Actress Academy Award. In *The Heiress*, de Havilland conveyed elegant pride and idealist hope at finding love despite being a plain mouse worn down by a lifetime of verbal abuse from her embittered, widowed father played by Best Supporting Actor nominee Ralph Richardson. Few plot resolutions satisfy like *The Heiress*, which owes it all to de Havilland's mesmerizing presence. The 1949 Best Actress race belonged to de Havilland from the start. After accepting her second consecutive New York Film Critics prize and first Golden Globe, she picked up her second Oscar in three years and became Oscar's most winning female star of the decade. de Havilland's movie career cooled in subsequent decades, but she emerged in other Oscar-nominated movies such as the romantic mystery *My Cousin Rachel* (1952) and two 1970s all-star disaster movies, *Airport '77* and *The Swarm*. de Havilland's elegance and wide-eyed beauty made her a favored Oscar presenter for many decades. Among the highlights were announcing John Ford's record fourth Best Director win for *The Quiet Man* in 1952, revealing that one of *Ben-Hur*'s historic eleven Oscars went to Best Supporting Actor Hugh Griffith, giving *Lawrence of Arabia* Best Picture in 1962, and introducing a glorious film tribute to 75 years of Oscar in 2003. Who better to lead into such a tribute than one of the few actors who lived through every one of those years?

27. *Fredric March*

1930/31 Best Actor as actor Tony Cavendish in *The Royal Family of Broadway*

1931/32 Best Actor as Dr. Henry Jekyll/Mr. Hyde in *Dr. Jekyll and Mr. Hyde*
1937 Best Actor as actor Norman Maine (Alfred Hinkel) in *A Star Is Born*
1946 Best Actor as veteran Al Stephenson in *The Best Years of Our Lives*
1951 Best Actor as salesman Willy Loman in *Death of a Salesman*

Handsome but not dashing, March wowed the Academy with nominated roles as a Broadway snob, mad scientist, drunken has-been, unsettled veteran, and deluded idealist. A Broadway star himself, March brought sardonic snap to *The Royal Family of Broadway*, which lampooned American theatre's sovereign Barrymores. The Barrymores, especially Ethel, so furiously objected to being the source of humor for Edna Ferber's and George S. Kaufman's hit play that it almost wasn't remade for movie audiences. As Tony Cavendish, March parodied suave, malcontented John Barrymore and was up for Best Actor at the fourth Academy ceremony. In either an ironic twist or a turn of poetic justice, he lost to Lionel Barrymore in *A Free Soul*. The next year March secured his place as a lead actor of his generation with a mesmerizing portrayal of the impassioned scientist and his demonic alter ego, *Dr. Jekyll and Mr. Hyde*. Part of the allure of the movie was its special effects, which allowed audiences to watch March's physical transformation, something earlier film techniques could not achieve so seamlessly. But the strength of the movie owes full credit to the power of March's performance, which the Academy honored with the Best Actor award. March's reign as the one and only Best Actor of that Oscar season lasted a few short minutes. Immediately after March accepted the award from Norma Shearer, an Academy vote tabulator noted that *The Champ*'s Wallace Beery trailed March by only a single vote. According to Academy rules at the time, Beery too deserved an Oscar. Immediately after Louis B. Mayer accepted Best Picture for MGM's *Grand Hotel*, ceremony host Conrad Nagel called Beery to the podium and gave him an Oscar, too. Consequently, March is the only person in Academy history to officially win his category, and then end up sharing the prize. The following year, March played two roles in Sidney Franklin's sentimental romance, *Smilin' Through*, which lost Best Picture to *Cavalcade* in 1932/33. Later that decade, March originated the role of Norman Maine in the first of (so far) three movie versions of *A Star Is Born*, all of which competed for Oscars. As a washed up actor who tried to dowse his burned professional bridges with alcohol, March turned the prism of his performance with every scene. He was alternately inspiring, infuriating, pathetic, caressable, and, ultimately, honorably hopeless. The Academy loved the performance, but they named Spencer Tracy in *Captains Courageous* as their Best Actor. World War II changed movie tastes.

While Frank Capra sentimentality drew audiences and awards before the global conflict, afterward audiences were more somber and analytical, and thus open to explorations of who people were and what impact World War II had on everyday life. As a result, William Wyler's contemplative 1946 drama *The Best Years of Our Lives* touched a nerve so precisely that the movie still tops many Best Movies of All Time lists. Much credit belongs to March as the central character among the three former soldiers who return home to rebuild their lives. That year's Best Actor race included some of the most famous performances in history. Besides strong work by Larry Parks in *The Jolson Story* and Gregory Peck in *The Yearling*, the category was dominated by Laurence Olivier as *Henry V*, James Stewart as George Bailey in *It's a Wonderful Life*, and March. Olivier's chances were diminished once the Academy decided to give him an honorary Oscar as actor, producer, and director of the Shakespeare history. Surprisingly, *It's a Wonderful Life* was not a big hit in 1946, so March took home his second Oscar. The following year, March was the first Oscar-winning actor ever to present Best Picture, announcing *Gentleman's Agreement* as 1947's winner. Although March turned down the role of Willy Loman in Arthur Miller's stage classic *Death of a Salesman*, he accepted the movie adaptation, and appeared one last time on Oscar's radar. He won the Golden Globe, for which Academy front runners Marlon Brando in *A Streetcar Named Desire*, Montgomery Clift in *A Place in the Sun*, and Oscar-victor Humphrey Bogart in *The African Queen* were not even nominated. Like his contemporary Spencer Tracy, March was more of a steady craftsman than movie star. Appropriately, in 1938 Tracy was the Academy's first double Best Actor winner. In 1946, March became the second.

26. Sean Penn

> 1995 Best Actor as prison inmate Matthew Poncelet in *Dead Man Walking*
> 1999 Best Actor as jazz guitarist Emmet Ray in *Sweet and Lowdown*
> 2001 Best Actor as coffee shop and diner worker Samuel John "Sam" Dawson in *I Am Sam*
> **2003 Best Actor as ex-convict/grocery store owner Jimmy Markum in *Mystic River***
> **2008 Best Actor as gay activist/San Francisco Supervisor Harvey Milk in *Milk***

When Jack Nicholson began his first acceptance speech with "I guess this proves there are as many nuts in the Academy as anywhere else," he suggested how difficult it could be for an eccentric outsider to so impress his peers that he could be rewarded with an Oscar. Early in his career, Penn's flagrant bad boy shenanigans could have interrupted the career momentum of a less profoundly talented actor. But when Penn finally did win the 2003 Academy Award for his fourth nominated performance, the crowd was so supportive that they whooped and shouted and rose to their feet. That moment was the first mountain top on a long upward climb. Penn's movie career began with teen hits such as *Taps*, cult favorite *Fast Times at Ridgemont High*, and the prophetically titled *Bad Boys*. News of his heated marriage to Madonna often overshadowed positive press about the fine work he was doing on both sides of the camera, even being recognized as a writer/director of projects such as *The Indian Runner* (1991) and *The Crossing Guard* (1993) at international film festivals. In 1995, *Dead Man Walking* confirmed his credibility as an actor. His depiction of an unapproachable, racist murderer for whom the audience develops compassion during his numbered days on death row speaks volumes about the intensity of his performance. For the first time, the Academy acknowledged his work, and he gave Nicholas Cage, whose performance in *Leaving Las Vegas* had won nearly every Best Actor prize of 1995, temporary pause about his lock on Oscar. As a musical talent but lost soul in Woody Allen's *Sweet and Lowdown*, Penn achieved the rare feat of joining Allen himself as the only two men to garner a Best Actor nomination for a Woody Allen film. Movies about developmentally disabled adults are either huge successes, like *Rain Man*, or cringing missteps. Penn's deft portrayal of a mentally challenged adult fighting for the custody of his daughter eased sentiment from authentic tension, giving Penn a showcase role in *I Am Sam*. Although Penn was consistently nominated for Best Actor awards that season, neither he nor Will Smith as *Ali* was a lead contender for the 2001 Oscar. Instead the contest favored Tom Wilkinson for *In the Bedroom*, Russell Crowe for *A Beautiful Mind*, and winner Denzel Washington self-destructing in *Training Day*. The 2003 Best Actor race was among the closest in recent history. Ben Kingsley's searing performance in *House of Sand and Fog* was considered his best leading role since *Gandhi*. Jude Law excelled in *Cold Mountain*. Johnny Depp finally won over the Academy with his eccentric take on pirate Jack Sparrow in *The Pirates of the Caribbean: The Curse of the Black Pearl*. But out front of the pack were Penn as a father shattered by his daughter's murder in Clint Eastwood's *Mystic River* and Bill Murray as a beleaguered foreign traveler *Lost in Translation*. Up through Oscar morning, no one could have predicted a sure winner, but Penn triumphed. In his acceptance speech, he acknowledged his fellow nominees and referenced fellow originals Jack Nicholson, Nicholas Cage, who'd beat him in his first Oscar competition, and other actors not nominated that year. He was a gracious and popular winner. In 2007, he directed Hal Holbrook to a Best Supporting Actor nomination for *Into the Wild*, and reinforced critics' enthusiasm for his skills behind as well as in front of the camera. When up for Oscar in the biopic *Milk*, Penn seemed primed to win. *The Curious Case of Benjamin Button* piqued so early during the 2008 awards season that it lost momentum leading up to the Oscars. As the title character, Brad Pitt still had a chance to win, but less than originally anticipated. Instead, Penn's closest rival for Best Actor was his friend, Mickey Rourke in a comeback role as *The Wrestler*. Penn so fully captured every mannerism and passion of slain gay rights activist Harvey Milk that comics joked they were surprised after the movie to discover that Penn was actually straight. The second time he accepted a golden boy at Oscar's dais, Penn was just as grateful, but more lighthearted, referring to the Academy with a grin as "you commie, homo-loving sons of guns." He followed by confessing, "I want it to be very clear that I do know how hard I make it to appreciate me." But appreciate him they do, and with five nominations and two wins, Penn is among the most appreciated actors in Oscar history.

25. Tom Hanks

1988 Best Actor as toy salesman/toy tester Josh Baskin in *Big*
1993 Best Actor as lawyer Andrew Beckett in *Philadelphia*
1994 Best Actor as veteran/entrepreneur/athlete Forrest Gump in *Forrest Gump*
1998 Best Actor as Army Captain/ranger company commander John H. Miller in *Saving Private Ryan*
2000 Best Actor as FedEx systems analyst Chuck Noland in *Cast Away*

A congenial Everyman sometimes considered the James Stewart of his generation, Hanks had a long stretch as an actor where he could do absolutely no wrong. In fact, from 1992 to 2000 all twelve of his movies were bonafide hits, most of them appearing multiple times on Oscar ballots. An earlier television appearance on *Happy Days* connected him with two people instrumental in making him a top movie star. When the nostalgic sitcom's star Ron Howard became a motion picture director, he cast Hanks as the lead in *Splash*, a 1984 Oscar nominee for Original Screenplay. When Penny Marshall of the *Happy Days* franchise left acting to direct, she cast Hanks in *Big*. It became the first movie directed by a woman to gross over $100 million. Key to the film's appeal was a thoroughly convincing and lovable Hanks as a 12-year-old whose wish to be big turns him into a grown man overnight. Classic scenes abound, especially his piano duet with Robert Loggia on an FAO Schwarz foot-operated electric keyboard. Though the Academy could be dismissive of comic performances, it embraced Hanks in *Big*. He lost to Dustin Hoffman in *Rain Man*, but already he was beloved by audiences and his colleagues. Reteaming with director Penny Marshall to make *A League of Their Own* in 1992 began one of the most auspicious streams of hits in any actor's career. He and Meg Ryan became the ideal romantic comedy team of the

1990s with *Sleepless in Seattle*. While it was still pulling in worldwide box office revenues, Hanks came out in *Philadelphia*. At the time, being an established actor playing a gay character could be career-shattering, but Hanks embraced the part of a lawyer with AIDS fighting the homophobic firm that fired him. Under the direction of Jonathan Demme, and with a haunting soundtrack from greats like Bruce Springsteen and Neil Young, Hanks gave one of the most resonant performances on celluloid. Despite a truckload of trophies leading up to Oscar night, Hanks was still a longshot, if only because the Academy was not always as quick to embrace diversity as some other organizations. Daniel Day-Lewis followed his Oscar-winning turn in *My Left Foot* with a second nomination as a falsely accused slacker in *In the Name of the Father*. Laurence Fishburne was menacing as abusive Ike Turner in *What's Love Got to Do with It*. On the heels of his win for *The Silence of the Lambs*, Anthony Hopkins was affectingly restrained as a butler in *The Remains of the Day*. But the strongest doubts of a Hanks victory came from Liam Neeson as the title character in *Schindler's List*, a destined classic that showed all the signs of taking the top prizes. *Schindler's List* did win Best Picture, Director, and Screenplay, but Hanks won Best Actor. With a congratulatory slap on the back from Hopkins and a jubilant standing ovation from his peers, Hanks reached the stage. His lower lip trembling, he honored a gay teacher and high school friend, and shared a compassionate plea in remembrance of the thousands who'd succumbed to AIDS to that time.

With the help of new technology, Hanks next interacted with pivotal figures from the 1960s and 1970s as wisdom-spouting simpleton *Forrest Gump*. Thanks to innumerable classic lines coined "Gumpisms," *Forrest Gump* spawned food

As wise simpleton *Forrest Gump* (1994), Tom Hanks became the fifth star to win Academy Awards in consecutive years.

products (shrimp gumbo, shrimp Creole, shrimp cocktail) and impersonations ("Life is like a box of chocolates," "Run, Forrest, run") that pervaded pop culture. No one doubted that *Forrest Gump* would win Best Picture, but could Hanks reach the heights of Luise Rainer, Spencer Tracy, Katharine Hepburn, and Jason Robards, Jr., by winning back-to-back acting Oscars? Indeed he could, and did. The hits continued. He was expected to be up for his third consecutive Best Actor award for *Apollo 13*, but wasn't. The same year he starred in that Best Picture nominee, he first voiced cowboy Woody in *Toy Story*, a franchise that continues to thrive. In 1998 he earned his fourth nomination for *Saving Private Ryan*. Two years later, he alone kept audiences rapt as a *Cast Away*, vying again for Oscar in a race won by Russell Crowe in *Gladiator*. In 2002 AFI made 46-year-old Hanks the youngest recipient of their Lifetime Achievement Award. Hanks reached a new peak in 2013 as *Captain Phillips*. Although his anticipated Best Actor nod didn't materialize, the Best Picture nominee provided a fresh reminder of the versatility of one of Hollywood's most affable stars.

24. James Stewart

> 1939 Best Actor as scout leader Jefferson Smith in *Mr. Smith Goes to Washington*
> **1940 Best Actor as tabloid reporter Macaulay "Mike" Connor in *The Philadelphia Story***
> 1946 Best Actor as savings and loan officer George Bailey in *It's a Wonderful Life*
> 1950 Best Actor as alcoholic eccentric Elwood P. Dowd in *Harvey*
> 1959 Best Actor as defense attorney Paul Biegler in *Anatomy of a Murder*
> **1984 Honorary lifetime achievement award "for his fifty years of memorable performances, for his high ideals both on and off screen, with the respect and affection of his colleagues"**

Read the autobiography of any actor who worked with James Stewart and you will find praise, testimonials, and a fond evocation of memories equivalent to any statuette a motion picture organization could bestow. No matter what the role, Stewart was the stalwart embodiment of strong character with whom audiences identified and for whom they rooted. Despite Stewart's varied career that explored everything from Hitchcockian darkness to Capraesque warmth and levity, the Academy's response to Stewart paralleled the public's. All five of his nominations came for playing virtuous, grass roots figures. Stewart's early alliances with director Clarence Brown gave him vehicles that attracted Oscar's attention. He did fine work in *The Gorgeous Hussy* (1936) and *Of Human Hearts* (1938) but both earned Beulah Bondi, not Stewart,

Academy Award nominations. Also in 1938 he made *You Can't Take It with You*, the first of three classic collaborations with director Frank Capra. Though Stewart and Jean Arthur were the stars, it was Capra's puppeteering of the zany shenanigans in the Sycamore household that brought the movie Best Director and Best Picture Oscars. The next year Stewart reunited with Jean Arthur and director Frank Capra to trumpet a message of integrity that secured his place as the legendary spokesman of honest values and courage in the face of power and corruption in *Mr. Smith Goes to Washington*. In a movie unabashedly similar to *Mr. Deeds Goes to Town*, which had earned his buddy Gary Cooper his first Oscar nod, Stewart had to give his character nuances that touched even deeper chords. He rose to the challenge with a climactic filibuster, paving his first road to Oscar so smoothly only the iconic work of Clark Gable as Rhett Butler in *Gone with the Wind* and Laurence Olivier as Heathcliff in *Wuthering Heights* seemed to toss pebbles on his path to victory. The Academy is nothing if not redemptive, and because they failed to give Robert Donat the Best Actor prize the previous year for *The Citadel*, they made up for it by naming *Goodbye, Mr. Chips'* Donat Best Actor over Stewart, Gable, Olivier, and young Mickey Rooney in *Babes in Arms*. The same psychology that kept Stewart from being an Oscar winner in 1939 made him one the following year. 1940's Best Actor race was led by another of Stewart's friends, Henry Fonda of *The Grapes of Wrath*, and again, Laurence Olivier, this time in *Rebecca*. Despite a less demanding role that supported Cary Grant and Katharine Hepburn as battling exes in George Cukor's *The Philadelphia Story*, Stewart's subtle comic delivery and a delectably calibrated intoxication scene were enough for the Academy to decide he should immediately be redeemed for the previous year's oversight, and Stewart won his only competitive Oscar. After World War II, Stewart reunited with Capra for *It's a Wonderful Life*. Considering its classic status today, it's surprising that the affirming holiday movie was not well received in 1946, but Stewart was so powerful that the Academy recognized him for his third Best Actor nomination. The latter scenes opened darker paths than Stewart ever trod on screen before, thereafter branching his career into harsher territories in Westerns and Hitchcock mysteries. Despite dynamic reviews and box office revenues, these movies never prompted Academy votes. Instead, Oscar liked the lighter Stewart. He started the 1950s with a nomination as amiable tippler, and perhaps mental case, Elwood P. Dowd, companion to a huge, imaginary rabbit named *Harvey*. He ended the decade with his last Oscar competition as a cool, clever small town lawyer in Otto Preminger's risqué *Anatomy of a Murder*. A quarter century later, with Stewart again on top of Hollywood's golden mountain thanks to repeated holiday broadcasts of *It's a Wonderful Life*, the Academy took new stock of the breadth of Stewart's work, which could easily have earned him Oscar nominations for projects as varied as his

Westerns (*Winchester '73* and *The Man Who Shot Liberty Valance*), mysteries (*Rear Window* and *Vertigo*), dramas (*The Glenn Miller Story* and *The Flight of the Phoenix*), and Oscar winners (*The Greatest Show on Earth* and *How the West Was Won*). Aptly, Stewart ended his acceptance speech for his lifetime achievement award by thanking audiences for giving him a wonderful life. His fans and the Academy agreed that he had actually done the same for them.

23. George Clooney

2005 Best Supporting Actor as CIA operative Bob Barnes in *Syriana*
2005 Best Director of *Good Night, and Good Luck*
2005 Best Original Screenplay as co-screenwriter (with Grant Heslov) of *Good Night, and Good Luck*
2007 Best Actor as law firm fixer Michael Clayton in *Michael Clayton*
2009 Best Actor as corporate downsizer Ryan Bingham in *Up in the Air*
2011 Best Actor as lawyer Matt King in *The Descendants*
2011 Best Adapted Screenplay as co-screenwriter (with Grant Heslov and Beau Willimon) of *The Ides of March*
2012 Best Picture as co-producer (with Ben Affleck and Grant Heslov) of *Argo*

Although Clooney had been in show business for decades before he reached Oscar's door, when he arrived the Academy opened it to Clooney in a big way. Before he became a nominee himself, Clooney joined future Oscar winners Adrien Brody, Sean Penn, and Jared Leto at the end of Terrence Malick's sprawling World War II Best Picture nominee of 1998, *The Thin Red Line*. Clooney started the new millennium with consecutive hits, *The Perfect Storm* and *O Brother, Where Art Thou?*, both of which competed for Academy Awards of 2000. By mid-decade, he not only had multiple films competing at the 2005 Oscars, but he was also up in three categories, a feat previously achieved by only a handful of greats like Charlie Chaplin, Orson Welles, Warren Beatty, Woody Allen, and Clint Eastwood. Clooney's star power gave him top billing in the labyrinthine political thriller *Syriana*, but the movie's multiple storylines fractured screen time among a vast array of players, justifying the Academy's placement of Clooney in the supporting category. Clooney was more prominently represented for a project even closer to his heart. He co-scripted, directed, and starred in *Good Night, and Good Luck*, a vintage black and white feature tracing the 1950s conflict between television journalist Edward R. Murrow and Communist-hunting Senator Joseph McCarthy. Up for Best Original Screenplay (against *Syriana*) and Best Director, Clooney seemed poised to win at least one award, ideally as Best Director. The first award of the night went to Clooney as Best Supporting Actor. Clooney conveyed his political savvy and welcome candor when he began his thank you speech by noting, "Alright, so I'm not winning Director." He was right, of course, as Best Director went to Ang Lee for *Brokeback Mountain*. But Clooney's performance as CIA Operations Officer Bob Barnes, the binding center point of an unraveling global web, was too intense and complex to be considered mere consolation. Thereafter, Clooney balanced his "sexiest man alive" grandeur with insightful performances that brought him back to Oscar's inner circle time and again. After multiple critic circles named Clooney their Best Actor of 2007 as law firm fixer *Michael Clayton*, Clooney went into Oscar night a potential winner, but the Academy favored Daniel Day-Lewis in *There Will Be Blood*. Two years later, *Up in the Air* tapped the slowing pulse of the public and examined the impact of corporate downsizing by inserting commentary by people who'd actually lost their jobs. Clooney, the frequent flyer who traveled to companies to inform employees they had been fired, was poised to win Best Actor throughout most of the 2009 award season. But the film's early pique fizzled, and his initial momentum drained into the coffer of Jeff Bridges in *Crazy Heart*.

The year 2011 proved another tidal wave year for Clooney, as two hits,

Painful secrets compromised an island paradise for Alexandra (Shailene Woodley), Matt (Best Actor nominee George Clooney), Scottie (Amara Miller) and Sid (Nick Krause) in *The Descendants* (2011).

The Descendants and *The Ides of March*, once again gave him two shots at an Oscar in a single year. With only one nomination, *The Ides of March* was not expected to take Best Adapted Screenplay, and lost to Clooney's other hit, *The Descendants*. It was for this second movie that Clooney was again a top competitor for Best Actor. As a man learning of his wife's infidelity almost immediately after facing her impending death from a boating accident, Clooney embodied the confusion, fear, anger, and helplessness inherent in the two colliding revelations. Reminiscent of Marlon Brando's soliloquy to his wife's corpse in *Last Tango in Paris*, Clooney's bedside summation of how his wife's love and her affair awakened him to his own character demonstrated the impact of Clooney's talent and appeal. A frontrunner for Best Actor that year, Clooney's victory was usurped by late-season excitement for *The Artist*, which took most of the big prizes of 2011, including Best Actor for Jean Dujardin. As a producer of *Argo* the following year, Clooney set an Academy record as the only person in history to be nominated in six categories. In part to atone for snubbing director Ben Affleck, the Academy honored the thrilling, retro political caper's producers Affleck, Grant Heslov, and Clooney with the Best Picture Academy Award. Clooney has it all: actor's instinct, director's eye, writer's insight, and producer's vision. That he has parlayed each into record-breaking Oscar contention is testimony to his appeal, talent, and status as one of Hollywood's greatest artists.

22. *Michael Caine*

1966 Best Actor as seducer Alfie Elkins in *Alfie*
1972 Best Actor as hair salon owner Milo Tindle in *Sleuth*
1983 Best Actor as college professor Dr. Frank Bryant in *Educating Rita*
1986 Best Supporting Actor as adulterous husband Elliot in *Hannah and Her Sisters*
1999 Best Supporting Actor as abortionist/orphanage director Dr. Wilbur Larch in *The Cider House Rules*
2002 Best Actor as journalist Thomas Fowler in *The Quiet American*

In recent years, Michael Caine has been the recipient of multiple lifetime achievement honors and film festival retrospectives where his career is flashed before him and the audience in video montages. Rather than bask in the immensity of his achievements as an actor, he instead says that watching himself age in such quick succession leaves him feeling sad about the brevity of life. That kind of heartfelt perspective has informed all of his performances since he first became an international success as the fourth-wall-breaking Cockney gadabout *Alfie*. The movie and Caine were quick international sensations, and Caine's Best Actor victory from the National Society of Film

Critics boded well for the success to continue at the Oscars. The tight race with three Brits leading the pack—Caine, Richard Burton in *Who's Afraid of Virginia Woolf?*, and Paul Scofield in *A Man for All Seasons*—ended with the award going to Scofield. In 1972, Caine and Laurence Olivier were on the same Best Actor ticket for matching each other scene for scene in the adaptation of Anthony Shaffer's cat and mouse charade, *Sleuth*. It was the year of Marlon Brando and *The Godfather*, so Caine did not get the Oscar, but he was a central figure at the 1972 ceremony because he hosted with Carol Burnett, Charlton Heston, and Rock Hudson, and even lent a hand in presenting Best Costume Design with Marisa Berenson. In 1975, Caine and Sean Connery were hot as the desert setting of *The Man Who Would Be King*. Although the movie earned four Oscar nominations, none was for acting. Caine and Maggie Smith spent time on the red carpet of the 1977 Academy Awards filming a segment of the upcoming *California Suite*, in which Smith's character is Oscar nominated. At that ceremony, they presented the Best Supporting Actor award to absent Jason Robards, Jr., of *Julia*, and then accepted on his behalf. The following year Smith won for her *California Suite* performance, and said she wished Caine were there with her so the award could be split down the middle. Caine reached a new pinnacle in the 1980s when he gained 35 pounds and reunited with *Alfie* director Lewis Gilbert to portray a disillusioned professor re-enchanted with life and learning thanks to offbeat pupil Julie Walters in *Educating Rita*. The milestone role perfectly suited Caine, who won his first BAFTA and Golden Globe, and was again up for Oscar. The Best Actor race pitted Caine against Robert Duvall as a cowboy in *Tender Mercies*. When Sylvester Stallone came on stage with Dolly Parton to present his category, Caine thought, "If they had a country and western star to give out the award, I wasn't going to win." Duvall won. But three years later Caine earned his first Oscar as the unfaithful husband whose affair with his sister-in-law has him "walking on air" in *Hannah and Her Sisters*. As usual, Caine was maintaining his frantic schedule of making multiple films in a single year, and so was in the Bahamas filming *Jaws: The Revenge* when Jeff Bridges and Sigourney Weaver presented that year's Best Supporting Actor prize, making him the only male actor to date to win an Academy Award for a performance directed by Woody Allen. In 1998 Caine won a lead actor Golden Globe for *Little Voice* but was inexplicably left off that year's Academy Awards roster. But he came on strong the next year for his supporting role as an ether addicted abortionist in *The Cider House Rules*. Caine won one of the tightest races in history against Tom Cruise in *Magnolia*, Michael Clarke Duncan in *The Green Mile*, Jude Law in *The Talented Mr. Ripley*, and Haley Joel Osment in *The Sixth Sense*. Caine graciously acknowledged each of his fellow actors in his acceptance speech. When *The Quiet American*'s Caine and *About Schmidt*'s Jack Nicholson were both nominated for Best Actor in 2002, they joined Laurence Olivier as the only actors in history to vie for Oscars in five consecutive decades. Uniquely, Caine is the only person recognized so often by Oscar to have all his nominations and wins separated by category. He lost each time he was up for Best Actor, and won every Best Supporting Actor race. Among international stars, few have had the impact and staying power of Caine. Into his 80s, Caine still packs his schedule with multiple movies each year, raising box office and enhancing a film's chances of award recognition.

21. Maggie Smith

1965 Best Supporting Actress as daughter/wife Desdemona in *Othello*
1969 Best Actress as teacher Jean Brodie in *The Prime of Miss Jean Brodie*
1972 Best Actress as spinster/traveling chaperone Aunt Augusta Bertram in *Travels with My Aunt*
1978 Best Supporting Actress as actress Diana Barrie in *California Suite*
1986 Best Supporting Actress as cousin/chaperone Charlotte Bartlett in *A Room with a View*
2001 Best Supporting Actress as noblewoman Constance, Countess of Trentham in *Gosford Park*

Statuesque as a 1920s fashion model, Smith entered films conveying a range that runs from soul-melting sorrow to deep-freeze wit. Academy members first savored Smith's captivating range as Miss Mead, lovelorn secretary of failing businessman Rod Taylor in *The V.I.P.s*, but the movie's Supporting Actress nod and win went to co-star Margaret Rutherford. A shattering Desdemona to Olivier's *Othello*, Smith and Joyce Redman as her attendant Emilia were both nominated for the 1965 Supporting Actress Oscar, which went to Shelley Winters in *A Patch of Blue*. Four years later Smith took the coveted film role of Jean Brodie, an elitist Edinburgh schoolteacher whose impact on her "gairls" is both inspiring and destructive in Ronald Neame's adaptation of Muriel Spark's popular *The Prime of Miss Jean Brodie*. The towering performance gave her a chance to manipulate ("If scandal is to your taste, Miss Mackay, I shall give you a feast!"), pontificate, and wither in a story that takes tragic turns, and Oscar came through with her first Best Actress nomination. Not expected to win over Jane Fonda in *They Shoot Horses, Don't They?*, Smith asked American actress friend Alice Ghostley to attend in her stead. Smith won, Ghostley accepted, and Smith's performance has gone down in Oscar history as one of the greats. Smith was a dark horse again in 1972 when *Travels with My Aunt* put her up against winner Liza Minnelli in *Cabaret*.

Smith attended the 1977 ceremony with Michael Caine so that director Herbert Ross could get authentic red carpet footage of them in character as an Oscar-nominated actress and her husband for the 1978 Neil Simon comedy *California Suite*.

When filming outside was done, Smith and Caine presented the Best Supporting Actor award to *Julia*'s Jason Robards, Jr. The next year, after Smith won Best Actress, Musical or Comedy and Dyan Cannon took Best Supporting Actress for *Heaven Can Wait*, they went head to head for the Best Supporting Actress Oscar. In previous years, actresses including Janet Gaynor and Judy Garland lost Oscar competitions for performances in which their characters won Academy Awards. Smith did the opposite by winning the Oscar playing Diana Barrie, an actress who loses her bid for an Oscar in a "nauseating little comedy" entitled *No Left Turns* in *California Suite*. Whether fretting over her looks ("I have a definite hoomp on my left showlder") or deflecting Caine's catty barbs ("That's not funny, Sidney, that's bizarre"), no one interpreted a Neil Simon one-liner quite like Smith. This Oscar win was landmark. The year after Richard Dreyfuss won for the Neil Simon penned *The Goodbye Girl*, Smith registered the only Oscar-winning performance by

As husband and wife Sidney Cochran and Diana Barrie in *California Suite* (1978), Michael Caine offered caustic support to Maggie Smith, who won the Oscar playing an actress competing for an Oscar.

a female in a Neil Simon work. Maggie Smith led a unique stream of Oscar winners in this category with the initials M.S. After her, Best Supporting Actress went to Meryl Streep, Mary Steenburgen, and Maureen Stapleton. Smith's 1978 victory also put her in the exclusive company of Helen Hayes, Jack Lemmon, and Ingrid Bergman as the only actors to win Oscars in both acting categories. All of them reached that milestone in the 1970s. Subsequently, Robert De Niro, Meryl Streep, Jack Nicholson, Gene Hackman, Jessica Lange, Kevin Spacey, Denzel Washington, and Cate Blanchett have joined them. In the 1980s Smith set and maintains the BAFTA record for most Best Actress victories. Having already won for *The Prime of Miss Jean Brodie*, Smith added to her trophy case BAFTAs for *A Private Function* (1984), *A Room with a View* (1986), and *The Lonely Passion of Judith Hearne* (1987). Thanks to multiple supporting wins, only Smith's friend Judi Dench has more BAFTAs overall. Of Smith's 1980s work, the Academy singled out her performance as manipulative chaperone Charlotte Bartlett in *A Room with a View* for a nomination, in the supporting category. Smith won her second of (so far) three Golden Globes for the part, but the avalanche of critical awards that rolled Dianne Wiest's way for *Hannah and Her Sisters* portended her Oscar win. In 2001, Smith and fellow British Dame Helen Mirren enjoyed strong odds for winning Best Supporting Actress for Robert Altman's *Gosford Park*, but they lost to Jennifer Connelly in the year's Best Picture, *A Beautiful Mind*. In her seventh decade as an actor, Smith continues to rack up awards for movies (*Quartet*, *The Best Exotic Marigold Hotel*), theatre (*The Lady from Dubuque*), and especially television (Violet Crawley, Dowager Countess of Grantham in *Downton Abbey* is a small screen legend). High class or lowbrow, regal or ravaged, Maggie Smith has earned her status as one of the world's finest actors.

20. Jessica Lange

1982 Best Actress as actress Frances Farmer in *Frances*
1982 Best Supporting Actress as actress Julie Nichols in *Tootsie*
1984 Best Actress as farmer Jewell Ivy in *Country*
1985 Best Actress as singer Patsy Cline in *Sweet Dreams*
1989 Best Actress as lawyer Ann Talbot in *Music Box*
1994 Best Actress as military wife Carly Marshall in *Blue Sky*

Perhaps more than any other actor on the list, Jessica Lange proved that no one ever achieved great success without taking great risks. Early in her career, she starred in two remakes that could have spelled disaster. When Fay Wray took the role of helpless victim of *King Kong* in the original 1933 beauty and the beast tale, she was forever identified with the classic. So when Lange accepted the same part in Dino De Laurentiis' big budget 1976 remake, the film could have been a huge bomb, damaging a fledgling career, or it could have been a huge hit that typecast her as a screaming sex symbol rather than A-list talent. Mixed reviews but box office attention resulted in Lange being named the Golden Globe's New Female Star of the Year. Lange's screen presence was so powerful that Bob Fosse created for her his angel of death character in 1979's *All That Jazz*, which put Lange in her first Best Picture Oscar-nominated movie. Lange took her next big risk by daring to reprise Lana Turner's classic turn as a murderously complicit, unfaithful wife in *The Postman Always Rings Twice*. In the hands of director Bob Rafelson and screenwriter David Mamet, this cable television version took liberties with sexual and violent content that could never have passed the 1946 censors. Again, Lange's performance and the movie polarized critics, but in the cutting room, editor Graeme Clifford found the lead for his directorial debut film, *Frances*. Beneath her palpable sexuality, Lange's power, singed with rage and determination, was ideal for playing Frances Farmer, the rebel actress destroyed by converging forces at home and work. That performance cemented her status as a dynamic actress. Any other year, the role might have given her a lock on Best Actress, but in 1982 Meryl Streep made *Sophie's Choice*. At Oscar time, no one doubted that Streep would be the year's Best Actress. But Lange celebrated another victory that night. As *Frances* confirmed Lange's ability to penetrate deep into the troubled psyche of her character, she warmed audience's hearts as a young mother and daytime soap actress who came into her own as a woman able to stand up for herself and a better relationship in Sydney Pollack's beloved *Tootsie*. As Julie Nichols, Lange's bold and tender complexity impressed audiences and the Academy. Lange became only the fourth person, after Fay Bainter, Teresa Wright, and Barry Fitzgerald, to be nominated for an Oscar in both acting categories the same year. Like her predecessors, Lange took the supporting prize, and like Teresa Wright, who beat Dame May Whitty, her co-star in *Mrs. Miniver*, Lange won in her category despite competition from *Tootsie* co-star Teri Garr. Thereafter a Hollywood leading lady who often developed her own film projects, Lange excelled in subsequent nominated roles as a desperate farm wife in *Country*, iconic singer Patsy Cline in *Sweet Dreams*, and a myopic lawyer whose eyes are opened to sordid details about her father, whom she's defending, in *Music Box*. Early the following decade, Lange ravenously devoured the part of a sexually charged, bi-polar army wife in *Blue Sky*, but a series of setbacks kept the movie from distribution. The studio's bankruptcy and director Tony Richardson's death put *Blue Sky* on the shelf for three years. When the movie was finally released in 1994, many hailed Lange's visceral performance as her best. A domino of Best Actress victories preceded her voyage to Oscar, where her closest competition seemed to be Jodie Foster as *Nell*, not likely to win a third Oscar in six years, and Susan Sarandon, whom the Academy was ready to honor, but preferably for a movie they were more enthusiastic about than *The Client*. As anticipated, Lange triumphed, giving her an acting Oscar the longest time after a film was completed. Lange remains cutting edge because of her fearless choices on projects and approaches to characterization. On stage or screens large and small, she has triumphed with award-winning interpretations of everyone from Maggie in *Cat on a Hot Tin Roof* and Blanche DuBois in *A Streetcar Named Desire* to Edith "Big Edie" Beale in *Grey Gardens* and Mary Tyrone in *Long Day's Journey into Night*. Like her multiple Emmy-winning turns in *American Horror Story*, there is no telling the depth of her wellspring of acting talent and courage.

19. Cate Blanchett

1998 Best Actress as British monarch Queen Elizabeth I in *Elizabeth*
2004 Best Supporting Actress as actress Katharine Hepburn in *The Aviator*
2006 Best Supporting Actress as teacher Sheba Hart in *Notes on a Scandal*
2007 Best Actress as British monarch Queen Elizabeth I in *Elizabeth: The Golden Age*
2007 Best Supporting Actress as singer Jude Quinn (Bob Dylan) in *I'm Not There*
2013 Best Actress as socialite Jeanette "Jasmine" Francis in *Blue Jasmine*
2015 Best Actress as wife Carol Aird in *Carol*

The Academy's most honored Australian actor, Blanchett has the subtle, transformative skills of an autumn oak. For her supporting role in *Thank God He Met Lizzie*, she won her first of so far six competitive Australian Academy Awards (at the time called the Australian Film Institute Award, now the Australian Academy of Cinema and Television Arts Award), but the Australian hit did not come to the U.S. for award consideration. Blanchett needn't have felt shortchanged. The next year *Elizabeth* was a global sensation, and Blanchett swept most of the world film festival and critical honors playing a fiery, morally clenched Elizabeth I. Blanchett's 1998 award reign seemed as indomitable as the monarch's until another film with Elizabeth I in it, *Shakespeare in Love* began enchanting late-season award voters. The shift began at the Golden Globes when Blanchett took Best Actress, Drama and Gwyneth Paltrow won Best Actress, Musical or Comedy. More telling were the SAGs, which favored Paltrow. The Academy nominated *Shakespeare in Love* for almost twice as many Oscars as *Elizabeth*, so by awards night, the momentum clearly pointed toward Paltrow's victory. In 1998 only Judi Dench won for playing Elizabeth I, in the Best Supporting Actress category for *Shakespeare in Love*. At the time, Blanchett had to settle for becoming part of the first pair of actors both nominated in a single year for playing the same character in different movies. She ended the decade with a supporting BAFTA nomination for *The Talented Mr. Ripley*, and then won supporting awards for an astounding four feature films in 2001. The National Board of Review named her Best Supporting Actress for *The Lord of the Rings: The Fellowship of the Ring*, *The Man Who Cried*, and *The Shipping News*, while the Hollywood Foreign Press nominated her lead performance in *Bandits*. Appearing in all three *Lord of the Rings* megahits increased her international box office prowess and brought her multiple Best Cast honors. Since then, Blanchett's hits have continued to arrive in bundles, with multiple movies all earning her award consideration in a single season. 2004 brought her various accolades for three diverse motion pictures. Blanchett was nominated for individual recognition playing herself and a fictitious cousin in a vignette from *Coffee and Cigarettes* and cast nods for *The Life Aquatic with Steve Zissou*. But it was *The Aviator* that gave her arms full of statuettes, including her first Oscar. Her startling immersion as Katharine Hepburn in her vivacious, athletic prime made Blanchett the first and still only actor to win an Academy Award playing another Academy Award-winning actor. Two years later both *Babel* and *Notes on a Scandal* contended for an array of Oscars, and Blanchett was nominated again in the supporting category as a naive art teacher who enchants a lonely lesbian colleague in *Notes on a Scandal*. Next award season, Blanchett again earned awards recognition for multiple projects. As Jude Quinn, one variation of Bob Dylan at his most creative and irascible in *I'm Not There*, Blanchett magnetized more awards. Not since Linda Hunt in *The Year of Living Dangerously* had Oscar nominated a female for playing a male character. That same year, Blanchett's lead nomination in *Elizabeth: The Golden Age* made her the first female actor to be nominated for playing the same character twice. Bing Crosby, Peter O'Toole, Al Pacino and Paul Newman preceded her; Sylvester Stallone followed in 2015. Only one performance of 2013 was a sure winner going into Oscar night. Blanchett added an astonishing 29 more awards to her mantle as a crumbling socialite in *Blue Jasmine*. Her win made Blanchett only the third actor, after Meryl Streep and Jessica Lange, to rise from Supporting Actress to lead Actress Academy Award winner, and the second, after Diane Keaton in *Annie Hall*, to win a lead acting Oscar under the direction of Woody Allen. In her acceptance speeches, Blanchett emphasized how *Blue Jasmine* proved that movies about women could be international successes, and rallied for more projects featuring central female characters. Having excelled as everyone from Elizabeth I to Katharine Hepburn, her compelling argument helped bring her the title role in *Carol*, adding yet another nomination to her Oscar achievements.

18. Robert De Niro

1974 Best Supporting Actor as grocery store employee/criminal/ mafia don Vito Corleone in *The Godfather Part II*
1976 Best Actor as taxi driver Travis Bickle in *Taxi Driver*
1978 Best Actor as steel worker/U.S. Army sergeant Michael Vronsky in *The Deer Hunter*
1980 Best Actor as boxer Jake LaMotta in *Raging Bull*
1990 Best Actor as encephalitis lethargica patient Leonard Lowe in *Awakenings*
1991 Best Actor as former inmate Maximilian "Max" Cady in *Cape Fear*
2012 Best Supporting Actor as father Pat Solitano, Sr., in *Silver Linings Playbook*

    Few collaborations have detonated on screen so precisely and consistently as Robert De Niro's acting under the direction of Martin Scorsese. But to think his most powerful screen moments have come in Scorsese movies is to overlook a trunk full of performances as large as one needed to stash corpses in *Goodfellas*. De Niro unsuccessfully auditioned for multiple roles in *The Godfather* (1972), but instead secured work in two very different movies released the following year. *Bang the Drum the Slowly* gave De Niro his first Oscar profile, as he played a dim, terminally ill baseball catcher coached by Best Supporting Actor nominee Vincent Gardenia. In De Niro's other 1973 hit, he first worked with fledgling director Scorsese in *Mean Streets*, a much grittier, local view of the poorer element of mafia life than the international scope of *The Godfather*. Comparing the style of the two similarly themed works might lead one to see how much better suited De Niro seemed for conveying the harsh seediness of that milieu. But then came *The Godfather Part II*. Director Francis Ford Coppola remembered De Niro's earlier auditions, and cast him as the young Vito Corleone. Handsome De Niro glided through every scene with a quiet sleekness that conveyed the lofty dreams and moral compromise that made Corleone a don. Oscar loved the sequel even more than the original, and De Niro set three records with his win: he was the first (and still only) actor to win in a category where two of his co-stars (Michael V. Gazzo and fellow method actor Lee Strasberg) were nominated. Speaking several dialects of Sicilian, as well as an occasional English phrase, De Niro became the first actor to win a supporting award for a foreign language performance. Winning as Vito Corleone after Marlon Brando did the same two years earlier made them the first actors to both win Oscars for playing the same fictitious character. Reteaming with Scorsese for *Taxi Driver* in 1976, De Niro and his Travis "Are you talkin' to me?" Bickle became instant movie classics. His slow dissolve shocked audiences like a Hitchcock shower, and the Academy put De Niro in his first Best Actor competition, won posthumously by Peter Finch for *Network*. Two years later his silence grounded in sadness the horror of Vietnam in *The Deer Hunter*, which the Academy embraced as the Best Picture of the year. With Warren Beatty, Gary Busey, and Laurence Olivier, De Niro lost Best Actor to Jon Voight as an equally scarred Vietnam vet in *Coming Home*. De Niro and Scorsese joined forces again in 1980 for *Raging Bull*, a brutal boxing biography so astounding it was instantly slated as the best film of the decade, a ranking that never diminished after nine more years of impressive films. In full method actor immersion, De Niro gained 60 pounds, mastered boxing, and so dominated the Best Actor category of 1980 that his name was all but etched into the trophy before Sally Field announced him the winner.

By now a film legend, De Niro continued a run of expansive performances throughout the decade, then had two Oscar hits in 1990. He excelled as one of Scorsese's *Goodfellas*, "Jimmy the Gent" Conway, but got the Oscar nomination as catatonic patient Leonard Lowe who experienced one of doctor Robin Williams' miraculous *Awakenings*. For the Penny Marshall film, De Niro joined a relatively small group of actors, such as Ruth Chatterton in Dorothy Arsner's *Sarah and Son* (1928/29) and Giancarlo Giannini in Lina Wertmüller's *Seven Beauties* (1976) nominated for a lead acting Oscar for a movie directed by a woman. The next year, De Niro stalked Nick Nolte and his family to another Best Actor bid in Scorsese's hugely successful remake of J. Lee Thompson's *Cape Fear*. Even De Niro at his harrowing best couldn't out-menace Anthony Hopkins as Hannibal Lecter in *The Silence of the Lambs*. In 2012, twice victorious De Niro vied for Best Supporting Actor against all previous winners, *Argo*'s Alan Arkin, *The Master*'s Philip Seymour Hoffman,

A trimmed down Robert De Niro had gained 60 pounds for some scenes in *Raging Bull*, for which he handily won the 1980 Best Actor Academy Award.

Lincoln's Tommy Lee Jones, and *Django Unchained*'s Christoph Waltz. It was anyone's to win, and sentiment bode well for De Niro to join the prestigious few triple Oscared actors. In the end, the *Django Unchained* star Waltzed off with Oscar. Amid his nearly 100 features, Robert De Niro has conquered every genre, and seeped into the cracks between the more evident nuances of each character he's played. Dedicated and intense, De Niro has embraced and personalized The Method to astounding results.

17. Jane Fonda

1969 Best Actress as aspiring actress/marathon dancer Gloria Beatty in *They Shoot Horses, Don't They?*
1971 Best Actress as prostitute/aspiring actress Bree Daniels in *Klute*
1977 Best Actress as playwright Lillian Hellman in *Julia*
1978 Best Actress as veteran's hospital volunteer Sally Hyde in *Coming Home*
1979 Best Actress as television news reporter Kimberly Wells in *The China Syndrome*
1981 Best Supporting Actress as executive/daughter Chelsea Thayer Wayne in *On Golden Pond*
1986 Best Actress as actress Alex Sternbergen in *The Morning After*

In no other acting dynasty has an actor so distinctly emerged from a parent's shadow to cast an even vaster one of her own than Jane Fonda. Her father Henry ranked 6th on AFI's list of the greatest legends of the 20th century, yet in less than a decade of acting, Jane Fonda outpaced her father in Oscar nominations and became the first family member to win. Jane also deserved some credit for her father's countdown status, for Jane secured the rights to *On Golden Pond* to fulfill her long sought vision to act with her father, and to give her dad a role so distinctive that, in his capable hands, it would bring him an Oscar, too. Jane was a siren of sorts for Oscar. While she was building her own momentum toward Oscar competition, she often chose projects that Oscar favored, too. Early films such as *Period of Adjustment* and *Walk on the Wild Side* got Academy notice in artistic categories, but it was *Cat Ballou* that set the foundation for trailblazing Fonda. As the title character, she played the first young female protagonist of the Western genre, and Oscar responded to the film with five nominations and a Best Actor trophy for Lee Marvin. *Barbarella* made her an international sex symbol, and the romantic *Barefoot in the Park* showed that her peers in the Academy were still most comfortable honoring her comedies. Then Fonda rocked the acting world with *They Shoot Horses, Don't They?* conveying depths of determination, frustration, and a disillusionment that Fonda personally overcame with a dynamism that made her one of the top entertainers and entrepreneurs of her generation. Her peers loved the movie and her performance. After winning Best Actress from the New York Film Critics, Fonda was poised to win the Oscar until dark horse Maggie Smith took the award for *The Prime of Miss Jean Brodie*. Two years later, *Klute* gave Fonda a broad field for exploring the complexity of fear, self-destruction, and cautious hope. As prostitute and aspiring actress Bree Daniels, Fonda released an arsenal of divergent emotions, often in a single line or gesture. The New York Film Critics again honored her, followed by so many other awards that, unless her peers in the Academy voted against her politics, she was sure to win Oscar. She did. More grounded in her advocacy later in the decade, she had an ideal project in *Julia*, Lillian Hellman's memory piece of two women's friendship and their courageous stance against Nazism spreading in World War II Europe. Languidly paced and beautifully evocative, *Julia* gave Fonda a role of a woman willing to test her courage for a cause. The Academy responded with 11 nominations, including Fonda's third for Best Actress. She might have beat Diane Keaton as *Annie Hall* if the Academy were not already expecting to honor Fonda the following year for her dream project set for release: a sensitive treatment of the Vietnam War's personal impact on returning soldiers and their loved ones called *Coming Home*. As anticipated, Fonda was a frontrunner for the 1978 Best Actress prize, with her strongest competition from Jill Clayburgh as *An Unmarried Woman*. A triumphant Fonda began her acceptance speech in sign language, then ended it by vocalizing her belief that, beyond entertaining, movies can inspire and teach and heal. *The China Syndrome*'s timeliness made it headline news and one of the following year's top Oscar contenders, but Sally Field had a lock on Best Actress as *Norma Rae*. Fonda's homage to her father Henry put her up for a supporting Oscar in 1981's *On Golden Pond*. Given special permission by the Academy to accept for her ailing father if Henry won Best Actor, Jane is the only proxy besides Peter Finch's widow and Heath Ledger's family to accept an Oscar on behalf of someone else since the Academy banned the practice after Marlon Brando sent Sacheen Littlefeather to decline his 1972 victory. But Jane returned to lead acting contention, once again playing an actress, in Sidney Lumet's *The Morning After*. The year Jane won her second Oscar, father Henry was feted with an AFI Life Achievement Award. In 2014, Jane won it, too, giving her the final stride out of a lengthy shadow. Fittingly, Jane acknowledged the positive impact her father had on her life and her craft, proving that their shadows were never competing, but always converging.

16. Dustin Hoffman

1967 Best Actor as college graduate Benjamin "Ben" Braddock in *The Graduate*

1969 Best Actor as con man Enrico Salvatore "Ratso" Rizzo in *Midnight Cowboy*
1974 Best Actor as standup comic Lenny Bruce in *Lenny*
1979 Best Actor as advertising executive Ted Kramer in *Kramer vs. Kramer*
1982 Best Actor as actor Michael Dorsey/Dorothy Michaels in *Tootsie*
1988 Best Actor as autistic savant Raymond Babbitt in *Rain Man*
1997 Best Actor as movie producer Stanley Motss in *Wag the Dog*

Anyone familiar with Dustin Hoffman's talent and temperament could recognize traces of his own life in the opening scenes of *Tootsie* where his character, a determined but artistically testy actor, argued against every prompt to leave his audition. "[You're the wrong height.] I can be taller. [No, we're looking for someone shorter.] Look, I don't have to be this tall. See, I'm wearing lifts, I can be shorter. [We're looking for somebody different.] I can be different." True to his character in the movie, thanks to grinding ambition and artistic courage, Hoffman can be almost anything. In the 1950s, he and fellow classmate Gene Hackman were voted "least likely to succeed" in their Pasadena Playhouse acting class. Hackman quit and headed to New York, but unrelenting Hoffman stayed awhile longer before rooming with Hackman and enrolling in the Actors Studio. Few actors had a breakthrough quite like Hoffman in *The Graduate*, who made confused, dispassionate Benjamin Braddock the poster child of his entire generation. Hoffman's short stature and unconventional looks set a new precedent for movie stardom that resonated worldwide, earning him New Star of the Year awards from the Golden Globes and BAFTA. Nominated for the Best Actor Oscar, Hoffman later confessed that he was relieved to lose to *In the Heat of the Night*'s Rod Steiger, for he felt unsettled about his new stardom. As gimp drifter Ratso "I'm walkin' he-a" Rizzo in *Midnight Cowboy*, Hoffman confirmed his transformative talent, and found himself in contention for Oscar against co-star Jon Voight and victor John Wayne of *True Grit*. The following year, Hoffman made the Guinness Book of World Records for "Greatest Age Span Portrayed by a Movie Actor" (aged 17 to 121) as Custer's Last Stand survivor Jack Crabb. Despite stellar reviews, *Little Big Man* garnered one Oscar nod, for Best Supporting Actor nominee Chief Dan George. Hoffman found favor again with Oscar in 1974 taking controversial comic Lenny Bruce up through fame and down through self-destruction in Bob Fosse's *Lenny*. A top contender along with Jack Nicholson of *Chinatown* and Al Pacino of *The Godfather Part II*, Hoffman alienated some voters by calling the Academy Awards "obscene, dirty, and no better than a beauty contest." Now associated with recent Oscar winners and refusers George C. Scott and Marlon Brando, Hoffman might never have won over the Academy if his output of work were not so consistently varied and brilliant. Though neither was nominated in 1976, stars Hoffman and Robert Redford helped elevate *All the President's Men* to its 8-nomination, 4-win status. That same year, his Oscar profile was expanded as the *Marathon Man* stalked by Best Supporting Actor nominee Laurence Olivier.

In 1979, *Kramer vs. Kramer* brought award gold from the New York and LA Film Critics, the Golden Globes, and ultimately the Academy. Humorous and humble in his Oscar acceptance speech, Hoffman confessed to having mixed feelings about his win, but focused graciously on the talent of not only the night's nominees, but also the vast family of actors that included legions of aspiring stars who would never know such a moment as his that night. In a single speech, he endeared himself to his peers. The 1980s brought him two more iconic roles, as Michael Dorsey/Dorothy Michaels, cross-dressing champion of women's integrity in *Tootsie*, and then toothpick counting, affection resistant autistic savant Raymond Babbitt in *Rain Man*. Three H's led the 1988 Best Actor race: Hoffman, Hackman, and Hanks. Hackman's early lead for *Mississippi Burning* dwindled amid questions of the film's historical accuracy, and as an Oscar newcomer in a comedy, Hanks would need to build his film vitae before voters checked his name. Such powerful momentum mounted for *Rain Man* that Hoffman was easily swept to the podium for his

Inattentive husband Ted (Dustin Hoffman) was stunned when wife Joanna (Meryl Streep) left him—with their son—in *Kramer vs. Kramer* (1979).

second Best Actor win in less than ten years, a feat achieved by only a handful of actors before him. Hoffman again proved warm and accessible, confessing that he should be jaded at that point in his career, but was grateful, and then highlighting the impact and value of the disabled in society. Thanks mostly to two heartfelt Oscar acceptance speeches, Hoffman disengaged himself from George C. Scott and Marlon Brando as Oscar antagonists, and instead became associated with other beloved double Best Actor winners like Spencer Tracy and Gary Cooper. They are indeed fine company among whom Hoffman rightly belongs.

15. Denzel Washington

1987 Best Supporting Actor as South Africa's Black Consciousness Movement leader Stephen Biko in *Cry Freedom*
1989 Best Supporting Actor as escaped slave/U.S. Civil War Private Trip in *Glory*
1992 Best Actor as minister/human rights activist Malcolm X in *Malcolm X*
1999 Best Actor as boxer/prison inmate Rubin "Hurricane" Carter in *The Hurricane*
2001 Best Actor as police detective Alonzo Harris in *Training Day*
2012 Best Actor as pilot William "Whip" Whitaker, Sr., in *Flight*
2016 Best Actor as waste collector Troy Maxson in *Fences*
2016 Best Picture as co-producer (with Todd Black and Scott Rudin) of *Fences*

With a tilted stare and generous row of front teeth, Washington has bit into some of the most intense roles in recently film history, pausing in some scenes for audiences to savor the emotional impact of his vulnerability, or chewing through the script and spitting out the contents in a daunting display of hubris. He excelled as an athlete and actor at Fordham College, honing his craft with leads in O'Neill's *The Emperor Jones* and Shakespeare's *Othello*. He was in movies for ten years before he interpreted Oscar material in a Best Picture nominee of 1984, *A Soldier's Story*. Reprising his role from the Pulitzer Prize-winning *A Soldier's Play*, Washington portrayed Private First Class Melvin Peterson, one of many suspects questioned about the murder of their sergeant, Best Supporting Actor nominee Adolph Caesar. Three years later, Washington's rousing anti-apartheid speeches and haunting flashlit image of his captivity as Steve Biko gave Richard Attenborough's epic political biography *Cry Freedom* an intimate resonance that had Academy members bringing Washington into their fold as a Best Supporting Actor nominee. As a newcomer, Washington had little chance of upsetting the lock that movie icon Sean Connery of *The Untouchables* had on the category. Two years later, Washington was the Best Supporting Actor to beat as a wary, proud, unrelenting soldier in *Glory*. The image of Washington's character, a scarred former slave, staring down commanding officer Matthew Broderick as he is about to be whipped is seared into the pantheon of great movie moments. On his tail for the Oscar were Dan Aykroyd contending with an aging mother in *Driving Miss Daisy*, Marlon Brando making an Academy comeback in *A Dry White Season*, morally compromising Martin Landau in *Crimes and Misdemeanors*, and Washington's closest rival Danny Aiello instigating the climactic violence in Spike Lee's *Do the Right Thing*. Although *Glory* was overlooked for a deserving Best Picture nod, Washington triumphed, and thanked, among others, the Black soldiers of the 54th depicted in *Glory*. By the 1990s, Washington was a steamrolling headliner. His performance as *Malcolm X* earned him Best Actor at the Berlin Film Festival and from the New York Film Critics Circle, and brought him his first lead acting Oscar nomination. No surprise, the Academy was ready to finally honor Al Pacino that year for *Scent of a Woman*. The following year Washington guided uninformed movie audiences through a gradually enlightened perspective of AIDS in *Philadelphia*, which earned Tom Hanks the Best Actor Oscar. A biographical role later that decade, as boxer Rubin Carter in *The Hurricane*, gave Washington a TKO performance so impressive that the film's director, Norman Jewison, praised it as the best acting he'd seen in any of his films. Washington went the distance to take Best Actor, Drama at the

Posing with Halle Berry, the night's other lead acting winner of 2001, Denzel Washington joined an elite handful of actors who've won Oscars in both the supporting and lead acting categories.

Golden Globes, but was felled at the Oscars by Kevin Spacey in *American Beauty*. Two years later, Washington swaggered his way into Oscar record books by bookending his Supporting Actor Oscar for *Glory* with a Best Actor triumph for *Training Day*. Few actors could have made such a corrupt character so entrancing, and Washington's victory capped off a landmark year for African-American actors when he came to the stage to accept his Oscar after Halle Berry became the Academy's first Black Best Actress winner and Sidney Poitier accepted a lifetime achievement award. Washington acknowledged Berry by starting his speech with, "Two birds in one night, huh?" and then honoring Poitier by looking toward the groundbreaking actor and confessing that there was nothing he would rather do than follow in his footsteps.

Washington is to the NAACP Image awards what Meryl Streep is to the Oscars. To date, he has 23 nominations and 17 Image Awards, putting him well ahead of Laurence Fishburne with 17 nominations and 5 wins, Will Smith with 15 nominations and 4 wins, and Morgan Freeman with 13 nominations and 7 wins. His Academy record is as impressive. But beyond being the most nominated and winning African-American actor in Academy history, Washington's impact transcends race, as he has infused many Oscar films, such as *Crimson Tide*, *The Preacher's Wife*, and *America Gangster* with a modulated resolve that leaves an indelible impression. He was again in top form as a heroic pilot hiding a potentially deadly secret in *Flight* and directing himself in *Fences,* keeping him one of today's Hollywood legends still impressing audiences and his peers in the Academy.

14. Jack Lemmon

1955 Best Supporting Actor as navy Ensign Pulver in *Mister Roberts*
1959 Best Actor as musician Jerry (Gerald)/"Daphne" in *Some Like It Hot*
1960 Best Actor as insurance office employee C. C. "Bud" Baxter in *The Apartment*
1962 Best Actor as publicist Joe Clay in *Days of Wine and Roses*
1973 Best Actor as garment manufacturing executive Harry Stoner in *Save the Tiger*
1979 Best Actor as nuclear plant shift supervisor Jack Godell in *The China Syndrome*
1980 Best Actor as actor Scottie Templeton in *Tribute*
1982 Best Actor as father Edmund Horman in *Missing*

As a Harvard graduate, Lemmon not surprisingly gave studied, textured performances. But it was Lemmon's ability to let loose in character after the cerebral planning that made his performances, especially his comic ones, among the most unforgettable of his generation. He may have drawn from his experience as a navy ensign to get in character for *Mister Roberts*. In one of his first movies, he achieved something nearly impossible by stealing the show from legends William Powell, James Cagney, and Henry Fonda, who reprised his Tony-winning title character for the movie. At the 1955 Oscars, *Mister Roberts* vied for Best Picture, but Lemmon was the only cast member in contention. Like his sudsy Ensign Pulver, he cleaned up his category over newcomers Sal Mineo (*Rebel without a Cause*) and Joe Mantell (*Marty*) as well as two veteran stalwarts named Arthur: O'Connell, who reprised his Broadway role as Howard Bevans in *Picnic*, and Kennedy, who had won the Golden Globe for *Trial*. Lemmon's first two Best Actor-nominated roles came for collaborating with director Billy Wilder. Lemmon let loose as a 1920s musician hiding from the mob with pal Tony Curtis by posing as women in *Some Like It Hot*. And hot it was, ultimately taking top honors as AFI's greatest comedy of all time. Both Lemmon and Marilyn Monroe won their respective lead acting categories at the Golden Globes, but, as he had in *Mister Roberts*, Lemmon garnered the film's only acting Oscar nomination, losing to Charlton Heston as *Ben-Hur*. Lemmon reteamed with Wilder the following year for *The Apartment*, filmdom's seminal social consciousness comedy. As Bud Baxter, Lemmon embodied the moral middle man who must find the courage to live from integrity and open his heart to love amid corporate corruption and social cynicism. With Lemmon and Shirley MacLaine as anchors, the film navigated, and thus smoothed to some degree, the choppy social milieu of the 1960s. Lemmon lost to Burt Lancaster as *Elmer Gantry*, but the movie was the night's big winner, taking five of its ten categories, including Best Picture. Two years later, Lemmon aligned with another frequent collaborator, director Blake Edwards, for *Days of Wine and Roses*, which depicted the haunting underbelly of addiction like no other film to date. The dark drama earned Lemmon another of his record-setting 22 Golden Globe nominations, the most of any male actor. His record has only been bested by female actor Meryl Streep. His Golden Globe streak entered him in seven Globe competitions from 1960 to 1970. Always impressive as characters down on their luck, Lemmon pursued MacLaine in *The Apartment* (1960) and *Irma La Douce* (1963), Lee Remick in *Days of Wine and Roses* (1962), Carol Lynley in *Under the Yum Yum Tree* (1963), and Natalie Wood in *The Great Race* (1965). Later his luck ran even dryer, left by his wife in *The Odd Couple* (1968) and then struggling through nightmarish vacation mishaps with Sandy Dennis in *The Out-of-Towners* (1970). Oscar came calling again when Lemmon slowed the tempo of his delivery as another morally compromised businessman, Harry Stoner, in *Save the Tiger*. That year's Best Actor race leaned toward Robert Redford as the potential victor for *The Sting*, but Lemmon was the surprise winner. In his enthusiastic acceptance speech, he expressed being thrilled at receiving "one hell of an honor." Although Helen Hayes beat him by three years to become the first actor to win Oscars in both lead and supporting categories, Lemmon became the first male to reach that milestone, and the first to rise up the ranks, winning Best Supporting Actor first and subsequently earning Best Actor.

Academy Award nominations continued through the next decade, and honors, nominations, and trophies streamed toward Lemmon up to his death in 2001. Near the end of his life, the generous, talented Lemmon was even honored at award shows where he didn't win or wasn't present. One of the most famous moments in Golden Globe history occurred when Ving Rhames as boxing promoter *Don King* beat Jack Lemmon of *12 Angry Men*, then called Lemmon to the podium to give him his trophy. The following year, Kevin Spacey dedicated his Best Actor Oscar win for *American Beauty* to Lemmon, whom Spacey considered a friend, mentor, and father figure. A frequent presenter and nominee, and even director of Walter Matthau's Best Actor-nominated performance as *Kotch*, Lemmon set records as an Academy favorite who represented for many of his generation the good-hearted common man whose integrity cut light through the fog of moral uncertainty.

Reporter Kimberly Wells (Jane Fonda) watched Jack Godell (Jack Lemmon) suffer a meltdown in the face of nuclear disaster in *The China Syndrome* (1979).

13. Marlon Brando

1951 Best Actor as brother-in-law Stanley Kowalski in *A Streetcar Named Desire*
1952 Best Actor as revolutionary Emiliano Zapata in *Viva Zapata!*
1953 Best Actor as Roman politician and general Marc Antony in *Julius Caesar*
1954 Best Actor as dockworker Terry Malloy in *On the Waterfront*
1957 Best Actor as U.S. Air Force Major Lloyd "Ace" Gruver in *Sayonara*
1972 Best Actor as mafia don Vito Corleone in *The Godfather*
1973 Best Actor as hotel owner Paul in *Last Tango in Paris*
1989 Best Supporting Actor as barrister Ian McKenzie in *A Dry White Season*

Anyone seeking fault with the Academy can and has used brilliant and brash Brando as proof of the argument. Woody Allen, a 24-time nominee with four Oscars who has been infamously indifferent to the Academy his entire career, attributes his disillusionment to Brando's 1951 loss for Best Actor in *A Streetcar Named Desire*. That happened when Allen was a teenager. But the Academy has the history and power to weather any storm, and it handled its volatile relationship with Brando so that both ended up looking like winners. Brando redefined acting as Stanley Kowalski, and was an obvious lead contender for the Best Actor prize when Academy Award nominations were announced. But Hollywood legend Humphrey Bogart, after having lost his only other Oscar race for *Casablanca*, decided he wanted to win for *The African Queen*, and hosted soirees for his peers while young newcomer Brando was busy etching his rebel niche in Hollywood by shunning Oscar promotions. In that context, it seems less surprising that Bogart won, and that it took several more compelling performances for the Academy to acknowledge Brando's genius with a golden statuette. With each subsequent performance, Brando's rebel roles came closer to honing in on a sense of justice that could make him identifiable as well as admired for his originality. His Emiliano Zapata was a righteous fighter, but nowhere near the isolated savior 1952 Best Actor winner Gary Cooper was as Will Kane in *High Noon*. Despite a few grumbles about Brando's mumbles as Marc Antony, the public and critics embraced his take on Shakespeare, but with fellow nominee Richard Burton also donning ancient garb in *The Robe*, voters more distinctly noticed William Holden in *Stalag 17*, and named him Best Actor of 1953. But then Brando went *On the Waterfront*. Until the social conscious classic, no one imagined that another Brando line could become even more memorable than his agonized "Stellaaa!" from *A Streetcar Named Desire*. By reaching even deeper to tell brother Rod Steiger that he "coulda been a contender …

coulda been somebody," Brando expanded his domination of classic movie lexicon. In the 1954 Best Actor race, *A Star Is Born*'s James Mason and *The Country Girl*'s Bing Crosby were awash with alcoholic bravado, Dan O'Herlihy was an international sensation in *Adventures of Robinson Crusoe*, and, *The Caine Mutiny*'s Humphrey Bogart offered Brando a chance for Academy redemption for his loss as Stanley Kowalski. As anticipated, *On the Waterfront* dominated the 1954 Oscars. When Bette Davis called his name as Best Actor, an ebullient Brando rushed to the stage and accepted his first Oscar, graciously observing, "I don't think that ever in my life have so many people been so directly responsible for my being so very, very glad. It's a wonderful moment and a rare one and I'm certainly indebted." He rounded out the 1950s with a fifth nomination as a soldier awakened to military injustice toward interracial marriage in *Sayonara*. With the exception of the 1962 remake of *Mutiny on the Bounty*, the Academy didn't favor any project with which Brando was associated during that turbulent decade. But then came the 1970s and *The Godfather*.

The film was an instant sensation, and Brando's understated performance was so mesmerizing that few realized his was among the shortest performances to compete for Best Actor. Leading up to the Oscars, Best Actor prizes were meted out among many actors, with Brando only winning some local critics circle honors and then the Golden Globe for Best Actor, Drama. The entire award season, Brando's elusiveness seemed merely a product of his familiar eccentricity, so his sending Sacheen Littlefeather to refuse his Oscar created the very shock Brando was likely to have savored. His refusal notwithstanding, the Academy remained steadfast to its commitment to honor excellence, and nominated Brando again the following year for the X-rated *Last Tango in Paris*, a performance that some critics said no one but Brando could have pulled off so effectively. In 1989, the Academy cited Brando's work as an enigmatic lawyer in *A Dry White Season* for his first Supporting nod, but as expected, Brando was nowhere to be found on Oscar night. Startlingly virile, complex, and mercurial, Brando recreated the craft of acting and inspired layers of character development for which Stanley Kowalski, Terry Malloy, and Vito Corleone will forever be inspiring models.

12. *Spencer Tracy*

1936   Best Actor as priest Father Tim Mullen in *San Francisco*
1937   Best Actor as fisherman Manuel Fidello in *Captains Courageous*
1938   Best Actor as priest Father Flanagan in *Boys Town*
1950   Best Actor as father Stanley T. Banks in *Father of the Bride*
1955   Best Actor as war veteran John J. Macreedy in *Bad Day at Black Rock*
1958   Best Actor as fisherman The Old Man in *The Old Man and the Sea*

Although son Michael (Al Pacino) looked up to his father, Vito Corleone (Marlon Brando), he resisted taking over his criminal dynasty in *The Godfather* (1972).

- 1960 Best Actor as defense attorney Henry Drummond in *Inherit the Wind*
- 1961 Best Actor as chief justice Judge Dan Haywood in *Judgment at Nuremberg*
- 1967 Best Actor as newspaper owner Matt Drayton in *Guess Who's Coming to Dinner*

Perhaps his everyday looks, devil-may-care demeanor, and casual, even rumpled posturing were magically deceptive, but Spencer Tracy spent four decades impressing audiences and the Academy with performances that looked effortless. He so seamlessly fit the character of a solid guy whom everyone trusted, it's not surprising that two of his earliest Oscar nominations came for playing heroic priests. With only 17 minutes of screen time in *San Francisco*, Tracy so impressed the Academy that they nominated him for Best Actor over the film's headline star, Clark Gable in a much flashier role of a roustabout gambler. It likely helped that Tracy had starred in four hits for MGM that year, and that two of his movies, *San Francisco* and *Libeled Lady*, both competed for Best Picture. Tracy lost his first competition to Paul Muni in *The Story of Louis Pasteur*. The next year Tracy took the difficult role of a Portuguese-American fisherman whose patience and compassion for a spoiled young passenger transformed the boy in *Captains Courageous*. Although he had second billing to child star Freddie Bartholomew, Tracy again overshadowed his movie's star and netted a Best Actor Oscar nomination. This time Tracy was favored to win. Laid up by appendicitis on Oscar night, Tracy missed the ceremony and his first victory. When his statuette arrived, Spence was surprised to see it mis-inscribed "to Dick Tracy," a rare mistake that has since become Oscar lore. Tracy's screen chemistry with young Freddie Bartholomew turned *Captains Courageous* into the studio's biggest hit that year. Taking note of his previous two nominations, MGM combined elements of both successes by putting Tracy back in priest's garb and matching him with a battalion of wayward youth in *Boys Town*. This time, Mickey Rooney, who had a small role as a shipmate on Tracy's schooner in *Captains Courageous*, was Tracy's most challenging ward. The two played so effectively opposite one another that the Academy nominated Tracy again for Best Actor and singled out Rooney for an honorary juvenile award for that dramatic work and his song-and-dance-and-youthful-romance films as Andy Hardy. Rooney must have brought Tracy Oscar luck, because Tracy won again, becoming the first male actor, and second star after Luise Rainer, to win back-to-back Oscars. Tracy spent most of his speech honoring Father Flanagan, whom he portrayed, concluding, "If you have seen him through me, then I thank you." Tracy's onscreen partnership with Katharine Hepburn began in 1942 with *Woman of the Year*, for which Hepburn was nominated, but Tracy was not. In fact, it wouldn't be until the end of their alliance with *Guess Who's Coming to Dinner* that Tracy and Hepburn were both nominated for one of their nine collaborations. Even though he starred in many Oscar contenders throughout the 1940s, such as *Tortilla Flat*; *The Seventh Cross*; *Edward, My Son*; and *Adam's Rib*, the Academy didn't nominate another Tracy performance until his heartrending portrait of a father letting go of his baby girl on her wedding day as *Father of the Bride*. Even in 1950, Vincente Minnelli's film had nostalgic warmth compared to the more jaded Oscar contenders *All About Eve* and *Sunset Boulevard*. Tracy lost to José Ferrer as *Cyrano de Bergerac*, but the new decade opened Tracy to parts as older, wearier, but even more determined heroes. Throughout Oscar history, no other actor's nominations fell so neatly into distinct pairs. In two movies he played a priest (*San Francisco*, *Boys Town*), in two a sailor (*Captains Courageous*, *The Old Man and the Sea*), in two a legal representative (back-to-back *Inherit the Wind* and *Judgment at Nuremberg*, both under the direction of Stanley Kramer), and in two a father confronting an issue with a grown daughter (*Father of the Bride* and *Guess Who's Coming to Dinner*). Only his character in *Bad Day at Black Rock* stands alone, which is fitting considering the character he played did exactly that against a town full of complicit racist killers.

Sick throughout the filming of *Guess Who's Coming to Dinner*, Tracy persevered, capping his career with one of his most heartfelt, enduring performances. His final speech, with onscreen wife and real-life love Katharine Hepburn's eyes glistening with tears behind him, is a tour de force, made more poignant by the fact that Tracy died just 17 days after the film wrapped.

In *Bad Day at Black Rock*, Spencer Tracy (as John J. Macreedy) overcame Ernest Borgnine's (as Coley Trimble) antagonism as Sam (Walter Sande) looked on, but at that year's Academy Awards, Tracy lost Best Actor to Borgnine in *Marty* (1955).

11. Walter Brennan

1936 Best Supporting Actor as pal Swan Bostrom in *Come and Get It*
1938 Best Supporting Actor as horse raiser Peter Goodwin in *Kentucky*
1940 Best Supporting Actor as Judge Roy Bean in *The Westerner*
1941 Best Supporting Actor as pastor Rosier Pile in *Sergeant York*

Brennan's movie beginnings as a film extra paved the way for his status as Hollywood's quintessential character actor and the Academy's first member to win three acting Oscars. Resilient and industrious, Brennan used everything in his repertoire to enhance his characterizations. The early loss of his front teeth, premature balding, and a voice that he could make wheeze and quiver at will enabled Brennan to emerge from the throngs of extras into memorable character roles, usually playing old men who served as supportive sidekicks, comic relief, and occasional wiry villains. Though primarily remembered for his work in Westerns, Brennan enhanced films in every genre, including roles in Oscar-nominated horror (an unbilled peasant in *Bride of Frankenstein*), historical dramas (Edward G. Robinson's sidekick, named Old Atrocity, in *Barbary Coast*), social dramas (a taxi driver in *These Three* with Best Supporting Actress nominee Bonita Granville), biographies (as sportswriter Sam Blake in *The Pride of the Yankees* with lead acting nominees Gary Cooper and Teresa Wright), and thrillers (as a conscious stricken dentist who helps Best Actor nominee Spencer Tracy improve his *Bad Day at Black Rock*). When the Academy introduced its supporting acting categories in 1936, Brennan's revered status among the Union of Film Extras gave him instant alliances with a massive block of Academy voters. To take nothing away from his outstanding performances, Brennan's beloved status among extras helped him not only launch the Best Supporting Actor category, but also dominate it the first five years of its existence. William Wyler and Howard Hawks, who both kept Brennan on their cast rosters for multiple film projects, directed him in *Come and Get It*, a grand scale adaptation of Edna Ferber's epic about lumbering. Playing Edward Arnold's Swedish sidekick Swan Bostrom, Brennan brought lively humor and humanity to the film, and *Daily Variety* correctly predicted Brennan's victory over closest competitor Akim Tamiroff as the diabolical Chinese title character in *The General Died at Dawn*. Two years later, Brennan made horse breeder Peter Goodwin less appealing but no less essential to the success of *Kentucky*. His performance brought the lush drama its only nomination. In three of the four acting categories of 1938, Best Supporting Actor Brennan, Best Actress Bette Davis, and Best Actor Spencer Tracy earned their second career Oscars and joined 1936 and 1937 Best Actress Luise Rainer as the first four performers to win two acting Academy Awards. In 1940, Brennan was the first to reach a landmark three. In *The Westerner*, "by gobs," Brennan dominated the film. Though his was the supporting role opposite frequent collaborator and good pal Gary Cooper, Brennan was in nearly every scene playing antagonistic Roy Bean, the dictatorial town judge whose obsession with lovely traveling entertainer, his "Jersey Lilly," Lilly Langtry became his Achilles' heel.

1940 was a great year for Best Supporting Actor, with Brennan up against Albert Bassermann as a murdered (or was he?) Dutch statesman in Hitchcock's *Foreign Correspondent*, William Gargan as a foreman with questionable loyalties in *They Knew What They Wanted*, Jack Oakie hilariously pooching his lips to parody Mussolini in *The Great Dictator*, and James Stephenson, dying of cancer during production, defending accused murderer Bette Davis in *The Letter*. That Brennan earned a record-setting third Academy Award over such a stellar cadre of performances is testimony to his work in the movie, and the reverence he engendered from his peers. Brennan set another Oscar record with William Wyler's classic *The Westerner*: He became the first

Cole Harden (Gary Cooper) and Judge Roy Bean (Walter Brennan) toasted in *The Westerner* (1940), the film that made Brennan the first person to win three acting Oscars.

star to give two Academy Award-winning performances under the same director. Brennan remains the only person in Oscar history with three supporting Oscars, and he leads the small, unprecedented roster of competitive triple crowners: Katharine Hepburn (the only star to eventually best his total wins, winning four for Best Actress); Ingrid Bergman, Jack Nicholson, and Meryl Streep (who all earned two lead and one supporting Oscar); and Daniel Day-Lewis (whose three wins were all for Best Actor). Because most of the hundreds of other roles he played were in Westerns, which the Academy is slow to recognize, Brennan played parts in only two movies besides all the aforementioned that competed for Oscars. In 1948, *Red River* was up for two Academy Awards, and 1963's *How the West Was Won* was victorious in three of its eight nominated categories. Rather than rely on false affectation in any of his performances, Brennan used eccentricities to flesh out his characterizations, proving long before he became a TV icon that he had always been the real McCoy.

10. *Elizabeth Taylor*

    1957 Best Actress as belle Susanna Drake in *Raintree County*
    1958 Best Actress as wife Maggie Pollitt in *Cat on a Hot Tin Roof*
    1959 Best Actress as cousin Catherine Holly in *Suddenly, Last Summer*
    1960 Best Actress as model Gloria Wandrous in *BUtterfield 8*
    1966 Best Actress as professor's wife Martha in *Who's Afraid of Virginia Woolf?*
    1992 Jean Hersholt Humanitarian Award

Inimitable violet eyes that glistened on screen as startlingly as the massive gems Richard Burton rained on her during their headline-dominating affair. A perfect figure that had Maggie Pollitt's pastel chiffon clinging to every curve like a cat on a hot tin roof. A ferocious independence and Cleopatran confidence that made her the first actor to earn a million dollars per picture. A career that blossomed amid the rubble of a collapsing studio system, making her the last movie star of Hollywood's golden era. These are the qualities that made Elizabeth Taylor a legend. But it was her commitment to her craft and a willingness to transform her personal hardships, of which she had more than a lifetime to endure, that gave Taylor respect from her colleagues in the industry, and the ear of a society only willing to acknowledge the universal impact of AIDS when heard through her lilting pleas. Like contemporary and friend Roddy McDowall, Taylor left England and took Hollywood by storm as a child star who partnered with animals for her most famous early roles. In *Lassie Come Home*, which earned an Oscar nomination in 1943, it was Taylor's character Priscilla who had the courage to release the collie to make its way back to McDowall. 1945's *National Velvet* brought Taylor a lead role worthy of her talents. Riding "The Pie" to a national championship brought the 13-year-old the international acclaim she sustained until her death at age 79. She was a porcelain doll as Amy Marsh in the 1949 remake of *Little Women*, and she radiated in white lace as the daughter swept into a new life, leaving behind her befuddled but enriched *Father of the Bride*, Best Actor nominee Spencer Tracy. In *A Place in the Sun* the next year, 19-year-old Taylor was the only member of the love triangle formed with Montgomery Clift and Shelley Winters not up for the Oscar. But, as filmed in stark close up by director George Stevens, Taylor's passion permeated the screen, and instantly she reigned over the Hollywood heavens. In 1956, she again was the Academy's only overlooked member of a *Giant* love triangle, this one with onscreen husband Rock Hudson and roustabout wildcatter James Dean. That changed the following year when she reteamed with *A Place in the Sun* star and personal friend Montgomery Clift to play a scheming Southern belle in Edward Dmytryk's *Raintree County*. That first Best Actress nod started a domino effect of nominations that continued until she won in 1960 for *BUtterfield 8*. Between them, she sizzled atop that hot tin roof as Paul Newman's sexually dismissed wife in Tennessee Williams' Pulitzer Prize classic. Her character's underlying forlorn desperation came from the immediate grief Taylor suffered during filming at the loss of third husband, producer Mike Todd. The following year, Montgomery Clift once again brought Taylor Academy luck when they appeared together in *Suddenly, Last Summer*. Winning the Golden Globe for her performance as Catherine gave Taylor an edge to win the 1959 Best Actress Oscar, but Simone Signoret made *Room at the Top* for the Oscar statuette that went to her instead. The next year, everything aligned for Taylor's first Oscar victory. Neither ungenerous reviews for *BUtterfield 8* nor Taylor's derision of the film, which she was forced to make in order to accept the million dollar role of *Cleopatra*, could stand in her way. Her recent brush with death and frail ascent to the Academy stage aided by new husband Eddie Fisher made Taylor's win historic. Her subsequent relationship with Richard Burton launched a tabloid frenzy, and the talented pair's big screen collaborations throughout the 1960s were all Oscar winners. *Cleopatra* won four, *The V.I.P.s* gave Margaret Rutherford a Best Supporting Actress trophy, and "The Shadow of Your Smile" from *The Sandpiper* won Best Song. But *Who's Afraid of Virginia Woolf?* surpassed every previous hit.

Taylor was lauded for not only her braying and brittle interpretation of husband-crushing Martha, but also her courage for jeopardizing her beautiful screen image by gaining weight and tackling a character much older than her 34 years. While censors balked at the adult content, audiences embraced the film, and the Academy honored Taylor with her second Oscar in six years. Three decades later, Taylor stood at Oscar's podium to accept the Jean Hersholt

Martha (Elizabeth Taylor) regaled Nick (George Segal) with insulting tales of husband George (Richard Burton) in the searing *Who's Afraid of Virginia Woolf?* (1966).

Humanitarian Award from Angela Lansbury, who played her older sister in *National Velvet*. Taylor's acting made her a legend in Hollywood, but her fight against AIDS, partly prompted by the death of Rock Hudson, the friend who played her husband in *Giant*, made her a worldwide heroine.

9. Gary Cooper

    1936 Best Actor as tallow works co-owner Longfellow Deeds in *Mr. Deeds Goes to Town*
    1941 Best Actor as army sergeant Alvin C. York in *Sergeant York*
    1942 Best Actor as baseball player Lou Gehrig in *The Pride of the Yankees*
    1943 Best Actor as American university instructor Robert Jordan in *For Whom the Bell Tolls*
    1952 Best Actor as sheriff Will Kane in *High Noon*
    1960 Honorary lifetime achievement award "for his many memorable screen performances and the international recognition he, as an individual, has gained for the motion picture industry"

Part I. The Countdown

With lips pursed as tight as his concerned, often wary eyes, Gary Cooper never had to say much on screen. His mere presence assured audiences that he alone was willing to carry the weight of the world. That heroism first embedded him naturally in romantic war hero roles. Near the beginning of his career, Cooper made a brief but impactful impression as Cadet White in *Wings*, which was named Best Picture of 1927/28 at the Academy's first ceremony. Three years later, the Academy next noticed Cooper in Josef von Sternberg's Best Director-nominated *Morocco*. As Légionnaire Private Tom Brown, Cooper fell for a risqué nightclub singer played by Best Actress nominee Marlene Dietrich. He donned a World War I uniform to play an archetypal Hemingway hero, Frederic Henry in the 1932 adaptation of *A Farewell to Arms*, which was up for Best Picture but which earned no acting nods. Having Hemingway say he considered Cooper the embodiment of his autobiographical central character helped the world connect to its favorite author of the time through a different medium. As Lieutenant Alan McGregor in 1935's *The Lives of a Bengal Lancer*, Cooper was in his last Best Picture-nominated film before he too started amassing nominations. Frank Capra chose Cooper to play the title character in *Mr. Deeds Goes to Town*, enabling Cooper to embody multiple nuances of the persona for which he would remain most beloved.

Tall and laconic, he carried his small town integrity with a bashfulness that made his tuba-playing greeting card poet comically approachable, while his moral clarity made Deeds a fearless champion of values that audiences trusted most. His chance at Oscar during his first competition was bolstered by the fact that he was also in *The General Died at Dawn*, which put Akim Tamiroff in the Best Supporting Actor race. Despite Oscar newcomer Cooper's appeal as Deeds, the Academy was determined to finally honor the decade's dominating actor, Paul Muni in *The Story of Louis Pasteur*. As foils to star Cooper in future projects, other actors after Tamiroff contended for supporting Oscars, including nominee Brian Donlevy in *Beau Geste* (1939) and 1940's winner, Walter Brennan in *The Westerner*. As the U.S. entered World War II, Cooper found the perfect vehicle to inspire Europe-bound American soldiers and engender hope that honor can win global combats as *Sergeant York*, a pacifist who becomes an unsuspecting war hero. Like Hemingway, the real Alvin York thought Cooper embodied him perfectly, and had in fact insisted that he would only sell the film rights to his story if Cooper portrayed him. Already a top box office attraction for many years leading to his first Oscar-winning performance, Cooper was the main reason *Sergeant York* became the top moneymaker of 1941. At that year's Oscars, Cooper again had multiple hit movies in contention, as he shone opposite Best Actress nominee Barbara Stanwyck in *Ball of Fire*, a screwball comedy that, like *Sergeant York*, was directed by Howard Hawks. James Stewart,

Even with the help of butler Walter (Raymond Walburn), Longfellow Deeds (Gary Cooper) couldn't get a foothold on his new prestige in *Mr. Deeds Goes to Town* (1936).

Cooper's close friend and the previous year's Best Actor winner, presented him the Oscar, which Cooper shyly, and humorously accepted by admitting that when he dreamed of this moment he always made a good speech. Cooper was on an Oscar roll in the early 1940s, and followed that win with a portrayal of Lou Gehrig in *The Pride of the Yankees*, which concluded with Cooper's iconic "luckiest man on the face of the Earth" speech. Cooper played another Hemingway hero, Robert Jordan in *For Whom the Bell Tolls*, ringing in his fourth nomination in 1943. With age and a heavy heart chiseling lines into his face, Cooper conveyed the same heroic persona transformed by time as Will Kane, the marshal who alone defended Hadleyville from a vengeful bandit arriving at *High Noon*. On Oscar night, the absent Cooper's prize was accepted by friend John Wayne, who drew laughs by using the moment to question why Cooper got the part of Kane instead of him. Three days after Cooper underwent surgery for prostate cancer in 1961, the Academy honored him with a lifetime achievement award. Only close friends in the industry knew Coop's fatal prognosis, but it became apparent to all when James Stewart began weeping while accepting the honor on Cooper's behalf. Less than a month later, Cooper died, leaving behind the legacy of motion picture's most staid and accessible hero.

8. Daniel Day-Lewis

1989 Best Actor as author/painter/poet Christy Brown in *My Left Foot*
1993 Best Actor as son/suspected terrorist Gerry Conlon in *In the Name of the Father*
2002 Best Actor as gang leader Bill "The Butcher" Cutting in *Gangs of New York*
2007 Best Actor as mineral prospector Daniel Plainview in *There Will Be Blood*
2012 Best Actor as U.S. President Abraham Lincoln in *Lincoln*

The first time Day-Lewis held a golden trophy on Oscar's stage, he grinned, "You've just provided me with the makings of one hell of a weekend in Dublin." With the devilish delivery of his quip and hair cascading to his shoulders, he gave the impression of a free spirit driven by artistic whims of a Dionysian appetite. Nothing is farther from Day-Lewis' career focus, commitment, and selectivity. Day-Lewis has always had an uncanny ability to choose and then help create classics. At age 14, he vandalized cars in 1970 Best Director nominee John Schlesinger's groundbreaking *Sunday Bloody Sunday*. Day-Lewis expanded his on screen thuggery by bullying Best Actor Ben Kingsley in the 1982 Best Picture *Gandhi*. International stardom came in 1985 with *My Beautiful Laundrette*, which the Academy cited for its screenplay. Day-Lewis bathed in a richer Oscar pool as comic, split-infinitive criticizing snob Cecil Vyse in *A Room with a View*, which entered the 1986 Oscar race with eight nominations. The New York Film Critics and the National Board of Review named Day-Lewis Best Supporting Actor for both performances, but Oscar nominated *A Room with a View* co-star Denholm Elliott instead. By 1989, Day-Lewis fully immersed himself in the role of physically and spiritually mangled Christy Brown in Jim Sheridan's film adaptation of the bestselling 1954 autobiography, *My Left Foot*. Irate, sexual, and diversely creative, Day-Lewis' Christy Brown was no endearing *Charly* or *Rain Man*. But that wasn't the only reason Day-Lewis was not favored to win that Best Actor Oscar. This was his first nomination, and for a small Irish drama. Dustin Hoffman had only the year before won Best Actor for another challenged character in *Rain Man*. Tom Cruise, also in a wheelchair as Ron Kovic in *Born on the Fourth of July*, was heavily favored over Day-Lewis for his masterful rendering of a difficult role. Robin Williams inspired as teacher

John Keating in *Dead Poets Society*. Morgan Freeman was ever patient as Hoke in *Driving Miss Daisy*, and Kenneth Branagh motivated as *Henry V*. When Day-Lewis won he paid tribute to the legacy of Christy Brown. In a throwback to his early hooligan roles, Day-Lewis reunited with director Sheridan in 1993 to play a wrongly convicted Guildford Four bomber in *In the Name of the Father*. Although Day-Lewis also had *The Age of Innocence* on Oscar ballots that year, the exposure couldn't overshadow Tom Hanks in *Philadelphia*. Though physically dirty, he remained unbesmirched standing on principle as John Proctor in *The Crucible*, but only Joan Allen as his wife earned an Oscar nod in 1996. As violent ringleader Bill the Butcher in Martin Scorsese's *Gangs of New York*, Day-Lewis remained on the wrong side of the law. The Academy leaned toward him or Jack Nicholson of *About Schmidt* to take Best Actor in 2002, but newcomer Adrien Brody slipped through as *The Pianist*. Then came *There Will Be Blood* and *Lincoln*. His two characters embodied divergent aspects of the same cultural manifestation. The image of Day-Lewis staring out the window at the empire awaiting him tapped into the American dream from its industrial foundation in *There Will Be Blood*. But that same profile of him bearded with eyes downturned as a President laden by the burden of reuniting a nation reached for the American dream from its loftiest philosophical heights. He was favored to win in 2007, and took the prize easily.

In 2012, he joined Henry Fonda of *On Golden Pond* and Meryl Streep of *Sophie's Choice* as perhaps the most certain victors of any Oscar race. Selective Day-Lewis has the highest ratio of movies-to-award honored performances of any multiple Academy Award-

His penetrating depiction of *Lincoln* (2012) made Daniel Day-Lewis the first male to win three lead acting Academy Awards.

winning star in history. In only 23 motion pictures, Day-Lewis has garnered 128 nominations and 95 victories. For *Lincoln*, he won 29 of the 43 acting competitions, among the most for any single performance ever. In the history of movie awards, only six actors have won an Oscar, BAFTA, Golden Globe, SAG, and Critic's Choice Best Actor for a single performance. Of those six, Day-Lewis is the only one to reach that milestone twice, for *There Will Be Blood* and *Lincoln*. His most recent Academy Award win placed him with Walter Brennan and Jack Nicholson as the only male actors to win three competitive acting Oscars, but above them because he is the only one to earn all his awards for leading roles. No female matches his three lead acting victory record, and only Katharine Hepburn, who won four Best Actress prizes, surpasses it. A solid, sinewy craftsman, Day-Lewis splits his characters at the bone to convey their marrow. Audiences and the Academy are appropriately awed.

7. Bette Davis

1935 Best Actress as actress Joyce Heath in *Dangerous*
1938 Best Actress as belle Julie Marsden in *Jezebel*
1939 Best Actress as socialite/heiress Judith Traherne in *Dark Victory*
1940 Best Actress as murderer Leslie Crosbie in *The Letter*
1941 Best Actress as aristocrat Regina Hubbard Giddens in *The Little Foxes*
1942 Best Actress as spinster Charlotte Vale in *Now, Voyager*
1944 Best Actress as socialite Fanny Trellis Skeffington in *Mr. Skeffington*
1950 Best Actress as actress Margo Channing in *All About Eve*
1952 Best Actress as actress Margaret Elliot in *The Star*
1962 Best Actress as former child star Jane Hudson in *What Ever Happened to Baby Jane?*

Davis carved her own fate in the Hollywood pantheon and aptly chose motion pictures as the medium so it could be sustained on celluloid. Ravenously determined to establish a soaring star legacy, Davis could be abrasive. But the polished cinematic results gave her backstage combativeness a delicious intrigue that made Bette Davis as interesting off screen as on. Between and during takes, Davis held nothing back. Through her uniquely voracious acting style, she summoned a vast, mannered repertoire, penetrated with dominating eyes, and calibrated her line delivery to the rhythm of a stalling car. She loved the Oscars not only because competitiveness inspired her like a race horse, but also because she could not help but respond to the adoration the Academy tossed toward her like wreaths of roses. She was still building a career until she devoured Leslie Howard in *Of Human Bondage*. But the glaring omission of Davis from the 1934 Best Actress list, which only included three actresses, inspired the Academy's first write-in campaign. After Davis lost to *It Happened One Night*'s Claudette Colbert, the Academy atoned by handing Davis the Best Actress trophy the following year for *Dangerous*. Although Davis publicly badmouthed the film, winning that first Oscar quickened her competitive blood, and she set a goal to become the Academy's winningest actor. She missed that achievement by one year. In 1937, Luise Rainer became the most Oscared actress by winning her second prize for *The Good Earth*. The next year, Davis tied that record in the same category by taking her second Oscar as a defiant Southern *Jezebel*le. That same year, Best Supporting Actor Walter Brennan also won his second Oscar, and two years later he won a third, an achievement Davis never reached. Davis allegedly was offered the role in *Jezebel* as consolation for not getting to play Scarlett O'Hara, a rejection that cut deeply. Davis likely found small comfort in beating Vivien Leigh by one year to become the first to win Best Actress for playing a Southern spitfire. Though Davis missed setting the record as most Oscared star, she set many others, and is included in more Oscar lore than most any star. She took credit for naming the Academy's statuette Oscar, a not-entirely disputed legend that seems more accurately accredited to early Academy board secretary Margaret Herrick. But Davis' take, that the trophy's posterior looked like her ex-husband's (Harmon Oscar Nelson), is more scintillating than Herrick's pronouncement that the statue reminded her of her Uncle Oscar. Davis' 1938 Academy Award nomination began an unprecedented run of nominations in five consecutive years, a feat soon tied by Greer Garson but never surpassed. Davis' performances during that stretch were all classics. She wrung tears from even the most jaded moviegoers with her heroic surrender to a "prognosis negative" in *Dark Victory*. She set another Academy record the following year by being nominated as murderous Leslie Crosbie in *The Letter*, the same role for which Jeanne Eagels was up in 1928/29. One would think that being an unfaithful wife, killer, and litigious manipulator would be the most unsympathetic character Davis could find, but she outdid herself the following year as mendacious Regina in *The Little Foxes*. Expected to win, Davis surprisingly lost to Joan Fontaine in *Suspicion*. That loss may have occurred because Davis, elected the Academy's first female president that year, resigned the post after only two months. Movie fans could more easily root for Davis in her fifth consecutive nominated performance as an abused waif who blossoms thanks to a shipboard romance with Paul Henried in *Now, Voyager*. Two years later, she took advantage of a vulnerable *Mr. Skeffington* to earn her seventh nomination. In her last three spins in the Best Actress circle, Davis played fading or former stars. As *All About Eve*'s vain, aging thespian, Davis swaggered up the stairs, trademark cigarette in hand, to warn guests to "fasten your seat belts. It's going to be a bumpy night,"

Part I. The Countdown

As the crazed sister of Blanche (Joan Crawford) and title character in *What Ever Happened to Baby Jane?* (1962), Bette Davis became the first to earn ten Academy Award nominations for acting.

creating one of the most repeated, montaged scenes in film history. As *The Star*, her career was behind her by a few years. In *What Ever Happened to Baby Jane?*, it lay in the dusty recesses of a doll-immortalized childhood.

That tenth nod in 1962 made Davis the first with double digit acting nominations. In the fifty plus years since Davis reached that milestone, only Laurence Olivier has tied her, while 12-time nominees Katharine Hepburn and Jack Nicholson, and 20-times pegged Meryl Streep have surpassed her. Ambitious Davis wanted to be Oscar's greatest star. Add to her bevy of bravura performances the drama of a lifelong list of backlot brawls, and Davis may actually have succeeded.

6. *Ingrid Bergman*

1943 Best Actress as guerrilla María in *For Whom the Bell Tolls*
1944 Best Actress as opera star trainee Paula Alquist in *Gaslight*
1945 Best Actress as nun Sister Mary Benedict in *The Bells of St. Mary's*

1948 Best Actress as crusader Joan of Arc in *Joan of Arc*
1956 Best Actress as daughter of Russian Tsar or imposter Anna Koreff in *Anastasia*
1974 Best Supporting Actress as missionary Greta Ohlsson in *Murder on the Orient Express*
1978 Best Actress as pianist Charlotte Andergast in *Autumn Sonata*

While watching the Swedish language movie *Intermezzo*, David O. Selznick saw in young starlet Ingrid Bergman an angelic freshness that veiled as yet untapped darker emotions all strongarming for dominant revelation. At the time he couldn't know that a series of childhood tragedies that took from Bergman her parents and multiple guardians opened a vast wellspring of emotions that Bergman could access to play a rebel, victim, visionary, conqueror, suicidal amnesiac, religious fanatic, and virtuoso. Each of those seven personae brought Bergman to Oscar's table, where she feasted on one of the most sumptuous, and briefly soured, careers in international film history. Selznick introduced Bergman to American audiences in an English remake of *Intermezzo*. The 70-minute film earned two Oscar nominations and made Bergman so instantly beloved that the studio groomed her career with a seraphim of roles that made her so increasingly angelic she literally graduated to playing a nun in *The Bells of St. Mary's* to a martyred saint in *Joan of Arc*. The final casting proved prophetic. Rising to that pivotal career moment, however, Bergman would become one of the world's most respected stars. Her fresh beauty required little makeup, inviting the camera to see nuances of expression that seemed to intensify her screen impact. In 1943, the Academy faced a tough decision: for which of her two brilliant performances should they nominate her? In the most famous role of her career, she played Ilsa to Humphrey Bogart's Rick in the timely World War II romance *Casablanca*. Yet she was more unique as a shorthaired, dark complected Spanish rebel in *For Whom the Bell Tolls*. At Oscar time, Bogart and his "beautiful friendship" with Claude Rains brought only them acting nominations for *Casablanca*. Instead, Bergman stepped up to the Best Actress race via *For Whom the Bell Tolls* as the expected champion over fellow first-time nominees Jean Arthur (*The More the Merrier*) and Jennifer Jones (*The Song of Bernadette*), and recent winners, *The Constant Nymph* Joan Fontaine, and, as *Madame Curie*, Greer Garson, who opened the Best Actress envelope and announced Jones the winner. A gracious Jones found Bergman later that night to apologize for taking her Oscar. The Academy made up for Bergman's loss the next year by naming her Best Actress as the young wife slowly driven mad by husband Charles Boyer in the shadows of a flickering *Gaslight*. Bergman's third and fourth consecutive nominations moved her from a convent to a burning stake. But at the end of the decade where she, Bette Davis, and Greer

Garson dominated the Oscars, her sainted image was defiled when she fell in love with *Stromboli* director Roberto Rossellini. Although they divorced their spouses and wed, disillusioned Hollywood rebuked Bergman. The industry didn't reconcile with Bergman until she divorced Rossellini. It extended its most blatant apology by awarding Bergman her second Best Actress statuette for *Anastasia*. Still in exile in Europe where she'd continued her career, Bergman did not attend the 1956 Oscars, and friend Cary Grant accepted on her behalf. To present Best Picture two years later, Grant called to Oscar's stage "a great actress and a great lady. Welcome back, Ingrid Bergman." With her standing ovation rattling the Pantages Theatre, Bergman knew that, as she put it, she went "from saint to whore and back to saint again." At the 1968 Oscars, Bergman had the memorable task of announcing the first Best Actress tie in Academy history, recognizing the absent Katharine Hepburn and extending Oscar to Barbra Streisand. When gathering his illustrious cast to take part in a gruesome late night *Murder on the Orient Express*, director Sidney Lumet asked Bergman to play ghost-white Princess Dragomiroff. But Bergman was more intrigued by shriveling, penitent Greta Ohlsson.

Though her character was featured prominently in only two scenes, astute Lumet knew to leave the camera on Bergman and let her spin her shuddering comic magic. The result: Bergman set a new Oscar record as the first person with three acting Oscars to win in both lead and supporting categories. Before her, the only actors with three victories were Walter Brennan, all Best Supporting Actor wins, and Katharine Hepburn, all for Best Actress. (Hepburn's fourth came seven years after Bergman won her last Oscar.) Only a person who has just tied a record-setting number of Oscar wins could get away with using the line "It's always nice to win an Oscar" as a subordinate clause to a more relevant point

Ingrid Bergman (as Greta Ohlsson) co-starred with so many other actors suspected of *Murder on the Orient Express* (1974), hers was the shortest performance to win an actor a third Academy Award.

during an acceptance speech. In lieu of the usual thank-yous, Bergman apologized to expected winner Valentina Cortese of *Day for Night* for taking her Oscar. That gracious, sophisticated gesture epitomized Bergman's true character, which history has embraced and the Academy wisely acknowledged.

5. *Paul Newman*

1958 Best Actor as ex-football star Brick Pollitt in *Cat on a Hot Tin Roof*
1961 Best Actor as pool hustler "Fast Eddie" Felson in *The Hustler*
1963 Best Actor as cowboy Hud Bannon in *Hud*
1967 Best Actor as convict Luke Jackson in *Cool Hand Luke*
1968 Best Picture as producer of *Rachel, Rachel*
1981 Best Actor as liquor wholesaler Michael Gallagher in *Absence of Malice*
1982 Best Actor as lawyer Frank Galvin in *The Verdict*
1985 Honorary lifetime achievement award "in recognition of his many and memorable compelling screen performances and for his personal integrity and dedication to his craft"
1986 Best Actor as pool hustler/liquor salesman/stakehorse "Fast Eddie" Felson in *The Color of Money*
1993 Jean Hersholt Humanitarian Award
1994 Best Actor as freelance construction worker Sully in *Nobody's Fool*
2002 Best Supporting Actor as organized crime boss John Rooney in *Road to Perdition*

Like his characters, which added swagger to the antiestablishment idealism of a new generation, Newman was a beautiful rebel. Reticent to indulge the excessive adulation heaped upon him by movie lovers, he graciously accepted the Academy's long delayed recognitions later in his career. It took the Academy over three decades, but when the accolades came, Newman pocketed the victories like a Fast Eddie pool shot where the balls finally align to be sunk in quick succession. First famous as Rocky Graziano in *Somebody Up There Likes Me*, everyone seemed to except the Academy, who nominated the movie for three 1956 Oscars, but not for acting. The Southern heat agreed with Newman in 1958. He won Best Actor at Cannes for *The Long, Hot Summer*, and was Oscar-tagged as Brick Pollitt, hobbled by a broken leg, fractured family, and sexual secrets in *Cat on a Hot Tin Roof*. "Too hungry" as *The Hustler*, Fast Eddie Felson, Newman embodied the new rebel of the 1960s.

His ambition and ambivalence struck a chord with the public and the Academy, and Newman seemed destined to win an Oscar as Felson. He would, a quarter century after losing the 1961 Best Actor race to Maximilian Schell in *Judgment at Nuremberg*. Every major player except Newman was

In 1961 George C. Scott (as Bert Gordon) watched *The Hustler* Paul Newman clear the table as Fast Eddie Felson, a character that would eventually earn Newman his long-awaited Best Actor prize.

nominated in 1962 for *Sweet Bird of Youth*, but he was back on the roster in 1963. Newman combined his family displeasure in *Cat on a Hot Tin Roof* with his emotional rootlessness of *The Hustler* to portray *Hud* as a spoiled, demanding cowboy. Given the choice to embrace one aspect of that era's social upheaval, the Academy opted for racial inclusion by selecting Sidney Poitier for *Lilies of the Field* over Hud's hedonistic disregard of his elders. 1967's Best Actor race was anyone's to win. Newman added an egg-bloated gut full of humor to his antiheroism as inmate *Cool Hand Luke*, but was the only Best Actor nominee from a film not up for Best Picture. Newman, *The Graduate* Dustin Hoffman, Warren Beatty in *Bonnie and Clyde*, and Spencer Tracy in *Guess Who's Coming to Dinner* all lost to Rod Steiger solving a crime committed *In the Heat of the Night*. Then Newman expanded his film contribution by producing and directing his wife Joanne Woodward to an Oscar nod in *Rachel, Rachel*. Newman was up, too, not for Best Director, but as producer in the Best Picture category. Neither won. Finally in the 1980s the pool balls started aligning. He was up for *Absence of Malice*, but 1981 belonged to Henry Fonda in *On Golden Pond*. The following year, Newman bared his soul in *The Verdict* as a shamed lawyer seeking redemption from a past still clinking in his head like liquor-soaked ice cubes. In another great year for Best Actor, Newman was favored to win over veterans Dustin Hoffman as dress-donning *Tootsie*, Jack Lemmon searching for a *Missing* son and ideology, and swashbuckling Peter O'Toole in *My Favorite Year*. But *Gandhi* dominated in 1982, and Ben Kingsley's epic performance in an epic film gave the newcomer the prize. After nearly thirty years of losing Oscar competitions, his lifetime achievement award may have seemed rueful consolation to Newman, who accepted via satellite in 1985. But to everyone's delight, the following year Newman easily took the Best Actor prize as a wiser and not-quite-so Fast Eddie in *The Color of Money*, Martin Scorsese's sequel to *The Hustler*. In 1993, the Academy's Board of Governors unanimously selected Newman for his "bottomless compassion" to receive the Jean Hersholt Humanitarian Award. Superstitious about attending in competitive years, Newman was finally present to accept his third Academy Award. His reputation for professionalism added heft and complexity to Oscar contenders throughout the decades. He was a formidable presence in grand scale features such as *Exodus* (1960) and *The Towering Inferno* (1974), box office shattering buddy pics *Butch Cassidy and the Sundance Kid* (1969) and *The Sting* (Best Picture of 1973), and features that brought him two final Oscar nominations, *Nobody's Fool* and *The Road to Perdition*. His long, stellar career helped define a generation, and then inspired some of the most impactful altruistic efforts, both acknowledged by the Academy.

4. Laurence Olivier

1939 Best Actor as foundling Heathcliff in *Wuthering Heights*
1940 Best Actor as aristocratic widower Maxim de Winter in *Rebecca*
1946 Best Actor as nobleman/King of England Henry V in *Henry V*
1946 Honorary award "for his outstanding achievement as actor, producer and director in bringing *Henry V* to the screen"
1948 Best Actor as prince of Denmark Hamlet in *Hamlet*
1948 Best Director for *Hamlet*
1956 Best Actor as Lord Protector/King of England Richard III in *Richard III*
1960 Best Actor as music hall stage performer Archie Rice in *The Entertainer*
1965 Best Actor as Moor of Venice Othello in *Othello*
1972 Best Actor as writer/country squire Andrew Wyke in *Sleuth*
1976 Best Supporting Actor as dentist/fugitive Nazi war criminal Dr. Christian Szell in *Marathon Man*

1978 Best Actor as Nazi hunter Ezra Lieberman in *The Boys from Brazil*
1978 Honorary lifetime achievement award "for the full body of his work, for the unique achievements of his entire career and his lifetime of contribution to the art of film"

Laurence Olivier holds the enviable status as the quintessential thespian, grand lord master of the craft of acting. Logically, his most admired performances universally connect him with William Shakespeare, who shares that unprecedented status as a writer. On the London stage, Olivier's first affiliation with The Bard came for a 1935 production of *Romeo and Juliet*. The following year, the first film adaptation of the tragic love story to earn Academy Award consideration cast Leslie Howard as Romeo opposite Best Actress nominee Norma Shearer's Juliet. But Hollywood would not take long to beckon Olivier for interpreting, not Shakespeare, but Emily Brontë. Olivier's brooding avenger Heathcliff cast a pall from Thrushcross Grange to *Wuthering Heights*. Just months before Olivier married Vivien Leigh, both were nominated for their first Oscars, with Leigh winning Best Actress for *Gone with the Wind* and Olivier losing Best Actor to fellow Brit Robert Donat in *Goodbye, Mr. Chips*. Olivier was up again the next year, this time grieving for his irreplaceable (new bride Joan Fontaine finds out a little too late) dead wife *Rebecca*. The Hitchcock hit won Best Picture, but Best Actor went to James Stewart in *The Philadelphia Story*. After World War II, the Academy again recognized Olivier and his film, *Henry V*. He might have been a lead contender for Best Actor of 1946 had the board of governors not ensured an Oscar victory

When the Academy voted Laurence Olivier Best Actor of 1948 for *Hamlet*, he became the first star to direct himself to a competitive acting Oscar.

by preparing for him an honorary award for starring in, producing, and directing *Henry V*. Prior to 1950 the Academy gave the Best Picture trophy to the production company, not the producers, so Olivier, *Henry V*'s sole producer, was not recognized as a nominee for his own film. The same rang true two years later when he adapted *Hamlet*, which won Best Picture.

For *Hamlet* Olivier did earn nominations as Best Director, which went to John Huston for *The Treasure of the Sierra Madre*, and Best Actor. At the time, Olivier seemed to have competition for the 1948 Best Actor prize primarily from young Montgomery Clift in *The Search*, with some consideration going to Clifton Webb in his third nomination, and first as lead actor, as persnickety Mr. Belvedere in *Sitting Pretty*. In retrospect, Olivier was sitting pretty on Oscar's perch since *Hamlet*, trimmed and simplified for the general public, proved a box office hit, and the New York Film Critics named Olivier their Best Actor. When he won at the Oscars, absent Olivier had friend Douglas Fairbanks, Jr., accept for him. Besides setting and duplicating his Academy record as the only actor to win doing Shakespeare, Olivier was also the first honorary Oscar winner to earn a competitive acting trophy. Two more Best Actor bids came for Shakespeare on celluloid, first directing himself as *Richard III*, then giving Stuart Burge the honors in *Othello*. Amid those nominations, Olivier continued to mesmerize the Academy in character studies (*The Entertainer*), mysteries (*Sleuth*), and thrillers, where his dental torture of *Marathon Man* Dustin Hoffman ranked him among the cruelest villains in movie history. In 1978, Olivier duplicated his 1946 success by competing for a Best Actor Oscar the same year he was guaranteed an honorary win. Presenting the lifetime achievement award, Cary Grant aptly summed up Olivier's career impact by beaming, "no man has graced his profession better than Larry Olivier has graced ours. He represents the ultimate in acting. He is the actor's most admired actor.... A remarkable achievement unmatched in range or stature."

3. *Jack Nicholson*

1969 Best Supporting Actor as lawyer George Hanson in *Easy Rider*
1970 Best Actor as oil rig worker Robert Eroica Dupea in *Five Easy Pieces*
1973 Best Actor as U.S. Navy Signalman First Class Billy "Bad Ass" Buddusky in *The Last Detail*
1974 Best Actor as detective J. J. Gittes in *Chinatown*
1975 Best Actor as recidivist criminal Randle Patrick McMurphy in *One Flew Over the Cuckoo's Nest*
1981 Best Supporting Actor as playwright Eugene O'Neill in *Reds*

1983 Best Supporting Actor as former astronaut Garrett Breedlove in *Terms of Endearment*
1985 Best Actor as mob hit man Charley Partanna in *Prizzi's Honor*
1987 Best Actor as homeless former baseball player Francis Phelan in *Ironweed*
1992 Best Supporting Actor as Commanding Officer/U.S. Army Colonel Nathan R. Jessep in *A Few Good Men*
1997 Best Actor as novelist Melvin Udall in *As Good as It Gets*
2002 Best Actor as actuary Warren Schmidt in *About Schmidt*

Aptly, Oscar's ultimate bad boy earned his first Academy Award nomination as a character who abandons his traditional job as a lawyer to hitch a motorcycle ride with psychedelic American Dreamers Peter Fonda and Dennis Hopper in *Easy Rider*. Because Nicholson always pushed the envelope, it took a little while for his name to be called whenever it was opened on Oscar night. He lost his first Oscar competition to Gig Young in *They Shoot Horses, Don't They?*, but he was back the following year for another road film. With *Five Easy Pieces*, Nicholson graduated from supporting player to central figure not only of the movie, but also as a voice of a disillusioned generation. The confrontation building to his table-clearing outburst in *Five Easy Pieces* epitomized the madness of a society built on freedom but unwilling to honor individuality. In the early 1970s, the Academy wasn't afraid of controversy, as its choice for Oscar-rebuking George C. Scott proved. But even then, Nicholson may have been a bit too fringe to hit the Oscar bullseye. In *The Last Detail*, his rabblerousing sailor illustrated an appealing hunger for savoring life to the marrow, but Oscar honored instead Jack Lemmon in the more somber *Save the Tiger*. The 1974 Best Actor bout placed *Chinatown*'s Nicholson and *The Godfather Part II*'s Al Pacino at the center of the ring. Thanks in part to the Old Hollywood noir atmosphere of *Chinatown*, Nicholson's J.J. Gittes appealed to both his hipper young followers and more traditional older Academy members who expressed previously underappreciated respect for Nicholson's craft. Oscar waxed nostalgic again, giving the prize to multiple Emmy-winning comedy star Art Carney in *Harry and Tonto*. When *One Flew Over the Cuckoo's Nest* and *Dog Day Afternoon* ushered in a menagerie of nominations in 1975, Nicholson and Pacino went head-to-head for Best Actor as frontrunners in their third consecutive Best Actor competition. Both were groundbreaking performances in classic films, but it was Nicholson who first broke through as an Oscar-winning actor. Fully aware of his reputation and the role of McMurphy in a mental ward, Nicholson began his thank-yous with, "Well, I guess this proves there are as many nuts in the Academy as anywhere else."

That win ended his 1970s run of Oscar nominations, but he returned in

As R. P. McMurphy, a frustrated rebel confined to a mental hospital in *One Flew Over the Cuckoo's Nest* (1975), Jack Nicholson won his first of three Academy Awards.

the 1980s as a revered master of his craft. He was a haunting Eugene O'Neill in *Reds*, and delighted the Academy to his second victory as a comical retired astronaut sporting a belly round as Jupiter in *Terms of Endearment*. With the win, Nicholson became the first previous Best Actor winner to add a Best Supporting Actor Oscar to his credits. In 1985, critics Gene Siskel and Roger Ebert marveled at his comic brilliance in *Prizzi's Honor*, pointing out how he could stir emotions, even guffaws, by acting with his back to the camera. Once again amid the Best Actor ranks, there was no doubt Nicholson reigned as the master actor of his generation. When he alternated back to Best Actor winner as an OCD-suffering misanthrope in *As Good As It Gets*, Nicholson was first to zigzag his victories as lead, then supporting, then lead winner. In the nearly 100 years of Oscar, only five pairs of actors won Best Actor and Best Actress for the same movie. Two of those pairs included Jack Nicholson, whose *One Flew Over the Cuckoo's Nest* antagonist Louise Fletcher and *As Good As It Gets* sidekick Helen Hunt shared with him Oscar night victories. As a presenter, he has, by far, revealed Best Picture the most. To date, he has presented it eight times, by himself in 1971, 1976, 1977, 1992, and 2005 ("And the Oscar goes to *Crash*—whoa!"), with Warren Beatty in 1989, with Diane Keaton in 2006, and indirectly with First Lady Michelle Obama live from the

White House while Nicholson was on Oscar's stage in 2012. His signature crinkled brow and sunglasses are mere visual aids. It is his expressive delivery of the insights to his characters that has made Nicholson Oscar's most beloved male actor.

2. *Katharine Hepburn*

1932/33 Best Actress as actress Eva Lovelace in *Morning Glory*
1935 Best Actress as daughter Alice Adams in *Alice Adams*
1940 Best Actress as socialite Tracy Lord in *The Philadelphia Story*
1942 Best Actress as journalist Tess Harding in *Woman of the Year*
1951 Best Actress as missionary Rose Sayer in *The African Queen*
1955 Best Actress as traveler Jane Hudson in *Summertime*
1956 Best Actress as spinster/farmer Lizzie Curry in *The Rainmaker*
1959 Best Actress as mother Mrs. Venable in *Suddenly, Last Summer*
1962 Best Actress as wife/mother Mary Tyrone in *Long Day's Journey into Night*
1967 Best Actress as wife/mother Christina Drayton in *Guess Who's Coming to Dinner*
1968 Best Actress as British monarch Queen Eleanor of Aquitaine in *The Lion in Winter*
1981 Best Actress as wife/mother Ethel Thayer in *On Golden Pond*

Some men's interest in pursuing a woman is piqued by her feigned nonchalance about his advances. Other times, a woman's genuine disinterest makes a man obsessively fascinated by her. Such was always the case between Oscar and dynamic, independent Katharine Hepburn, who never once gave the Academy the least attention, and who ended up winning an unprecedented four acting awards. 1932/1933 was the only year none (in this case, because there were only two acting categories, neither) of the winning actors attended the Academy Award ceremony. Charles Laughton didn't make the trip from England, and Katharine Hepburn wasn't interested in an award that, at the time, did not have the professional heft or global impact it has today. In *Morning Glory*, she was an unknown actress hungry for success, and that year's Oscar board favored her performance over May Robson in *Lady for a Day* and Diana Wynyard in the year's Best Picture, *Cavalcade*. Her next nomination came for one of her most appealing characters, *Alice Adams*, a sincere young woman struggling to impress wealthy suitor Fred MacMurray by hiding her family's recent destitution. In 1935, the Academy revealed its vote tallies, and Hepburn came in second to Bette Davis in *Dangerous* to take Best Actress. The late 1930s was Hepburn's infamous "box office poison" phase, which she conquered, in very Hepburn style, by creating her own new opportunity.

She barnstormed Broadway as combative socialite Tracy Lord in *The Philadelphia Story*, then bought the film rights, hired George Cukor to direct, and helped select as cast mates two of Hollywood's hottest male properties, Cary Grant and James Stewart, to create with her a comic love triangle. The result was a classic film, a revived movie career for Hepburn, and a third Best Actress nomination. In 1942, she first teamed with Spencer Tracy as a headstrong professional whose attempts at domesticity drew the most laughs in *Woman of the Year*, and Oscar called again. As before, Hepburn showed no interest. She and Bogie were both considered top contenders in 1951 for *The African Queen*. Bogie triumphed, but Hepburn lost to Vivien Leigh in *A Streetcar Named Desire*. In 1955 desire freed her character Jane Hudson from her shell of isolation as romance blossomed for her on a *Summertime* European vacation. At her most enchanting and vulnerable, Hepburn was up for the Oscar, as was her director, David Lean, but those were *Summertime*'s only nominations, and neither won. But that performance started her on a new

Supported by John Halliday (rear, as Seth Lord), James Stewart (as Mike Connor), Ruth Hussey (rear, as Elizabeth Imbrie) and Cary Grant (as C.K. Dexter Haven), Katharine Hepburn (as Tracy Lord) reignited her movie career with *The Philadelphia Story* (1940).

roll of nominations. She was tomboyish in *The Rainmaker*, and ascended gloriously toward madness about the demise of her relationship with her son ("Sebastian and Violet, Violet and Sebastian") in *Suddenly, Last Summer*, the only movie for which she competed for Best Actress against a co-star (Elizabeth Taylor). Hepburn's tour de force as morphine addict Mary Tyrone in Sidney Lumet's *Long Day's Journey into Night* is considered by some the most powerful interpretation of Eugene O'Neill's iconic character. As they had been in 1935, Hepburn and Bette Davis were both front runners for Best Actress in 1962. Like Hepburn in *Summertime*, Davis played a character named Jane Hudson in *What Ever Happened to Baby Jane?*, and both lost to Anne Bancroft as *The Miracle Worker*. So it seemed that uninterested Hepburn would go down in Oscar history for a single win that helped launch her movie career. Then her record-setting streak began. In 1967 she used her genuine love and anticipated grief over the impending death of the love of her life, *Guess Who's Coming to Dinner* co-star Spencer Tracy, to convey a feast of emotions that the Academy devoured. The next year, as unrelenting exile Eleanor of Aquitaine, she tamed *The Lion in Winter* and tied Best Actress with Barbra Streisand in *Funny Girl*. Her back-to-back wins aligned her Academy legacy with Spencer Tracy, as she became the third actor in Oscar history, after Luise Rainer and her beloved Spence, to win acting Oscars in consecutive years. Thirty-five years after winning her first Academy Award, the Great Kate held the record as the only person with three lead acting Oscars. She broke that record in 1981 and still reigns as the only person to win four acting Academy Awards when she won Best Actress as grounding, morale-boosting wife to declining Henry Fonda during their summer *On Golden Pond*. Of course, Hepburn was not there to accept that award either. Though unimpressed by Oscar, she was neither unkind about nor oblivious to the Academy's generosity. Once in her career, in 1973, Hepburn did grace Oscar's stage to present the Irving G. Thalberg Award to producer, and personal friend, Lawrence Weingarten. Her appearance was kept secret until David Niven introduced her. As she stepped forward in an understated black slack outfit, the audience rose to give Hepburn a standing ovation. She responded, "Thank you very, very much. I am naturally deeply moved. I'm also very happy that I didn't hear anyone call out, 'It's about time.' I'm the living proof that a person can wait 41 years to be unselfish." A towering talent, an indestructible individualist, and finally, a gracious guest, Katharine Hepburn conveyed with dignity and humility why she deserved Oscar's unrequited love.

1. *Meryl Streep*

1978 Best Supporting Actress as grocery store employee/girlfriend Linda in *The Deer Hunter*

1979 Best Supporting Actress as wife/mother Joanna Kramer in *Kramer vs. Kramer*
1981 Best Actress as Victorian woman/contemporary actress Sara Woodruff/Anna in *The French Lieutenant's Woman*
1982 Best Actress as concentration camp survivor/Polish immigrant to U.S. Zofia "Sophie" Zawistowski in *Sophie's Choice*
1983 Best Actress as metallurgy worker Karen Silkwood in *Silkwood*
1985 Best Actress as baroness/coffee plantation owner/writer Karen Blixen (Isak Dinesen) in *Out of Africa*
1987 Best Actress as homeless girlfriend Helen Archer in *Ironweed*
1988 Best Actress as wife/mother Lindy Chamberlain in *A Cry in the Dark*
1990 Best Actress as actress Suzanne Vale in *Postcards from the Edge*
1995 Best Actress as farm wife Francesca Johnson in *The Bridges of Madison County*
1998 Best Actress as wife/mother Kate Gulden in *One True Thing*
1999 Best Actress as music teacher Roberta Guaspari in *Music of the Heart*
2002 Best Supporting Actress as author Susan Orlean in *Adaptation*
2006 Best Actress as magazine editor-in-chief Miranda Priestly in *The Devil Wears Prada*
2008 Best Actress as school principal Sister Aloysius Beauvier in *Doubt*
2009 Best Actress as chef Julia Child in *Julie & Julia*
2011 Best Actress as British Prime Minister Margaret Thatcher in *The Iron Lady*
2013 Best Actress as wife/mother Violet Weston in *August: Osage County*
2014 Best Supporting Actress as witch The Witch in *Into the Woods*
2016 Best Actress as opera singing socialite Florence Foster Jenkins in *Florence Foster Jenkins*

So far, Meryl Streep doesn't have the most competitive Oscar wins. She's one behind Katharine Hepburn. She has yet to win an honorary or lifetime achievement Oscar. But her unwavering favor from the Academy and consistent respect from peers for her daunting talent and munificent comradery on set make the probability for such further accolades great. The year after she debuted in the multiple Oscar-winning movie *Julia*, Streep set her foundation of Oscar nominations that would ultimately tower gargantuanly over every other actor. As Linda in *The Deer Hunter*, she was so tender and raw that the audience clung to her responses as a safe place to anchor their vulnerability about the atrocities that barrel, Russian roulette-style, from the screen. The following year she won her first Oscar as Joanna in *Kramer vs.*

Kramer by drawing sympathy for the confusion of a woman willing to abandon her young son. *The French Lieutenant's Woman* was a test of the highest order. Her single glance had to convince audiences that Jeremy Irons would abandon a happy life and spotless reputation for the allure of a stranger. Streep made the grade and earned her first Best Actress Oscar nomination. She probably didn't need to work so hard to convince Alan J. Pakula to make her his *Sophie's Choice*. Through her interpretation, Streep made fragile, complex, and horrifically identifiable Sophie *the* tragic character of cinema. Winning Best Actress for the performance made Streep the first female actor to win Oscars in both acting categories first as a supporting player, and then as a lead actress. The only male actor to do the same before her was Jack Lemmon. Among the twelve actors with Oscars as both lead and supporting players, Streep earned hers the fastest, taking both categories in just three years. Streep's impeccable dialects first gained recognition with *Sophie's Choice*, and would enhance her full embodiment of each character's unique life, mannerisms, and conscience. In 1983 she was a rough but righteous blue collar champion as Karen *Silkwood*. Two years later she depicted, with a single grasp of Robert Redford's hand while flying over Kenya, the engulfing sweep of being awed by life and achingly in love as Karen Blixen. Though a lead contender for 1985's Best Actress for *Out of Africa*, Streep was the first to leap to her feet to honor Geraldine Page's win for *The Trip to Bountiful*. Throughout the decades, Streep's nominations mounted. She was lost as a rootless *Ironweed*, condemned *In the Dark*, singularly aware of *One True Thing*, and ruthlessly truth tellin' in *Osage County*. In every performance, there was a trademark Streep moment when she gave the audience a gasp-worthy glimpse into her character's soul. For Francesca Johnson, it came through agonized hesitation of reaching for a car door handle. For Susan Orlean, it was psychotropic drug-induced euphoria. For Amanda Priestly, it erupted in, then choked back, unacceptable tears. For Sister Aloysius it burst in a windswept confession of *Doubt*. Even for Margaret Thatcher, it emerged through a haze of dementia. Further testament of Streep's talent is the roll call of directors with whom she has created characterizations revered by the Academy. Besides Mike Nichols, who directed her to Oscar nominations twice (for *Silkwood* and *Postcards from the Edge*), all of Streep's others were for working with different directors. For many of those directors (Carl Franklin of *One True Thing*, Wes Craven of *Music of the Heart*, David Frankel of *The Devil Wears Prada*, Nora Ephron of *Julie & Julia*, and Phyllida Lloyd of *The Iron Lady*) hers is the only performance to bring any of their films an acting Oscar nod.

It took 29 years, but the Academy honored Streep with her third victory in 2011. During her acceptance speech for *The Iron Lady*, Streep may have miscalculated her own impact by professing, "I really understand I'll never be up here again." Without a misstep throughout her career, she continues to build on a reputation as a consummate professional and artistically generous colleague. How could the Academy help but want its romance with Streep to continue, and rightfully, with more honors on the horizon?

After her humorous ("Her? Again?") and heartfelt acceptance speech, triumphant Meryl Streep raised her third golden statuette at the 2011 Academy Awards.

PART II. THE RUNNERS-UP: ACTORS WHO DIDN'T MAKE THE COUNTDOWN

1

So Close and Yet So Far

Actors One Nomination from the Countdown

Clark Gable

> 1934 Best Actor as reporter Peter Warne in *It Happened One Night*
> 1935 Best Actor as mutineer sailor Fletcher Christian in *Mutiny on the Bounty*
> 1939 Best Actor as speculator Rhett Butler in *Gone with the Wind*

Had Clark Gable any idea what Frank Capra's *It Happened One Night* would have done for his career, he might have been more enthusiastic about the project. Before *It Happened One Night* became the first film in history to sweep all five top Oscars (Picture, Actor, Actress, Director, and Screenplay), Gable had appeared in *A Free Soul* (1930), the first movie to earn two Oscar nominations for performances (Best Actor winner Lionel Barrymore and Best Actress nominee Norma Shearer). Despite little Oscar attention, Gable was a major star before the Capra classic, but he was "King of Hollywood" thanks to his priceless comic flair as a reporter chasing the story of runaway heiress Claudette Colbert. He followed his Oscar win, for which his entire acceptance speech consisted of two words, "Thank you," by playing Fletcher Christian in *Mutiny on the Bounty*.

The adventure at sea won the Academy's top prize, making Gable the first to star in two consecutive Best Pictures. Nominated with Gable were co-stars Charles Laughton and Franchot Tone, making them the only actors to fill three slots in a lead acting category for a single film. When *Gone with the Wind* headed into production, Gable indisputably had to play Rhett Butler. "Frankly, my dear," no one could have done it quite like him. His presence in the film served as grounding balance to Vivien Leigh's flittering Scarlett

O'Hara. Beyond the movie's ambitious artistic excellence, their chemistry made the movie *the* classic screen love story. Although he lost the 1939 Oscar to Robert Donat in *Goodbye, Mr. Chips*, Gable's performance remains at the top of the greatest nominated performances not to win gold.

Teresa Wright

- 1941 Best Supporting Actress as daughter Alexandra Giddens in *The Little Foxes*
- 1942 Best Actress as wife Eleanor Gehrig in *The Pride of the Yankees*
- 1942 Best Supporting Actress as daughter-in-law/wife Carol Beldon in *Mrs. Miniver*

For his performance as Fletcher Christian, Clark Gable competed for Best Actor against his *Mutiny on the Bounty* (1935) co-stars Charles Laughton and Franchot Tone, the only time in history three actors from the same movie were all nominated for a lead acting Oscar.

When she was only 23, Teresa Wright earned her first Supporting Actress nomination as Bette Davis' daughter in *The Little Foxes*. Her chance at a win may have been diminished by the fact that established London stage actress Patricia Collinge, in a showier role from the movie, was up for the same award. They lost to Mary Astor in *The Great Lie*. The next year, Wright followed Fay Bainter as the only stars to date to be nominated for a lead and supporting performance in a single year. Only 24 at the time, Wright was, and remains, the youngest actor with that achievement. She shone as Lou Gehrig's supportive wife in *The Pride of the Yankees*, but that film highlighted Gary Cooper's performance throughout. The 1942 Academy Awards belonged to *Mrs. Miniver*, with Greer Garson in the title role beating Wright for Best Actress. But Wright, as Garson's courageous daughter-in-law, gave a glowing performance that earned her a well-deserved honor as Best Supporting

Actress. Getting three nominations and one win in her first three movies is also a rare Academy achievement. Although not nominated in 1946, Wright also appeared in the other biggest Oscar winner of the 1940s, *The Best Years of Our Lives*.

Joan Fontaine

    1940 Best Actress as wife, the second Mrs. De Winter in *Rebecca*
    1941 Best Actress as wife Lina McLaidlaw in *Suspicion*
    1943 Best Actress as Belgian gamine Teresa "Tessa" Sanger in *The Constant Nymph*

Less ambitious than her sister, Olivia de Havilland, Joan Fontaine slipped leisurely into an acting career, and temporarily usurped her older sibling as Oscar's favorite. Olivia earned the first nomination, as a supporting player in *Gone with the Wind*, but the next year Fontaine was up as lead actress of the Best Picture winner, *Rebecca*. The following year they became the first siblings to compete for an acting Academy Award. Gossip columnists capitalized on the sisters' contentious relationship to help that Oscar race become one of the tensest in Academy history. Fontaine's victory and alleged snub of de Havilland's supposed attempt at scene-stealing graciousness escalated their feud and remains a most titillating bit of Oscar lore. When de Havilland won Best Actress five years later, she and Fontaine became the first, and still only siblings to both win acting Oscars. Fontaine's performance in *Suspicion* also made her the only star in history to win an Academy Award under the direction of Alfred Hitchcock. Fontaine had two hits in 1943, as the title heroine in *Jane Eyre*, and nominated for her third Oscar for *The Constant Nymph*. In the movie, cited as her personal favorite, Fontaine aged from her early teens to full womanhood as a poor, physically fragile musician secretly pining for composer Charles Boyer. In 1952 the always lovely Fontaine appeared in another Best Picture competitor, playing Lady Rowena, love interest of *Ivanhoe*.

Claudette Colbert

    1934 Best Actress as heiress Ellie Andrews in *It Happened One Night*
    1935 Best Actress as psychiatrist Jane Everest in *Private Worlds*
    1944 Best Actress as wife/mother Anne Hilton in *Since You Went Away*

The Academy first met French-born Claudette Colbert when Maurice Chevalier fell in love with her in his Best Actor-nominated performance in the 1930 romantic comedy, *The Big Pond*. The following year she reteamed with Chevalier in *The Smiling Lieutenant*, which competed for Best Picture of 1931/32. Two years later, Colbert was headlining her own projects, impressively starring in three movies that competed for Best Picture. She tempted and schemed as pampered *Cleopatra*, bonded with Black housekeeper Louise Beavers in the beloved race-conscious drama *Imitation of Life*, and famously flashed her car-stopping calf in the Best Picture winner *It Happened One Night*. Frank Capra's screwball comedy became the first to sweep the five major Oscar categories, and Colbert's 6-minute appearance at that Academy Awards is history-making high drama. Assuming she wouldn't win, Colbert was boarding a train as the ceremony ensued. When host Irving S. Cobb announced Colbert Best Actress, Columbia Studio employees raced to the station to sweep her back to the Biltmore in time for Shirley Temple to hand Colbert her statuette before the night's ceremony closed. The following year, she was up again as a doctor at a mental institution in *Private Worlds*, and subsequently received Oscar nominated support from Edna May Oliver in *Drums along the Mohawk* (1939), Paulette Goddard in *So Proudly We Hail!* (1943), and Marjorie Main in *The Egg and I* (1947). She was nominated one last time as a mother keeping the home fires burning in the sensitive World War II family drama *Since You Went Away*. From seductive to silly to sincere, Colbert could springboard any emotion into an unforgettable film moment.

Charles Coburn

    1941 Best Supporting Actor as department store tycoon John P. Merrick in *The Devil and Miss Jones*
    1943 Best Supporting Actor as retired millionaire Benjamin Dingle in *The More the Merrier*
    1946 Best Supporting Actor as great-grandfather Alexander Gow in *The Green Years*

One of the most dependable and standout supporting players of his generation, Coburn could squint with arrogance, smile with melting charm, and win over the heart of any audience while befuddling every character he played opposite. His delightful characterizations were often enhanced by colorful, often playful character names. He was Charles Shingle opposite Best Supporting Actress nominee Beulah Bondi in *Of Human Hearts*, Mr. Dingle matchmaking for Joel McCrea and Jean Arthur in *The More the Merrier*, and Sir Francis "Piggy" Beekman, the diamond mine owner who prompted a diamond-dazed Marilyn Monroe to sing about a girl's best friend in *Gentlemen Prefer Blondes* in 1953. Coburn teamed with Jean Arthur in 1941 to play her crabby boss, Mr. Merrick in *The Devil and Miss Jones*, losing that Academy Award to fellow senior actor Donald Crisp of *How Green Was My Valley*. Two years later, Coburn reunited with Arthur as her unexpected roommate in *The*

More the Merrier, and earned his second nomination. At the 1943 Oscars, Coburn faced stiff competition for Supporting Actor, especially from Claude Rains as Renault in *Casablanca*, but as the central figure who propelled the action and delivered the most comic goods in *The More the Merrier*, Coburn was a clear and popular winner. He appeared in Best Picture nominees *Kings Row* in 1942 and *Wilson* in 1944, then filled another Supporting Actor slot in 1946 as the understanding great-grandfather who helps see Tom Drake through *The Green Years* of adolescence.

Anne Revere

> 1943 Best Supporting Actress as mother Louise Soubirous in *The Song of Bernadette*
> **1945 Best Supporting Actress as mother Mrs. Araminty Brown in *National Velvet***
> 1947 Best Supporting Actress as mother Mrs. Green in *Gentleman's Agreement*

If producers were looking for a solid, no-nonsense mother who could run a gamut of profiles from severe to serene, they needed look no further than Anne Revere. Her first nomination came as Best Actress winner Jennifer Jones' mother in *The Song of Bernadette*. At first unwilling to suffer the illusionary foolishness of a zealously pious daughter, Revere allowed her stiff caste to melt as she came to recognize the sincerity of the child's faith. In 1945 she starred with Best Actor nominee Gregory Peck in *The Keys of the Kingdom*, and was nominated again as Elizabeth Taylor's mother in *National Velvet*. This time, Revere maintained her sturdy backbone, but shone with understanding for her daughter's childlike hope. That combination proved irresistible to her Academy peers, and Revere won Best Supporting Actress over stalwart competition from wisecracking Eve Arden and selfish Ann Blyth, both from *Mildred Pierce*, innocent songbird Angela Lansbury in *The Picture of Dorian Gray*, and bad girl and bad student Joan Lorring in *The Corn is Green*. Revere reunited with Gregory Peck in 1947 to play his mother, and was highlighted for another Oscar nomination. This time she lost to another star from *Gentleman's Agreement*, Celeste Holm. Revere's final appearance in a Best Picture-nominated hit was as Montgomery Clift's heartbroken missionary mother in *A Place in the Sun*.

Celeste Holm

> 1947 Best Supporting Actress as fashion editor Anne Dettrey in *Gentleman's Agreement*

1949 Best Supporting Actress as French nun Sister Scholastica in *Come to the Stable*
1950 Best Supporting Actress as playwright's wife Karen Richards in *All About Eve*

Although Eve Arden was most identified as the spitfire, wisecracking sidekick in movies of their era, Holm offered the same, then added a softened edge that gave her performances a nuance that the Academy loved. In only her second year in movies, Holm won the role of insightful fashion editor Anne Dettrey in *Gentleman's Agreement*. Despite tense Best Supporting Actress competition from co-star Anne Revere as Gregory Peck's mother, Ethel Barrymore in a small role in *The Paradine Case*, Gloria Grahame's scene-stealing appearance in *Crossfire*, and Marjorie Main's introduction as Ma Kettle in *The Egg and I*, Holm began her movie career as an Oscar winner. She was an engaging French nun aided by fellow Best Supporting Actress nominee Elsa Lanchester in *Come to the Stable*, and she set the delicious tone as narrator of Best Picture nominee, and Best Director and Screenplay winner *A Letter to Three Wives* in 1949. Holm's Karen Richards was among the many victims duped before they figure out *All About Eve* in 1950. Playing a loyal friend with a hint of moral superiority, Holm gave a performance as savory as the rest of the cast's, and vied once more for Oscar. She and co-star Thelma Ritter both lost to Josephine Hull in *Harvey*. Among actors with three nominations, Holm stands out as the one actor whose every Oscar competition put her in contention against another star from the movie that earned her a nomination.

Joan Crawford

1945 Best Actress as restaurant owner Mildred Pierce in *Mildred Pierce*
1947 Best Actress as nurse Louise Howell in *Possessed*
1952 Best Actress as Broadway playwright Myra Hudson (Blaine) in *Sudden Fear*

No one worked harder or marketed herself more ferociously than Joan Crawford. The Academy's initial appreciation of her came in 1931/32 Best Picture winner *Grand Hotel*, for which none of the illustrious cast members was nominated. She impressed as *The Gorgeous Hussy* in 1936, but the Academy only nominated supporting star Beulah Bondi. In 1945, Crawford reached the height of her fame as fervently devoted mother *Mildred Pierce*. When the title role brought her an Academy Award nomination, Crawford used Oscar night to build sympathy by claiming to be ill and remaining in bed wearing full makeup and elegant bed jacket, with photographers at the ready should the radio airwaves waft in her favor. They did, and the savvy marketer capitalized on a uniquely golden moment. Crawford earned another Oscar nomination for the second movie she made called *Possessed*, this one a noir in which she played a mentally unstable woman obsessed with a former love. In her third nominated role, she was the victim rather than cause of a bad relationship, as new husband, Best Supporting Actor nominee Jack Palance, turned sinister early in their marriage, causing her *Sudden Fear*. When the Academy overlooked Crawford but nominated notorious rival Bette Davis for *What Ever Happened to Baby Jane?*, Crawford exacted her revenge by volunteering to accept the Best Actress award for any other nominee unable to attend the 1962 Oscars. Unsuspecting Anne Bancroft, on stage in New York when she won for *The Miracle Worker*, agreed, and Crawford took the spotlight from Davis and dominated photos of the 1962 Oscar winners. *What Ever Happened to Baby Jane* at that year's Academy Awards? She got upstaged by a calculating, publicity-savvy Joan Crawford.

José Ferrer

1948 Best Supporting Actor as The Daughin, Charles VIII in *Joan of Arc*
1950 Best Actor as poet/swordsman Cyrano de Bergerac in *Cyrano de Bergerac*
1952 Best Actor as painter Henri de Toulouse-Lautrec and as painter's father Alphonse Charles de Toulouse-Lautrec in *Moulin Rouge*

With a voice as ruddy as his countenance and enough compelling talent to earn him a lead actor Oscar, Puerto Rico-born José Ferrer is the first Hispanic to win an acting Academy Award. After conquering Broadway as an actor and director, Ferrer turned to film, earning an Oscar nomination for his first movie performance, as morally malleable Charles VIII in *Joan of Arc*. He lost to Walter Huston of *The Treasure of the Sierra Madre*. Two years later he triumphed with a Best Actor Oscar as lovelorn *Cyrano de Bergerac*, a role he had played to Tony-winning success in 1947. The year he won Oscar he was also nominated for an Emmy for his body of television work, making him the first star to be up for both awards in a single year. In 1956 he brought *Cyrano de Bergerac* to the small screen and earned a second Emmy nomination, making him one of the few actors to compete for theater's, motion pictures,' and television's highest honors for adaptations of the same work. His Best Actor nomination for playing a father and son in *Moulin Rouge* made him one of the only actors to be nominated for playing multiple roles in a single movie. Ferrer's long, impressive career also included appearances in other Oscar-nominated movies over the decades. He had supporting roles in *The Caine Mutiny* (1954), *The Greatest Story Ever Told* and *Ship of Fools* (both 1965), *Voyage of the Damned* (1976), and *To Be or Not to Be* (1983). Initially hesitant about accepting the small role as the Turkish Bey in 1962's Best Picture *Lawrence of Arabia*, Ferrer considered that performance his best five minutes on film.

Humphrey Bogart

1943 Best Actor as American expatriate Rick Blaine in *Casablanca*
1951 Best Actor as boat captain Charlie Allnut in *The African Queen*
1954 Best Actor as naval Lieutenant Commander Philip Francis Queeg in *The Caine Mutiny*

Bogart curled his upper lip, drove his dark stare into his victims or gun molls, and ultimately became AFI's greatest male legend of the 20th century. To his own surprise, his biggest hit cast him as a romantic lead in *Casablanca* and brought him his first Academy Award nomination.

Paul Henried (playing Victor Laszlo) stood behind Humphrey Bogart, whose most iconic role as Rick Blaine in *Casablanca* (1943) brought Bogie his first Academy Award nomination.

1. So Close and Yet So Far

Though the script included indelible lines ("Here's looking at you, kid"; "Louie, I think this is the beginning of a beautiful friendship"), it was Bogart's delivery that embossed them into American movie gold. Usually indifferent to Hollywood politicking, Bogart launched a unique and successful campaign to win Best Actor for *The African Queen* by treating Academy pals to drinks at Romanoff's. His win was only controversial to those who thought Marlon Brando should have won that year for *A Streetcar Named Desire*. But Oscar can be equitable. When Brando won his first Best Actor prize three years later for *On the Waterfront*, he beat Bogie as crazed, ball-bearing fumbler Queeg in *The Caine Mutiny*. Though Bogart and Ingrid Bergman's romance earned *Casablanca* Best Picture and Best Director for Michael Curtiz, Oscar most often favored Bogart's alliances with director John Huston. In 1941, *The Maltese Falcon* made Bogart a superstar. In 1948, his un-nominated performance as prospector Dobbs in *The Treasure of the Sierra Madre* is considered one of Oscar's most startling omissions, and *The African Queen* sailed Bogart into Oscar's elite winner's circle.

Bing Crosby

1944 Best Actor as priest Father O'Malley in *Going My Way*
1945 Best Actor as priest Father O'Malley in *The Bells of St. Mary's*
1954 Best Actor as actor Frank Elgin in *The Country Girl*

With his tired eyes and languid line delivery, Crosby didn't seem to fit the standard for matinee idols during the 1940s. Already being one of the great singers of the century would seem to have made his transition to movie stardom all the more challenging, but Crosby succeeded so resoundingly that he ultimately ranked seventh among the Top Ten All-Time Moneymaking Stars in motion picture history. He starred in movies throughout the 1930s, but Oscar only recognized two, and both in great part thanks to Crosby's singing. He introduced the title song from *Pennies from Heaven* to a Best Song nomination in 1936. The following year his rendition of "Sweet Leilani" during the *Waikiki Wedding* won Best Song. His depiction of compassionate, progressive young priest Father O'Malley won him the Best Actor prize over such solid performances as devious Charles Boyer in *Gaslight*, destitute Cary Grant in *None But the Lonely Heart*, and staunch Alexander Knox as Woodrow Wilson. In his category, Crosby also beat fellow *Going My Way* actor Barry Fitzgerald, who was also nominated as, and won, Best Supporting Actor for *Going My Way*. Crosby set an Academy record by becoming the first person nominated twice for playing the same character when he reprised his Father O'Malley role the following year in *The Bells of St. Mary's*. In 1951 he sang another Best Song winner, "In the Cool, Cool, Cool of the Evening" in *Here*

Comes the Groom, and in 1954 proved his dramatic prowess with a staggering turn as a has-been actor, washed up because he'd been washing in alcohol too long, in *The Country Girl*. That same year, Crosby also starred in *White Christmas*, the sequel to *Holiday Inn* (1942), the film in which Crosby introduced "White Christmas," which won Best Song and went on to become the biggest selling single in music history. Besides his musical and dramatic roles, Crosby owed most of his box office stronghold for teaming with Bob Hope in seven *Road* comedies that took them from Singapore in 1939 to Hong Kong in 1962. Near the middle of that successful run, Crosby and Hope shared a cameo as circus spectators in 1952's Best Picture, *The Greatest Show on Earth*.

Claire Trevor

1937 Best Supporting Actress as prostitute Francey in *Dead End*
1948 Best Supporting Actress as mistress Gaye Dawn in *Key Largo*
1954 Best Supporting Actress as single woman Mary Holst in *The High and the Mighty*

Trevor admitted that the most intimidating scene she ever played was having to keep Humphrey Bogart, Lauren Bacall, and Edward G. Robinson rapt by her singing as a nervous captive on *Key Largo*. That mesmerizing moment may have tipped the scales in her favor over powerhouse performances including Jean Simmons as Ophelia in *Hamlet* and heartwarming narrator Barbara Bel Geddes in *I Remember Mama* to earn the 1948 Best Supporting Actress prize. That Oscar win was bookmarked by Trevor's two other nominated performances in the same category. In the Academy's second Best Supporting Actress competition, she brought sad compassion as Francey, a prostitute roaming the *Dead End* slums of New York, but lost to Alice Brady as Mrs. O'Leary in *In Old Chicago*. In 1954, Trevor played a fading beauty and flight passenger along with fellow Best Supporting Actress nominee Jan Sterling in *The High and the Mighty*, a competition that brought Eva Maria Saint the Oscar for the year's Best Picture *On the Waterfront*. Among Trevor's non-nominated performances, she is best remembered as Dallas, a classier prostitute than Francey, riding on John Ford's Old West *Stagecoach* in 1939.

James Cagney

1938 Best Actor as gangster Rocky Sullivan in *Angels with Dirty Faces*
1942 Best Actor as entertainer George M. Cohan in *Yankee Doodle Dandy*
1955 Best Actor as gangster Martin Snyder in *Love Me or Leave Me*

One Oscar-nominated screenplay had Cagney, engulfed in *White Heat*, shouting the immortal line, "Made it, Ma! Top of the world!" Another, *The Public Enemy*, called for him to grind half a grapefruit into Mae Clarke's face. But those aren't the movies for which his peers in the Academy honored him. After roles in Best Picture nominees *Here Comes the Navy* (1934) and *A Midsummer Night's Dream* (1935), Cagney earned the New York Film Critics prize and his first Best Actor Oscar nomination as the lifelong criminal whose boyhood friend, priest Pat O'Brien, tried to save in *Angels with Dirty Faces*. Midway through World War II, Cagney hoofed his way through jaunty patriotic numbers as fast-talking showman George M. Cohan. The New York Film Critics chose him again as their Best Actor, and this time, so did Oscar. 1955 was a landmark year for Cagney, who starred in the Best Picture–nominated *Mister Roberts* while earning his last Best Actor nod as "Moe the Gimp," a gangster enraptured by singer Ruth Etting (Doris Day) in *Love Me or Leave Me*. Twice more in his career Cagney came close to an Oscar nomination. In 1961 Academy buzz swarmed around Cagney for his demanding role in Billy Wilder's rapid-fire comedy, *One, Two, Three*. Director Miloš Foreman coaxed Cagney out of retirement twenty years later to play Commissioner Waldo in his epic, turn of the century *Ragtime*. Although anticipation for a supporting nomination never materialized, Oscar consideration put him once again on "top of the world."

Charles Laughton

1932/1933 Best Actor as British monarch Henry VIII in *The Private Life of Henry VIII*
1935 Best Actor as Captain Bligh in *Mutiny on the Bounty*
1957 Best Actor as barrister Sir Wilfrid Robarts in *Witness for the Prosecution*

The first star to win an Academy Award for a non–Hollywood production, robust British actor Charles Laughton exaggerated a pouting expression and laconic speech pattern into some of cinema's most memorable characterizations. He was not present to accept his 1932/1933 Oscar as Henry VIII. Of the three actors nominated for playing the colorful king, Laughton, Robert Shaw in *A Man for All Seasons* (1966) and Richard Burton in *Anne of the Thousand Days* (1969), Laughton was the only one to win. That Best Picture contender began a string of Best Picture nominees starring Laughton. He was the incestuously possessive father of Best Actress nominee Norman Shearer in *The Barretts of Wimpole Street* (1934), and then had lead roles in three Best Picture contenders of 1935: hilariously low key as the title manservant, *Ruggles of Red Gap*, obsessively vengeful as Javert in *Les Misérables*, and nominated for Best Actor along with Clark Gable and Franchot Tone in the Best Picture winner, *Mutiny on the Bounty*. Wife Elsa Lanchester had played Henry's fourth wife, Anne of Cleves, in *The Private Life of Henry VIII*, and in 1957 both were nominated as barrister and doting nurse in *Witness for the Prosecution*. Two years before his 1962 death, Laughton appeared in his last Oscar-winning film, in a supporting role as Roman nobleman Sempronius Gracchus in *Spartacus*. A revered stage director, Laughton helmed the movie thriller *The Night of the Hunter*, which in 1955 was dismissed by critics, audiences, and the Academy, but is now considered a classic that in 1992 was selected for preservation in the Library of Congress' National Film Registry.

Fay Bainter

1938 Best Actress as peddler/housekeeper Hannah in *White Banners*
1938 Best Supporting Actress as Aunt Belle Massey in *Jezebel*
1961 Best Supporting Actress as grandmother Mrs. Amelia Tilford in *The Children's Hour*

In only the third year since Oscar added supporting acting categories to his roster, Bainter did what no other actor had done before and only ten others have done since: she competed as both a lead and supporting player the same year. Bainter used her expressive eyes and long, thin lips to convey the pathos of a struggling woman who becomes the domestic for a young family in *White Banners*, earning the film's only Academy Award nomination, as Best Actress. She stood out among a solid supporting cast of William Wyler's *Jezebel* as the traditional, reproving aunt of scandalously independent Bette Davis. At the 1938 Oscars, Bainter lost the Best Actress race to *Jezebel* lead, Bette Davis, but took the supporting prize. The following year, she presented both supporting player awards, to Thomas Mitchell and Hattie McDaniel. Most often cast as the solid matriarch or friendly voice of reason, Bainter supported Best Actress nominee Katharine Hepburn in *Woman of the Year* in 1942 and was Best Actor nominee Mickey Rooney's mother in *The Human Comedy* in 1943. At age 68, Bainter made an Oscar comeback as a grandmother unwittingly swept into her wrathful granddaughter's vengeance against two teachers in *The Children's Hour*. Like *Jezebel*, the nomination came for a film directed by William Wyler.

Wendy Hiller

1938 Best Actress as flower vendor Eliza Doolittle in *Pygmalion*
1958 Best Supporting Actress as hotel proprietress Pat Cooper in *Separate Tables*

1966 Best Supporting Actress as English Lady Alice More in *A Man for All Seasons*

One of history's greatest playwrights, George Bernard Shaw insisted that Wendy Hiller be cast as Eliza Doolittle, the cockney spitfire he created in the movie version of his classic *Pygmalion*. She took the part, opposite Leslie Howard as Henry Higgins, and both competed for lead acting Oscars in 1938. Because Audrey Hepburn fell victim to a Best Actress snub for the 1964 musical adaptation *My Fair Lady*, Hiller remains the only star nominated for playing the bloomin' flower vendor who became a blossomed lady. Preferring stage work, Hiller only accepted movie roles that intrigued her, and was not up for another Oscar until she took the supporting role of the hotel manager aware of the secrets all the guests conceal at *Separate Tables*. She lost the Golden Globe to Hermione Gingold in *Gigi*, but when the Academy bypassed Gingold for a nomination, Hiller took home Oscar. Playing Sir Thomas More's lion of a wife in *A Man for All Seasons* piqued Oscar's interest in Hiller once more. As a Best Supporting Actress winner, she has the rare distinction of starring in multiple films that earned someone else a nomination or win in that category. Among those films were *Sons and Lovers* (1960), for which Mary Ure was up, *Voyage of the Damned* (1976), which brought Lee Grant her fourth nomination, and *Murder on the Orient Express* (1974), which netted Ingrid Bergman a record-setting win.

Rod Steiger

1954 Best Supporting Actor as lawyer Charley "The Gent" Malloy in *On the Waterfront*
1965 Best Actor as concentration camp survivor/pawnbroker Sol Nazerman in *The Pawnbroker*
1967 Best Actor as Police Chief Bill Gillespie in *In the Heat of the Night*

Marlon Brando's backseat "I coulda been a contender" scene in *On the Waterfront* is often used to highlight his brilliance as an actor, but many fail to notice that supporting him in that scene, and helping make it work, was 1954 Best Supporting Actor nominee Rod Steiger as the brother who sold him out. With co-stars Lee J. Cobb and Karl Malden in the same category as Steiger, they likely split votes, leaving room for Edmond O'Brien to win for *The Barefoot Contessa*. Steiger, who had originated the role of Marty Pilletti on live television, didn't take the role in the big screen adaptation of *Marty*, which won Best Picture, and Best Actor for Ernest Borgnine in 1955. A decade later, Steiger was favored to win as an embittered concentration camp survivor in Sidney Lumet's *The Pawnbroker*. He won the 1965 BAFTA, but lost Oscar to Lee Marvin's comic dual roles in *Cat Ballou*. But in 1967 Steiger pulled off one of the greatest wins in Oscar history when his performance as a bigoted, gum-chomping Mississippi police chief beat out Spencer Tracy's heartfelt swansong, *Guess Who's Coming to Dinner*, Paul Newman's egg-stuffed antihero *Cool Hand Luke*, and iconic, generation-defining wanderers Warren Beatty in *Bonnie and Clyde* and Dustin Hoffman in *The Graduate*.

Gig Young

1951 Best Supporting Actor as alcoholic Boyd Copeland in *Come Fill the Cup*
1958 Best Supporting Actor as psychologist Dr. Hugo Pine in *Teacher's Pet*
1969 Best Supporting Actor as dance marathon emcee Rocky in *They Shoot Horses, Don't They?*

Tall, fine-featured Gig Young was a supporting character actor who always strove to be a leading man. He began his career with uncredited roles in two Best Picture nominees of 1941, *Sergeant York* and *One Foot in Heaven*. Ten years later, Young earned his first of three Best Supporting Actor Oscar nominations as an unfaithful husband in *Come Fill the Cup*. He was a charming cad in *Teacher's Pet*, but lost the 1958 Oscar to Burl Ives of *The Big Country*. But the 1969 race was his to win from the beginning of award season. As Rocky, the corrupt dance marathon emcee who goaded weary competitors with an increasingly drowsy, "Yowsah, yowsah, yowsah," Young embodied the cruelty that poked at the Depression era dancers' desperate despair. The film secured Young's reputation as a stalwart supporting player, but, from personal reports, was also the performance that he believed kept him from his dream of becoming a lead actor.

Walter Matthau

1966 Best Supporting Actor as lawyer Willie H. Gingrich in *The Fortune Cookie*
1971 Best Actor as retired traveling salesman Joseph P. Kotcher in *Kotch*
1975 Best Actor as retired vaudeville comedian Willy Clark in *The Sunshine Boys*

Scene stealer and hangdog curmudgeon Walter Matthau caused a row in Oscar circles when he won Best Supporting Actor of 1966 as Jack Lemmon's scheming shyster lawyer, Whiplash Willie in *The Fortune Cookie*. His gut-splitting performance clearly deserved to win, but some argued that he shared the lead with Lemmon, and thus unfairly took a shot at a supporting win from fellow nominees Mako of *The Sand Pebbles*, James Mason in *Georgy Girl*, George Segal from *Who's Afraid of Virginia Woolf?*, and Robert Shaw in *A Man for All Seasons*. Matthau's win capped off a challenging year, as Matthau suffered a massive heart attack during film production and then came to that year's Oscars facially bruised and with a cast on his arm from a serious bike accident. With usual dry wit, Matthau began his acceptance speech, "The other day, as I was falling off my bicycle...." Good pal and frequent co-star Jack Lemmon directed Matthau to his first lead actor nomination as senior runaway *Kotch*. Four years later, Matthau's pairing with fellow comic veteran George Burns made *The Sunshine Boys* one of Neil Simon's biggest hit movies. Burns won the Best Supporting Actor Academy Award, but Matthau, despite winning the Golden Globe for Best Actor, Musical or Comedy, lost the Best Actor Oscar to *One Flew Over the Cuckoo's Nest* star Jack Nicholson.

Faye Dunaway

1967 Best Actress as bank robber Bonnie Parker in *Bonnie and Clyde*
1974 Best Actress as widow Evelyn Cross Mulwray in *Chinatown*
1976 Best Actress as television network producer of entertainment programming Diana Christensen in *Network*

At age 27, newcomer Faye Dunaway won the coveted role of Bonnie Parker over Ann-Margret, Leslie Caron, Cher, Jane Fonda, Carol Lynley, Sue Lyon, Tuesday Weld, and Natalie Wood. It catapulted her to revered actress, fashion icon, and worldwide A-list star, verified by a Best Newcomer BAFTA victory. Dunaway's performance was on the roster of most indelible Best Actress characterizations in history. 1967 had her competing against other frontrunners Anne Bancroft as Mrs. Robinson in *The Graduate* and winner Katharine Hepburn as Christina Drayton in *Guess Who's Coming to Dinner*. Dunaway's scintillating cat and mouse chase of Steve McQueen in *The Thomas Crown Affair* expanded her influence as actor and fashion trendsetter. 1974 saw Dunaway in two Best Picture nominees, *The Towering Inferno* and *Chinatown*, for which she gave the Best Actress race its greatest chance for an upset as fragile femme fatale Evelyn Mulwray. The Oscar went to frontrunner Ellen Burstyn in *Alice Doesn't Live Here Anymore*. Then Sidney Lumet cast Dunaway as UBS's soul-less *Network* executive Diana Christensen, and she sailed right into the Academy Award winner's circle. In her acceptance speech, she said she didn't expect to win the Oscar so early in her career. But in the nine years since she first dazzled moviegoers and the Academy, Dunaway clearly earned her Oscar-winning status.

William Holden

1950 Best Actor as screenwriter/gigolo Joe Gillis in *Sunset Boulevard*
1953 Best Actor as World War II P.O.W. Sergeant J.J. Sefton in *Stalag 17*
1976 Best Actor as television network news division president Max Schumacher in *Network*

William Holden dominated the 1950s as an Academy mainstay and one of cinema's top ranking box office stars. He floated to Academy recognition with a Best Actor nod as a corpse recounting the circumstances leading to his drowning on *Sunset Boulevard*. That same year, Holden established his beloved persona as a morally upright intellectual who helps Best Actress winner Judy Holliday realize she wasn't *Born Yesterday*. He won Best Actor in 1953 as a mistrusted prisoner of war at *Stalag 17*, and played opposite Oscar contenders year after year. He romanced Best Actress nominees Maggie McNamara in *The Moon is Blue* (1953), Audrey Hepburn in *Sabrina* (1954), and Jennifer Jones in *Love is a Many-Splendored Thing* (1955). He supported to lead acting victories Grace Kelly in *The Country Girl* (1954) and Alec Guinness in *The Bridge on the River Kwai* (1957). Supporting nominees Nina Foch of *Executive Suite* (1954) and Arthur O'Connell of *Picnic* (1955) also shone in scenes impacted by Holden. His career resurged in the 1970s with Best Picture nominees *The Towering Inferno* and *Network*. While Peter Finch deservedly won praise and the 1976 Oscar as *Network* newscaster Howard Beale, many critics considered fellow Best Actor nominee Holden's the more difficult role, as he alone sought moral high ground against the madness corrupting the airways. Till the end, that upright image suited Holden, and always impressed fans and the Academy.

Maximilian Schell

1961 Best Actor as defense attorney Hans Rolfe in *Judgment at Nuremberg*
1975 Best Actor as industrialist/Nazi death camp survivor Arthur Goldman in *The Man in the Glass Booth*
1977 Best Supporting Actor as friend Johann in *Julia*

Darkly handsome Austrian/Swiss Maximilian Schell originated the role of defense attorney Hans Rolfe in *Playhouse 90*'s television production of *Judgment at Nuremberg*. In 1961, director Stanley Kramer selected Schell to recreate his performance on the big screen. As a relative film unknown, Schell was billed fifth among the prestigious ensemble. Schell won Best Actor from the New York Film Critics and the Hollywood Foreign Press, and he and

Spencer Tracy were both nominated for the lead acting Oscar for the courtroom drama. When Schell won, he became the first actor to win an Academy Award for a performance he originated on the small screen, and remains the lowest billed star to win a lead acting Oscar. Schell earned *The Man in the Glass Booth*'s only Oscar nomination in 1975, and, as he did in 1961, found himself competing against another actor from the same movie when he and Jason Robards, Jr., were up for Best Supporting Actor for *Julia* in 1977. This time, Schell's co-star won instead of him. Although his sister Maria Schell had roles in such Oscar hits as *The Brothers Karamazov* (1958), *The Mark* (1961), and *Voyage of the Damned* (1976), Maximilian remained their only family member to compete for Academy Awards.

Julie Andrews

1964 Best Actress as English nanny Mary Poppins in *Mary Poppins*
1965 Best Actress as aspiring nun/governess/wife Maria in *The Sound of Music*
1982 Best Actress as singer Victoria Grant/Count Victor Grazinski in *Victor Victoria*

Although Julie Andrews was a revered Tony-nominated Broadway star for her roles as Eliza Doolittle in *My Fair Lady* and Guinevere in *Camelot*, and a television sensation seen by more than 100 million viewers as *Cinderella*, producers of the film adaptation of *My Fair Lady* found her too big a box office risk, and cast Audrey Hepburn as their Eliza instead. Did Andrews prove them wrong! Instead of playing Henry Higgins' fair lady, she took the role of magical nanny *Mary Poppins*, which became the biggest moneymaker of any live action film in Disney Studio history. At the Oscars that year, Academy members rallied behind Andrews by not even nominating Hepburn for *My Fair Lady* and then awarding Andrews the Best Actress prize for *Mary Poppins*. The next year, Andrews played Maria, a postulant turned governess in *The Sound of Music*, which broke worldwide box office records, trailing only *Gone with the Wind* as the biggest moneymaker of all time, and led to a string of hits that made Andrews the most successful film star of the mid–1960s. Andrews was again up for Oscar, but another Brit named Julie, Julie Christie, was the Academy's 1965 Best Actress *Darling*. Andrews charmed in *Thoroughly Modern Millie* in 1967, but the Oscar nomination went to supporting player Carol Channing. The following year, she reunited with *The Sound of Music* director Robert Wise to play Gertrude Lawrence in *Star!* Although the movie earned seven Oscar nominations, tapering box office indicated that the public's reverence for traditional musicals was dwindling. Years later, appearances in *10* and *S.O.B.* reigniting her star and led to her final Oscar-nominated role, as a woman posing as a man posing as a woman in *Victor Victoria*. Andrews has remained a perennial favorite. Her continued popularity resounded clearly at the 2014 Academy Awards when she stepped on stage to a rousing ovation after Lady Gaga's musical tribute to her and the 50th anniversary of *The Sound of Music*.

Anjelica Huston

> **1985 Best Supporting Actress as Mafia don's daughter Maerose Prizzi in *Prizzi's Honor***
> 1989 Best Supporting Actress as Holocaust survivor/wife Tamara Broder in *Enemies, A Love Story*
> 1990 Best Actress as con artist Lilly Dillon in *The Grifters*

With a nasally New York delivery, Anjelica Huston made, "You wanna do it, Charley?" one of the most quotable lines of 1985. The statuesque daughter of director John Huston moved from modeling to acting, enjoying her two earliest hits with her spouse at the time, Jack Nicholson, playing his lover in both *The Postman Always Rings Twice* (1981), and *Prizzi's Honor*. As Walter and John Huston had been in 1948 thanks to their work on *The Treasure of the Sierra Madre*, John and Anjelica made the Huston's the royal family of the 1985 Academy Awards, with 79-year-old John becoming Oscar's oldest Best Director nominee, and Anjelica becoming the first daughter directed to Oscar victory by her father. Two years later she was a glowing Greta in *The Dead*, her father's last directorial effort and the only movie so far to earn her screenwriter brother, Tony Huston, an Academy Award nomination. She and Lena Olin both vied for a 1989 Oscar that went to Brenda Fricker for *My Left Foot*, and the following year Huston rose to lead actress contender as one of *The Grifters* in Stephen Frears' neo-noir. Thanks to her nominations and win, Anjelica helped make the Huston dynasty Oscar's most honored family.

Jack Palance

> 1952 Best Supporting Actor as actor Lester Blaine in *Sudden Fear*
> 1953 Best Supporting Actor as gunslinger Jack Wilson in *Shane*
> **1991 Best Supporting Actor as trail boss Curly Washburn in *City Slickers***

Jack Palance never lacked talent or courage. Before he made his film debut as a plague-carrying fugitive in *Panic in the Streets*, which won a screenplay Oscar in 1950, he had the daunting task of taking over Marlon

Brando's role of Stanley Kowalski in the Broadway run of *A Streetcar Named Desire*. Tall, with chiseled, sinister features, the powerful former boxer found quick success as movie villains. He caused Joan Crawford's *Sudden Fear* as her ambitious, murderous husband, and both were Oscar nominated in 1952. He was up for another Supporting Actor Oscar the following year as an even more psychopathic antagonist in *Shane*. His second Oscar race had him competing against *Shane*'s youngest star Brandon deWilde, but neither had much of a chance against comeback kid Frank Sinatra in the year's Best Picture, *From Here to Eternity*. The next year, *The Silver Chalice* was up for two Academy Awards, but none for acting. The Academy didn't recognize another Palance film until he played a bandit in *The Professionals*, which earned three Oscar nominations in 1966, including Best Screenplay and Best Director for Richard Brooks. Palance kept extending his résumé until, almost forty years after his first Academy bid, he barnstormed the Oscars with a tongue-in-cheek sendoff of his dastardly image as smug, catty trail boss Curly in the comedy *City Slickers*. Among a handful of actors to win Oscar and an American Comedy Award for the same performance, Palance spontaneously made his acceptance speech one of Oscar's most memorable by dropping down at the podium to demonstrate his ability to still do one-armed pushups at age 73. The image continues to be one of the most indelible in Academy history.

Martin Landau

1988 Best Supporting Actor as financier Abe Karatz in *Tucker: The Man and His Dream*
1989 Best Supporting Actor as ophthalmologist Judah Rosenthal in *Crimes and Misdemeanors*
1994 Best Supporting Actor as actor Bela Lugosi in *Ed Wood*

For decades Martin Landau was the shadowy supporting actor lurking behind unique characterizations in such Oscar-nominated hits as *North by Northwest*, *The Greatest Story Ever Told* and *Meteor*. TV audiences knew him well from the 1960s hit *Mission: Impossible*, but it was twenty years later, when Landau was in his sixties, that he secured the kinds of roles that the Academy nominated. A 1988 Golden Globe win increased his Oscar chances as the New York financier who supported *Tucker: The Man and His Dream*, but Kevin Kline came up the surprise winner for *A Fish Called Wanda*. Landau became one of the few male actors nominated for an Oscar under Woody Allen's direction as an ophthalmologist conscious-plagued by his *Crimes and Misdemeanors*, but 1989 supporting actor *Glory* belonged to Denzel Washington. In 1994, Landau dominated his race as late-in-life, drug-addicted horror star Bela Lugosi being directed by crackpot crossdresser *Ed Wood*. Landau's tragicomic performance was a tour de force homage to an actor never acknowledged by the Academy.

Russell Crowe

> 1999 Best Actor as research scientist Jeffrey Wigand in *The Insider*
> **2000 Best Actor as Roman general/gladiator Maximus Decimus Meridius in *Gladiator***
> 2001 Best Actor as mathematics student/professor John Nash in *A Beautiful Mind*

A New Zealand rogue with cheeks like a cherub, Russell Crowe entered Oscar circles via Hollywood noir investigating murder and mayhem in *L.A. Confidential*. Kim Basinger got the Best Picture nominee's only acting consideration, which she capped with a victory. Two years later Crowe went from *Confidential* to confidentiality as *The Insider* who knows dirty secrets concerning the tobacco company that just fired him. Early award season gave him multiple awards and genuine hopes of winning the Best Actor Oscar, if not upset by equally lauded Denzel Washington as Rubin "*Hurricane*" Carter. By Oscar night, the intoxicating scent of *American Beauty* transfixed the Academy, and the movie became the big winner, giving Kevin Spacey the Best Actor prize. Big biceps, big budget, and big box office made *Gladiator* Russell Crowe a certain contender for Best Actor of 2000. Beyond his powerful performance, Crowe likely also earned votes from Academy members who thought he should have won the year before. For his second Best Actor battle, Crowe remained the last contender standing in Oscar's arena. The next year his beautiful performance in *A Beautiful Mind* left pundits suspecting he might join Spencer Tracy and Tom Hanks as the only back-to-back Best Actor winners, but Denzel Washington turned his *Training Day* into a victorious night.

Kathy Bates

> **1990 Best Actress as nurse/kidnapper Annie Wilkes in *Misery***
> 1998 Best Supporting Actress as political advisor Libby Holden in *Primary Colors*
> 2002 Best Supporting Actress as mother Roberta Hertzel in *About Schmidt*

Before she caused James Caan *Misery* in 1990, Bates had earned a 1983 Tony nomination as the suicidal daughter in *'night, Mother* and enjoyed a long run in *Frankie and Johnny in the Clair de Lune*. But at first, her powerful presence wasn't an easy Hollywood sell, and those roles respectively went to Sissy Spacek and Michelle Pfeiffer in film adaptations that the Academy ignored. But Oscar quickly became Bates' "number one fan" when she blended terrifying odiousness with "cocky-doodie" comic relief in Rob Reiner's adaptation of Stephen King's *Misery*. As the only nominees from their respective films, Bates and *Pretty Woman* Julia Roberts were neck and neck going into the 1990 Academy Awards, with both still riding their Best Actress wins at the Golden Globes, Bates for Drama and Roberts for Musical or Comedy. On Oscar night, Bates, who had also played Mrs. Green in the Oscar-nominated *Dick Tracy*, seemed to have the late-season momentum, and Daniel Day-Lewis announced her the winner. Bates followed that hit with *Fried Green Tomatoes*, a film that grossed twice as much at the box office and earned Jessica Tandy a Best Supporting Actress Oscar nomination. Bates portrayed Molly Brown in the 1997 Best Picture *Titanic*, but playing the unsinkable stalwart didn't bring her an Oscar nomination as it had Debbie Reynolds in 1964. But Bates was a lead contender in her next two Academy Award races, both as a supporting player. As volatile powerhouse Libby Holden, she conveyed multiple *Primary Colors*, and shared with Lynn Redgrave of *Gods and Monsters* the best shot at upsetting Judi Dench's expected win for *Shakespeare in Love*. In 2002, Bates' nude hot tub scene in *About Schmidt* gave her extended press, but that race ultimately came down to Meryl Streep in *Adaptation* and winner Catherine Zeta-Jones in the year's big winner, *Chicago*. Since then, Bates has spent most of her time directing for and acting in television programs to Emmy-winning success, and doing occasional movies including Oscar winners *The Blind Side* (2009) and *Midnight in Paris* (2011).

Renée Zellweger

 2001 Best Actress as publishing worker/journalist/TV news correspondent Bridget Jones in *Bridget Jones's Diary*
 2002 Best Actress as showgirl Roxie Hart in *Chicago*
 2003 Best Supporting Actress as farmer Ruby Thewes in *Cold Mountain*

While going to school in her native Texas, Renée Zellweger recorded in her diary her dream of one day working with Meryl Streep. Less than a decade later, her dream was fulfilled when she played Streep's daughter in *One True Thing*, which earned Streep, but not Zellweger, an Oscar nomination. The same fate befell her two years earlier when she was expected to earn a Best Actress, or even a Best Supporting Actress, bid opposite Tom Cruise in *Jerry*

Maguire, but only Cruise and eventual Supporting Actor winner Cuba Gooding, Jr., locked in enough Academy votes to appear on Oscar ballots. The new millennium was groundbreaking for Zellweger, who overcame the controversy of being an American cast in the coveted role as beloved British ne'er-do-well Bridget Jones in the adaptation of Helen Fielding's bestselling novel. Zellweger competed for and lost the Oscar to Halle Berry in *Monster's Ball*. The following year *Chicago* razzle-dazzled the Academy, and Zellweger, *Far From Heaven*'s Julianne Moore, and initial longshot Nicole Kidman of *The Hours* led the Best Actress race, with Kidman taking the prize. The following year Zellweger joined forces with Kidman to survive and farm *Cold Mountain*. Playing rustic independent Ruby Thewes dropped Zellweger to the supporting race, which she handily won over potential spoiler Shohreh Aghdashloo of *House of Sand and Fog*.

Marisa Tomei

1992 Best Supporting Actress as fiancée Mona Lisa Vito in *My Cousin Vinny*
2001 Best Supporting Actress as girlfriend/mother Natalie Strout in *In the Bedroom*
2008 Best Supporting Actress as stripper Cassidy/Pam in *The Wrestler*

In 1992 Marisa Tomei's career achieved "positraction" as Joe Pesci's wedding-ready, mechanically adept girlfriend in *My Cousin Vinny*. Initially a longshot to win Best Supporting Actress, Tomei's chances were buoyed by her appearance as Mabel Normand opposite Best Actor nominee Robert Downey, Jr., as *Chaplin*, and by the fact that in her supporting actress category she was the sole American nominee against four Brits, a pattern that often provides a home team advantage. Presenter Jack Palance chided that all the contenders were foreign, four English and one from Brooklyn, before announcing Tomei the winner. Her comic gem of a performance has gone down in Oscar history as a favorite. The following decade, her supporting performance as the woman indirectly responsible for the death of Sissy Spacek's and Tom Wilkinson's son brought all three actors into Oscar contention for director Todd Field's debut feature film, *In the Bedroom*. Tomei lost to Jennifer Connelly for *A Beautiful Mind*, but was up again seven years later for *The Wrestler* in a competition against winner Penélope Cruz of *Vicky Cristina Barcelona*. Although Tomei brought something sparkling and original to all her nominated performances, some film critics in 2008 sited her textured performance as an aging stripper wooed by *The Wrestler* as career-topping.

Penélope Cruz

    2006 Best Actress as restaurant manager Raimunda in *Volver*
    2008 Best Supporting Actress as ex-wife Maria Elena in *Vicky Cristina Barcelona*
    2009 Best Supporting Actress as mistress/wife Carla Albanese in *Nine*

Like other international beauties such as Melina Mercouri of Greece, Sophia Loren of Italy, and Anouk Aimée of France, Spanish beauty Cruz needed just one performance to gain worldwide fame and astonish the Academy enough to bring her into the ranks of lead actress contenders. She found that vehicle in Pedro Almodóvar's *Volver* as the central character of a family of eccentric working class women going to deep-freeze lengths to survive. Despite the film's stellar reviews, the Academy overlooked it for any awards but Best Actress, a nomination that continued Cruz's award season run of recognition that began with Cruz and the other actresses from the movie sharing Best Actress honors at the Cannes Film Festival. Had 2006 not belonged to Helen Mirren as *The Queen*, Cruz might have expected to be called up to Oscar's stage to accept a statuette. That honor came just two years later as the riled, impassioned ex-wife of Javier Bardem in *Vicky Cristina Barcelona*. Cruz took many Supporting Actress prizes that season, but lost the Golden Globe to Kate Winslet in *The Reader*. When Oscar bumped Winslet up to the Best Actress category, Cruz was an obvious Supporting Actress victor over such other fine performances as Amy Adams and Viola Davis in *Doubt*, Taraji P. Henson in *The Curious Case of Benjamin Button*, and Marisa Tomei in *The Wrestler*. The following year, Cruz was singled out among several fine female performances of Rob Marshall's *Nine* for its only acting nomination as Daniel Day-Lewis' lusty, uninhibited but not always secure mistress. The following year, Cruz married fellow Oscar-winner Javier Bardem, placing them among the rare married acting pairs of Oscar-winning actors such as Vivien Leigh and Laurence Olivier, and Joanne Woodward and Paul Newman.

Javier Bardem

    2000 Best Actor as author Reinaldo Arenas in *Before Night Falls*
    2007 Best Supporting Actor as hitman Anton Chigurh in *No Country for Old Men*
    2010 Best Actor as father Uxbal in *Biutiful*

With his expressionless visage framed by a drab pageboy, and his methodic trudge in blood-soaked socks, Javier Bardem gave as menacing an Oscar-winning performance as Anthony Hopkins as the liver-sucking, chianti-sipping Hannibal Lecter in *The Silence of the Lambs*. 2007 belonged to the Coen Brothers' *No Country for Old Men*, and few Oscar victories seemed as guaranteed as Bardem's for Best Supporting Actor. Bardem appropriately gave part of his acceptance speech in Spanish, as he became the first Spaniard to win an acting Oscar. The following year, Penélope Cruz became the second. The year after that, they wed. Bardem started this millennium an international star as gay poet Reinaldo Arenas trying to escape persecution in Cuba *Before Night Falls*. The performance earned him Best Actor from the National Board of Review, National Society of Film Critics, and the Independent Spirit award, but that Oscar went to *Gladiator* Russell Crowe. After a *Biutiful* reception at the 2010 Cannes Film Festival where he was named Best Actor, Bardem earned another Oscar nomination, again as lead actor, playing a dying drug addict with an awakened conscience and a plan to secure a future for his children after he's gone.

Gena Rowlands

> 1974 Best Actress as housewife/mother Mabel Longhetti in *A Woman under the Influence*
> 1980 Best Actress as mobster's girlfriend Gloria Swenson in *Gloria*
> **2015 Honorary lifetime achievement award to "Gena Rowlands, who has illuminated the human experience through her brilliant, passionate and fearless performances"**

Fourteen years into Rowlands' marriage to John Cassavetes, their professional collaborations ignited interest from critics and the Academy with the groundbreaking film *Faces*. One of the first independent projects to impress the Academy, *Faces* appeared in three Oscar categories, reflecting Cassavetes' only writing nomination, and featuring Seymour Cassel and Lynn Carlin as longshots in their respective supporting acting categories. Rowlands herself stepped onto Oscar's red carpet as a favorite to win Best Actress of 1974 as *A Woman under the Influence*. Crumbling through director Cassavetes' long unflinching scenes, Rowlands captivated with her complex, sometimes excruciating characterization. She won that year's Best Actress from the National Board of Review and Best Actress, Drama at the Golden Globe over other Oscar front-runners, Faye Dunaway in *Chinatown* and Ellen Burstyn as the title character in *Alice Doesn't Live Here Anymore*. Burstyn won the Oscar, but Rowlands broke ground for indie films and female protagonists. She competed against Burstyn again in 1980 as *Gloria*, a tough pistol packer on the lam with a child in tow. The diametric extremes of her two Oscar-nominated performances attested to the range she mastered as an actor, making her a welcome and deserving recipient of the Academy's lifetime achievement award in 2015.

Christian Bale

2010 Best Supporting Actor as boxing trainer Dicky Eklund in *The Fighter*
2013 Best Actor as con artist Irving Rosenfeld in *American Hustle*
2015 Best Supporting Actor as physician/hedge fund manager Michael Burry in *The Big Short*

The Gregor Samsa of non–Method actors, Christian Bale infuses every aspect of his body and psyche to metamorphose into characters that rank among the most indelible in recent film history. At age 13, he anchored the visual splendor of *Empire of the Sun*, which competed for six artistic Academy Awards that all went to *The Last Emperor*. He supported Oscar nominees Kenneth Branagh as *Henry V* (1989) and Winona Ryder in *Little Women* (1994). As *The Dark Knight* in 2008 he protected Gotham City from posthumous winner Heath Ledger before becoming one of the dominating Oscar contenders of the 2010s. He started the decade by winning Best Supporting Actor as *The Fighter*'s emaciated trainer and ostracized brother with the hair-trigger temper. He was almost unrecognizable masterminding an *American Hustle* with Amy Adams, which earned them both their first lead acting nods from the Academy. Bale was the only member of *The Big Short*'s impressive cast to rustle an acting nomination as the bleary but stonily self-assured predictor of the financial collapse that netted his character over 100 million dollars. With an eye for quality writing as sharp as his acting skill, Bale knows how to pick powerful material and bring it to life with award-worthy results.

Viola Davis

2008 Best Supporting Actress as mother Mrs. Miller in *Doubt*
2011 Best Actress as maid Aibileen Clark in *The Help*
2016 Best Supporting Actress as wife/mother Rose Maxson in *Fences*

With only three performances, Viola Davis' impact on the Academy intensified from a subtle rumble to a seismic implosion. Academy attention on the actors from *Doubt* initially focused on the triangle of opposing forces played by Meryl Streep, Philip Seymour Hoffman and Amy Adams. But Viola Davis' brief scenes opposite Streep were so indelible that the Academy nominated her, along with Adams, as Best Supporting Actress of 2008. As the 2011 Oscars approached, Davis was favored to win Best Actress after her often-repeated "You is kind. You is smart. You is important" affirmation to her young wards in *The Help* seeped into the movie-going zeitgeist of the era. When Streep won that competition for *The Iron Lady*, she stopped to acknowledge Davis with a hug before reaching the stage. After becoming the first African American to win a Lead Actress in a Drama Series Emmy for *How to Get Away with Murder*, and a Tony for *Fences*, Davis joined costar and film director Denzel Washington in recreating their stage roles in the movie adaptation. Davis dominated the Best Supporting Actress category that entire award season, and handily punctuated her victories with an Oscar win as well.

Natalie Portman

    2004 Best Supporting Actress as stripper Alice Ayres/Jane Jones in *Closer*
    2010 Best Actress as ballerina Nina Sayers/The Swan Queen in ***Black Swan***
    2016 Best Actress as First Lady Jackie Kennedy in *Jackie*

A late-season Golden Globe victory for *Closer* launched Natalie Portman into the cluster of frontrunners for 2004 Best Supporting Actress with Virginia Madsen from *Sideways* and the ultimate winner, Cate Blanchett in *The Aviator*. Six years later, her harrowing portrayal of a prima ballerina psychologically succumbing to the darker aspects of her role in *Swan Lake* brought even higher hopes that her name would be pulled from the envelope on Oscar night. Although Annette Bening's performance in *The Kids Are All Right* left room for a possible Best Actress upset, on Academy Awards night, Portman seemed to have her competition well in hand. By the end of that night, she had a tight grip on her very own Oscar, too. Portman joined a prestigious handful of actresses (Beula Bondi in *The Gorgeous Hussy*, Joan Allen in *Nixon* and Sally Field in *Lincoln*) when she earned an Oscar nomination playing a First Lady in *Jackie*. This time, the First Lady, not the President was the focal point of the film, and she captured Jackie's persona with haunting perfection. Early award season praise suggested Portman would lead the Best Actress Oscar race, but mixed reviews for the movie and weak box office evened the chances for all five Best Actress nominees. Although she appeared on a "Mean Tweets" segment and was featured in a Best Actress montage, a very pregnant Portman was the only Oscar nominated actor not in attendance at the 2016 Academy Awards.

Most Nominated Non-Winners

Richard Burton

    1952 Best Supporting Actor as aristocrat Philip Ashley in *My Cousin Rachel*

1. So Close and Yet So Far

1953 Best Actor as Roman tribune Marcellus Gallio in *The Robe*
1964 Best Actor as Archbishop of Canterbury/saint Thomas Becket in *Becket*
1965 Best Actor as spy Alec Leamas in *The Spy Who Came in from the Cold*
1966 Best Actor as history professor George in *Who's Afraid of Virginia Woolf?*
1969 Best Actor as English monarch King Henry VIII in *Anne of the Thousand Days*
1977 Best Actor as psychiatrist Dr. Martin Dysart in *Equus*

Burton started strong with the Academy in the early 1950s, rising from supporting to lead actor nominee in two dramas from director Henry Koster. Suspecting his beloved *Cousin Rachel* of murder brought Burton a New Male Star of 1952 Golden Globe and made him a Hollywood leading man, yet Oscar placed him in the supporting category in a race he lost to Anthony Quinn in *Viva Zapata!* The Academy honored *The Robe* with five nominations in 1953, including Best Picture and Best Actor for Burton. Scant Oscar-winning costumes shot imposingly through CinemaScope could not detract from Burton's performance, where he grappled with guilt expressed through a liquid Welsh accent. While his Academy peers nominated Peter O'Toole and him more than any other actors throughout the 1960s, they failed to honor either with a win. Burton blamed his losses on personal indulgences and excesses. In the 1950s, when the Academy first embraced him with nominations, a drunk Burton made unflattering remarks about Hollywood at a party that dimmed his rising star. In the 1960s, he confessed to squandering his talent, which originally drew comparisons to Olivier, on his romance with Elizabeth Taylor. Though their teaming inspired some of his strongest performances, his work was constantly overshadowed by tabloid hysteria fueled by his drinking, spending, and public shows of affection. He and *Becket* co-star Peter O'Toole may have canceled each other's Best Actor votes in 1964, but his loss to Lee Marvin in a comic Western role in 1965's *Cat Ballou* suggested that his favor with the Academy remained marginal. He triumphed with wife Elizabeth Taylor in *Who's Afraid of Virginia Woolf?*, and both were nominated in the lead acting categories. On Oscar night, she won, but Burton lost to fellow Brit Paul Scofield in *A Man for All Seasons*. Rave reviews for *Anne of the Thousand Days* couldn't overcome John Wayne's impact in *True Grit*. The 1977 Oscars held the most promise for the Academy to finally acknowledge Burton, as his *Equus* soliloquies were among the most searing in film history. When Oscar opted for Richard Dreyfuss in the romantic comedy *The Goodbye Girl*, Burton set a record as most nominated actor never to win. His record still stands.

Thelma Ritter

1950 Best Supporting Actress as dresser Birdie in *All About Eve*
1951 Best Supporting Actress as hamburger stand owner/mother Ellen McNulty in *The Mating Season*
1952 Best Supporting Actress as nurse Clancy in *With a Song in My Heart*
1953 Best Supporting Actress as waterfront tie peddler Moe Williams in *Pickup on South Street*
1959 Best Supporting Actress as housekeeper Alma in *Pillow Talk*
1962 Best Supporting Actress as mother Elizabeth Stroud in *Birdman of Alcatraz*

If a mid–20th century script called for a wise, and wise-cracking, supporting female, Thelma Ritter usually got the part, and an Oscar nomination. Ritter definitely knew a good script when she saw one, as three of her first performances came in movies that won Best Screenplay Oscars: she was a Macy's shopper in *Miracle on 34th Street*, the neighbor who chugged beer and provided comic relief in *A Letter to Three Wives*, and then Margo Channing's always-suspicious-of-Eve-and-not-afraid-to-say-"I told you so" dresser in *All About Eve*. That role started a run of four consecutive Oscar nominations that kept her a dominating presence of the Oscars throughout the first half of the 1950s. In Mitchell Leisen's screwball comedy *The Mating Season*, her comic characterization as a mother mistaken for a hired cook was singled out for Oscar consideration. Her best shot at Oscar might have been as the weary necktie vendor who proved a useful informant in Samuel Fuller's downbeat *Pickup on South Street*. That year, *From Here to Eternity*'s Donna Reed beat Ritter. Other Oscar-nominated roles called for a nurse's uniform in *With a Song in My Heart*, a maid's simple attire (with pockets large enough for her stash of booze) in *Pillow Talk*, and a hardened old mother's overcoat and hat in *Birdman of Alcatraz*, but the Brooklynese barbs were all Ritter. Her *Pickup on South Street* nomination made her the first, and still only, actor with supporting Oscar nominations in four consecutive years. She became the most nominated supporting player with her *Pillow Talk* nomination, then broke her own record when nominated in the same category for *Birdman of Alcatraz*. The fact that she never won for any of these performances also set a record as the most recognized supporting player never to take home Oscar.

Glenn Close

1982 Best Supporting Actress as nurse/writer Jenny Fields in *The World According to Garp*

1983 Best Supporting Actress as doctor Sarah Cooper in *The Big Chill*
1984 Best Supporting Actress as girlfriend/mother Iris Gaines in *The Natural*
1987 Best Actress as publishing editor/mistress Alex Forrest in *Fatal Attraction*
1988 Best Actress as French aristocrat Marquise de Merteuil in *Dangerous Liaisons*
2011 Best Actress as hotel waiter Albert Nobbs in *Albert Nobbs*

Few stars had the Oscar track record of Glenn Close in the 1980s. Her big screen debut was a powder keg that ignited her career. As fierce feminist Jenny Fields, Close shaped *The World According to Garp* by modeling for her son the benefits of eccentric nonconformity. The following year, she was the only member of *The Big Chill*'s ensemble to vie for Oscar, and entered the category for her third year in a row literally glowing as an angelic symbol in *The Natural*. Close ascended to lead acting nominations soon after. Despite playing one of *the* ubiquitous movie characters of the decade as a jilted lover whose *Fatal Attraction* won't let her be ignored, Close lost a tight Best Actress race to Cher in *Moonstruck*. Expected to take the category the following year, she lost to longshot Jodie Foster in *The Accused*. Strong competition, rather than any dissatisfaction from the Academy, accounts for her being the most nominated female actor to grace both categories and leave every Oscar ceremony empty-handed. She's had much better award fortune in other media. Television performances in *The Lion in Winter* (2004) netted her a SAG and Golden Globe, while the series *Damages* brought her another Globe and two Emmys to add to the previous Emmy she earned for *Serving in Silence*. For her stage work she's won three Tonys, for the dramas *The Real Thing* (1984) and *Death and the Maiden* (1992) as well as the musical *Sunset Boulevard* (1995). The year she earned her first Oscar nomination, she won an Obie for the stage play *The Singular Life of Albert Nobbs*. Three decades later, she brought her passion project to the big screen. Oscar took note and recognized her with a sixth nomination. With a record like hers, Close must certainly be on the minds of the Academy when considering lifetime achievement honors.

Irene Dunne

1930/31 Best Actress as settler/wife Sabra Cravat in *Cimarron*
1936 Best Actress as author Theodora Lynn in *Theodora Goes Wild*
1937 Best Actress as wife Lucy Warriner in *The Awful Truth*
1939 Best Actress as music teacher Terry McKay in *Love Affair*
1948 Best Actress as matriarch Marta "Mama" Hanson in *I Remember Mama*

Author Edna Ferber did well by Irene Dunne, who had her two first big hits, and initial Oscar nomination playing Ferber characters. Director Wesley Ruggles' adaptation of *Cimarron* brought both leads, Irene Dunne and Richard Dix, acting nominations and won Best Picture. In 1936, Dunne reprised her star-making stage role of Magnolia Hawks in *Show Boat* for the best-reviewed movie adaptation of the Kern and Hammerstein classic, and then proved adept at screwball comedy with an Oscar-nominated performance as an incognito author in *Theodora Goes Wild*. The following year she was up for an even more popular movie in the same genre, *The Awful Truth*. For the second year in a row, she lost Best Actress to Luise Rainer. Dunne shone during her 1939 *Love Affair* with Charles Boyer, but that Best Actress race belonged to Vivien Leigh as Scarlett O'Hara. Almost a decade later, Dunne played yet another vastly different character from her previous nominated turns. This time she was the quietly solid matriarch of a Swedish immigrant family in George Stevens' *I Remember Mama*. Every bit as lovely and loveable here as in her romantic performances, Dunne again found herself in one of the toughest Best Actress categories in Academy history. Ingrid Bergman was one of the first females to carry an epic as *Joan of Arc*; director Anatole Litvak showcased Olivia de Havilland and Barbara Stanwyck respectively battling insanity in *The Snake Pit* and *Sorry, Wrong Number*, and winner Jane Wyman silently conveyed the horror of rape as a deaf mute in *Johnny Belinda*. In 1939, Dunne was up for Best Actress for *Love Affair*, but Deborah Kerr was not nominated when cast in Dunne's role in the 1957 remake, *An Affair to Remember*. In 1946, Dunne was overlooked for Best Actress in *Anna and the King of Siam*, but Kerr was nominated for the 1956 musical remake, *The King & I*. Equally talented and beloved, both career-entwined actors had multiple lead actress Oscar nods, but no competitive wins. Why the Academy decided to honor Kerr with a lifetime achievement accolade but never Dunne remains an unanswered Oscar mystery.

Arthur Kennedy

1949 Best Supporting Actor as brother/boxing manager Connie Kelly in *Champion*
1951 Best Actor as U.S. Army sergeant Larry Levins in *Bright Victory*
1955 Best Supporting Actor as lawyer Barney Castle in *Trial*
1957 Best Supporting Actor as father Lucas Cross in *Peyton Place*
1958 Best Supporting Actor as brother Frank Hirsh in *Some Came Running*

Sandy-haired chameleon Arthur Kennedy was best known for his stage interpretations of Arthur Miller characters. His rendering of morally confused

Biff in *Death of a Salesman* earned him the 1949 Tony Award. That same year, Kennedy was up for his first Oscar, supporting boxing *Champion* Kirk Douglas as his weak-willed brother and manager. When *Death of a Salesman* was adapted for the big screen in 1951, Kevin McCarthy got the role of Biff and the supporting Oscar nomination. But Kennedy had little time to fret, for that year he competed in the lead actor category as a veteran reaching a *Bright Victory* in overcoming physical blindness and his racial prejudices. Kennedy was a consistent figure in the Best Supporting Actor races of the latter half of the 1950s. His attorney brought *Trial* its only Oscar nomination, but he was in good company when he and four other *Peyton Place* stars dominated the acting categories of 1957. He may have lost some votes to co-star Russ Tamblyn, but as a poor alcoholic who raped his daughter (Best Supporting Actress nominee Hope Lange), Kennedy made his dastardly character unforgettable. *Some Came Running* to name him Best Supporting Actor in his fifth competition, but Burl Ives was such a dominating presence in 1958 playing two pugnacious patriarchs, Big Daddy in *Cat on a Hot Tin Roof* and Rufus Hannassey in *The Big Country* that the Best Supporting Actor question that year was not so much who would win, but for which role Burl Ives would take the prize. He won for the latter, and Kennedy remained without an Oscar. Kennedy continued to make hit movies throughout the 1960s, with roles in Academy Award winners *Elmer Gantry*, *Lawrence of Arabia*, and *Fantastic Voyage*.

Albert Finney

    1963 Best Actor as foundling Tom Jones in *Tom Jones*
    1974 Best Actor as detective Hercule Poirot in *Murder on the Orient Express*
    1983 Best Actor as actor Sir in *The Dresser*
    1984 Best Actor as British consul Geoffrey Firmin in *Under the Volcano*
    2000 Best Supporting Actor as lawyer Ed Masry in *Erin Brockovich*

Two landmark 1960 movies brought British charmer Albert Finney instant success. He first came into Oscar's view supporting Best Actor nominee Laurence Olivier in *The Entertainer*, directed by Tony Richardson. But he established himself in the "angry young man" mold of British imports in *Saturday Night and Sunday Morning*, for which BAFTA named his Most Promising Newcomer, but which the Academy bypassed entirely. Director Richardson reteamed with Finney in 1963 for the lusty comic adaptation of Henry Fielding's 1749 novel *Tom Jones*. As the charmingly roguish title character, Finney cemented his status as a worldwide star, and earned his first Academy Award nomination. In 1974 Finney investigated a *Murder on the*

Orient Express as Agatha Christie's fastidious, thick-tongued Belgian sleuth Hercule Poirot. A longshot for Best Actor that year, Finney managed to bump Gene Hackman of *The Conversation* out of a 1974 Best Actor slot, earning his second lead actor nomination. Finney's Oscar heyday came in the 1980s with back-to-back Best Actor bids. He was unforgettable as an aging, bombastic actor in *The Dresser*, but being nominated against Tom Courtenay as his dresser may have lessened both their chances for a win. *Under the Volcano* would likely have gone under Oscar's radar if not for Finney's towering performance. If ever the Academy had an opportunity to honor Finney's lifetime of powerhouse work with a late-career Best Supporting win, it would have been in 2000. But *Erin Brockovich* remained a vehicle for Best Actress winner Julia Roberts, and the Best Supporting Actor race of 2000 was dominated all season by Benicio Del Toro of *Traffic*. But with his filmography and reputation, Finney may well follow in the footsteps of fellow Brits like Alec Guinness, Laurence Olivier, and Peter O'Toole by earning a lifetime achievement Oscar.

Amy Adams

2005 Best Supporting Actress as wife Ashley Johnsten in *Junebug*
2008 Best Supporting Actress as schoolteacher Sister James in *Doubt*
2010 Best Supporting Actress as bartender Charlene Fleming in *The Fighter*
2012 Best Supporting Actress as wife Peggy Dodd in *The Master*
2013 Best Actress as con artist Sydney Prosser/Lady Edith Greensly in *American Hustle*

Whether fair, fowl, frail, or ferocious, Amy Adams has already unveiled a gamut of varied characterizations that have dazzled Oscar. He first caught a glimpse of the pale, usually strawberry blonde as a nurse in Steven Spielberg's *Catch Me If You Can* (2002), which brought Christopher Walken a Best Supporting Actor nomination. Adams became a fixed feature of the Best Supporting Actress category starting three years later in a showcase role as Ashley Johnsten, pregnant with rosy optimism in *Junebug*. With a Cannes Film Festival win followed by an Academy Award nomination, she seemed on the fast track to joining the likes of Eva Marie Saint, Shirley Jones, and Anjelica Huston and launching a stellar career by winning in her first Oscar competition. Instead, the Academy voted for Rachel Wiesz as a more politically driven mother-to-be in *The Constant Gardener*. Adams' next two nominated performances caught interference from other cast members, as Viola Davis was also up for *Doubt* and Melissa Leo took the prize over her for *The Fighter*. Adams proved to be the fierce sustaining force behind *The Master*'s charisma in 2012, and the next year she found herself for the first time vying for lead actress of the year as the mercurial Sydney Prosser, doing an *American Hustle* with a British accent. Like Thelma Ritter and Glenn Close before her, Adams has been a glistening find for several consecutive Oscar competitions without shimmering with gold in hand. But Adams and her career are both young and hot, which keep her prospects glowing.

Claude Rains

- 1939 Best Supporting Actor as Senator Joseph Paine in *Mr. Smith Goes to Washington*
- 1943 Best Supporting Actor as police captain Louis Renault in *Casablanca*
- 1944 Best Supporting Actor as stockbroker Job Skeffington in *Mr. Skeffington*
- 1946 Best Supporting Actor as relocated Nazi Alexander Sebastian in *Notorious*

London-born Rains started in silent movies, but made his greatest contribution to motion pictures as a supporting character actor in some of the greatest classics in film history. He played in the Best Picture-nominated *The Adventures of Robin Hood* in 1938, and the following year found himself competing against his *Mr. Smith Goes to Washington* co-star Harry Carey for Best Supporting Actor. Thomas Mitchell of *Stagecoach* won instead, but Rains eased into the next decade as one of the most sought after supporting players for directors from Frank Capra and Michael Curtiz to Alfred Hitchcock and Sam Wood. He played the title character in *Here Comes Mr. Jordan*, a big winner at the 1941 Academy Awards, but James Gleason, not Rains, was nominated for Best Supporting Actor. He began a beautiful friendship with Humphrey Bogart in *Casablanca*, and the two actors were the only cast members nominated from the Best Picture winner. He was up for Supporting Actor for another title character, *Mr. Skeffington*, but *Going My Way* was the year's big winner, and Barry Fitzgerald won that Oscar. Rains perfected the ultimate screen villain in Hitchcock's *Notorious*, but in 1946 the Academy cast most of its votes for *The Best Years of Our Lives*. Even though they were already giving Harold Russell an Honorary Oscar for his performance, Academy members doubled up and named him Best Supporting Actor as well. Rains' list of Oscar-favored movies include classics such as *Juarez*; *Kings Row*; *Now, Voyager*; and even *Lawrence of Arabia*. Though small in stature, Rains always stood tall with characterizations that rang true with every word and gesture.

Agnes Moorehead

1942 Best Supporting Actress as spinster aunt Fanny Minafer in *The Magnificent Ambersons*
1944 Best Supporting Actress as French baroness Aspacia Conti in *Mrs. Parkington*
1948 Best Supporting Actress as aunt Aggie MacDonald in *Johnny Belinda*
1964 Best Supporting Actress as housekeeper Velma Cruther in *Hush ... Hush, Sweet Charlotte*

Like Walter Brennan, revered thespian Agnes Moorehead began playing characters much older than she from an early age. A member of Orson Welles' Mercury Players, she had the pivotal role of young Charles Foster Kane's mother in *Citizen Kane*. She was named the New York Film Critics Best Actress and earned her first Oscar nomination under Welles' direction as Tim Holt's Aunt Fanny in *The Magnificent Ambersons*. She took the Golden Globe and was nominated for Oscar as French aristocrat Aspacia Conti opposite Greer Garson as *Mrs. Parkington*. Oscar's 1944 ballot was filled with Agnes Moorehead movies, as she also starred in *Since You Went Away*, *The Seventh Cross*, and *Dragon Seed*. With her drooping gaze and saltwater taffy line delivery, Moorehead specialized in griping doubters, and was nominated as one in *Johnny Belinda*. She had such chemistry with Best Actress winner Jane Wyman that Moorehead supported her in Wyman's next two Oscar nominated movies, *The Blue Veil* (1951) and *Magnificent Obsession* (1954). In the 1960s, Moorehead caught up in age to her characters, and hit her professional stride. During the run of popular TV sitcom *Bewitched*, Moorehead won an Emmy for guest starring on *Wild, Wild West* and was up for Oscar once more as the haggard housekeeper who figures out the deadly goings-on in Robert Aldrich's *Hush ... Hush, Sweet Charlotte*. Moorehead's final scene is among the most compelling, and shocking, in horror film history. Although she lost the Oscar that year to Lila Kedrova of *Zorba the Greek*, she earned another Golden Globe. Moorehead stood out in Oscar contenders including *The Stratton Story*, *Caged*, *Raintree County*, *How the West Was Won*, and, reteaming with director Robert Aldrich, *What's the Matter with Helen?* A fair question: What would have been the matter with giving Moorehead, one of filmdom's greatest character actresses, an Academy Award?

Marsha Mason

1973 Best Actress as prostitute Maggie Paul in *Cinderella Liberty*
1977 Best Actress as dancer Paula McFadden in *The Goodbye Girl*

1979 Best Actress as soap opera actress Jennie MacLaine in *Chapter Two*
1981 Best Actress as actress Georgia Hines in *Only When I Laugh*

The year 1973 started a peak in Marsha Mason's life and career by enchanting two entertainment powerhouses: the pillar of quick-quip comedy, playwright/screenwriter Neil Simon, and the little golden boy named Oscar. That year Mason starred in Neil Simon's Broadway play *The Good Doctor* and the movie *Cinderella Liberty*. Working with Simon led to their 10-year marriage, and starring as a hard-luck prostitute opposite James Caan led Mason to her first Oscar competition for Best Actress. Her next three nominations came for interpreting Neil Simon works. She was a romance-shy dancer dodging the sparks generated with Best Actor winner Richard Dreyfuss in *The Goodbye Girl* and an alcoholic mother to Kristy McNichol in *Only When I Laugh*. In 1979, she reteamed with James Caan to portray a character based on herself in Neil Simon's autobiographical romance *Chapter Two*. All four of her Oscar-nominated performances are considered exceptional. She won a Golden Globe as Best Actress, Drama for *Cinderella Liberty*, and another as Best Actress, Musical or Comedy for *The Goodbye Girl*. For both *Only When I Laugh* and *Chapter Two* her performances generated enthusiastic praise, with some critics citing the latter as the strongest of her career.

Jane Alexander

1970 Best Actress as girlfriend Eleanor Bachman in *The Great White Hope*
1976 Best Supporting Actress as informer The Bookkeeper in *All the President's Men*
1979 Best Supporting Actress as abandoned wife/neighbor Margaret Phelps in *Kramer vs. Kramer*
1983 Best Actress as wife/mother Carol Wetherly in *Testament*

Jane Alexander launched her stage and screen careers on *The Great White Hope*, first winning the Tony Award for Best Featured Actress in a Play, and then reprising her role to a Best Actress Oscar nomination in the film version with Broadway and cinema co-star James Earl Jones. Alexander lost her first Oscar competition to Glenda Jackson in *Women in Love*. Two subsequent nominations in the 1970s came in the supporting category. The 1976 Best Supporting Actress race was anyone's to win, with Alexander especially strong as a reticent whistleblower in *All the President's Men*. Also favored was Piper Laurie in *Carrie*, but no one counted out young Jodie Foster in *Taxi Driver*. Longshots that year were Lee Grant for *Voyage of the Damned* and surprise winner Beatrice Straight in *Network*. After her role in *Kramer vs. Kramer* was modified to highlight Meryl Streep's more pivotal character, Joanna, the lead female in the film, Alexander was understandably disappointed when the Academy nominated and awarded Streep the Oscar over Alexander in the supporting category. Alexander again contended for lead actress in 1983, and might have won as a mother struggling to save her children after a nuclear holocaust had that year's Best Actress race not been so clearly dominated all award season by Shirley MacLaine in *Terms of Endearment*.

Ed Harris

   1995 Best Supporting Actor as NASA flight director Gene Kranz in *Apollo 13*
   1998 Best Supporting Actor as television show creator and director Christof in *The Truman Show*
   2000 Best Actor as artist Jackson Pollock in *Pollock*
   2002 Best Supporting Actor as author Richard Brown in *The Hours*

Every year Ed Harris has competed for an Academy Award, he arrived at the ceremony as most pundits' pick to take his category, only to go home empty-handed. His dynamic portrayal of NASA Flight Director Gene Kranz in *Apollo 13* made him the favorite to win Best Supporting Actor of 1995, with James Cromwell of *Babe* thought to be a possible upset. Instead, Kevin Spacey snuck into the winner's circle as one of *The Usual Suspects*. In 1998, Harris made his interpretation of Christof in *The Truman Show* a character so indelible his presence pervaded every scene. Such command from a supporting performance often results in an Oscar, but that year the Academy waxed nostalgic, and honored beloved character actor James Coburn in *Affliction*. Harris directed himself in the biopic of abstract expressionist painter Jackson *Pollock*, and the Best Actor race teased with the hope of a win until *Gladiator* built late-season momentum and went on to win Best Picture, and Best Actor for Russell Crowe. It seemed the Academy might finally make amends for earlier oversights when Harris was up again in 2002 as a writer with AIDS who never reconciled the shattering desertion from his mother (Best Supporting Actress nominee Julianne Moore). But as the 2002 award season ensued, Chris Cooper gathered a bevy of trophies for *Adaptation*, and by Oscar night easily took their category. Regularly featured in Oscar-beloved movies, such as *The Right Stuff* (1983), *Swing Shift* and *Places in the Heart* (1984), *Sweet Dreams* (1985), *The Firm* (1993), and *Nixon* (1995), Harris still has a good chance to be singled out for an Oscar of his own.

Annette Bening

- 1990 Best Supporting Actress as girlfriend/grifter Myra Langtry in *The Grifters*
- 1999 Best Actress as real estate broker Carolyn Burnham in *American Beauty*
- 2004 Best Actress as actress Julia Lambert in *Being Julia*
- 2010 Best Actress as doctor Nicole "Nic" Allgood in *The Kids Are All Right*

Bening started the 1990s by winning over two of Hollywood's most sought after men: Warren Beatty and Oscar. The Academy nominated her supporting performance as potentially the most duplicitous of all *The Grifters* conning each other in Stephen Frears' suspenseful neo-noir. Although Bening was named the National Society of Film Critics' Best Supporting Actress of 1990, that Oscar race belonged to Whoopi Goldberg in *Ghost*. The next year Bening starred opposite Warren Beatty in *Bugsy*. Although Bening was one of the few lead cast members not up for a 1991 Oscar for the biopic, their collaboration made Bening the one Hollywood starlet in three decades of Beatty's romantic partnerships that inspired him to marry. Bening's first two Best Actress expectations were both dimmed by Hilary Swank. Bening led the competition throughout the 1999 award season until Swank swept in for an upset victory in the indie film *Boys Don't Cry*. Early in 2004, Bening was pegged to finally win Best Actress as talented but disillusioned thespian Julia Lambert in *Being Julia* until, again, Swank was nominated as Clint Eastwood's *Million Dollar Baby* boxer and TKO'd Bening and the other nominees for her second Best Actress victory in five years. Bening gave another strong showing at the 2010 Oscars as an obstetrician and dominant spouse shaken by the impact the reemergence of her children's biological father has on her family in *The Kids Are All Right*. Though Bening won the Golden Globe for Best Actress, Musical or Comedy that year, Academy momentum built toward Natalie Portman's Oscar victory as an emotionally fraying ballerina in *Black Swan*. With talent like Bening's, she'll likely find a project that finally allows her to place her Best Actress statuette next to Beatty's Best Director Oscar for *Reds*.

Michelle Williams

- 2005 Best Supporting Actress as wife Alma Beers Del Mar in *Brokeback Mountain*
- 2010 Best Actress as pre-med student Cindy Heller in *Blue Valentine*
- 2011 Best Actress as actress Marilyn Monroe in *My Week with Marilyn*

2016 Best Supporting Actress as ex-wife Randi in *Manchester by the Sea*

Whether in a lead or supporting role, mercurial Michelle Williams can use a simple inflection or uniquely turned phrase to make her character the focal point of any scene she plays. While *Brokeback Mountain*'s groundbreaking love affair between the characters played by Heath Ledger and Jake Gyllenhaal alone could have mesmerized audiences, Williams garnered equal attention, and an Oscar nomination along with her male costars, as Ledger's distraught wife. A potential winner that year, Williams lost her competition to Rachel Weisz for *The Constant Gardener*. A touching portrayal of volatile love made her a *Blue Valentine*, and a lead actress Oscar nominee, in 2010. The next year, courageous Williams accepted the daunting task of playing the most iconic pop culture phenomenon to star in movies—Marilyn Monroe. Rather than accentuate the affectations, Williams found new nuances to Monroe's magnetic mix of neediness and guile, inviting even Monroe's lifelong fans to consider new facets of the superstar. Williams again vied for a supporting Oscar in a briefer but equally powerful turn opposite 2016 Best Actor winner Casey Affleck in *Manchester by the Sea*. No matter the category, Williams seems destined to one day leave a future Oscar ceremony with a golden statuette of her own.

2

Legends and Trailblazers

Those Who Won an Oscar

Charles Boyer

1937 Best Actor as French Emperor Napoleon Bonaparte in *Conquest*
1938 Best Actor as thief Pepe Le Moko in *Algiers*
1942 Honorary Award "for his progressive cultural achievement in establishing the French Research Foundation in Los Angeles as a source of reference for the Hollywood Motion Picture Industry"
1944 Best Actor as opera tutor Gregory Anton in *Gaslight*
1961 Best Actor as pub owner César in *Fanny*

Staid, intellectual, and unmoved by adulation beyond Hollywood's limelight, Boyer's dazzling screen presence made him to talkies what Rudolph Valentino was to silent film: an unparalleled romantic hero. He shone as brightly as luminescent star Greta Garbo in *Conquest*, and earned his first Best Actor nomination from the Academy. He competed in the same category the next year as iconic thief on the lam Pepe Le Moko, evading the police through the Casbah of *Algiers*. He lost both Oscar competitions to Spencer Tracy. The following year, he wooed Irene Dunne through the often-remade *Love Affair*, but only lead actress Dunne and supporting Actress Maria Ouspenskaya made Oscar's final 1939 ballot. Boyer's research about France's people and culture was aimed at shattering French stereotypes and introducing Americans to a richer view of his country. His globally unifying effort in the midst of World War II so impressed the Academy that they recognized Boyer with an honorary award in the form of a certificate of merit. Subsequently the Academy continued nominating him for lead acting Oscars. In 1944, he was a Best Actor frontrunner as the suave, menacing husband to Best Actress winner Ingrid Bergman in *Gaslight*, but he lost in part to the Academy's enthusiasm for *Going My Way*, which included Best Actor honors for Bing Crosby. When Boyer's career outpaced all his romantic lead contemporaries, he became known as cinema's last great lover and, despite being fourth in the credits, earned one more lead actor Oscar nomination, as a Marseille bartender whose family is impacted by lovely Leslie Caron as *Fanny*. Boyer's death forever confirmed that he deserved his indelible romantic image, as he took his own life two days after his wife of 44 years, actress Patricia Paterson, died of cancer.

Rosalind Russell

    1942 Best Actress as reporter Ruth Sherwood in *My Sister Eileen*
    1946 Best Actress as Australian bush nurse Elizabeth Kenny in *Sister Kenny*
    1947 Best Actress as daughter Lavinia Mannon in *Mourning Becomes Electra*
    1958 Best Actress as aunt Mame Dennis in *Auntie Mame*
    1972 Jean Hersholt Humanitarian Award

Of all the Hollywood legends, Russell and Charles Boyer came closest to meeting the criteria to make the countdown. She had the requisite four nominations and one victory, but the Academy Award she received was not for acting, but for her humanitarian work. Yet what an actress she was. When it came to comedy stars of their generation, Jean Arthur's cricket-whisper voice accommodated sweet innocents; at the opposite extreme, the husky boom Russell gave to her lines afforded her the glut of comic roles for fast-talking, quick-thinking independents from *His Girl Friday* to *Auntie Mame*. In comic or dramatic roles, Russell used a startled-sized gaze to convey horror (*Night Must Fall*), understanding (*The Citadel*), and resignation (*My Sister Eileen*). Russell could shoot a quip faster and funnier than most of her contemporaries, and wring pathos from a tear-crescent sidelong glance. Regarding Oscar, Russell is forever associated with the biggest upset in award history. Already a shoo-in to win Best Actress of 1947 for *Mourning Becomes Electra*, Russell took no chances and hired Joan Crawford's 1945 publicist for *Mildred Pierce* to lock in votes with an impassioned campaign. During 1947, RKO changed hands, and new studio head Dore Schary put his considerable influence behind getting Loretta Young, star of his own production, *The Farmer's Daughter*, into the winner's circle. He succeeded, Russell lost, and she never ended up with a competitive Oscar. After her record-setting five wins in five nominations at the Golden Globes, Russell was honored by the Academy for her volunteer work with the sick. Battling recurring cancer since 1959, Russell held her golden statuette in arthritic hands and acknowledged those who helped her when she too was "not quite well." Though her body was failing, her powerful heart touched a worldwide audience that night.

Judy Garland

1939 Special Award "for her outstanding performance as a screen juvenile during the past year"
1954 Best Actress as actress Esther Blodgett/Vicki Lester in *A Star Is Born*
1961 Best Supporting Actress as hausfrau Irene Hoffman in *Judgment at Nuremberg*

When Judy Garland sang and acted, emotion seeped through her very pores. The results were immortalizing. As teens, she and Mickey Rooney saved the day with backyard shows in Andy Hardy hits like *Babes in Arms*, giving Garland box office clout before *The Wizard of Oz* made her a superstar. Both movies came out in 1939, and the Academy honored Garland with a special miniature statuette, presented to her by Rooney. During that ceremony, she accepted the award then performed "Over the Rainbow," the year's Best Song. Another signature Garland hit, "The Trolley Song" was one of *Meet Me in St. Louis*'s four unsuccessful bids for Oscar in 1944. Two years later, *The Harvey Girls* took Best Song for "On the Atchison, Topeka, and the Santa Fe," which Garland introduced in the movie with Ben Carter, Marjorie Main, Virginia O'Brien and Ray Bolger, her pal from *The Wizard of Oz*. The 1954 musical remake of *A Star Is Born* gave Garland a career resurgence and her first Oscar nomination. She was favored to win Best Actress and, though eight months pregnant, planned to attend the ceremony and perform *A Star Is Born*'s only nominated song, "The Man That Got Away." Son Joey arrived prematurely, leaving Garland to discover from a hospital bed that the Best Actress statuette went to Grace Kelly. Because son Joey was ill with an earache the night of the 1961 Oscars, he again kept Garland from attending. Despite being the anticipated winner once more, this time in a non-musical role as a brutalized hausfrau on the witness stand in *Judgment at Nuremberg*, she lost to Rita Moreno in the musical *West Side Story*. The next year, 39-year-old Garland became the youngest star to win the Hollywood Foreign Press Association's Cecil B. DeMille Lifetime Achievement Award.

Cary Grant

1941 Best Actor as newspaperman/father Roger Adams in *Penny Serenade*
1944 Best Actor as cockney Ernie Mott in *None But the Lonely Heart*
1969 Honorary Award "for his unique mastery of the art of screen acting with the respect and affection of his colleagues"

Cary Grant tempered the impact of seeing his suave physical beauty on the big screen with disarming humor, claiming once that even he wished he were Cary Grant. The Academy first noted Grant as the suitor Mae West invited to come up and see her in the 1932/1933 Best Picture nominated *She Done Him Wrong*. In 1937 he had the leads in two Oscar-contending comedies, *Topper* and *The Awful Truth*, but the Academy offered nothing for Grant's performances. The same occurred in 1940 when Grant was the only major player of *The Philadelphia Story* left off Oscar's ballot. But the Academy responded better to a more melancholy Grant, nominating him first for his poignant portrayal of a grieving father in *Penny Serenade*. Although he lost Best Actor that year to friend Gary Cooper as *Sergeant York*, Joan Fontaine, his wife in *Suspicion*, won Best Actress. In 1944 he starred in two more classics, the deadly funny *Arsenic and Old Lace* and the somber *None But the Lonely Heart*, and the Academy nominated Grant for drifting through rootless poverty in that Clifford Odets drama. Despite carrying such Oscar winners as *The Bishop's Wife*, *The Bachelor and the Bobby-Soxer* (both 1947), *To Catch a Thief* (1955), and *Father Goose* (1964), Grant never competed for another Oscar. But the Academy showed its appreciation for his immeasurable talent and appeal with a lifetime achievement award in 1969. Tearfully accepting the award, Grant acknowledged how lucky he was to be part of Hollywood's most glamorous era. How apt, for he made it so.

John Wayne

    1949 Best Actor as U.S. Marine Sergeant John M. Stryker in *Sands of Iwo Jima*
    1960 Best Picture as producer of *The Alamo*
    1969 Best Actor as U.S. Marshall Reuben J. "Rooster" Cogburn in *True Grit*

In 1939 *Stagecoach* may have earned Thomas Mitchell a supporting Oscar without even giving its strapping young star a nomination, but that stagecoach took John Wayne on an unprecedented film journey across the West, with occasional detours in war dramas and crime films that added to his decades-long, top box office status. With a signature gate and line delivery that was not method, but uniquely methodical, Wayne ambled through Best Picture nominees *The Long Voyage Home* (1940), *The Quiet Man* (1952), *The Longest Day* (1962), *How the West Was Won* (1963), and *The Alamo* (1960), which, as its producer, made Wayne one of the first actors to also compete for a Best Picture Academy Award. His two Best Actor nods came first as a hard but wise Marine in *Sands of Iwo Jima* and then indelibly as crusty one-eyed U.S. Marshal Rooster Cogburn in *True Grit*.

In 1952, Wayne accepted two Oscars for friends, Best Actor Gary Cooper in *High Noon* and director John Ford for *The Quiet Man*. He presented often, and in 1969, gave his own acceptance speech, beginning with "Wow! If I'd have known that, I would have put that patch on 35 years earlier."

Gene Kelly

1945 Best Actor as sailor Joseph Brady in *Anchors Aweigh*

1951 Honorary Award "in appreciation of his versatility as an actor, singer, director and dancer, and specifically for his brilliant achievement in the art of choreography on film"

John Wayne topped off thirty years as a popular star of war films and westerns with an Oscar-winning performance as Rooster Cogburn in *True Grit* (1969).

Gene Kelly blended balletic precision with bounding athleticism to elevate the Hollywood musical to its dazzling heyday. The ascent began with Kelly's film debut in *For Me and My Gal*. The National Board of Review gave him one of its Best Acting awards, but the Academy cited the movie only for its music. With each project Kelly commanded greater control over choreographing his contributions until he had full power in 1945's *Anchors Aweigh*. The impressive results brought him his only competitive Oscar nomination. In 1951, his creative direction over lengthy, story-encompassing dance routines helped turn Vincente Minnelli's *An American in Paris* into the year's Best Picture, and brought Kelly an honorary statuette. His performance earned him a Golden Globe nomination, but no Oscar nod for Best Actor. The following year, he and co-director Stanley Donen took musicals to their peak with *Singin' in the Rain*, eventually named the greatest movie musical of all time. It, like other musicals *The Pirate* (1948), *On the Town* (1949), *Brigadoon* (1954), and *Les Girls* (1957), all found modest favor with Oscar. Kelly was as commanding in romantic and dramatic roles, notably in Oscar-nominated hits like *The Three Musketeers* (1948), *Marjorie Morningstar* (1958), and *Inherit the Wind* (1960). In 1969 he earned a Best Director Golden Globe nomination for his splashy adaptation of *Hello, Dolly!* The Academy cited the movie with seven nominations, including Best Picture, and three wins, but Kelly did not compete. Since then Kelly's lifetime of achievements were feted by most every major international organization, from AFI to SAG to the César, for brilliant artistry, precise craftsmanship, and an exuberance in his feet that kept audiences rising to theirs in elation.

Grace Kelly

1953 Best Supporting Actress as wife Linda Nordley in *Mogambo*
1954 Best Actress as wife Georgie Elgin in *The Country Girl*

Like fellow legend James Dean, Kelly graced American cinema screens for a startlingly brief time. Yet her grand elegance and ivory allure rang so pitch-perfectly with audiences that the timbre of her film career still resonates more than half a century after she departed the Hollywood hills to reign over the landscape of Monaco. She became a movie star as Best Actor winner Gary Cooper's bride in *High Noon* in 1952, then was Oscar nominated herself as a young wife ill-equipped for the grueling safari or her lust stirred by guide Clark Gable in *Mogambo*. In 1954, three hit movies brought Kelly multiple honors. She played the mobile, clue-seeking accomplice who abetted wheelchair-bound James Stewart's voyeuring through his *Rear Window*, and the unfaithful wife of plotting Ray Milland in *Dial M for Murder*. Even more notably, she downplayed her beauty with flattened coif and somber diffidence as the loyal wife of alcoholic Bing Crosby in *The Country Girl*. The three performances earned her Best Actress honors from the National Board of Review and the New York Film Critics. Oscar singled out her performance as *The Country Girl* for a nomination. Kelly was the first presenter at that year's ceremony, but joyously returned to the Pantages Theatre stage when William Holden, who starred with Kelly in two Oscar contenders that year, *The Country Girl* and *The Bridges at Toko-Ri*, announced her as Oscar's Best Actress as well. Before leaving behind her brief but brilliant career, Kelly revisited Oscar to present the 1955 Best Actor prize to *Marty*'s Ernest Borgnine. She then exited the stage, and Hollywood, to live her life as royalty in Monaco.

Lillian Gish

1946 Best Supporting Actress as wife Laura Belle McCanles in *Duel in the Sun*

1970 Honorary Award "for superlative artistry and for distinguished contribution to the progress of motion pictures"

Few legends from Hollywood talkies worked as early in America's new movie industry as Lillian Gish. She started in silents with younger sister Dorothy, but Lillian eventually became such a dominating force that she was labeled "The First Lady of American Cinema." Her filmography boasted 75 titles even before the Academy came into existence, with her most famous pre–Oscar roles in D. W. Griffith's epic classics, *The Birth of a Nation* (1915) and *Intolerance* (1916), and as Hester Prynne in Victor Sjöström's *The Scarlet Letter* (1926). Perhaps because she was so selective about her roles, the Academy had fewer opportunities to nominate her than most other actors of her stature. Her collaborations with Jennifer Jones apparently impressed them, for she received her only Oscar nomination as Jones' guardian in King Vidor's ambitious *Duel in the Sun*, and two years later Gish as Mother Mary of Mercy and Jones as the title character were photographed with Oscar-nominated cinematography and winning Special Effects in *Portrait of Jennie*. One of Gish's most celebrated roles came in Charles Laughton's only directorial effort, playing the gun-toting protector of orphaned children running from sinister preacher Robert Mitchum in *The Night of the Hunter*. Though a classic now, the movie was not embraced in 1955 and was up for no Oscars. In 1987, Gish had all the early season award enthusiasm for her delicate, grounded portrayal as Bette Davis' tolerant sister in *The Whales of August*. A zealous nomination campaign by Sally Kirkland as *Anna* gave her a slot for Best Actress over Gish, who had already won a lifetime achievement award for her massive contribution to the advancement of cinema in its foundational years.

Fred Astaire

1949 Special Award "for his unique artistry and his contributions to the technique of musical pictures"
1974 Best Supporting Actor as con man Harlee Claiborne in *The Towering Inferno*

Fred Astaire's impact on making the Hollywood musical a relevant building block of early talkies is evident through Oscar's Best Songs. From 1934, when the Academy introduced the category, throughout that decade, a Fred Astaire song always competed. The first Best Song Oscar went to "The Continental," sung by Astaire and a cast of party-going hoofers in *The Gay Divorcee*. In 1935 "Lovely to Look At" was up for Best Song from *Roberta*, while *Top Hat* competed for Best Picture. The following year, Astaire's smoothly romantic "The Way You Look Tonight" won from *Swing Time*. At the next Oscars, *Shall We Dance*'s "They Can't Take That Away from Me" was up, and the year after that, "Change Partners" made a *Carefree* entrant in Oscar's big night competitions. But elegant dancing, not singing, made Astaire a movie legend and inspired his special Oscar in 1949. A favorite of the Hollywood Foreign Press, Astaire won the Best Actor, Musical or Comedy Golden Globe for 1950's *Three Little Words*, and was nominated in that category for the 1961 comedy *The Pleasure of His Company* as well as the 1968 musical *Finian's Rainbow*. His second Golden Globe victory came for a supporting role in Irwin Allen's red hot disaster film *The Towering Inferno*. Four decades after premiering in *Dancing Lady*, Astaire was up for his first competitive Oscar. "If I win," he promised, "I'll dance with the damn thing." However, his fine performance, even with a boost of sentiment, did not generate enough votes to overtake Robert De Niro in *The Godfather Part II*. Astaire's dramatic performances still sizzle, and his gravity-defying élan on the dance floor remain legendary.

Lauren Bacall

1996   Best Supporting Actress as mother Hannah Morgan in *The Mirror Has Two Faces*

2009   Honorary Award "in recognition of her central place in the golden age of motion pictures"

Simmering, sultry, and saddled for a lifetime with having to dodge first husband Humphrey Bogart's shadow, Lauren Bacall was a film icon in her twenties. Her nervous inexperience before the camera gave her "the look," a downturned head and veering eyes, that became her trademark and fueled the kinetic energy she and Bogie generated in 1944's *To Have and Have Not*. Their collaboration in *Dark Passage* and *The Big Sleep* didn't awaken any Oscar interest, but *Key Largo* earned Bacall's supporting female, Claire Trevor, an Academy Award. In her own Oscar-winning vehicles, Bacall excelled in every genre. She steadied the tumult created by alcoholic sister-in-law Dorothy Malone in the drama *Written on the Wind* (1956), seduced then sparred with Gregory Peck in the romantic comedy *Designing Woman* (1957), provided comic relief as a boisterous American passenger suspected of *Murder on the Orient Express* (1974), and searched for her writer client James Caan as he suffered *Misery* at the hands of 1990 Best Actress Kathy Bates in the popular thriller. In 1996, the Academy had an ideal opportunity to honor the legend when she gave a stark, insightful, and witty performance as Barbra Streisand's un-nurturing mother in *The Mirror Has Two Faces*. Everyone, from Barbara Walters in her pre–Oscar interview with Betty Bacall to the press to the critics to the red carpet interviewers, was primed for Bacall's acceptance speech that night. Gasps of disbelief rumbled through the Shrine Auditorium when Kevin Spacey announced Juliette Binoch of *The English Patient* the year's Best Supporting Actress. Thirteen years later the Academy made amends by recognizing the canon of Bacall's work with a lifetime achievement award.

Debbie Reynolds

1964 Best Actress as socialite Molly Brown in *The Unsinkable Molly Brown*
2015 Jean Hersholt Humanitarian Award

Personally and financially, Debbie Reynolds proved herself to be every bit as plucky as Molly Brown, the backwoods raised, high stepping and loyal socialite she portrayed in her only Oscar-nominated performance. Reynolds' star first shot like a nova when, at age 20, she shone as the musical protégé to hoofers Gene Kelly and Donald O'Connor in *Singin' in the Rain*. Although later named the best musical in the history of cinema, the movie garnered only two nominations from the Academy, one for its score and the other for Best Supporting Actress—not Reynolds, but Jean Hagen. Aptly, Reynolds got her big break in a movie about the history of movies, for she spent her adult life preserving that history by collecting movie costumes and then valiantly trying multiple times to house them at a single site. Besides that painful failure, she faced the public heartbreak of losing husband Eddie Fisher to Elizabeth Taylor, the financial and personal storms of other husbands who bankrupted her, and the challenge of caring for daughter Carrie Fisher through her bipolar disorder. Yet always, Reynolds has risen above her disappointments, including being overlooked for an anticipated Oscar nomination for *Mother* in 1996, with an altruism that the Academy acknowledged by giving her a Jean Hersholt Humanitarian Award in 2015.

Shirley Temple

1934 Special Award "in grateful recognition of her outstanding contribution to screen entertainment during the year 1934"

One of the great entertainers of all time, the tiny Kewpie doll with bobbing curls brought hope to millions during the Great Depression and helped break racial barriers by dancing hand-in-hand with African-American tap legend Bill "Bojangles" Robinson in four movies (*The Little Colonel* and *The Littlest Rebel* in 1935; *Rebecca of Sunnybrook Farm* and *Just around the Corner* in 1938), none of which was up for a single Oscar. Nevertheless, Temple set

Academy records many times over. She received her special award when she was only six years old, making her the youngest actor in history to receive an Academy Award. That record still stands. She was also the first star to receive the special miniature juvenile Oscar, an award likely created as a way to honor Temple's gargantuan contribution to the art of film in 1934, when she made nine motion pictures. A single Oscar for that many movies proved to be another Oscar record that no one else has matched in the past 80 years.

Temple's career continued through her teens and included two Oscar-winning features. In *Since You Went Away* (1944) she played Bridget "Brig" Hilton, daughter of Best Actress nominee Claudette Colbert and younger sister of Best Supporting Actress nominee Jennifer Jones. She had an even more prominent role in 1947 when she and Cary Grant played the title characters, *The Bachelor and the Bobby-Soxer* from Sidney Sheldon's Oscar-winning screenplay. Temple made a few special appearances on Oscar's stage. Especially memorable were her presenting an honorary Oscar to wounded veteran Harold Russell for *The Best Years of Our Lives* in 1946 and closing out the category she inspired by giving the last special juvenile award to *Pollyanna*'s Hayley Mills in 1960.

After Shirley Temple received the first special juvenile Academy Award in 1934, she presented the Best Actress trophy to Claudette Colbert.

Hattie McDaniel

1939 Best Supporting Actress as housekeeper Mammy in *Gone with the Wind*

When Fay Bainter stepped to the dais at the Coconut Grove, she began her 1939 Best Supporting Actress presentation by calling it "a tribute to a country where people are free to honor noteworthy achievements regardless of creed, race or color." Clearly, Hattie McDaniel's record as the first African-American actor to be nominated for and win an Oscar was a socially groundbreaking victory. McDaniel had built a career playing domestics with the wit and wisdom to call her employers on their idiocies. As Malena, McDaniel warned *Alice Adams* (Best Actress nominee Katharine Hepburn) of the shortfalls of putting on social airs. The following year, she worked for the Darnleys with Best Actress nominee Gladys George in *Valiant is the Word for Carrie* and also appeared as a maid in the Best Picture-nominated *Libeled Lady*. She didn't have to alter her costume much the next year as a maid in *Stella Dallas* opposite Oscar nominees Barbara Stanwyck and Anne Shirley. But *Gone with the Wind* showcased McDaniel's impeccable delivery of the robust, insightful, sometimes comically nonplussed Mammy. Though Jim Crow laws kept McDaniel from *Gone with the Wind*'s Atlanta premier and segregated her to a back table at the Academy Awards, her triumph remains a milestone of Oscar's reach past social limitations and toward honoring authentic talent whenever it makes an indelible mark on screen.

Ginger Rogers

1940 Best Actress as fashion executive Kitty Foyle in *Kitty Foyle*

Platinum blondes of the early sound era were often molded to replicate the unthreatening allure of Jean Harlow—sexy, but ditzy. Too astute to fall into that trap, Ginger Rogers used her prodigious musical talent to first impact Oscar by stopping traffic as Anytime Annie in the 1932/1933 Best Picture nominee *42nd Street*. She subsequently boarded her first of nine collaborations with Fred Astaire by *Flying down to Rio*. The movie earned a Best Song nomination for "Carioca," but it lost to "The Continental" from another Rogers/Astaire hit, the Best Picture-nominated *The Gay Divorcee*. Rogers glided through several more Oscar-nominated hits that decade, including *Roberta*, *Shall We Dance*, and *Carefree*, and occasionally traded in her dancing shoes for pavement-pounding pumps. She was a struggling actress rapping at fame's *Stage Door* with 1937's Best Supporting Actress nominee Andrea Leeds. In 1940, she had consecutive Oscar hits. To win the heart of Joel McCrea, she hid her poor shanty life and prostitute mother (Best Supporting

Actress nominee Marjorie Rambeau) behind a *Primrose Path*. In an even more compelling vehicle, Rogers debated two romantic choices in layered flashbacks to reveal the heart and headiness of struggling white collar saleswoman *Kitty Foyle*. With the help of enthusiastic campaigning from RKO, Rogers won Best Actress over her fellow frontrunners, Katharine Hepburn of *The Philadelphia Story* and *Rebecca*'s Joan Fontaine. The victory confirmed that Rogers was as powerful dramatically as musically. Interestingly, her final screen appearance was in 1965 as the contentious mother of Jean *Harlow* (Carol Lynley), the immortal star who created the blonde bombshell prototype that Rogers successfully defied to waltz into a niche of her own.

James Baskett

1947 Special Award "for his able and heart-warming characterization of Uncle Remus, friend and story teller to the children of the world in Walt Disney's *Song of the South*"

Most Oscar trivia buffs are aware that Sidney Poitier crossed color boundaries as the first Black actor to be nominated for a competitive acting Oscar in 1958 for *The Defiant Ones* and to win in 1963 for *Lilies of the Field*, but fewer realize that the first male African-American actor to receive an Oscar was James Baskett. Baskett had provided the voice of Preacher Crow in Disney's 1941 animated hit *Dumbo* before he auditioned at Disney again to voice another supporting animal for *Song of the South*. Walt Disney himself was so impressed by Baskett's range and appeal that he cast him as Uncle Remus in the mixed live action/animated feature. In addition to playing the lead, Baskett also voiced Brer Fox, and dubbed some lines as Brer Rabbit. Jean Hersholt and columnist Hedda Hopper provided the decisive arguments to convince the Academy's board of governors to honor Baskett, who accepted the award on Oscar night from presenter Ingrid Bergman. Already ailing from diabetes and heart troubles during the filming of *Song of the South*, Baskett died less than four months after receiving his groundbreaking accolade.

Harold Lloyd

1952 Honorary Award "to Harold Lloyd, master comedian and good citizen"

Large, horn rimmed spectacles personified Harold Lloyd just as oversized shoes and narrow mustache made Charlie Chaplin "the tramp." In searching for a persona with which audiences could identify his likeable incarnations of a cute, down on his luck optimist determined to impress a pretty girl, Lloyd donned a pair of glasses. The simple addition added an intellectual nuance to his characters that made his physical bumbling even funnier. More importantly, they made him look like any other non-movie star sitting in a theater identifying with his hard-luck antics. Like his Oscared contemporaries, Charles Chaplin and Buster Keaton, Lloyd cornered his own market on silent film comedy, and became so popular that he was identified as one of motion pictures' first icons. Artfully choreographed physical daring-do was essential for any top-flight silent film comedian, and no one was more courageous or dexterous than Lloyd. What made his feats unfathomably skilled, and dangerous, is that he did his own high-element stunts, even dangling from skyscrapers as he did in *Safety Last*, without a thumb and forefinger on his right hand. In 1919, Lloyd was holding what he thought was a prop bomb for a photo shoot when it detonated in his hand, blinding him temporarily, and desecrating half his hand. Suspecting that audiences would be too afraid to laugh at the danger of his stunts should they know of his handicap, Lloyd wore a prosthetic glove that is only obvious once a viewer is aware of it. The first year of the Academy Awards, Lloyd's hit, *Speedy*, earned Ted Wilde a Best Comedy Director nomination, the only time that category existed. At the Academy's silver jubilee in 1952, Oscar honored its "beloved freshman" with a lifetime achievement award for his extraordinary contribution to motion picture comedy. At the height of McCarthy's blacklisting many Hollywood A-listers, the award also made a political statement by acknowledging Lloyd's citizenship as well as his talent.

Miyoshi Umeki

1957 Best Supporting Actress as war bride Katsumi Kelly in *Sayonara*

Born in Otaru, Japan, Miyoshi Umeki gained international acclaim as a singer, rendering jazz classics with unique blends of alternating Japanese and English lyrics. Among her American standards were "My Foolish Heart" and "With a Song in My Heart," which share the title of movies that were Best Actress-nominated vehicles for Susan Hayward. Umeki's filmography featured only a handful of movies, beginning with *Sayonara* in which she played the demure Asian wife of White American soldier Red Buttons. The racially charged drama surged with Oscar excitement in 1957, earning ten nominations, and winning four, including both supporting acting categories for Buttons and Umeki. When she shuffled up the aisle to receive her golden prize from Anthony Quinn and offer a halting, gracious acceptance speech, Umeki was the first Asian star to win an acting Academy Award. Her achievement is still rare, as she has been joined by only three other actors, all male. Ben Kingsley, of South Asian descent, won Best Actor for *Gandhi* in 1982.

Cambodian Haing S. Ngor won Best Supporting Actor for *The Killing Fields* in 1984. Chinese actor/moviemaker Jackie Chan received an honorary Academy Award for lifetime achievement in 2016. While Oscar acknowledged Umeki only once, the Hollywood Foreign Press brought her into contention for a Golden Globe three times. In movies, she was up for her supporting role in *Sayonara*, and in 1961 as lead actress for the Rodgers and Hammerstein musical *Flower Drum Song*, a role she originated on stage to Tony-nominated success. On television, she played soft-spoken housekeeper Mrs. Livingston in *The Courtship of Eddie's Father* from 1969 to 1972, and competed as Best Supporting Actress in a Series, Miniseries or Television Film during the show's second season.

Buster Keaton

1959 Honorary Award "for his unique talents which brought immortal comedies to the screen"

Silent film's sadsack of comedy and conscience, Buster Keaton's output of movies throughout the 1920s was so powerful and prolific that some film critics, Roger Ebert among them, singled out Keaton as arguably the greatest actor-director in the history of movies. His masterpiece, *The General*, was released on December 31, 1926, just prior to the year the Academy first considered awarding films with a golden statuette. Keaton pantomimed the underwater "The Dance of the Sea" number in *The Hollywood Review of 1929*, the only plotless, filmed stage review ever nominated for a Best Picture Oscar. Keaton made cameos in three other Oscar favorites, appearing as himself in *Sunset Boulevard* (1950), as Jimmy the Crook in *It's a Mad, Mad, Mad, Mad World* (1963), and playing the train conductor from San Francisco to Fort Kearney in 1956's Best Picture winner *Around the World in 80 Days*. He had a more prominent role as former stage partner of his silent film actor/director contemporary Charlie Chaplin in 1952's *Limelight*. The movie wasn't shown in Los Angeles until twenty years after its release. Finally eligible for Oscar consideration in 1972, *Limelight* took home a much delayed Academy Award for Best Score. Between the height of his career as the stone-faced silent screen giant and his comedy comebacks later in life, Keaton was honored with a special Oscar in 1959. Uniquely, Keaton did not receive his award during the ceremony, but afterwards at the Governors Ball.

Laurel and Hardy

1960 Honorary Award "to Stan Laurel for his creative pioneering in the field of cinema comedy"

No two actors could stir up "a fine mess," let it simmer in slapstick, and cook up legendary laughs better than Stan Laurel and Oliver Hardy. The comic duo, brought together by writer/director Leo McCarey, who wrote some of their many films directed by Hal Roach, were each revered actors independently before they became silent screen sensations as a bumbling duet. They made an easy transition to talkies by remaining faithful to the physical comedy that worked in either medium. Once the Academy was formed, the comedy team had opportunities to be recognized for both their feature length and short films. Their first appearance in a sound film was as magicians for a skit entitled "Magic Act" in *The Hollywood Review of 1929*. The movie competed for the Best Picture Academy Award of the 1928/29 season, losing to *The Broadway Melody*. The following year, Laurel and Hardy were added late in the production of *The Rogue Song* to add levity and box office potential to the musical romance directed by Lionel Barrymore and starring Lawrence Tibbett, who competed for Best Actor. Subsequently, Laurel and Hardy appeared in two short films nominated for Oscars in the Best Short Subject (Comedy) category. "The Music Box" won the Oscar in 1931/32 for producer Hal Roach, and "Tit for Tat," another Roach production, was nominated in 1935. Although by 1960 Oliver Hardy had been dead three years and Stan Laurel was too ill to attend the ceremony, the Academy acknowledged their stellar contribution to filmmaking with an honorary Oscar for Stan Laurel, presented by fellow honorary Oscar-winning comic actor Danny Kaye.

Edward G. Robinson

1972 Honorary Award "to Edward G. Robinson who achieved greatness as a player, a patron of the arts and a dedicated citizen ... in sum, a Renaissance man, from his friends in the industry he loves"

Edward G. Robinson established his nasally insult-spewing gangster persona on Broadway in 1927's *The Racket*. The story was adapted into a silent film nominated for Best Picture the first year of the Academy Awards. Although Robinson didn't reprise his role for the movie, he soon dominated the film world with riveting performances in multiple Oscar-impressed hits. One of his most famous roles, as Rico in *Little Caesar*, failed to bring him into Best Actor contention in 1930/31, despite the movie's Best Writing nomination. The following Oscar season, *Five Star Final* was up for Best Picture, but Robinson, in the lead as tabloid city editor Joseph Randall, was again overlooked. Consistently fine work as headline star or strong support allowed Robinson to etch deep characterizations in many Oscar-nominated hits. He was a murder suspect on the *Barbary Coast* (1935), a groundbreaking physician in *Dr. Ehrlich's Magic Bullet* (1940), the sadistic captain of *The Sea Wolf*

(1941), and Israelite Dathan in *The Ten Commandments* (1956). In noir classics, he was Fred MacMurray's confidante in the 1944 Best Picture-nominated *Double Indemnity*, and in 1948, he was a gangster on the lam who held captive Bogart, Bacall, and friends, including Best Supporting Actress winner Claire Trevor, on storm-ravaged *Key Largo*. Before his death from bladder cancer, Robinson learned that the Academy was giving him a lifetime achievement award at the 1972 ceremony. He died before Charlton Heston, star of *The Ten Commandments* and Robinson's last movie, 1973's *Soylent Green*, presented the honorary trophy to Robinson's widow. In over 100 movies, Robinson used his squat frame and jack-o-lantern features to strong arm his co-stars, and warrant reverence from legions of fans.

The Marx Brothers

1973 Honorary Award "to Groucho Marx in recognition of his brilliant creativity and for the unequalled achievements of the Marx Brothers in the art of motion picture comedy"

When the American Film Institute ranked the funniest movies of all time in "100 Years ... 100 Laughs," Marx Brothers comedies occupied five slots. Midrange on the list were *Monkey Business* at 73, *Horse Feathers* at 65, and *A Day at the Races* at 59. But hovering near the top were their unforgettable classics, *A Night at the Opera*, crammed in at #12 and *Duck Soup* swimming with the best of the best at #5. Yet somehow, Oscar never took to their whip-sharp wit. Of all the Marx Brothers pictures, only one, *A Day at the Races*, was ever up for an Oscar, and it only competed in a single category. The number "All God's Chillun Got Rhythm" was nominated for Best Dance Direction, and lost to the "Fun House" number in *Damsel in Distress*. The fact that so much of their humor was spontaneous accounts for the fact that none of their movies was even given Best Screenplay consideration. Years after the comedy team disbanded, the Academy finally paid homage to the classic comedians by giving Groucho Marx an Honorary Oscar. Jack Lemmon's introduction made it clear that this special Oscar was a tribute to all the Marx Brothers. When accepting, Groucho gave special acknowledgment to his two brothers who had passed, Chico in 1961 and Harpo in 1964, and to Margaret Dumont, the straight woman who, Groucho claimed, never got any of his jokes.

Myrna Loy

1990 Honorary Award "in recognition of her extraordinary qualities both on screen and off, with appreciation of a lifetime's worth of indelible performances"

Because her work evolved on screen with such authenticity that each performance appeared effortless and she disappeared through the inflections and mannerisms of each character she played, it's easy to understand how the Academy somehow failed to nominate Myrna Loy for a competitive Oscar through more than a half-century in movies. Not that her films didn't consistently garner Oscar praise, as they often did, giving some of her leading men their greatest Oscar exposure. She and William Powell were the smart, sparring sleuths Nick and Nora Charles in the popular *The Thin Man* movies, the first of which earned Powell his initial Best Actor nomination in 1934. She was the understanding wife whose staid strength helped Best Actor winner husband Fredric March regain some domestic stability after returning from war in *The Best Years of Our Lives*. She shone in other Oscar-winning hits including cinema's first all-talking picture, *The Jazz Singer* (1927); Best Screenplay winners *Manhattan Melodrama* (1934) and *The Bachelor and the Bobby-Soxer* (1947); Best Picture nominees *Arrowsmith* (1931), *Libeled Lady* (1936), and *Test Pilot* (1938); and Best Picture winners *The Great Ziegfeld* (1936) and *The Best Years of Our Lives* (1946). In each, Loy used her languid eyes and pert lips to convey a rainbow of emotions that made movie fans eager to express their admiration. When Loy was 85, the Academy finally did, too, making her the first actress in history to receive a lifetime achievement award without ever having competed for an Oscar.

Halle Berry

2001 Best Actress as Leticia Musgrove in *Monster's Ball*

In Oscar's 74th year, *Monster's Ball* star Berry became the first African American to win Best Actress. Throughout the twentieth century, African Americans gained headway with nominations, and occasional victories in all acting categories, but a Best Actress victory eluded African-American actresses. Berry was only the seventh Black star up for Best Actress. Before her, representation of African-American lead actresses was spotty, at best. Historically, Best Actress nominations came in 1954 to Dorothy Dandridge as *Carmen Jones*, in 1972 to Diana Ross as Billie Holiday in *Lady Sings the Blues* and Cicely Tyson for *Sounder*, in 1974 to Diahann Carroll as *Claudine*, in 1985 to Whoopi Goldberg in *The Color Purple*, and in 1993 to Angela Bassett as Tina Turner in *What's Love Got to Do with It*. Amid sobs of stunned gratitude, Berry acknowledged many of those pioneers, including Dorothy Dandridge, whom she portrayed to Emmy-winning victory on television, Lena Horn, Diahann Carroll, and Angela Bassett, as well as contemporaries Jada Pinkett and Vivica Fox. Other Oscar recognition for Halle Berry movies include a Best Original Screenplay nomination for *Bulworth* in 1998 and a nod to the special effects in *X-Men: Days of Future Past* in 2014.

Jerry Lewis

2008 Jean Hersholt Humanitarian Award

Madcap, zany, elastic, genius—many terms lopped onto comic actor and tireless charity trailblazer Jerry Lewis offer a sense of the magnitude of his international impact. He and comedy partner Dean Martin shared billing in 17 motion pictures that drew an ever increasing fan base, but which never checked a single Oscar ballot. Lewis' long filmography with and without Martin spans more than sixty years, yet the only movies to garner Oscar recognition were those in which Lewis breezed through in blinkably short but memorable cameos: *Li'l Abner* (1959), *It's a Mad, Mad, Mad, Mad World* (1963), and *Mr. Saturday Night* (1992). Three movies did bring him serious Oscar consideration. In 1963, his potion-induced, personality-shifting pursuit of lovely student Stella Stevens gave Lewis the opportunity to demonstrate diversity and range as *The Nutty Professor*, a movie Lewis also co-wrote and directed. The Golden Globes' omission of him in either the Best Actor, Drama or, more expectedly, Musical or Comedy categories portended his oversight from the Academy. The Globes did nominate Lewis for the 1965 comedy *Boeing, Boeing*, but he lost to Lee Marvin who went on to win the Oscar for *Cat Ballou*. Critical praise and a BAFTA nomination for his surprisingly dark supporting role as a powerful talk show host kidnapped by Robert De Niro in *The King of Comedy* left many expecting Lewis to finally get his Oscar due. But the Academy seemed reticent to embrace Martin Scorsese's bleak black comedy, and the movie passed Oscar without a single nomination. But for Lewis' humanitarian efforts, most notably for his multibillion dollar fundraising as national chairman of the Muscular Dystrophy Association (MDA) and telethon host (1966–2010), the Academy gave Lewis commendation in the form of a Jean Hersholt Humanitarian Award. Eddie Murphy, a new generation's *Nutty Professor*, presented the award to Lewis. Having graced Oscar's stage multiple times as a presenter and even host, Lewis finally had the chance to step into the circular centerpiece of the Kodak Theatre stage and accept an Academy Award of his own.

Maureen O'Hara

2014 Honorary Award "to Maureen O'Hara, one of Hollywood's brightest stars, whose inspiring performances glowed with passion, warmth and strength"

A wild Irish rose and self-proclaimed tomboy, O'Hara exuded a green valley loveliness that made audiences swoon, and a combustible confidence that enabled her to wrangle with John Wayne in five hits, including the Oscar-winning *The Quiet Man*. Discovered by Charles Laughton, O'Hara entranced him as Esmeralda in *The Hunchback of Notre Dame* (1939). Director John Ford recognized her captivating command on camera and cast her as Angharad in *How Green Was My Valley*, which took Best Picture of 1941 and earned Ford his second Best Director award. Helped once more by O'Hara's igniting the screen, Ford won again for *The Quiet Man* in 1952. She portrayed the pragmatic businesswoman shielding daughter Natalie Wood from delusions of Santa Claus in the Best Picture-nominated *Miracle on 34th Street*, which won two writing awards and Best Supporting Actor for Edmund Gwenn as Kris Kringle. Despite praiseworthy performances in all these films, as well as other Oscar contenders such as *Sitting Pretty* (1948) and *The Parent Trap* (1961), O'Hara didn't generate a thrill of potential Oscar enthusiasm until she was 71 and wove multiple textures into her characterization of a tough mother afraid to lose the dependence of grown son John Candy in *Only the Lonely*. The nomination never materialized, but the Academy did come through nearly a quarter century later with a lifetime achievement award presented to her by Liam Neeson and Clint Eastwood. O'Hara joined Myrna Loy as the only actresses to be feted with an honorary Oscar after a career without a single competitive Academy Award nomination.

Mel Gibson

1995 Best Director for *Braveheart*
1995 Best Picture as co-producer (with Bruce Davey and Alan Ladd, Jr.) for *Braveheart*
2016 Best Director for *Hacksaw Ridge*

Swarthy Australian action and movie director Mel Gibson first found international fame thanks to the 1980's *Mad Max* franchise, but the Academy didn't take note of Gibson until 1983 when Linda Hunt won Best Supporting Actress playing opposite him in *The Year of Living Dangerously*. The next year, a new remake of *Mutiny on the Bounty*, this time called simply *The Bounty*, had Gibson as an intense Fletcher Christian. Though well-reviewed, it was the only of the three movie adaptations to get no Oscar recognition. Gibson bravely tackled Shakespeare's brooding Dane in a new interpretation of *Hamlet* (1990), a tough act to follow considering Laurence Olivier and the movie both won top Oscars back in 1948. But critics and audiences responded favorably to the film, and the Academy recognized its costumes and art direction with nominations. But it was Gibson's directing and producing *Braveheart*, in which he starred as Sir William Wallace, that shifted the timbre of the Academy's response to Gibson. By the end of the 1995 ceremony, Gibson had an Oscar in each hand. In the new millennium, Gibson tackled two controversial, newsworthy projects: *The Passion of the Christ* (2004) and *Apocalypto* (2006) generated extensive, if sometimes polarizing press. Both did impressive box office and each earned three Academy Award nominations. By starting from Down Under, Gibson made a dexterous leap to Oscar's highest honors.

Those Who Were Nominated for an Oscar

Montgomery Clift

- 1948 Best Actor as American army engineer Ralph Stevenson in *The Search*
- 1951 Best Actor as clothing factory worker George Eastman in *A Place in the Sun*
- 1953 Best Actor as U.S. Army private Robert E. Lee Prewitt in *From Here to Eternity*
- 1961 Best Supporting Actor as Nazi victim Rudolph Petersen in *Judgment at Nuremberg*

Slender, handsome, intense, and talented, Montgomery Clift had star quality from the start of his career. His first two movies, *Red River* and *The Search*, were Oscar favorites of 1948. While *Red River* was a vehicle for John Wayne, *The Search* showcased new acting sensation Clift as a compassionate soldier helping a displaced youth find his mother during World War II. Clift was nominated for Best Actor, losing to Laurence Olivier as *Hamlet*, and Ivan Jandl, the young boy Clift helps, was given a special juvenile Oscar. William Wyler capitalized on Clift's good looks to play the dashing suitor of 1949 Best Actress Olivia de Havilland, reserved and plain as *The Heiress*. The small role expanded Clift's fan base worldwide, and had directors clamoring to cast him. Billy Wilder and his fellow screenwriters wrote the part of narrator Joe Gillis in *Sunset Boulevard* for Clift. He refused it, and William Holden got the part and the Oscar nomination. Clift reached a new career high the next year as ambitious George Eastman in *A Place in the Sun*. Although he and Marlon Brando of *A Streetcar Named Desire* were Best Actor frontrunners, they lost to Humphrey Bogart in *The African Queen*. In 1953, William Holden took Oscar momentum from Clift again. Both were nominated for lauded performances as World War II soldiers: Clift in *From Here to Eternity* and Holden in *Stalag 17*. *From Here to Eternity* took Best Picture, and Holden won Best Actor. A 1956 automobile accident damaged Clift's features and career, but he still delivered intense performances in Oscar competitors, most notably opposite friend and Best Actress nominee Elizabeth

Taylor in *Raintree County* (1957) and *Suddenly, Last Summer* (1959). His brief scene on the witness stand as a laborer sexually sterilized under Nazi persecution in *Judgment at Nuremberg* was a tour de force that many thought would bring Clift his long-deserved Academy Award. He and co-star Judy Garland went into Oscar night expected winners, but both fell victim to a *West Side Story* sweep that gave the supporting Oscars to George Chakiris and Rita Moreno.

Natalie Wood

   1955 Best Supporting Actress as teenage girlfriend Judy in *Rebel without a Cause*
   1961 Best Actress as high school student Wilma Dean Loomis in *Splendor in the Grass*
   1963 Best Actress as Macy's Department Store salesperson Angie Rossini in *Love with the Proper Stranger*

Of Natalie Wood's performance in her first credited role in 1946's *Tomorrow is Forever*, star and fellow prodigy Orson Welles marveled "she was so good it was frightening." Beautiful as a child and even lovelier as an adult, Wood's naturalness on screen was enhanced by a voice that could boom finely calibrated emotion from every line. She became a bonafide star at age 9 for doubting Kris Kringle's authenticity until she witnessed a *Miracle on 34th Street*, then supported Best Actress nominees Jane Wyman in *The Blue Veil* (1951) and Bette Davis in *The Star* (1952) before a determined pursuit of the role of misunderstood "bad girl" Judy in *Rebel without a Cause* made her a teen sensation and Oscar nominee. She reached legend status with two of the top Oscar pictures of 1961, *West Side Story* and *Splendor in the Grass*. She carried the weight of the central love story as Puerto Rican innocent Maria in the musical, which took Best Picture, and competed for Best Actress for her kinetic portrayal of a young woman emotionally fraying from first love in Elia Kazan's *Splendor in the Grass*. Wood was favored to win that competition, but the Academy instead went international by voting in Sophia Loren for Italy's *Two Women*. In 1963, only an actor as respected as Wood could overcome the controversial themes of premarital sex and abortion in *Love with the Proper Stranger* to enter another Best Actress race, which ultimately went to Patricia Neal in *Hud*. Wood reteamed with *Love with the Proper Stranger* director Robert Mulligan for *Inside Daisy Clover*, the film some critics consider her finest work, but, like her 1969 hit *Bob & Carol & Ted & Alice*, acting nominations were relegated to only her supporting cast. Add to her filmography such characterizations as *Gypsy* (1962) and *Marjorie Morningstar* (1958), and it's easy to see why her legendary allure still simmers.

Tom Cruise

1989 Best Actor as Vietnam War veteran/anti-war activist Ron Kovic in *Born on the Fourth of July*
1996 Best Actor as sports agent Jerry Maguire in *Jerry Maguire*
1999 Best Supporting Actor as motivational speaker Frank T. J. Mackey in *Magnolia*

Fame is *Risky Business*, but Tom Cruise glided into it with stocking feet and hip swiveling verve while lip syncing to "Old Time Rock and Roll" when he was 21. In 1986 he was in two Oscared hits, highflying in *Top Gun* to the Best Song, "You Take My Breath Away," and learning to recognize *The Color of Money* thanks to Best Actor Paul Newman. In 1988 he was Dustin Hoffman's polished brother with a lot to learn in *Rain Man*, which won Best Actor for Hoffman and Best Picture. The following year Cruise found himself in the same position with his first Best Actor nod as Vietnam vet turned protester Ron Kovic in the Best Picture-nominated *Born on the Fourth of July*. His first Academy Award competition set the precedent for his going into every Oscar race the actor favored to win, only to lose momentum during award season or to suffer a surprise upset on Oscar night. Dark horse Daniel Day-Lewis of *My Left Foot* beat Cruise for Best Actor in 1989. In 1996, early season enthusiasm for *Jerry Maguire* looked like it would hold when a jubilant Cuba Goodling, Jr., and his Best Supporting Oscar trampolined on the Shrine Auditorium stage, but that turned out to be *Jerry Maguire*'s only victory. Critics and peers loved Cruise's interpretation of a profane self-help guru in *Magnolia*. Like his two previous Oscar-nominated roles, this performance again won him a Golden Globe, but no Academy Award. Instead, he was acknowledged from the podium by the victor in his category, Michael Caine from *The Cider House Rules*. Cruise has starred in films that brought other supporting players Oscar nominations, including Jack Nicholson in *A Few Good Men* (1992), Holly Hunter in *The Firm* (1993), Ken Watanabe in *The Last Samurai* (2003), Jamie Foxx in *Collateral* (2004), and Robert Downey, Jr., in *Tropic Thunder* (2008). It seems just a matter of time that the only star to rank #1 at the box office a record-setting seven times will one day similarly impact his peers and win Oscar gold.

Johnny Depp

2003 Best Actor as pirate captain Jack Sparrow in *Pirates of the Caribbean: The Curse of the Black Pearl*
2004 Best Actor as author Sir James Matthew (J.M.) Barrie in *Finding Neverland*

2007 Best Actor as barber Sweeney Todd in *Sweeney Todd: The Demon Barber of Fleet Street*

Magnetically eccentric Depp has etched a career that spans huge creative leaps while his independent approach to his life and craft distinguishes him among such legendary trailblazers as Bob Dylan and Willie Nelson. Most of his scenes as translator Lerner were cut from the final release of *Platoon*, but the 1986 Best Picture and Best Director-winning film served as Depp's invitation to Oscar territory. Depp found his niche in the 1990s with three movies the Academy, and movie fans, relished. In 1990 he played endearing outcast *Edward Scissorhands*, and in 1994 was the title character whose compassion consumed him in *What's Eating Gilbert Grape* and whose lack of talent never dampened his blind excitement for cranking out horrible horror as cross-dressing director *Ed Wood*. The movies put stars of each of those films in competition for Best Supporting Actor, with *Ed Wood*'s Martin Landau winning over a young Leonardo DiCaprio from *What's Eating Gilbert Grape*, but the lead actor competition did not have Depp on the ballot. His risky stretch generated comic brilliance as Jack Sparrow, leaving the Academy doubled over in laughter and then stepping up with his first Best Actor nomination for the first *Pirates of the Caribbean* movie. They repeated the acknowledgment the next year for his mourning-laced author in *Finding Neverland* and then his gruesome avenger *Sweeney Todd* in 2007. Frequent appearances in movies Oscar recognized, such as *Chocolat* (2000), *Charlie and the Chocolate Factory* (2005), and *Into the Woods* (2014), keep strong the anticipation that his magnetism will soon attract an 8½ pound statuette named Oscar.

James Dean

1955 Best Actor as bean growing business entrepreneur Cal Trask in *East of Eden*
1956 Best Actor as handyman/oil man Jett Rink in *Giant*

Except for James Dean, most every movie legend clocked hundreds, sometimes thousands of hours on celluloid. For his three credited big screen performances, the total combined running time of *East of Eden* (115 minutes), *Rebel without a Cause* (111 minutes), and *Giant* (201 minutes) was 7 hours and 17 minutes. Of course, Dean was not in every minute of each movie, especially the epic-length *Giant*, in which Dean took a supporting role to stars Elizabeth Taylor and fellow Best Actor nominee Rock Hudson. Such a vantage point gives richer perspective to the indelible impact Dean had in three movies, released in two consecutive years, the latter two of which came out after Dean's untimely death. One of the youngest actors ever accepted into The Actors Studio, Dean utilized his angst-filled Method to confront his mother (played to Best Supporting Actress victory by Jo Van Fleet) and brother (fellow screen newcomer Richard Davalos) in *East of Eden*. His acting so embodied teen displacement in *Rebel without a Cause* that he singularly encapsulated the wayward disenchantment of an entire generation. In 1955, the Hollywood Foreign Press posthumously designated an honorary Best Dramatic Actor award to Dean, and the Academy nominated him for Best Actor. He lost to Ernest Borgnine as *Marty*, but word already circulated that he would set an Academy record with a second posthumous nomination the next year for *Giant*. He did, and although he lost his second competition to Yul Brynner in *The King and I*, Dean's legacy was cemented so firmly he still stands with Humphrey Bogart, Marilyn Monroe, and Audrey Hepburn as the most represented icons in movie history.

Will Smith

2001 Best Actor as boxer Muhammad Ali in *Ali*
2006 Best Actor as salesman/broker Chris Gardner in *The Pursuit of Happyness*

Smith's journey that made *I Am Legend* more than a movie title, but a moniker, followed a diverging path from hip-hop innovator to small-screen royalty to leading star of the silver screen. He was a Grammy-winning artist by the time he moved to a starring role as television's *Fresh Prince of Bel-Air* in 1990. Within three years, he established himself as a thriving movie actor as the central character in *Six Degrees of Separation*, which showed up at the Oscar's in 1993 with a Best Actress nomination for Stockard Channing. Mountainous worldwide box office receipts from back-to-back hits *Independence Day* (1996) and *Men in Black* (1997) also brought him into clearer view of Oscar, as *Independence Day* won Best Visual Effects and *Men in Black* Best Makeup. Tackling the role of such a vivid, pervasive icon as boxer Muhammad Ali would have been daunting for any actor, but Smith pulled it off with such flair that he was Oscar nominated in 2001. He lost that race to Denzel Washington in *Training Day*. Five years later, Smith's nuanced and inspiring performance as a homeless man determined to make good as a model for his young son (played by his real-life son, Jaden Smith) in his *Pursuit of Happyness* kept it from being a small movie overlooked by Oscar. Instead he was in the ring to win Best Actor, this time losing to Forest Whitaker, who swept that year's awards for *The Last King of Scotland*. Energetic and electric on screen, Smith needs only the right vehicle to transport him directly into Oscar's winning circle.

Marlene Dietrich

1930/1931 Best Actress as singer Amy Jolly in *Morocco*

Only someone with Dietrich's charisma could make a disdainful gesture sexy or a scoffing comment suggest real heart beneath her seeming indifference. Her seven movies under the direction of Josef von Sternberg established the persona of aloof magnetism that remained her trademark through a lifetime of movies and cabaret performances. Oscar probably could have flipped a coin in 1930/31 to determine which of her two star-making roles as a nightclub vamp they should nominate. Dietrich introduced her signature "Falling in Love Again" as Lola Lola seducing men from the stage at *The Blue Angel*, but she intrigued the Academy more by cautiously dodging Gary Cooper's advances backstage at her theater in *Morocco*. Best Actress that year went to Marie Dressler in *Min and Bill*, but with back-to-back international hits— *The Blue Angel* from Germany, and *Morocco*, Dietrich's first American film— she had embossed her androgynous screen temptress into the psyche of world cinema. She maintained her exotic indifference aboard the *Shanghai Express*, a Best Picture nominee of 1931/32, then was crowded out of a packed Best Actress cavalcade in 1939 when she mastered comedy in *Destry Rides Again*. She had fun with her own image in a cameo as a saloon hostess in 1956's Best Picture *Around the World in 80 Days*, then judiciously revived her career in two of Oscar's most powerful courtroom dramas. In 1957, she was the pivotal *Witness for the Prosecution*, and in 1961, her insights to Spencer Tracy about everyday Germans' perspectives on the rise of the Nazis helped result in a harsher *Judgment at Nuremberg*. At age 60, Dietrich still had the legs, the looks, and the allure, but she introduced a softer sincerity befitting a woman who had conquered the world with an obtuse glare and sexy German inflection.

Carole Lombard

1936 Best Actress as socialite daughter Irene Bullock in *My Man Godfrey*

When a top-tier star dies suddenly in her prime, it is not unusual for colleagues to offer vociferous praise about how much they loved her. But Lombard had the more unique distinction of earning such admiration from studio heads, directors, stars, and even technicians on the set while she was still living. Lombard cut her comic teeth in Mack Sennett silent comedies. After earning solid reviews in films of varied genres, Lombard impressed the world, and Oscar, most in screwball comedies. Her only Academy Award nomination came in 1936 for *My Man Godfrey*, playing opposite frequent co-star and former husband William Powell. The first movie to earn nominations in all four acting categories, *My Man Godfrey* was also up for Best Picture and Best Screenplay. Although it won none, it endeared Lombard to critics, fans, and her peers in the Academy, and proved to be the quintessential performance of her career. Before her 1942 death in a plane crash while rallying for war bonds, Lombard's career had started the decade strong with two Oscar contenders. She played a waitress pursued by Best Supporting Actor nominee William Gargan in *They Knew What They Wanted* (1940), and had the lead opposite Jack Benny in Ernst Lubitsch's Nazi-skewing comedy *To Be or Not to Be* (1942). Released two months after Lombard's death, the movie earned an Academy Award nomination the following year for its musical score. Lombard's most famous alliance was with second husband Clark Gable, with whom she had starred in one movie, *No Man of Her Own*, three years before they wed. Upon her death, Gable and the world mourned, and the Academy never had the opportunity to appropriately recognize Lombard for the impression she left on her coworkers, fans, and the movie industry.

Robert Mitchum

1945 Best Supporting Actor as U.S. Army Captain/Lieutenant Bill Walker in *The Story of G.I. Joe*

Back when being a rabble-rouser usually ended a film career, Robert Mitchum played by his own rules, breaking some laws and serving prison time, and still managed to solidify his rightful place among Hollywood's 20th century legends. Through Oscar-nominated cinematography and Oscar-winning special effects, *Thirty Seconds over Tokyo* introduced handsome young Robert Mitchum to film audiences and the Academy. The following year, Mitchum was himself among the Oscar nominated for his supporting performance as an amiable, if exhausted lieutenant who defied his squadron and indulged journalist Ernie Pyle's inquisitive explorations in *The Story of G.I. Joe*. Having every 1945 Best Supporting Actor contender a first time nominee except for J. Carrol Nash helped even the chances for anyone to win. But because Mitchum could be singled out for giving the one supporting performance that catapulted him to instant star status, his chances of winning were strong. On Oscar night, the Academy gave the prize instead to established character actor James Dunn in *A Tree Grown in Brooklyn*. Thereafter, movies with Mitchum in the lead acting role found intermittent favor with Oscar. In 1947 he investigated a racially motivated military murder in the Best Picture nominee *Crossfire*. Later he played opposite Deborah Kerr in two of her Best Actress-nominated performances, first as the title character in *Heaven Knows, Mr. Allison* (1957) and then as her husband, an Irish-

Australian sheep drover in *The Sundowners* (1960). He was Brigadier General Norman Cota in the 1962 Best Picture-nominated war epic *The Longest Day*, and in 1970 he played the schoolmaster with whom Best Actress nominee Sarah Miles falls in love in David Lean's ambitious *Ryan's Daughter*. From his uncredited appearance as one of Barry Nelson's war buddies in *The Human Comedy* (1943) to his return to film noir as Philip Marlowe in *Farewell, My Lovely* with 1975 Best Supporting Actress nominee Sylvia Miles, Mitchum used his droopy-eyed, hard-knock life to become a silver screen rebel worth rooting for in more than a half-century of films.

Ava Gardner

1953 Best Actress as gold digger Eloise "Honey Bear" Kelly in *Mogambo*

A dark enchantress who excelled first in film noir, Gardner left Oscar a little melted when her beauty turned out to be the most powerful of *The Killers* in Robert Siodmak's sleeper hit of 1946. The movie appeared in four categories on Oscar ballots, though none for acting. Gardner's role as Julie LaVerne was expanded for the 1951 movie adaptation of *Show Boat*, the only version to compete for Academy Awards. Again, Oscar cited the movie for its technical merit, but entirely dismissed the acting. Gardner's talents caught up to her beauty by 1953 when her characterization of Honey Bear Kelly, whose jaded disillusionment is sometimes punctuated with surges of lusty entanglements with Clark Gable, placed her among the year's Best Actresses. It was a balanced category, with Gardner and *From Here to Eternity*'s Deborah Kerr heating up the screen, Maggie McNamara shocking the censors as a pre–*Lolita* nymphet, entrancing young Leslie Caron as *Lili*, and Audrey Hepburn as a runaway heiress on *Roman Holiday*. Hepburn took the prize. Gardner was billed as "The World's Most Beautiful Animal" in *The Barefoot Contessa* the following year, and Oscar took note and named Edmond O'Brien Best Supporting Actor. She brought O'Brien luck once again in 1964, as his only other nomination came for another Gardner film, *Seven Days in May*. Gardner was a featured player at the 1964 Academy Awards, as her other hit, *The Night of the Iguana* had led to speculation about a second Best Actress nod for Gardner. BAFTA and the Golden Globes registered their approval with nominations, but Oscar only acknowledged supporting star Grayson Hall. Like many A-listers, Garnder courted disaster in the 1970s by joining an all-star cast for a big budget trembler, Oscar-winning *Earthquake*. As lovely late in her career as she was in her prime, Gardner lit the screen for four decades, then found a new following thanks to Kate Beckinsale's portrayal of her in Martin Scorsese's Oscar-winning *The Aviator* in 2004.

Doris Day

1959 Best Actress as interior decorator Jan Morrow in *Pillow Talk*

Blonde big band singer Doris Day exuded such a balanced blend of wholesome sex appeal that she seemed destined for movie greatness, ultimately cornering the market on innuendo-driven romantic comedies that made her the top worldwide box office female for the better part of the 1950s and 1960s. In 1953, she introduced the Best Song winner "Secret Love" as title character *Calamity Jane*, then supported Best Actor nominee James Cagney in the biographical drama *Love Me or Leave Me* in 1955. The following year she sang "Que Sera, Sera" in Hitchcock's remake of his own *The Man Who Knew Too Much*, and it too won Best Song. Clark Gable enrolled in her course and became her *Teacher's Pet* in 1958, but it was supporting actor Gig Young who got the Oscar nomination.

The following year, Day teamed with Rock Hudson for a little *Pillow*

As Jan Morrow in *Pillow Talk* (1959), Doris Day began a series of flirtatious romantic comedies with Rock Hudson (here playing Brad Allen) that extended into the next decade her reign as top box office star.

Talk, bringing Day her only Academy Award nomination. Subsequent entendre-laced comedies, often with Rock Hudson or James Garner, engaged worldwide audiences and earned Day top box office prizes from the Golden Globes five times. Since retiring, Day has been recognized with lifetime achievement awards from such organizations as the Hollywood Foreign Press (1989), the Grammys (2008), and the Los Angeles Film Critics (2012). Rigorous campaigning by columnist Liz Smith and critic Rex Reed to honor Day with a lifetime achievement Academy Award suggests that it's only a matter of time before she has an honorary Oscar as well.

Steve McQueen

1966 Best Actor as naval Machinist's Mate 1st Class Jake Holman in *The Sand Pebbles*

In 1956 McQueen had a bit part in the Oscar-winning *Somebody Up There Likes Me* starring Paul Newman before each would dominate as the antiheroes of their generation. Two years later McQueen had his first starring role in the cult horror classic, *The Blob*, and two years after that he honed his reputation as a cool rebel as rootless Vin Tanner, one of *The Magnificent Seven*. Though not nominated in 1963, McQueen's presence was felt through two competing films, *The Great Escape*, which began his tenure as a top box office draw that lasted more than a decade, and *Love with the Proper Stranger* opposite Best Actress nominee Natalie Wood. Oscar did finally afford McQueen one nomination for Robert Wise's sprawling epic *The Sand Pebbles*. McQueen polished his shimmering chrome cool with two Oscar-winning box office bonanzas of 1968, *Bullitt*, whose legendary car chase precludes *The French Connection*'s by three years, and *The Thomas Crown Affair*, where his chess match against kinetic Faye Dunaway out-titillated Albert Finney and Joyce Redman's meat-tearing dinner foreplay in *Tom Jones*. After other Oscar-contending hits such as *The Reivers* (1969) and *Papillon* (1973), McQueen donned a fireman's uniform in 1974 and reteamed with Paul Newman, playing the architect of San Francisco's tallest building, to douse *The Towering Inferno*. Worldwide excitement for the film sustained McQueen's box office prowess and became his only movie besides *The Sand Pebbles* to compete for a Best Picture Oscar. Casually astride his motorcycle with his glistening eyes hidden behind dark glasses, the image of Steve McQueen still epitomizes the indomitable appeal of a breezy, magnetically aloof rebel.

Harrison Ford

1985 Best Actor as detective John Book in *Witness*

Harrison Ford's presence as supporting player Han Solo in the *Star Wars* franchise and as the central figure in the equally prosperous *Indiana Jones* dynasty easily put him in the top tier of all-time box office champions. But he began building bankability in George Lucas' 1973 ensemble nostalgia homage, *American Graffiti* and Francis Ford Coppola's *The Conversation* (1974), which were both up for Best Picture. Again under the direction of Coppola and with a stellar cast including Best Supporting Actor nominee Robert Duvall, Ford navigated the jungles of Vietnam as military intelligence officer Colonel Lucas in *Apocalypse Now*, another Best Picture nominee of the 1970s. He was the centerpiece of the similarly apocalyptic cult classic *Blade Runner*, which the Academy recognized only for its technical merit. Ford finally became a Best Actor contender as John Book, a detective who tracks his *Witness* to Amish country. In that 1985 competition, Ford was a frontrunner with a good chance to win over James Garner in *Murphy's Romance* and Jon Voight in *Runaway Train*, and in a tight race with Jack Nicholson defending *Prizzi's Honor* and ultimate winner William Hurt delusionally enchanted by the *Kiss of the Spider Woman*. He reteamed with *Witness* director Peter Weir on *The Mosquito Coast*, but Oscar didn't pay attention again until two years later when he tangled with *Working Girl* Melanie Griffith in Mike Nichols' 1988 Best Picture nominee. Griffith was up for lead actress while Sigourney Weaver and Joan Cusack filled two supporting slots, but Ford was left off the Academy roster. His next huge hit was the film version of TV's popular *The Fugitive*. Though he was bypassed by the Academy, Tommy Lee Jones, as his pursuer, won Best Supporting Actor. In all, Ford has been nominated for four Golden Globes, for those three performances as well as for the 1995 remake of *Sabrina* with Ford reprising the Bogart role, and in 2001 he earned their Cecil B. DeMille Award for lifetime achievement. Having been similarly lauded by the American Film Institute in 2000, it seems reasonable that the amicable actor whose good looks are balanced by crystal eyes and a scarred chin might anticipate similar acknowledgment from his peers in the Academy.

Burt Reynolds

1997 Best Supporting Actor as porn director Jack Horner in *Boogie Nights*

For the longest time, handsome man's man Burt Reynolds seemed to build comradery with every other powerful male in Hollywood except Oscar. His success on 1960s television led to a harrowing journey down the rapids and potentially to Oscar's stage in 1972's *Deliverance*. Talk proliferated throughout award season that Reynolds would be the one among the ensemble to get the Oscar nomination for the terrifyingly tense drama, but at nomination time, *The Godfather* dominated the male acting categories, leaving *Deliverance* a Best Picture nominee with no acting contenders. Football-themed *The Longest Yard* earned Reynolds his first Golden Globe nomination, but the Academy put it up only for Film Editing. In 1977 *Smokey and the Bandit* secured Reynolds' place among Hollywood's most popular box office draws, and again the Academy cited only the movie's editing. The following year *Hooper* was up for Best Sound, but then in 1979 Reynolds' hopes of finally earning the Academy's respect, and a nomination, ran high when Alan J. Pakula's *Starting Over* proved to be a critical smash and Reynolds was again up for a Golden Globe. Disappointment returned when Jill Clayburgh and Candice Bergen were nominated but his performance was ignored. 1982 was his "Best" year when Charles Durning was up for supporting actor for *The Best Little Whorehouse in Texas* and *Best Friends* was nominated for its song, "How Do You Keep the Music Playing?" But Reynolds finally hit his award-warranting stride as pornographic film director Jack Horner in Paul Thomas Anderson's daring and insightful *Boogie Nights*. Critics groups across the nation from LA to New York named him 1997's Best Supporting Actor, and momentum continued through his Golden Globe victory. A SAG loss to Robin Williams for *Good Will Hunting* put the stars in a dead heat for the Oscar, with Williams going home the winner. Yet Reynolds' nomination made up for much past disappointment, and finally he could respond to the Academy with a touch of the playful joy that punctuated his most popular comic performances.

Those Who Were Overlooked

Rudolph Valentino

As silent film's chic sheik, Rudolph Valentino gave the world the first glimpse of the power of a screen presence. Female fans purportedly often wept at the sight of his gorgeous presence on massive cinema screens. After his death from peritonitis at age 31, over 100,000 people attended his funeral, and some fans allegedly committed suicide because of his passing. Valentino's star shot into the heavens in great part thanks to his sexy tango as a directionless but favored son of a wealthy Argentine landowner in 1921's *The Four Horsemen of the Apocalypse*. The part established his screen persona as the ultimate swarthy lover, a status intensified later that year when he sweltered in the desert wearing a keffiyeh and a spellbinding gaze as *The Sheik*. Because Valentino's untimely death occurred in 1926, the year before the Academy formed and three years before it began giving out gold statuettes, Valentino's legacy could never converge with Oscar unless, like Kenneth Branagh as Laurence Olivier in *My Week with Marilyn* (2011), someone is nominated for, or, like Cate Blanchett as Katharine Hepburn in *The Aviator* (2004), someone wins an Oscar portraying Valentino in a movie.

Jean Harlow

Jean Harlow originated and embodied Hollywood's ultimate blond bombshell. That she achieved the staggering feat in 36 movies over only ten years before she died at age 26 makes her achievement all the more unprecedented. Unlike many who hungered for stardom, teenaged Harlow took bit parts in silent films to appease her ambitious mother. When talkies arrived, she was a perfect fit to replace similar foreign beauties whose thick accents ended their American motion picture careers. Such was the case with Harlow's breakthrough role as the surprisingly lusty Helen in Howard Hughes' big budget *Hell's Angels*. Originally begun as a silent film with Norwegian Greta Nissen playing Helen, the movie grew in Hughes' vision and became a sound motion picture, necessitating a new Helen, which Harlow took, mastered, and became a star as a result. At the 1929/30 Academy Awards, it was up for Best Cinematography. That same year Harlow played a lady in waiting in *The Love Parade*, a dominating hit at that same Oscar ceremony. It earned six nominations, including one for director Ernst Lubitsch and star Maurice Chevalier. At the 1930/31 Oscars, Harlow was the woman with a penchant for bad men like James Cagney in *The Public Enemy*, which competed for Best Original Story. Thanks to classic performances like Wallace Beery's spoiled wife in *Dinner at Eight* (1933), Harlow's star soared, and she was soon a top box office champ of the decade. With such bankability, Harlow was soon headlining her own pictures. She was the American showgirl named *Suzy*, in which her character (dubbed by Virginia Verrill) sang the 1936 Best Song–nominated "Did I Remember?" That same year, Harlow had the lead in *Libeled Lady*. Although the screwball comedy was up for Best Picture, it garnered no other nominations. Always frail from long-term effects of childhood illnesses, Harlow died the following year, but by then had left such an impression on movies that her platinum waves and mole-punctuated cheek remain emblematic of beauty buoyed by saucy sexuality, and a glint of fun. In 1965, her popularity resurged with two competing film biographies both entitled *Harlow*. In May, the first came out with Carol Lynley as Harlow; the next month, Carroll Baker did the honors. Although the Baker version earned Red Buttons a Golden Globe nomination for playing her compassionate agent, Arthur Landau, neither biopic translated into Oscar gold. No matter, Harlow's legacy was platinum.

Mae West

Like male contemporaries such as Charles Chaplin, Harold Lloyd, and Buster Keaton, Mae West knew that the key to a successful transition from a comedy writer for the stage to a career that put her in front of the public in theaters and cinemas hinged on developing an indelible persona. And what a persona her hip-shifting, eye-leering, Brooklynese-whispering sexpot was. More Sophie Tucker than Jean Harlow, West realized that her stocky build in the age of sprightly flappers could make sexual innuendoes coming from her more startling. West transformed her hit Broadway character, Diamond Lil into Lady Lou for her first starring movie role in 1933's *She Done Him Wrong*. Always keen-eyed for a handsome man with talent, West secured young unknown Cary Grant to be her suitor, and the Academy responded to their racy banter with a Best Picture nomination. Though she made only about a dozen motion pictures, her work as an actress/screenwriter gave cinema some of its greatest lines, including "Why don't you come up sometime and see me" (*She Done Him Wrong*) revised by West to the more familiar "Come up and see me sometime" (*I'm No Angel*), also opposite Cary Grant. Despite her box office gusto and enough envelope-pushing to keep the censors incensed and the public publicity-drenched, the Academy only recognized one more West film with a nomination, singling out *Every Day's a Holiday* for a Best Art Direction nomination in 1937. Always a compelling presence adorned by gorgeous men, West appeared at the 1957 Academy Awards, performing the Best Song winner of 1949, "Baby, It's Cold Outside" with Rock Hudson. While contemporaries Chaplin, Lloyd, and Keaton all eventually took home honorary Oscars, not even a late career comeback in the early 1970s moved the Academy to honor West's contribution to film. Like W.C. Fields, who starred with her in the 1940 box office hit, *My Little Chickadee*, she was a comic groundbreaker who remained a treasure egregiously overlooked by Oscar.

W. C. Fields

With a hazy squint, bulbous red nose, and affectations aided by his love of liquor, W. C. Fields synced his finger flutters to the rhythm of lines spilling sidelong from his tilted mouth and gave audiences a comic curmudgeon to love. Fields transformed his vaudeville juggling act in the Ziegfeld Follies into a silent film career and managed, as no one had before him, to make endearing on screen characters that people would have avoided in real life. Ill health prevented him from making many movies once talkies and the Academy Awards emerged, but Fields did fulfill a professional dream by playing the ultimately likeable Wilkins Micawber in *David Copperfield*. The movie, and Fields, were a huge success, with the film competing for Best Picture of 1935. Had the Dickens adaptation been released just a year later, when the Academy added supporting actor competitions, Fields would likely have been a contender. Instead, his supporting role registered rave reviews and admiration, but no Academy accolade. Oscar recognized only two subsequent movies that included appearances by Fields, and both in the Best Song category. *The Big Broadcast of 1938* featured Bob Hope and Shirley Ross singing the Oscar-winning "Thanks for the Memory." In 1944, *Follow the Boys*, in which Fields revived a trick pool shot routine he'd perfected on stage, contained the Oscar-nominated song, "I'll Walk Alone." In many ways, Fields did just that, pursuing a unique path to stardom that resulted in silver screen stardom, but no Oscar gold.

Rita Hayworth

Rita Hayworth built a career that simmered at a slow boil until she lit the screen as a ravishing, raven-haired seductress best remembered for her World War II pinup and her performance as the embittered femme fatale called *Gilda*. Hayworth's career built throughout the 1930s in three movies warmly received by Oscar. In 1936, *Dancing Pirate* earned a Best Dance Direction nomination, and the 1939 drama, *Only Angels Have Wings* was up for Best Cinematography and Special Effects. Though best known for her flaming red locks, Hayworth's career really heated up as *The Strawberry Blonde* in 1941. An accomplished dancer, she was the first to partner on film with both Fred Astaire (initially in *You'll Never Get Rich*, 1941) and Gene Kelly (in the Oscar-winning *Cover Girl*, 1944). By then, Hayworth was smoldering on screen year after year as a top box office star of such Oscar competitors as *My Gal Sal*, *Tonight and Every Night*, *The Loves of Carmen*, and *Miss Sadie Thompson*, reprising a role that earned Gloria Swanson an Oscar nomination in the Academy's first year. Despite never being nominated for an Oscar herself, Hayworth was in two of her highest Oscar profile films in the late 1950s with *Pal Joey*, which was up for four awards, and Best Picture nominee *Separate Tables*, which garnered David Niven and Wendy Hiller Oscar wins. Like other timeless beauties, Hayworth continues to impact popular culture. In 1982, Stephen King wrote the novella *Rita Hayworth and the Shawshank Redemption*. Her pinup served as a pivotal plot point in *The Shawshank Redemption*, a Best Picture nominee in 1994, more than half a century after Hayworth lit the torch that continues to illuminate her place in film history.

Roddy McDowall

The most trusted confidante to his moviemaking colleagues, Roddy McDowall is believed to have gone to his grave with more Hollywood secrets than Hedda Hopper and Louella Parsons revealed in both their columns. Even as a child star McDowall built friendships that lasted a lifetime. At age 12, McDowall immediately caught Oscar's attention as the youngest member of the Morgan family in John Ford's Best Picture of 1941 *How Green Was My Valley* opposite beloved stars Walter Pidgeon and Maureen O'Hara. Besides his starring roles opposite some of Hollywood's most successful four-legged characters, loyal to *My Friend Flicka* and hoping to see *Lassie Come Home*, McDowall also supported lead actor nominees of the era by following Monty Woolley as *The Pied Piper* (1942) and playing the younger version of Gregory Peck's character in *The Keys of the Kingdom* (1945). McDowall made the transition from child to adult movie star with Tony- and Emmy-winning forays on stage and television. Back on the big screen in 1962 he joined the legion of A-listers suffering through *The Longest Day* of World War II. The next year he was all but guaranteed a supporting nomination for his inflated Octavian in *Cleopatra* until 20th Century Fox accidentally submitted him for Best Actor consideration. The resulting oversight of McDowall is considered one of the worst studio gaffs in Oscar campaign history. His fan base grew behind Oscar-winning makeup as heroic chimp Cornelius in *Planet of the Apes* (1968) and as injured steward Acres hobbling toward safety through Academy Awarded special effects in *The Poseidon Adventure* (1972). McDowall died before the Academy recognized his acting with a nomination or honorary award, so they paid tribute to him by naming their massive still photograph collection in the Academy's Margaret Herrick Library "the Roddy McDowall collection."

Marilyn Monroe

Monroe burst onto the screen in two Oscar contenders of 1950. She had a small role as the impressed young starlet at Bette Davis' "bumpy night" in *All About Eve*. Monroe had more opportunity to convey her acting skills from Louis Calhern's couch in *The Asphalt Jungle*. Soon after, Monroe owned the decade, and established the persona of the salaciously sexy yet mournful object of desire, admiration, envy, and pity that would keep her the world's most beloved star more than a half century after her death. The Academy's failure to acknowledge Monroe with even a single nomination misleadingly suggests that Monroe's talents remained undervalued throughout her career. Not so. She was nominated for awards, just not from the Academy. In 1955, her skirt flew as high as world box office receipts in *The Seven Year Itch*, earning Monroe a Best Foreign Actress BAFTA nomination.

The following year, audiences and critics raved about her as showgirl Cherie in *Bus Stop*. The Hollywood Foreign Press nominated her for Best Actress, but Oscar nominated only supporting actor Don Murray. In 1957,

Marilyn Monroe earned her first serious Oscar consideration in 1956 for *Bus Stop* playing Chérie, an ambitious singer who aspired to be what Monroe already was— a beloved star.

The Prince and the Showgirl earned her a second BAFTA Best Foreign Actress nod, as well as victories in Italy and France, but Oscar dismissed that film entirely. The same held true for *The Misfits*, the vehicle that one-time husband Arthur Miller wrote to showcase Monroe's dramatic range. In 1959, she proved why *Some Like It Hot*, including the Academy. Members nominated the movie for six awards, with one for Jack Lemmon as Best Actor. But Oscar wasn't as sweet on Monroe's Sugar Kane as the Hollywood Foreign Press, who named Monroe Best Actress, Musical or Comedy. Monroe attended the Academy Awards only once, near the start of her career: she presented Best Sound Recording to *All About Eve*, her only movie to be nominated for, and win, Best Picture.

3

Double Threat: Filmmaker-Actors

Filmmakers Who Won Acting Oscars

Lionel Barrymore

1928/29 Best Director of *Madame X*
1930/31 Best Actor as defense attorney Stephen Ashe in *A Free Soul*

Lionel Barrymore's greatest movie contributions, and his Oscar successes, came for movies that spanned cinema's transition to talkies. In Oscar's first year, Barrymore played the antagonistic preacher set on destroying Best Actress nominee Gloria Swanson as good-time islander *Sadie Thompson*. Barrymore was among the first ten filmmakers up for Best Director thanks to *Madame X* for which he was nominated at the second Academy Awards. For that movie, Barrymore directed Ruth Chatterton to a Best Actress nod. The next year, he did the same for Lawrence Tibbett in the Best Actor category for *The Rogue Song*. Barrymore resumed work in front of the cameras in 1930 to tackle the demanding role of alcoholic attorney Stephen Ashe in *A Free Soul*. His climactic scene concluded with a 14-minute monologue, the longest uninterrupted speech in motion picture history. When Barrymore was nominated for Best Actor for the performance in Oscar's fourth year, he became the first person to compete for Academy Awards in different categories. Though he lost 1928/29 Best Director to Frank Lloyd for *The Divine Lady*, Barrymore won 1930/31 Best Actor in what is still considered one of the strongest Best Actor performances in history. Barrymore's lengthy résumé featured him in many Best Picture-vying classics. Of those that won, he played dying Otto Kringelein in *Grand Hotel* (1931/32) and eccentric patriarch Martin Vanderhof in *You Can't Take It with You* (1938). Of those nominated, he appeared as himself in *The Hollywood Review of 1929* (1928/29), fisherman

Mr. Peggotty in *David Copperfield* (1935), schooner captain Disko Troop in *Captains Courageous* (1937), airplane manufacturer Drake in *Test Pilot* (1938), and the town clergyman in *Since You Went Away* (1944). Though castmate James Stewart was the only actor nominated for the 1946 classic, *It's a Wonderful Life*, Barrymore's most familiar film legacy came as Mr. Potter, the wheelchair-bound curmudgeon set on owning every business and soul of Bedford Falls.

Barbra Streisand

1968 Best Actress as Ziegfeld performer Fanny Brice in *Funny Girl*
1973 Best Actress as Marxist activist Katie Morosky in *The Way We Were*
1976 Best Song as co-songwriter (with Paul Williams) of "Evergreen (Love Theme from *A Star Is Born*)" from *A Star Is Born* (music by Barbra Streisand; lyrics by Paul Williams)
1991 Best Picture as co-producer (with Andrew Karsch) of *The Prince of Tides*
1996 Best Song as co-songwriter (with Bryan Adams, Marvin Hamlisch, and Robert "Mutt" Lange) for "I Finally Found Someone" from *The Mirror Has Two Faces* (music and lyrics by all co-songwriters)

Superstardom is a moniker few people attain, but Barbra Streisand's work in only the 1960s and '70s warranted the impressive status. She was already a Broadway legend when she brought her interpretation of Fanny Brice from stage to screen in *Funny Girl*. When Ingrid Bergman opened the Best Actress envelope in 1968, "It's a tie!" brought Streisand to Oscar's stage to accept while her fellow winner, Katharine Hepburn of *The Lion in Winter*, was a predicted no-show. Streisand greeted her golden boy with "Hello, gorgeous," her first line in *Funny Girl*. Towering box office persisted through much of the next decade, and Streisand earned a second Best Actress bid for *The Way We Were*. Her rendering of the title song made it a shoo-in for the Best Song Oscar. Three years later, another of her movies, the third film version of *A Star Is Born*, not only won Best Song, but also made Streisand the first Oscared actor to win a second Academy Award in another, non-acting category. Always courageously testing the limits of her creative output, Streisand co-authored, directed, produced, and starred as *Yentl*. The hit musical earned five nominations in 1983, but to her understandable disappointment, none for her. Although Oscar didn't embrace her direction of *The Prince of Tides* either, Streisand's adaptation of Pat Conroy's novel did bring her a Best Picture nod as producer. For her next film, she directed, co-produced and starred in *The Mirror Has Two Faces*, which finally tagged legend

Lauren Bacall for her only competitive Oscar nomination and snagged Streisand a second bid for Best Song. Among her other Oscar-honored films, Streisand played matchmaker Dolly Levi in *Hello, Dolly!*, which was nominated for seven Oscars, including Best Picture of 1969, and won three. She worked hard to spearhead a continuation of Fanny Brice's story, finally bringing it to the screen as *Funny Lady*, which competed for five Academy Awards in 1975.

Ruth Gordon

- 1947 Best Original Screenplay as co-screenwriter (with Garson Kanin) of *A Double Life*
- 1950 Best Story and Screenplay as co-screenwriter (with Garson Kanin) of *Adam's Rib*
- 1952 Best Story and Screenplay as co-screenwriter (with Garson Kanin) of *Pat and Mike*
- 1965 Best Supporting Actress as mother The Dealer in *Inside Daisy Clover*
- **1968 Best Supporting Actress as neighbor Minnie Castevet in *Rosemary's Baby***

"I can't tell you how encouraging a thing like this is" quipped Ruth Gordon as she finally held an Oscar after winning Best Supporting Actress as Mia Farrow's devil-worshipping neighbor who coveted *Rosemary's Baby*. Already an established stage star, Gordon was making headway as a movie actress when she and husband Garson Kanin submitted a screenplay called *A Double Life*. Director George Cukor took on the project, cast Ronald Colman, and all four were Oscar nominated in 1947. Colman won, as did composer Dr. Miklos Rozsa. Gordon and Kanin used their subsequent friendship with Katharine Hepburn and Spencer Tracy to create the comic romances *Adam's Rib* and *Pat and Mike*. Both movies, directed by Cukor, were among the acting pair's sharpest hits. In 1965, Gordon earned a Best Supporting Actress Golden Globe as Natalie Wood's mentally fracturing mother in *Inside Daisy Clover*. Momentum for a repeat win at the Oscars diminished as Shelley Winters won favor and a record-setting second Best Supporting Actress Oscar for *A Patch of Blue*. Three years later, Gordon reaped another Best Supporting Actress win from the Hollywood Foreign Press, and sustained voter enthusiasm through Tony Curtis's opening the envelope to declare her Oscar's winner as well. In her acceptance speech, Gordon shared that she had been acting in motion pictures since 1915. Most memorably, she played the wives of two historical figures in 1940 movies that competed for Oscar. She was Mary Todd Lincoln to Best Actor nominee Raymond Massey's *Abe Lincoln in Illinois*, and she played Hedwig, wife of physician Edward G. Robinson, in *Dr. Ehrlich's*

Magic Bullet. Always endearingly clever, Gordon ended her Academy Award acceptance speech by thanking all those who voted for her. "And all of you who didn't," she smiled, "please excuse me."

John Houseman

> 1953 Best Picture as producer of *Julius Caesar*
> **1973 Best Supporting Actor as Harvard law professor Charles Kingsfield in *The Paper Chase***

Houseman first cut his teeth in show business as a theater producer, which gave him enough bite to withstand a volatile relationship with fellow auteur, the equally brilliant Orson Welles. Houseman and Welles collaborated on the infamous 1938 *War of the Worlds* radio broadcast, and together conceptualized and shaped the screenplay for *Citizen Kane* before a financial argument ended their relationships as business partners and friends. As sole producer, he helped bring to life classics including *The Blue Dahlia*, which was up for Best Original Screenplay of 1946; *Julius Caesar*, which competed for five Oscars, including Best Picture with Houseman as nominee, and won for Art Direction; and *Lust for Life* (1956), which brought Anthony Quinn the only win among its four nominations. Houseman found acting fame late in his career, and at age 62 played Vice Admiral Farley C. Barnswell opposite Best Supporting Actor nominee Edmond O'Brien in *Seven Days in May*. Houseman was 71 when given the Best Supporting Actor Golden Globe and Oscar for *The Paper Chase*. As the emotionally unreachable law professor whom student Timothy Bottoms identifies in front of class as a "son of a bitch," Houseman droned on in class, used eye contact for haughty intimidation, and proved to be a great law professor despite his social ineptitude. The movie proved so popular that it was recreated as a television series with Houseman continuing on as Kingsfield. Houseman's two Golden Globe nominations for the television series made him one of the few stars to play a single character that earned him Golden Globe nominations in both movie and television competitions.

Michael Douglas

> **1975 Best Picture as co-producer (with Saul Zaentz) of *One Flew Over the Cuckoo's Nest***
> **1987 Best Actor as corporate raider Gordon Gekko in *Wall Street***

To be nominated by the Academy for work as an actor and as a non-actor is in itself an impressive achievement. To win in both, a milestone. To win in both when those victories came from one's only nominations, an almost impossible coup. Yet actor/producer Michael Douglas did just that with two projects. In 1963, Michael's father Kirk had retained the film rights to his stage hit, *One Flew Over the Cuckoo's Nest*. After a decade without finding financial backing, Kirk gave the rights to Michael, who piqued United Artists' interest. With his dad now too old to play McMurphy, the part went to one of the day's hottest actors, Jack Nicholson, while unknown Louise Fletcher was cast as antagonist Nurse Ratched. *One Flew Over the Cuckoo's Nest* went into 1975's Oscar race the frontrunner, and exceeded everyone's expectations by matching *It Happened One Night*'s record of securing all five top prizes: Best Actor and Actress for Nicholson and Fletcher, Best Adapted Screenplay, Best Director, and Best Picture, which Douglas shared with Saul Zaentz. As producer and actor, Douglas followed with *The China Syndrome*, which earned four Oscar nominations in 1979, and *Romancing the Stone* which won the 1984 Best Picture, Musical or Comedy Golden Globe and was nominated for a film editing Oscar. "Greed, for lack of a better word, is good," avaricious *Wall Street* stockbroker Gordon Gekko attested, lulling movie fans and the Academy into his egocentric success. Douglas' victories mounted from international honors to Best Actor wins from the National Board of Review and Golden Globes, and ultimately to the Academy's Best Actor pick as well. Notable work in subsequent hits such as *Basic Instinct* (1992), *The American President* (1995) and *Solitary Man* (2009) brought Douglas nominations from other organizations, but never the Academy. Their brashest oversight came in 2000 when Douglas was touted for nominations in two Oscar-winning hits, *Traffic* and *Wonder Boys*, and came up empty-handed again. Regardless, going two-for-two in two different categories places Douglas in a success category all his own.

Tim Robbins

1995 Best Director for *Dead Man Walking*
2003 Best Supporting Actor as blue-collar worker Dave Boyle in *Mystic River*

Towering in physique and talent, Tim Robbins made his first impression on Oscar as a highflier in *Top Gun*, which won Best Song for "You Take My Breath Away" in 1986. Two years later, both Robbins and future spouse Susan Sarandon had high hopes for nominations in *Bull Durham*, which ended up with a single Academy Award bid for its original screenplay. Robbins won Best Actor at the 1992 Cannes Film Festival as unscrupulous movie exec Griffin Mill in *The Player*. The Academy responded to the film with three nominations, including Best Director for Robert Altman, but none for its cast. In

1994 *The Shawshank Redemption* garnered seven nominations, including Best Picture, but Morgan Freeman got the Best Actor nod instead of Robbins. He finally earned the Academy's praise with a nomination, not for acting, but for directing *Dead Man Walking* which brought Susan Sarandon the Best Actress prize of 1995. Taking the lion's share of Best Supporting Actor trophies leading to the 2003 Academy Awards boded well for Robbins to win the Oscar as well. Despite strong competition from Ken Watanabe in *The Last Samurai*, Robbins and Best Actor Sean Penn won *Mystic River*'s two victories amid its six nominations, finally making Robbins an Oscar winner.

Oscar-Winning Filmmakers Nominated for Acting Oscars

Charles Chaplin

1927/28 Special Award "for acting, writing, directing and producing *The Circus*"
1940 Best Actor as barber/Dictator of Tomania Adenoid Hynkel in *The Great Dictator*
1940 Best Original Screenplay as screenwriter of *The Great Dictator*
1947 Best Original Screenplay as screenwriter of *Monsieur Verdoux*
1971 Honorary Award "for the incalculable effect he has had in making motion pictures the art form of this century"
1972 Best Original Dramatic Score as co-composer (with Raymond Rasch and Larry Russell) for *Limelight*

In The Little Tramp, Charles Chaplin created an iconic character that first illustrated the impact of a single unique image on screen. More than 100 years after its incarnation, Chaplin's impish, waddling tramp is *the* indelible symbol of motion pictures. Chaplin was already the highest paid entertainer worldwide when the Academy first formed, and his tramp had been dodging fists and dining on shoe leather for thirteen years before the naked swordsman became a gold-plated statuette. As a world sensation, Chaplin had his share of detractors, some among them in the Academy's founding board. For the first Oscar ceremony, Chaplin was nominated for Best Actor and Best Director for *The Circus*, but the governors of the Academy withdrew his nominations and sent him a letter telling him he would become the first recipient of an honorary Oscar. Thereafter, the Academy bypassed such classics as *City Lights* (1931) and *Modern Times* (1936), until Chaplin courageously dared to skewer, through humor and a climactic impassioned plea, world-crushing dictator Adolf Hitler, in Chaplin's first talkie, *The Great Dictator*. After the

Tramp retired his oversized shoes and bowler hat, Chaplin impressed the Academy as murderous *Monsieur Verdoux* before he was exiled from the U.S. when his political views obscured his artistic contributions.

Chaplin's return to the Oscars at age 81 to be re-embraced by a more appreciative Academy remains one of the most touching moments in award history. He wept as he accepted an apologetic ovation from the Academy and his statuette from Jack Lemmon. The following year, his movie *Limelight*,

Encircled by his wife, Oona O'Neill, and Oscar winners Cloris Leachman, Ben Johnson and Gene Hackman, Charles Chaplin returned to Hollywood for an emotional reunion and a lifetime achievement award in 1971.

filmed way back in 1952, finally reached Los Angeles cinemas, and so became eligible for Oscar consideration. Near the end of his career, Chaplin won his first, and only, competitive Oscar, for *Limelight*'s score. Whether compressed through the massive cogs of industrialism or precariously bouncing a featherweight globe, Chaplin choreographed humor with a universal message, and did so as an actor, producer, director, writer, and composer. He achieved it all because he did it all, and helped develop the most powerful artistic form of his century.

Orson Welles

1941 Best Actor as newspaper magnate Charles Foster Kane in *Citizen Kane*
1941 Best Director for *Citizen Kane*
1941 Best Original Screenplay as co-screenwriter (with Herman J. Mankiewicz) of *Citizen Kane*
1970 Honorary Award "for superlative artistry and versatility in the creation of motion pictures"

Young wunderkind Orson Welles knew his talents, and never suffered the fools off-put by the confidence he sustained for his massive vision and execution. His Mercury Players, the ensemble that worked with him on stage, radio, or cinema, included revered thespians that won Oscars (Judy Holliday, Anne Baxter), were nominated for Oscars (Agnes Moorehead, Geraldine Fitzgerald, Arthur O'Connell), or were among the greatest actors overlooked by Oscar (George Coulouris, Joseph Cotton, Paul Stewart). After demonstrating the impact of radio by scaring the nation with his *War of the Worlds* radio broadcast on Halloween 1938, Welles co-wrote, produced, directed, and starred in what remains for many the greatest movie in cinema history, *Citizen Kane*. Wrapped in the compelling mystery (who or what is Rosebud?), Welles, like Kane's mistress Susan in the film, slowly laid out the huge pieces of the Charles Foster Kane puzzle, and assembled them gradually through symbols, new cinematic techniques with lighting and camera angles, and crisp writing that garnered Welles what he called "half an Oscar" for co-authoring the bold screenplay that dared pit him against real newspaper magnate William Randolph Hearst. At the 1941 Oscar ceremonies, 26-year-old Welles had detractors who actually booed each time his name was announced during the ceremony. Welles' first triumph remained his greatest, as the subsequent classics he created were, in Welles' opinion, toyed with and infected by others' input. *The Magnificent Ambersons* (1942) earned four Oscar nominations, including Best Picture. *The Third Man* (1950) was up for three, and won for its black and white cinematography. Rotund but never robust, cherubic though rarely cherished in his lifetime, Welles was a master film craftsman, a cinema scientist whose experiments inspired even the most seasoned directors. For his achievements, the Academy tempered its responses to the young Welles and honored the sometimes "difficult, unemployable" genius, at age 55. John Huston took to Oscar's 1970 stage to pay tribute to Welles, who accepted on film from Spain, for his lifetime contribution to original storytelling on celluloid.

John Huston

- 1940 Best Original Screenplay as co-screenwriter (with Norman Burnside and Heinz Herald) of *Dr. Ehrlich's Magic Bullet*
- 1941 Best Original Screenplay as co-screenwriter (with Harry Chandlee, Abem Finkel, and Howard Koch) of *Sergeant York*
- 1941 Best Screenplay as screenwriter of *The Maltese Falcon*
- **1948 Best Director of *The Treasure of the Sierra Madre***
- **1948 Best Screenplay as screenwriter of *The Treasure of the Sierra Madre***
- 1950 Best Director of *The Asphalt Jungle*
- 1950 Best Screenplay as co-screenwriter (with Ben Maddow) of *The Asphalt Jungle*
- 1951 Best Director of *The African Queen*
- 1951 Best Screenplay as co-screenwriter (with James Agee) of *The African Queen*
- 1952 Best Director of *Moulin Rouge*
- 1957 Best Adapted Screenplay as co-screenwriter (with John Lee Mahin) of *Heaven Knows, Mr. Allison*
- 1963 Best Supporting Actor as ecclesiastical leader Cardinal Glennon in *The Cardinal*
- 1975 Best Adapted Screenplay as co-screenwriter (with Gladys Hill) of *The Man Who Would Be King*
- 1985 Best Director of *Prizzi's Honor*

In the 1966 epic, *The Bible*, John Huston was the voice of God. It was an apt role probably not too difficult to perfect, as his languid baritone and supreme confidence in the worlds he created on film made him one of the most powerful and prolific filmmakers of the 20th century. Huston's Hollywood career began as a screenwriter, where he penned such Oscar winners as *Jezebel* (1938) and *Sergeant York* (1941), and nominees including *Juarez* (1939), *Dr. Ehrlich's Magic Bullet* (1940), and *The Killers* (1946). Ever eager to express his artistic vision and expand his influence, Huston convinced Warner Brothers to let him direct. He began with *High Sierra*. Although the Academy showed no interest, it established him as a solid director and turned his lead actor, Humphrey Bogart, into a star. From there, Huston's list of credits dominated the Academy Award nominations, and often winners' lists consistently throughout the 1940s to the 1960s, with occasional gems sprinkled through the two subsequent decades as well. He reteamed with Bogie for *The Maltese Falcon*, the first classic helmed by Huston, and then he made Oscar history by directing his father, Walter, to an Oscar-winning performance in *The Treasure of the Sierra Madra*, which brought Huston his own pair of Oscars, for directing and screenwriting the drama of duplicity and greed. *The Asphalt Jungle* was up for four Academy Awards and helped introduce to the world another top Hollywood legend, Marilyn Monroe. Bogart won his only Best Actor prize under Huston's direction in *The African Queen*. An artist in his youth, Huston had the vision to bring *Moulin Rouge* effectively to the screen, and his art director and costume designer won in those two of the Lautrec biography's seven Oscar categories. Huston excelled in front of the camera as well, bringing greater depth and vivacity to Otto Preminger's lingering epic, *The Cardinal*, and earned a Supporting Actor Oscar nomination.

Warren Beatty

1967 Best Actor as bank robber Clyde Barrow in *Bonnie and Clyde*
1967 Best Picture as producer of *Bonnie and Clyde*
1975 Best Original Screenplay as co-screenwriter (with Robert Towne) of *Shampoo*
1978 Best Actor as professional football backup quarterback Joe Pendleton (alias Leo Farnsworth, Tom Jarrett) in *Heaven Can Wait*
1978 Best Director as co-director (with Buck Henry) of *Heaven Can Wait*
1978 Best Picture as producer of *Heaven Can Wait*
1978 Best Adapted Screenplay as co-screenwriter (with Elaine May) of *Heaven Can Wait*
1981 Best Actor as journalist/writer John "Jack" Reed in *Reds*
1981 Best Director for *Reds*
1981 Best Picture as producer of *Reds*
1981 Best Original Screenplay as co-screenwriter (with Trevor Griffiths) of *Reds*
1991 Best Actor as gangster Benjamin "Bugsy" Siegel in *Bugsy*
1991 Best Picture as co-producer (with Mark Johnson and Barry Levinson) of *Bugsy*
1998 Best Original Screenplay as co-screenwriter (with Jeremy Pikser) of *Bulworth*
1999 Irving G. Thalberg Memorial Award

3. Double Threat: Filmmaker-Actors 267

When he embarked on a movie career in 1961, Shirley MacLaine's little brother was a chisel-cheeked, wavy-haired lothario over whom fans swooned and the Academy took notice. His first two hits were Oscar competitors, as *Splendor in the Grass* put Natalie Wood in contention for Best Actress and won William Inge a Best Story and Screenplay prize, while *The Roman Spring of Mrs. Stone* brought Lotte Lenya a Best Supporting Actress nod. At age 30, Beatty overcame the stigma of his matinee idol looks to make his mark as a bold filmmaker by producing *Bonnie and Clyde* in 1967. After the movie's initially unimpressive reception, Beatty remarketed the film until critics retracted earlier negative reviews and ultimately identified it as a seminal work of its era. In one of moviedom's strongest years, *Bonnie and Clyde* entered the Oscar race with ten nominations, and joined the sparse list of films in Academy history to earn five acting nominations, including one for Beatty. Supporting Actress Estelle Parsons won, as did cinematographer Burnett Guffey. Thereafter, Beatty had total control over his career, passionately fueling his prodigious energy into multiple roles before and behind the camera in hits of every genre. He tackled social commentary with *Shampoo*, an Oscar winner for Best Supporting Actress Lee Grant; comedy with the 9-times nominated and single-winning (for Best Art Direction) *Heaven Can Wait*; and political epic with *Reds*, which earned Beatty his first Academy Award, as Best Director. In 1990, *Dick Tracy* won three of its seven Oscar categories, and the following year *Bugsy* took two of its ten. Beatty's multiple trophies from the Writers Guild, LA Film Critics, Golden Globes, and other leading American and international film organizations had to make shelf space for one more from Oscar, an Irving G. Thalberg Memorial Award, presented to producers who have made an indelible impact on motion pictures. Beatty definitely earned his status among them.

Robert Redford

    1973 Best Actor as small-time con man Johnny Hooker in *The Sting*
    1980 Best Director of *Ordinary People*
    1994 Best Director of *Quiz Show*
    1994 Best Picture as co-producer (with Michael Jacobs, Julian Krainin, and Michael Nozik) of *Quiz Show*
    2001 Honorary Award "to Robert Redford: Actor, director, producer, creator of Sundance, inspiration to independent and innovative filmmakers everywhere"

As much as the Academy appreciates talent, some members have a hard time recognizing the acting skills of actors whose physical splendor overwhelms all other factors that make them a star. Such was the case initially for Robert Redford. He picked strong projects from very early in his career, teaming with Natalie Wood as distraught actors disillusioned with stardom in *Inside Daisy Clover* and reteaming with her the following year for Tennessee Williams' *This Property is Condemned*. He then partnered with Jane Fonda in *The Chase* and *Barefoot in the Park*. Both sets of partnerships brought a supporting female into an Oscar race, as Ruth Gordon was up for *Inside Daisy Clover* and Mildred Natwick competed for *Barefoot in the Park*. Superstardom came when Redford connected with fellow heartthrob Paul Newman, first in the comic misadventures of *Butch Cassidy and the Sundance Kid*, a Best Picture nominee of 1969, and as suave conmen in *The Sting*, Best Picture winner of 1973. That year, Redford was the favorite to win Best Actor for *The Sting*, and his chances seemed enhanced because the Oscar ballots also included several nominations for a hit in another genre, romance, opposite Best Actress nominee Barbra Streisand in *The Way We Were*. Instead of Redford, Oscar honored Jack Lemmon with his second Academy Award, for *Save the Tiger*. As an actor, Redford enjoyed many other Oscared hits, including *The Candidate* (1972), *The Great Gatsby* (1974), *All the President's Men* (1976), and *Out of Africa* (1985). But when Redford went behind the camera, any peers who hesitated to vote for him as an onscreen presence supported him fully. In his directorial debut for 1980's *Ordinary People*, Redford took Best Director and his film won Best Picture. His Sundance Film Festival in large part inspired Oscar to honor Redford's lifetime achievement. In 2013, at age 77, Redford won Best Actor from the New York Film Critics and seemed destined for another Best Actor Oscar nod for *All is Lost*, in which he captivated the audience for 105 minutes as the only character in an almost wordless role as a shipwrecked yachtsman. Pundits shortlisted Redford, then expressed shock when he was absent from the final roster of nominees. Like seasoned contemporaries such as Clint Eastwood and Warren Beatty, Redford continues to awe with boundless energy and talent before and behind the cameras.

Woody Allen

- 1977 Best Actor as comedian Alvy Singer in *Annie Hall*
- **1977 Best Director of *Annie Hall***
- **1977 Best Original Screenplay as co-screenwriter (with Marshall Brickman) of *Annie Hall***
- 1978 Best Director of *Interiors*
- 1978 Best Original Screenplay as screenwriter of *Interiors*
- 1979 Best Original Screenplay as co-screenwriter (with Marshall Brickman) of *Manhattan*
- 1984 Best Director of *Broadway Danny Rose*
- 1984 Best Original Screenplay as screenwriter of *Broadway Danny Rose*

1985 Best Original Screenplay as screenwriter of *The Purple Rose of Cairo*
1986 Best Director of *Hannah and her Sisters*
1986 Best Original Screenplay as screenwriter of *Hannah and Her Sisters*
1987 Best Original Screenplay as screenwriter of *Radio Days*
1989 Best Director of *Crimes and Misdemeanors*
1989 Best Original Screenplay as screenwriter of *Crimes and Misdemeanors*
1990 Best Original Screenplay as screenwriter of *Alice*
1992 Best Original Screenplay as screenwriter of *Husbands and Wives*
1994 Best Director of *Bullets over Broadway*
1994 Best Original Screenplay as co-screenwriter (with Douglas McGrath) of *Bullets over Broadway*
1995 Best Original Screenplay as screenwriter of *Mighty Aphrodite*
1997 Best Original Screenplay as screenwriter of *Deconstructing Harry*
2005 Best Original Screenplay as screenwriter of *Match Point*
2011 Best Director of *Midnight in Paris*
2011 Best Original Screenplay as screenwriter of *Midnight in Paris*
2013 Best Original Screenplay as screenwriter of *Blue Jasmine*

Because of his one Best Actor nomination for *Annie Hall*, Woody Allen holds the record as the most nominated person in Oscar history ever to compete for an acting Academy Award. With 24 nominations, four victories, and a new movie every year that Oscar seldom ignores, Allen shows every indication of expanding his Academy influence as one of the most honored filmmakers in history. Yet like Katharine Hepburn, Allen has never shown the tiniest modicum of interest in any of Oscar's attention. Oscar lore has it that, when Allen was just a teen, his watching Marlon Brando of *A Streetcar Named Desire* lose the 1951 Best Actor trophy to Humphrey Bogart of *The African Queen* so discredited the Academy in Allen's mind that he never got over it. His indifference has never kept Oscar from recognizing Allen's monumental contribution to motion pictures, and so the nominations mount. As impressive as his own nominations are, Allen also ranks behind only William Wyler, Elia Kazan (who directed Brando in *A Streetcar Named Desire*), George Cukor, Martin Scorsese, and Fred Zinnemann as the filmmakers to have directed the most actors to Academy Award nominations and wins. Of those ahead of him, only Scorsese is still alive and making movies. As of Sally Hawkins' nomination and Cate Blanchett's win for *Blue Jasmine* in 2013, Allen has directed 18 performances nominated for Oscar, with seven of those winning. Of all those nominations, Michael Caine, Martin Landau, Chazz Palminteri, Sean Penn, and Allen himself are the only male nominees, and Caine's Best

Supporting Actor victory for *Hannah and Her Sisters* made him Allen's only male winner to date. Allen has a ways to catch number one director William Wyler: he directed 37 actors to nominations, and 14 of them to wins. Again like Katharine Hepburn, Allen did attend one Academy Award ceremony in a year he was not nominated. At the 2002 ceremony, the first after the 9/11 terrorist attacks, Allen introduced a film montage created by Nora Ephron in tribute to his beloved New York City.

Christine Lahti

1984 Best Supporting Actress as singer/riveter Hazel Zanussi in *Swing Shift*
1995 Best Live Action Short Film as director (with co-winner, producer Jana Sue Memel) of *Lieberman in Love*

Oscar lore has it that Lahti's captivating performance as a heartbroken former singer so mesmerized in *Swing Shift* that star and executive producer Goldie Hawn scrapped some of her scenes so Lahti would not outshine the leads. Whether or not that is actually how or why her performance was cut to the length of its ultimate release, Lahti wowed critics, audiences, and award organizations, and took home a bookcase of trophies before losing the Golden Globe and Oscar to Peggy Ashcroft of *A Passage to India*. In 1995, Lahti directed a 39-minute Short Film based on W. P. Kinsella's "Lieberman in Love," and ended up with an Oscar.

Oprah Winfrey

1985 Best Supporting Actress as wife Sofia in *The Color Purple*
2011 Jean Hersholt Humanitarian Award
2014 Best Picture as co-producer (with Christian Colson, Dede Gardner and Jeremy Kleiner) of *Selma*

Before her local talk show went into national syndication, Oprah Winfrey had been spellbound by the character of Sofia in Alice Walker's Pulitzer Prize novel, *The Color Purple* and set her sights on playing the part in Steven Spielberg's movie adaptation. The journey from striving for the role, being told she lost it to Alfre Woodard, then ultimately getting it once she prayerfully released it to Woodard, became a pivotal spiritual message that Winfrey called life-changing. At the 1985 Oscars, Whoopi Goldberg in the lead category, and Winfrey and Margaret Avery in supporting, made *The Color Purple* the first movie to earn Academy Award nominations for three African-American cast members. Winfrey won rave reviews, and was the possible longshot spoiler behind shoo-in Anjelica Huston under the direction of her father John in *Prizzi's Honor*. After Huston won, Winfrey waited 26 years before the Academy honored, not her acting, but her inspiring worldwide humanitarianism. Since then, her acting and producing have returned her to Oscar's center stage. Hope loomed large for a Best Supporting Actress nod as Gloria Gaines, strong-willed wife of *Lee Daniel's The Butler*, but the Academy dismissed the movie entirely in 2013. The following year, Winfrey's performance crackled as courageous civil rights activist Annie Lee Cooper, determined to vote as a citizen of *Selma*. But it was as one of its producers that Winfrey earned another Oscar nomination when *Selma* joined the prestigious ranks of the eight movies up for Best Picture of 2014. A social phenomenon and driving force of change and empowerment, Winfrey has conquered all media, and impressed her Academy peers for her acting, filmmaking, and especially altruism.

Clint Eastwood

    1992 Best Actor as widower/former bandit Bill Munny in *Unforgiven*
    1992 Best Director for *Unforgiven*
    1992 Best Picture as producer of *Unforgiven*
    1994 Irving G. Thalberg Memorial Award
    2003 Best Director for *Mystic River*
    2003 Best Picture as co-producer (with Judie G. Hoyt and Robert Lorenz) of *Mystic River*
    2004 Best Actor as boxing trainer Frankie Dunn in *Million Dollar Baby*
    2004 Best Director for *Million Dollar Baby*
    2004 Best Picture as co-producer (with Tom Rosenberg and Albert S. Ruddy) of *Million Dollar Baby*
    2006 Best Director for *Letters from Iwo Jima*
    2006 Best Picture as co-producer (with Robert Lorenz and Steven Spielberg) of *Letters from Iwo Jima*
    2014 Best Picture as co-producer (with Bradley Cooper, Andrew Lazar, Robert Lorenz, and Peter Morgan) of *American Sniper*

It took a while for Oscar to recognize the significant artistic impact that soft-spoken, steely-eyed Eastwood made to the film industry. Throughout the 1960s and '70s collaborating with director Sergio Leone to play no-named antiheroes in multiple spaghetti Westerns, and subsequently portraying cold-hearted cop *Dirty Harry* made Eastwood a top box office star. Yet Oscar wanted no part of any of these hits, not even recognizing Ennio Marricone's infectious themes of hits like *The Good, the Bad, and the Ugly*. Instead, the Academy nominated Eastwood's 1969 musical, *Paint Your Wagon* for Best

Score, and in 1974, Eastwood's young sidekick, Jeff Bridges, was up for Best Supporting Actor for the caper *Thunderbolt and Lightfoot*. In 1992 Oscar finally recognized the power and majesty of an Eastwood production. *Unforgiven* garnered nine nominations, with three just for Eastwood. It was the big winner of the year, taking home four Oscars, for Supporting Actor Gene Hackman, editor Joel Cox, and Best Director and Best Picture for Eastwood. Just reaching his stride as a filmmaker, Eastwood received the Thalberg Award for his producing well before he became one of the 2000's most honored filmmakers. In 2003, *Mystic River* won Oscars for its lead and supporting actors, Sean Penn and Tim Robbins. The following year, Eastwood duplicated his *Unforgiven* victories with *Million Dollar Baby*, and directed Hilary Swank and Morgan Freeman to acting Oscars. Well into his eighties, Eastwood continues to star in, direct, produce, and score ever more diverse and penetrating films. Oscar's initially cold response to Eastwood's work heated up like the bathtub water he shared with Best Actress nominee Meryl Streep in *The Bridges of Madison County*. With *American Sniper*, Eastwood once again created filmmaking sparks, stoking love from Oscar that shows no signs of cooling.

Brad Pitt

    1995 Best Supporting Actor as psychiatric ward patient Jeffrey Goines in *12 Monkeys*

    2008 Best Actor as tugboat sailor Benjamin Button in *The Curious Case of Benjamin Button*

    2011 Best Actor as professional baseball general manager Billy Beane in *Moneyball*

    2011 Best Picture as co-producer (with Michael De Luca and Rachael Horovitz) of *Moneyball*

    2013 Best Picture as co-producer (with Dede Gardner, Anthony Katagas, Jeremy Kleiner, and Steve McQueen) of *12 Years a Slave*

    2015 Best Picture as co-producer (with Dede Gardner and Jeremy Kleiner) of *The Big Short*

Any way you add them up, Brad Pitt's movies equal success. Audiences first saw the sinewy actor as a thief whose life intersects with *Thelma & Louise*, the Best Original Screenplay winner of 1991, and then as a rebel son lit with Oscar-winning cinematography in *A River Runs through It* (1992). Pitt's numbers added up to Oscar recognition in 1995: despite New Line Cinema's campaign to get the lead actors of *Se7en* Oscar nominations, the Academy only cited it for Film Editing. However, actor Pitt ran his first Oscar race as a pulsating, animal-obsessed mental patient in Terry Gilliam's neo-noir thriller,

12 Monkeys. Other films that scratched the surface of Oscar's interest included nominated *Interview with the Vampire* (1994), *Fight Club* and *Being John Malkovich* (both 1999), and *Troy* (2004). Once he also became a producer, Pitt hit his Oscar stride. In 2006, he produced two Best Picture nominees: *Babel* (in which he also starred) and *The Departed*. For the latter Pitt secured rights to adapt the Hong Kong crime drama *Infernal Affairs*, and was listed with Brad Grey and Graham King as a producer of *The Departed*. But the Academy's recently tightened restrictions on what qualifies a producer to be an Oscar nominee left only King in contention, so only he departed the Kodak Theatre with a Best Picture statuette that year. The 2008 award season had Pitt and *The Curious Case of Benjamin Button* piquing too soon to win on Oscar night. In 2011 Pitt had both *Moneyball* and *The Tree of Life* in the running for Best Picture, with critics begging to finally see Pitt win. He did two years later, not as an actor, but as the producer whom director Steve McQueen credited with bringing *12 Years a Slave* to production. For his first nomination, *12 Monkeys* made him an Oscar nominee. *12 Years* made him a winner. Oscar's jury has reached a verdict: 12 is Pitt's lucky number.

Matt Damon

    1997 Best Actor as janitor Will Hunting in *Good Will Hunting*
    1997 Best Original Screenplay as co-screenwriter (with Ben Affleck) of *Good Will Hunting*
    2009 Best Supporting Actor as rugby team captain Francois Pienaar in *Invictus*
    2015 Best Actor as botanist Mark Watney in *The Martian*
    2016 Best Picture as co-producer (with Lauren Beck, Chris Moore, Kimberly Steward and Kevin J. Walsh) of *Manchester by the Sea*

Damon burst onto the screen as the title character in *Good Will Hunting*. During the 1997 award season, he became a bona fide A-list star. Any disappointment for losing the Best Actor race to Jack Nicholson of *As Good As It Gets* was short-lived. Three awards later, Damon, along with collaborating screenwriter and co-star Ben Affleck, won Best Original Screenplay. A top box office draw for the *Bourne* movie series, Damon consistently appears in Oscar-favored films. He played the title soldier in *Saving Private Ryan*, which earned Steven Spielberg Best Director in 1998. His trustworthy good looks served him well as *The Talented Mr. Ripley* (1999) opposite Best Supporting Actor nominee Jude Law. Confident grasp of his craft helped him stand out among the large ensembles of *Syriana* (2005), even though George Clooney won the Best Supporting Actor Oscar, and *The Departed*, the Best Picture of 2006 that earned Mark Wahlberg a Best Supporting Actor nomination.

Damon ended the decade with his second acting Academy Award nomination, this time as a supporting player with a South African accent as champion rugby flanker Jacobus Francois Pienaar in *Invictus*. He lost to Christoph Waltz in *Inglourious Basterds*. He reprised the Glen Campbell role of Texas Ranger La Boeuf in the Coen Brothers' 2010 remake of *True Grit*, and appeared as Dr. Mann in *Interstellar*, which was nominated for five Oscars and won for Visual Effects in 2014. Amid several installments of the *Bourne* movie franchise, Damon reinvigorated the Academy's admiration for his talents with yet another Best Actor nomination in 2015 as a resourceful stranded astronaut in *The Martian*.

Non–Oscar-Winning Filmmakers Nominated for Acting Oscars

Bradley Cooper

- 2012 Best Actor as teacher Patrick "Pat" Solatano, Jr., in *Silver Linings Playbook*
- 2013 Best Supporting Actor as FBI agent Richard "Richie" DiMaso in *American Hustle*
- 2014 Best Actor as U.S. Navy SEAL Chris Kyle in *American Sniper*
- 2014 Best Picture as co-producer (with Clint Eastwood, Andrew Lazar, Robert Lorenz, and Peter Morgan) of *American Sniper*

Movie audiences first fell in love with Bradley Cooper as one of the *Wedding Crashers* (2005) who woke the morning after with *The Hangover* (2009, 2011, 2013) that made him box office gold. But he enthralled Academy members for his intense, Actors Studio–perfected characterization of Pat, a former mental patient struggling with bipolar disorder by seeking the positive in life through his *Silver Linings Playbook*. Despite universal awe at his range and intensity, Cooper and fellow nominees Hugh Jackman (*Les Misérables*), Joaquin Phoenix (*The Master*) and Denzel Washington (*Flight*) watched nearly every Best Actor prize of 2012 go to Daniel Day-Lewis as *Lincoln*. Cooper stood out as the FBI Agent duping (or duped by?) fellow nominees Christian Bale and Amy Adams doing their *American Hustle*. Cooper again found himself competing against an award landslider, as Jared Leto swept most Best Supporting Actor awards, including Oscar, for *Dallas Buyers Club*. Controversy over the heroism of his *American Sniper* character gave Cooper endless press leading up to the 2014 Oscars, and placed him as a front runner to win alongside Michael Keaton as *Birdman* and Eddie Redmayne in *The Theory of Everything*. Although he lost to Redmayne, Cooper was the only actor in the competition double nominated that year, as he also co-produced the film in which he starred. One of the few actors in Academy history to earn four Oscar nominations in his first three years to compete, Cooper's strong support among his Academy peers seems to promise an Oscar win soon.

Ethan Hawke

- 2001 Best Supporting Actor as police officer Jake Hoyt in *Training Day*
- 2004 Best Adapted Screenplay as co-screenwriter (with Julie Delpy, Kim Krizan, and Richard Linklater) of *Before Sunset*
- 2013 Best Adapted Screenplay as co-screenwriter (with Julie Delpy and Richard Linklater) of *Before Midnight*
- 2014 Best Supporting Actor as father Mason Evans, Sr., in *Boyhood*

Hawke's collaborations with director Richard Linklater have given cinema some of its most revered and innovative projects. They worked together on the *Before* series, comprised of *Before Sunrise* (1995), *Before Sunset* (2004), and *Before Midnight* (2013). Their minimalist views of the relationship between stars Hawke and Julie Delpy brought the trio two Oscar nominations for screenwriting. Equally ambitious was the Hawke/Linklater *Boyhood* project, which resulted in a single movie twelve years in the making as it literally followed a young boy (Ellar Coltrane) from ages six to eighteen. The groundbreaking concept turned into a revered motion picture, which went into the 2014 Oscars a frontrunner to win the biggest prizes. Late season momentum for *Birdman* gave it the Best Picture award, but Hawke earned his second Best Supporting Actor nomination as Coltrane's father, and Patricia Arquette earned the movie's only Academy Award when she won Best Supporting Actress as his mother. Hawke's introduction to Oscar came in 2001 when he earned a Best Supporting Actor nod for spending a *Training Day* with Best Actor winner Denzel Washington. Hawke lost that competition to Jim Broadbent of *Iris*.

Dyan Cannon

- 1969 Best Supporting Actress as wife Alice Henderson in *Bob & Carol & Ted & Alice*
- 1975 Best Live Action Short Film as co-producer (with Vince Cannon) of *Number One*
- 1978 Best Supporting Actress as wife/mistress Julia Farnsworth in *Heaven Can Wait*

Just as Lauren Bacall had to prove herself in order to escape the shadow of her marriage to Humphrey Bogart, Dyan Cannon found professional light after her brief marriage to Cary Grant with memorable performances punctuated by one of the most powerful, contagious laughs on any film soundtrack. She employed the laugh in a hilarious scene with fellow supporting nominee Elliott Gould as her husband in *Bob & Carol & Ted & Alice*, which earned Cannon her first Oscar nomination. Highlighting her second nominated performance for Best Supporting Actress was not a laugh, but a panicked, piercing scream at seeing Warren Beatty, the husband she thought she'd just killed in *Heaven Can Wait*. She lost her first acting competition to Goldie Hawn in *Cactus Flower* and the second to Maggie Smith in *California Suite*. In between, Cannon won kudos and another Oscar nod for starring in, producing, directing, writing, and editing the live action short film about adolescent sexual curiosity, *Number One*, co-produced by her longtime manager, Vince Cannon (no relation).

John Cassavetes

> 1967 Best Supporting Actor as gangster/killer/soldier Victor Franko in *The Dirty Dozen*
> 1968 Best Story and Screenplay as screenwriter of *Faces*
> 1974 Best Director of *A Woman under the Influence*

Innovative actor and filmmaker John Cassavetes started his own alternative method acting workshop in 1956 New York before opening the door for all independent filmmakers by raising the funds for his writing and directing debut project, *Shadows* which won the critics' Pasinetti Award at the 1959 Venice Film Festival. Thereafter, Cassevetes often financed his own projects by working in mainstream movies, and in the process fascinating his Academy peers. He was up for Best Supporting Actor in 1967, the only member of *The Dirty Dozen* to be so recognized, then followed it by playing Mia Farrow's ambitious actor/husband willing to give to the devil his and *Rosemary's Baby*. That year, he was up for Best Screenplay, and two supporting actors, Seymour Cassel and Lynn Carlin, were Academy Award nominated for Cassevetes' independent film, *Faces*. In later years, his wife Gena Rowlands earned both her Best Actress Oscar nominations, for *A Woman under the Influence* (1974) and *Gloria* (1980), under his direction. Although the Academy never honored Cassevetes with a competitive or special Oscar for his groundbreaking, opportunity-opening approach to making and financing his movie visions, the Independent Spirit Awards did, introducing in 1999 the Independent Spirit John Cassavetes Award, given to the creative team of the best movie budgeted at $500,000 or less. The first movie to win that prize was the unique international hit thriller, *The Blair Witch Project*.

Vittorio De Sica

1957 Best Supporting Actor as Italian army surgeon Major Alessandro Rinaldi in *A Farewell to Arms*

Neorealist director and actor Vittorio De Sica is best known through the Academy for directing several Best Foreign Language Film winners and directing Sophia Loren to both her Best Actress nominated performances, in *Two Women* (1961) and *Marriage Italian Style* (1964). *Two Women* brought Loren the Oscar and made De Sica the first person to direct an actor in a foreign language film to a competitive Academy Award win. De Sica's tenure as a director of Best Foreign Language films is also record-setting. Before the Academy made Best Foreign Language Film a regular category in 1956, De Sica's *Shoeshine* (released in the U.S., and thus eligible for Academy consideration in 1947) was the first foreign movie to inspire the Academy to honor it with a special Academy Award from the Board of Governors. Two years later, De Sica's tragic *The Bicycle Thief* earned the same special honor. In the history of the Academy, only Vittorio De Sica and French filmmaker René Clément (*The Wall of Malapage* in 1950 and *Forbidden Games* in 1952) directed two foreign language movies to win special awards. Once Best Foreign Language Film appeared regularly on Oscar ballots, De Sica directed two to victories, with *Yesterday, Today and Tomorrow*, starring Sophia Loren, winning the same year she was nominated for *Marriage Italian Style*, and with *The Garden of the Finzi Continis* taking the statuette in 1971. Although he acted in very few English language films, De Sica picked up a Best Supporting nod in 1957 as charming and courageous Major Rinaldi in Charles Vidor's remake of the Ernest Hemingway classic *A Farewell to Arms*. He lost that Academy Award competition to another soldier, Red Buttons as Sergeant Joe Kelly in *Sayonara*.

4

Special Acclaim

Multiple Wins in a Single Category

Emil Jannings

1927/28 Best Actor as Tsarist Russian officer General Dolgorucki (Grand Duke Sergius Alexander) in *The Last Command*; as bank clerk August Schilling in *The Way of All Flesh*

Emil Jannings' imposing presence helped him become a towering success in silent films. The only actor to win a single Academy Award for performances in two different movies, Jannings effectively contrasted his daunting stature with his ability to wither from the defeat of tragic choices in both his Oscar-winning roles. In Josef von Sternberg's *The Last Command*, his abusive Grand Duke in Tsarist Russia crumbled into an aged, withered Hollywood extra. *The Way of All Flesh* took his character from a happy banker to a homeless wanderer unrecognizable to his own family. The Academy launched their awards initiative as talkies overtook silent movies. With a German accent thick as his barrel chest, Jannings realized he had no future in American talking pictures, and booked permanent passage back to Europe prior to being notified that he had earned the Academy's first Best Actor prize. Before he disembarked, the Academy gave Jannings his award, making him the first recipient of an Oscar statuette. Jannings and his golden prize already settled in Germany by the time the Academy's inaugural ceremony commenced on May 19, 1929, at the Hollywood Roosevelt Hotel. Before returning home, Jannings had already filmed *The Patriot*, which was up for Best Picture in Oscar's second year.

Janet Gaynor

1927/28 Best Actress as Parisian waif Diane in *7th Heaven*; as Neapolitan girl Angela in *Street Angel*; as farmer's wife The Wife in *Sunrise*
1937 Best Actress as actress Esther Blodgett/Vicki Lester in *A Star Is Born*

At the first Academy Awards, 22-year-old doe-eyed waif Janet Gaynor set records as Oscar's first Best Actress, the first female to win an Academy Award in any category, the only star in Academy history to win a single Oscar for three performances, and the only female actor to win her Oscar for silent movies. She played prostitutes in *7th Heaven* and *Street Angel*, and a cuckolded young wife in *Sunrise*. Gaynor again competed for Best Actress in 1937, this time in the original version of *A Star Is Born*. To enhance authenticity of the scene where rising star Vicki Lester wins an Academy Award, Gaynor used the statuette she had won ten years earlier. In the 1937 Best Actress race, Gaynor competed against Irene Dunne hiding *The Awful Truth*, Greta Garbo in *Camille*, Barbara Stanwyck as *Stella Dallas*, and Luise Rainer farming *The Good Earth*. Because Gaynor and Rainer had both won previously, a victory for either would have made them Oscar's first actor with two Academy Awards. Rainer took that honor. Nevertheless, because she was forever his first female winner, Oscar invited Gaynor back regularly to participate in the Academy's illustrious night. In 1952 she announced Gary Cooper Best Actor for *High Noon*, gave Best Picture to *Around the World in 80 Days* in 1956, and co-presented Best Director with Ryan O'Neal in 1970. To commemorate Oscar's fiftieth birthday, Gaynor returned to crown *Annie Hall*'s Diane Keaton Best Actress of 1977.

Multiple Nominations in a Single Category

George Arliss

1929/1930 Best Actor as British Prime Minister Benjamin Disraeli in *Disraeli*; as Oxonian, the Rajah of Rukh in *The Green Goddess*

A versatile and imposing predecessor to other greats like Charles Laughton and Peter Ustinov, George Arliss holds the Oscar record as the first British actor to win a competitive Academy Award (Chaplin received an honorary Oscar as actor, director, and writer of *The Circus* in 1927/28). In 1929/30 he received one nomination for two movies. He was the mysterious kidnapper in *The Green Goddess*, but the nomination disappeared without explanation when Arliss was announced that year's Best Actor for only *Disraeli*. The role of the determined, visionary prime minister is one Arliss had honed over many transformations. He had played the part on stage for five years and had made a silent film version of it in 1921 before recreating it for one of the earliest sound pictures in 1929. When he won that year's Best Actor, he became the first to earn an Oscar for recreating a role. Born in 1868, Arliss also set records as the earliest-born star ever to win an Academy Award, and the first actor over age 60 to win a competitive Oscar. Arliss later played two characters, Mayer Rothschild and his son, Nathan, in the 1934 Best Picture–nominated *The House of Rothschild*. In 1942 Arliss might have been up for Oscar once more if he had accepted the offer to play *The Pied Piper*. Monty Woolley took the role that Arliss declined, and was up for Best Actor.

Maurice Chevalier

 1929/30 Best Actor as Venetian tour guide Pierre Mirande in *The Big Pond*; as husband of Sylvania's Queen Louise, Count Alfred Renard in *The Love Parade*
 1958 Honorary Award "for his contributions to the world of entertainment for more than half a century"

"Thank heaven for little girls," a twinkling-eyed Chevalier crooned in the classic, *Gigi*, which went 9-for-9 at the 1958 Oscars to become the first movie to win every category for which it was nominated. But the accolades didn't stop there, as the Academy also chose that year to present Chevalier an honorary award for his half century of acting, singing, and romancing a worldwide audience. He first charmed audiences at the turn of the century in Paris, established himself as a European star when performing live in London, then was one of the first international superstars of the 20th century when he conquered Hollywood. Though Chevalier himself thought little of his work in silent pictures, even he couldn't deny that his French-tinged savoir-faire translated perfectly to sound pictures. He was double-nominated in 1929/30, but lost to George Arliss for *Disraeli*. He was so charming in 1930/31 that the Academy nominated two of his starring vehicles for Best Picture: *One Hour with You* and *The Smiling Lieutenant*. At the 1955 Oscars, first Chevalier performed the nominated song "Something's Gotta Give" from *Daddy Long Legs*, a Fred Astaire movie in which Chevalier did not appear. Then he presented the Best Song award to "Love is a Many-Splendored Thing." Rosalind Russell gave Chevalier his honorary Oscar in 1958, and he responded by thanking her with a kiss. Long before Oscar limited acceptance speeches and hurried winners off the stage with music, the orchestra at the

1958 Oscar mistakenly thought Chevalier's kiss was his acceptance, and drowned out his subsequent thank-yous. Always gracious, Chevalier realized the error and walked off stage arm-in-arm with Russell. For such a gentleman, Hollywood could "thank heaven," indeed.

Record-Setting Honorary Winners

Bob Hope

- 1940 Special Award "in recognition of his unselfish services to the Motion Picture industry" (silver plaque)
- 1944 Special Award "for his many services to the Academy" (Life Membership in the Academy of Motion Picture Arts and Sciences)
- 1952 Honorary Award "for his contribution to the laughter of the world, his service to the motion picture industry, and his devotion to the American premise" (statuette)
- 1959 Jean Hersholt Humanitarian Award (statuette)
- 1965 Honorary Award "for unique and distinguished service to our industry and the Academy" (gold medal)

Bob Hope was always a comic, and his movies were only a forum for funneling his jokes through a cohesive plot that sustained his humor for about ninety minutes of

Besides emceeing many more Academy Awards ceremonies (including this one in 1967) than any other host, Bob Hope's record for most honorary Oscars still far exceeds everyone else in the film industry.

entertainment. And entertaining he was. The Golden Globes nominated Hope for the Best Actor, Musical or Comedy awards for *The Facts of Life* (1960) and *Bachelor in Paradise* (1961), but Oscar never did. Leave it to Hope to capitalize on that fact during the record 18 times he hosted Academy Award ceremonies ("Welcome to the Academy Awards, ladies and gentlemen. Or, as we call it at our house, Passover"). In his first full-length film, *The Big Broadcast of 1938*, Hope and Shirley Ross sang "Thanks for the Memory," which won a Best Song Oscar and gave Hope his trademark tune. In *The Paleface* Hope sang "Buttons and Bows," which became the biggest selling record of his career and also won the 1948 Best Song Oscar.

Despite no competitive consideration, Hope outranks every honorary Oscar winner by receiving an unprecedented five honorary prizes, which came in various forms, and most of which were created solely as unique ways to recognize Hope for his treasured contribution to world entertainment. Besides unique awards, the Academy also sought original ways to acknowledge Hope at the ceremonies. For his last accolade, the Academy surprised Hope by having Arthur Freed interrupt Jack Lemmon's announcement of 1965's Best Picture to honor him with a gold medal. The always quick-witted Hope told the audience that they could later view the medal at his place—in his shrine.

Danny Kaye

1954 Honorary Award "for his unique talents, his service to the Academy, the motion picture industry, and the American people"

1981 Jean Hersholt Humanitarian Award

Danny Kaye was a nimble, hair-flying, gibberish-spouting phenomenon who made every production an unforgettable, if exhausting, extravaganza. Throughout his 50+ years as an entertainer, Kaye made relatively few motion pictures, and among them only a handful were nominated for Academy Awards. In 1944, *Up in Arms* was up in two music categories, for score and for the song "Now I Know." The following year, *Wonder Man* vied for four Oscars, two for music, and won for Best Visual Effects. In 1949, "It's a Great Feeling" represented the film of the same name in the Best Song category. By far Kaye's best chance at a nomination came in 1952 when the Academy cited *Hans Christian Andersen* in six categories, but all for artistic design and music, and none for acting. Other unrealized chances for Oscar nominations came in 1951 for *On the Riviera* and in 1958 for *Me and the Colonel*, both of which brought Kaye Golden Globe awards as Best Actor, Musical or Comedy. Nevertheless, the red-topped ball of energized cleverness has the rare distinction of earning two honorary Academy Awards without a single competitive nomination or a movie that competed in any of the five major categories. The Academy honored Kaye's grand showmanship with one golden statuette in 1954, and then another for his charitable work with UNICEF securing help for impoverished children around the world.

Landmark Single-Year Honors

Harold Russell

1946 Best Supporting Actor as disabled veteran Homer Parrish in *The Best Years of Our Lives*
1946 Special Award "for bringing hope and courage to his fellow veterans through his appearance in *The Best Years of Our Lives*"

Though not a motion picture or stage actor, Harold Russell was a World War II Army instructor who made training films. During one, a malfunctioning explosive he was holding detonated in his hands and left him with two prosthetic hooks. Director William Wyler selected Russell to play Homer Parrish, the young sailor who returned to his family and fiancée after being wounded in World War II in *The Best Years of Our Lives*, the big winner at the 1946 Academy Awards. Russell wrung such pathos and courage in scenes revealing his adjustment to a familiar life made unreachable without hands that the Academy nominated him for Best Supporting Actor. But because he was a Hollywood unknown without an acting background competing against four veterans (Charles Coburn, William Demarest, Claude Rains, and Clifton Webb), the Academy's governing board decided to honor Russell with a special Oscar to ensure recognition of his inspiring performance. Russell called receiving that award early in the 1946 telecast "the proudest and happiest moment of my life." Only moments later, Russell was back on stage accepting his Best Supporting Actor prize with, "Two in a night is just too much! Thanks a lot." The double victory made Russell the only actor to receive two Oscars for a single performance.

Barry Fitzgerald

1944 Best Actor as priest Father Fitzgibbon in *Going My Way*
1944 Best Supporting Actor as priest Father Fitzgibbon in *Going My Way*

With a squint of his suspicious eyes and a chin tucked with comic contemplation, Irish-brogued character actor Barry Fitzgerald won the hearts of many a moviegoer, and stands as the only actor with a single performance nominated for both a lead and supporting actor Oscar. A favorite of director John Ford, Fitzgerald appeared in two of Ford's Best Picture nominees and one Best Picture winner. He took vengeance as a steward named Cocky during *The Long Voyage Home* (1940), served as village matchmaker in *The Quiet Man* (1952), and helped teach bullied Roddy McDowall to box in *How Green Was My Valley*, Oscar's big winner of 1941. But it was in Leo McCarey's beloved *Going My Way* that Fitzgerald did what can never be done at the Oscars again unless the Academy changes its nominating policy. Although Bing Crosby had top billing as progressive Father O'Malley in *Going My Way*, Fitzgerald had as integral a role as the older, more traditional Father Fitzgibbon at St. Dominic's. Lightly rippling with comic frustration throughout most of the film, Fitzgerald brought a tidal wave of genuine sentiment to the conclusion of the movie, and earned enough Academy votes in each acting category to compete in both races on Oscar night. Right after his *None But the Lonely Heart* co-star Ethel Barrymore was named Best Supporting Actress, Fitzgerald won Best Supporting Actor, then lost Best Actor to Crosby, rounding out *Going My Way*'s seven victories that included two writing awards, Best Director for McCarey, and Best Picture.

Jamie Foxx

2004 Best Actor as singer Ray Charles in *Ray*
2004 Best Supporting Actor as taxi driver Max Durocher in *Collateral*

Biopics of musicians and biopics of the physically handicapped handily impress Oscar. When Jamie Foxx gave an uncannily perfect performance as blind gospel-tinged rhythm and blues soul singer Ray Charles, the Academy, and nearly every other award-issuing organization that year, could not help but be awed. Foxx won prize after prize throughout the 2004 award season. Although dominating every other award made his subsequent Oscar victory in *Ray* deservedly inevitable, he reinforced his chances of a win by also earning a Best Supporting Actor nomination that same year as Tom Cruise's captive cabdriver in *Collateral*. As expected, Foxx saw the supporting competition go to Morgan Freeman in *Million Dollar Baby*, and heard Charlize Theron call his name as winner for Best Actor. He became only the third actor, after Al Pacino in 1992 and Holly Hunter in 1993, to earn nominations in both acting categories and go home with the prize for leading actor. Before he inspired movie audiences, and then award givers to rise to their feet with excitement for his performances and his award victories, Foxx appeared as Muhammad Ali's vibrant assistant and cornerman Drew Bundini Brown in the 2001 biopic *Ali*. Although Foxx was billed in the movie right below Best Actor nominee

Will Smith in the title role, it was Jon Voight as equally colorful Howard Cosell who received the supporting nomination for *Ali*. Since his Oscar win, Foxx has had leads as record executive Curtis Taylor, Jr., in *Dreamgirls* in 2006 and as the title character in Quentin Tarantino's uncompromising *Django Unchained* in 2012. Both films won respective supporting acting awards for Jennifer Hudson and Christoph Waltz.

Sigourney Weaver

> 1986 Best Actress as space ship warrant officer Ellen Ripley in *Aliens*
> 1988 Best Actress as naturalist Dian Fossey in *Gorillas in the Mist*
> 1988 Best Supporting Actress as financial executive Katharine Parker in *Working Girl*

Weaver broke ground a few times in the Academy. In 1986, her powerhouse performance as Ripley in *Aliens* depicted women as strong, complex, action hero dynamos in a way movies had rarely shown women before. Earning a Best Actress nomination for the thriller, a science fiction horror adventure sequel, gave her Oscar recognition for a movie from multiple genres the Academy historically ignored. Until 1988, any actors who received both a lead and supporting acting nomination in a single year went home with an Oscar for the supporting performance, and usually lost the lead to the star they supported. The 1988 Oscars seemed to promise similar results, especially after Weaver was nominated for both Oscars, broke Golden Globe records by winning Best Actress in a Drama for *Gorillas in the Mist* and Best Supporting Actress for *Working Girl,* and her *Working Girl* co-star, Melanie Griffith was in contention for a Best Actress Oscar. But Weaver became the first double acting nominee to go home empty-handed, losing the early night competition to Geena Davis in *The Accidental Tourist* and Best Actress to Jodie Foster in *The Accused*. In 1997 Weaver won a Best Supporting Actress BAFTA and was nominated for the Golden Globe for *The Ice Storm*, but the Academy turned a cold shoulder to her performance and the film. Three actresses have earned two nominations in a single year, but lost both competitions. Emma Thompson lost both her 1993 competitions the year after she won Best Actress for *Howards End*. Julianne Moore lost both her 2002 competitions, but won Best Actress in 2014 for *Still Alice*. That leaves Sigourney Weaver as the only non-winning actor nominated for two Oscars in a single year.

Countdown List

108. Angela Lansbury
107. Kirk Douglas
106. Ronald Colman
105. Maureen Stapleton
104. Lee Grant
103. Ethel Barrymore
102. Tommy Lee Jones
101. Alan Arkin
100. Walter Huston
99. Robin Williams
98. Philip Seymour Hoffman
97. Frances McDormand
96. Julia Roberts
95. Nicole Kidman
94. Geoffrey Rush
93. Helen Mirren
92. Ben Kingsley
91. George C. Scott
90. Holly Hunter
89. Jennifer Lawrence
88. Anthony Hopkins
87. William Hurt
86. Jon Voight
85. Julie Christie
84. Diane Keaton
83. Joanne Woodward
82. Jane Wyman
81. Burt Lancaster
80. Barbara Stanwyck
79. Greta Garbo
78. Morgan Freeman

77. Julianne Moore
76. Jennifer Jones
75. Susan Sarandon
74. Anne Bancroft
73. Susan Hayward
72. Paul Muni
71. Shirley MacLaine
70. Deborah Kerr
69. Vanessa Redgrave
68. Norman Shearer
67. Leonardo DiCaprio
66. Ellen Burstyn
65. Sissy Spacek
64. Jeff Bridges
63. Kate Winslet
62. Angelina Jolie
61. Frank Sinatra
60. Charlton Heston
59. Mary Pickford
58. Sidney Poitier
57. Sophia Loren
56. Henry Fonda
55. Christoph Waltz
54. Kevin Spacey
53. Hilary Swank
52. Vivien Leigh
51. Helen Hayes
50. Luise Rainer
49. Dianne Wiest
48. Melvyn Douglas
47. Jason Robards, Jr.

46. Peter Ustinov
45. Judi Dench
44. Robert Duvall
43. Greer Garson
42. Sally Field
41. Mickey Rooney
40. Emma Thompson
39. Anthony Quinn
38. Shelley Winters
37. Jodie Foster
36. Glenda Jackson
35. Alec Guinness
34. Peter O'Toole
33. Al Pacino
32. Geraldine Page
31. Audrey Hepburn
30. Gregory Peck
29. Gene Hackman
28. Olivia de Havilland
27. Fredric March
26. Sean Penn
25. Tom Hanks
24. James Stewart
23. George Clooney
22. Michael Caine
21. Maggie Smith
20. Jessica Lange
19. Cate Blanchett
18. Robert De Niro
17. Jane Fonda
16. Dustin Hoffman
15. Denzel Washington
14. Jack Lemmon
13. Marlon Brando
12. Spencer Tracy
11. Walter Brennan
10. Elizabeth Taylor
9. Gary Cooper
8. Daniel Day-Lewis
7. Bette Davis
6. Ingrid Bergman
5. Paul Newman
4. Laurence Olivier
3. Jack Nicholson
2. Katharine Hepburn
1. Meryl Streep

Bibliography

Academy Awards Database. Academy of Motion Picture Arts and Sciences: http://awards.database.oscars.org/ Web. 21 Sept. 2016.
Blake, Michael F. *A Thousand Faces: Lon Chaney's Unique Artistry in Motion Pictures.* Lanham, MD: Vestal, 1995.
Borgnine, Ernest. *Ernie: The Autobiography.* New York: Citadel, 2008.
Clarke, Gerald. *Get Happy: The Life of Judy Garland.* New York: Delta, 2000.
Curtis, Tony, with Peter Golenbock. *American Prince: A Memoir.* New York: Harmony, 2008.
Edwards, Anne. *Streisand: A Biography.* Boston: Little, Brown, 1997.
Fox, Julian. *Woody: Movies from Manhattan.* New York: Overlook Press, 1996.
Gebert, Michael. *The Encyclopedia of Movie Awards.* New York: St. Martin's, 1996.
Grant, Lee. *I Said Yes to Everything: A Memoir.* New York: Plume, 2014.
Jewison, Norman. *This Terrible Business Has Been Good to Me: An Autobiography.* Toronto: Key Porter, 2004.
Jones, Shirley, with Wendy Leigh. *Shirley Jones: A Memoir.* New York: Gallery, 2013.
Karney, Robyn, ed. *Cinema Year by Year, 1984–2002.* London: Dorling Kindersley, 2002.
Katz, Ephraim. *The Film Encyclopedia,* 4th ed. New York: HarperResource, 2001.
Kaufman, David. *Doris Day: The Untold Story of the Girl Next Door.* New York, Virgin, 2008.
Kobel, Peter, and the Library of Congress. *Silent Movies: The Birth of Film and the Triumph of Movie Culture.* New York, Little, Brown, 2007.
Kramer, Stanley, with Thomas M. Coffey, *A Mad, Mad, Mad, Mad World.* New York: Harcourt Brace, 1997.
Lee, Betty. *Marie Dressler: The Unlikeliest Star.* Lexington: University Press of Kentucky, 1997.
Leslie, Roger. *Film Stars and Their Awards: Who Won What for Movies, Theater and Television.* Jefferson, NC: McFarland, 2008.
Meyers, Jeffrey. *Bogart: A Life in Hollywood.* Boston: Houghton Mifflin, 1997.
Monush, Barry. *The Encyclopedia of Hollywood Film Actors from the Silent Era to 1965.* New York: Applause, 2003.
O'Neil, Tom. *Movie Awards: The Ultimate, Unofficial Guide to the Oscars, Golden Globes, Critics, Guild, & Indie Honors.* New York: Perigee, 2003.
Pickard, Roy. *The Oscar Movies.* New York: Facts on File, 1994.
_____. *The Oscar Stars from A–Z.* London: Headline, 1996.
Pilato, Herbie J. *Twitch upon a Star: The Bewitched Life and Career of Elizabeth Montgomery.* New York: Taylor Trade, 2012.
Pond, Steve. *The Big Show: High Times and Dirty Dealings Backstage at the Academy Awards.* New York: Faber & Faber, 2005.
Quinlan, David. *The Illustrated Encyclopedia of Movie Character Actors.* New York: Harmony, 1985.

Reynolds, Debbie, and Dorian Hannaway. *Unsinkable: A Memoir.* New York: William Morrow, 2013.
Scarfone, Jay, and William Stillman. *The Wizard of Oz: The Official 75th Anniversary Companion.* New York: HarperCollins, 2013.
Schroeder, Alan. *Charlie Chaplin: The Beauty of Silence.* Danbury, CT: Franklin-Watts, 1997.
Shale, Richard. *The Academy Award Index: The Complete Categorical and Chronological Record.* Westport, CT: Greenwood, 1993.
Sperber, A. M., and Eric Lax. *Bogart.* New York: William Morrow, 1997.
Starr, Michael Seth. *Art Carney: A Biography.* New York: Fromm International, 1997.
Swenson, Karen. *Greta Garbo: A Life Apart.* New York: Scribner's, 1997.
Thomson, David. *The New Biographical Dictionary of Film,* 4th ed. London: Little, Brown, 2003.
Walker, John, ed. *Halliwell's Who's Who in the Movies.* New York: HarperResource, 2003.
Wiley, Mason, and Damien Bona. *Inside Oscar: The Unofficial History of the Academy Awards.* New York: Ballantine, 1986.
Winters, Shelley. *Shelley, Also Known as Shirley.* London: Granada, 1981.
_____. *Shelley II: The Middle of My Century.* New York: Simon & Schuster, 1989.
Yudkoff, Alvin. *Gene Kelly: A Life of Dance and Dreams.* New York: Back Stage, 1999.

Index

Numbers in **_bold italics_** indicate pages with photographs.

Abe Lincoln in Illinois 15, 75, 259
About Schmidt 133, 164, 175, 202, 203
Abraham, F. Murray 50, 64, 112, 114
Abraham Lincoln 15
Absence of Malice 95, 170, 171
The Academy Awards: A Pictorial History 1
The Accidental Tourist 31–32, 103, 285
The Accused 103, 211, 285
Ace in the Hole 7
Adams, Amy 25, 95, 205, 207, 214–215, 274
Adams, Bryan 258
Adams, John Quincy 30
Adam's Rib 154, 259
Adaptation 180, 181, 203, 218
The Adventures of Robin Hood 121, 215
Adventures of Robinson Crusoe 152
An Affair to Remember 212
Affleck, Ben 130, 132, 273
Affleck, Casey 220
Affliction 218
The African Queen 81, 101, 124, 151, 177, 178, 190, 191, 240, 265, 266, 269
Afterglow 33, 34, 89
The Age of Innocence 164
Agee, James 265
Aghdashloo, Shohreh 204
Agnes of God 49, 50, 113
The Agony and the Ecstasy 70
Aiello, Danny 147
Aimée, Anouk 205
Airport 9, **_10_**, 81, 82
Airport '77 122
Aladdin 17
The Alamo 224
Albert, Eddie **_115_**
Albert Nobbs 211
Albertson, Jack 68, **_102_**
Aldrich, Robert 216
Alexander, Jane 103, 105, 217–218

Alfie 101, 132, 133
Algiers 221
Ali 32, 33, 125, 244, 284, 285
Ali, Muhammad 33, 244, 284, 285
Alice 269
Alice Adams 177, 231
Alice Doesn't Live Here Anymore 60, 61, 197, 206
Aliens 285
All About Eve 50, 155, 165, 166–167, 188, 210, 255, 256
"All God's Chillun Got Rhythm" 236
All Is Lost 268
All That Jazz 137
All That Money Can Buy 15, 64
All the King's Men 118
All the President's Men 86, 87, 103, 145, 217, 268
"All the Way" 68
Allen, Irwin 228
Allen, Joan 164, 208
Allen, Woody 3, 9, 35, 76, 77, 84, 92, 113, 125, 130, 133, 139, 151, 201, 268–270
Almodóvar, Pedro 205
Almost Famous 19
Altered States 31
Altman, Robert 19, 24, 33, 45, 62, 136, 261
Amadeus 64
American Beauty 77, 78, 79, 148, 150, 202, 219
American Gangster 148
American Graffiti 250
American Horror Story 138
American Hustle 28, 29, 207, 214, 215, 274
An American in Paris 225
The American President 261
American Sniper 271, 272, 274
Amistad 30
Anastasia 54, 82, 168, 169

291

Index

Anatomy of a Murder 26, 69, 128, 129
Anchors Aweigh 67–68, 225
... And Justice for All 110, 111
Anderson, Paul Thomas 18, 45, 251
Anderson, Wes 120
Andrews, Julie 33, 49, 121, 199–200
Angels with Dirty Faces 192, 193
Ann-Margret 105, 197
Anna 227
Anna and the King of Siam 212
Anna Christie 41, 42
Anna Karenina 42
Anne Frank Museum 101
Anne of Cleves 194
Anne of the Thousand Days 32, 193, 209
Annie Hall 3, 35, 36, 50, 113, 139, 143, 268, 269, 279
Anthony Adverse 121
Antoinette, Marie 56, 58
Antonioni, Michelangelo 55
Antony, Marc 151
The Apartment 52, 53, 78, 116, 148, 149
Apocalypse Now 91, 92, 250
Apocalypto 240
Apollo 13 77, 128, 218
The Apostle 91, 92
Arden, Eve 187, 188
Arenas, Reinaldo 205, 206
Argo 14, 15, 76, 130, 132, 141
Arkin, Alan 14–15, 76, 141, 287
Arliss, George 8, 57, 279–280
Arnold, Edward 156
Aronofsky, Darren 61
Around the World in 80 Days 9, 234, 245, 279
Arquette, Patricia 275
Arrowsmith 8, 237
Arsner, Dorothy 141
Arthur, Jean 8, 46, 80, 129, 168, 186, 222
The Artist 132
As Good As It Gets 34, 76, 89, 175, 176, 273
Ashcroft, Peggy 113, 270
The Asphalt Jungle 255, 265, 266
Astaire, Fred 47, 64, 116, 227–228, 231, 254, 280
Astor, Mary 184
Atlantic City 38, 39, 47
Attenborough, Richard 25, 146
Audrey Hepburn's Enchanted Tales 117
August: Osage County 20, 21, 180, 181
Auntie Mame 51, 222
Austen, Jane 65, 98
Autumn Sonata 168
Avery, Margaret 270
The Aviator 43, 58, 59, 79, 87, 138, 139, 208, 247, 252
Avrakotos, Gust 17, 18
Awakenings 17, 140, 141

Away from Her 33, 34–35, 45
The Awful Truth 83, 211, 212, 224, 279
Aykroyd, Dan 147

Babe 77, 218
Babel 139, 273
Babes in Arms 95, 96, 129, 223
"Baby, It's Cold Outside" 253
Bacall, Lauren 192, 228–229, 236, 259, 276
The Bachelor and the Bobby-Soxer 224, 230, 237
Bachelor in Paradise 282
The Bad and the Beautiful 6, 7, *7*, 69
Bad Boys 125
Bad Day at Black Rock 152, 155, **155**, 156
Bainter, Fay 137, 184, 194, 231
Baker, Carroll 252
The Balcony 11
Bale, Christian 29, 207, 274
Ball of Fire 40, 41, 161
The Ballad of Cable Hogue 87
Ballard, Carroll 96
Balsam, Martin **34**, 87
Bancroft, Anne 35, 49–50, 53, 72, *72*, 113, 179, 189, 197, 287
Bandits 139
Bang the Drum the Slowly 140
Barbarella 142
Barbary Coast 156, 235
Bardem, Javier 18, 205, 205–206
The Barefoot Contessa 195, 247
Barefoot in the Park 142, 268
The Barker 71
The Barretts of Wimpole Street 56, *57*, 58, 193
Barrie, Sir James Matthew (J.M.) 242, 243
Barrow, Buck 118
Barrow, Clyde 266
Barrymore, Drew 12
Barrymore, Ethel 11–12, 118, 123, 188, 284, 287
Barrymore, John 12, 123
Barrymore, Lionel 12, 81, 123, 183, 235, 257–258
Barrymore, Maurice 12
The Barrymores 15
Bartholomew, Freddie 154
Barton Fink 19
Basic Instinct 261
Basinger, Kim 202
Baskett, James 232
Bassermann, Albert 157
Bassett, Angela 237
Bates, Alan 14
Bates, Kathy 21, 37, 202–203, 228
Batiatus, Lentulus 87, 88
Batman Forever 22
Baxter, Anne 50, 264
Beale, Edith "Big Edie" 138
Bean, Judge Roy 156, 157

Beane, Billy 272
Beatty, Warren 2, 11, 30, 32, 33–34, 35, 92, 119, 130, 141, 171, 176, 196, 219, 266–267, 268, 276
Beau Geste (1926 movie) 8
Beau Geste (1939 movie) 50, 161
A Beautiful Mind 24, 125, 136, 202, 204
Beauty and the Beast 6
Beavers, Louise 186
Beck, Lauren 273
Becket 108, 109, 209
Becket, Thomas 209
Beckinsale, Kate 247
Bedknobs and Broomsticks 6
Beery, Wallace 123, 252
Before Midnight 275
Before Night Falls 205, 206
Before Sunrise 275
Before Sunset 275
Being John Malkovich 66, 273
Being Julia 79, 219
Being There 85, 86, 92, 96, 111
Belfort, Jordan 58, 60
Bel Geddes, Barbara 192
The Bells of St. Mary's 167, 168, 191
Ben-Hur 26, 69, 122, 149
Benét, Stephen Vincent 15
Benigni, Roberto 74
Bening, Annette 29, 45, 79, 208, 219
Bennett, Joan 80
Benny, Jack 246
Benton, Robert 94
Berenson, Marisa 133
Bergen, Candice 251
Bergman, Ingrid 5, 38, 41, 46, 54, 78, 136, 158, 167–170, **169**, 191, 195, 212, 221, 232, 258, 288
Bernhardt, Curtis 38
Berry, Halle 73, **147**, 148, 204, 237
Bertrand, Clay (AKA Clay Shaw) 13
The Best Exotic Marigold Hotel 136
Best Friends 251
The Best Little Whorehouse in Texas 251
The Best Man (movie) 75
The Best Man (theater) 85
The Best Years of Our Lives 32, 117, 123, 124, 185, 215, 230, 237, 283
Bewitched 216
The Bible 265
The Bicycle Thief 277
Big 126
The Big Broadcast of 1938 254, 282
The Big Chill 31, 211
The Big Country 118, 196, 213
Big Eyes 25
The Big Pond 185, 280
The Big Short 207, 272
The Big Sky 7, 99
The Big Sleep 228

Biko, Stephen 146
Bill 96
Billy Bathgate 22
Billy Budd 86, 88
Binoch, Juliette 229
The Birdcage 17
Birdman 274, 275
Birdman of Alcatraz 38, 39, 210
The Birth of a Nation 227
The Bishop's Wife 224
Bite the Bullet 119
Biutiful 205, 206
Black, Karen 9
Black, Todd 146
Black Fury 52
Black Narcissus 54
The Black Stallion 95, 96
Black Swan 22, 29, 208, 219
Blade Runner 250
The Blair Witch Project 276
Blakley, Ronee 11
Blanchett, Cate **44**, 45, 78, 82, 90, 113, 136, 138–139, 208, 252, 269, 288
The Blind Side 25, 203
Blixen, Karen 180, 181
The Blob 249
Blood and Sand 99
Blood Diamond 58, 59
Blood Simple 19
Blossoms in the Dust 92, 93
Blowup 55
The Blue Angel 245
The Blue Dahlia 260
Blue Jasmine 138, 139, 269
Blue Sky 13, 136, 137
Blue Valentine 219, 220
The Blue Veil 37, 38, 216, 241
Blyth, Ann 187
Bob & Carol & Ted & Alice 241, 275, 276
Body and Soul 8
Body Heat 31
Boeing, Boeing 238
Bogart, Humphrey 116, 119, 124, 151, 152, 168, 178, **190**, 190–191, 192, 215, 228, 236, 240, 244, 250, 266, 269, 276
Bogdanovich, Peter 63
The Bold and the Brave 95, 96, 100
Boleyn, Anne 55
Bolger, Ray 223
Bonaparte, Napoleon 221
Bondi, Beulah 15, 85, 128, 186, 188, 208
Bonham Carter, Helena 89
Bonnie and Clyde 118, 119, 171, 196, 197, 266, 267
Bono, Sonny 1
Boogie Nights 17, 18, 44, 45, 250, 251
Booth, Shirley 39, 61
Borgnine, Ernest 68, **155**, 195, 226, 244
Born on the Fourth of July 43, 163, 242

Born Yesterday 198
The Bostonians 55, 56, 95
Bottoms, Timothy 260
The Bounty 239
Bourne movies 273, 274
Boyer, Charles 5, 42, 168, 185, 191, 212, 221–222
Boyhood 275
Boys Don't Cry 45, 66, 78, 79, 219
The Boys from Brazil 118, 173
Boys Town 96, 152, 154, 155
Brackett, Charles 42
Bradlee, Ben 86, 87
Brady, Alice 192
Branagh, Kenneth 97, 164, 207, 252
Brando, Marlon 1, 39, 68, 99, 107, 110, 111, 124, 132, 133, 140, 143, 144, 146, 147, 151–152, **153**, 191, 195, 200–201, 240, 269, 288
Braveheart 239
Breakfast at Tiffany's 73, 115, 116
Brennan, Walter 76, 85, 100, 156–158, **157**, 161, 165, 166, 216, 288
Brice, Fanny 258, 259
Brickman, Marshall 268
Bride of Frankenstein 156
The Bridge on the River Kwai 106–107, 198
Bridges, Jeff 63–64, 131, 133, 272, 287
The Bridges at Toko-Ri 226
The Bridges of Madison County 49, 180, 181, 272
Bridget Jones's Diary 203, 204
Brierley, Sue 21
Brigadoon 225
Bright Victory 212, 213
Broadbent, Jim 26, 275
Broadcast News 27–28, 31
Broadway Danny Rose 268
The Broadway Melody 71, 235
Brockovich, Erin 20, 21
Broderick, Matthew 147
Brody, Adrien 130, 164
Brokeback Mountain 131, 219, 220
Brontë, Emily 173
Brooks, Albert 27
Brooks, James L. 27–28, 77
Brooks, Mel 49, 88
Brooks, Richard 39, 201
The Brothers Karamazov 199
Brown, Christy 163, 164
Brown, Clarence 37, 42, 96, 128
Brown, Drew Bundini 284
Brown, Molly 203, 229
Browning, Elizabeth Barrett 56, 57, 58
Browning, Robert 57
Bruce, Lenny 144
Bruce Almighty 43
Bryant, Louise 35
Brynner, Yul 7, 54, 244
Bugsy 25, 30, 219, 266, 267

Bull Durham 47, 261
Bulldog Drummond 8
Bullets Over Broadway 24, 76, 84, 85, 269
Bullitt 249
Bullock, Sandra 25
Bulworth 237, 266
The Bunker 30
Burge, Stuart 174
Burnett, Carol 113, 133
Burns, George 197
Burnside, Norman 265
Burstyn, Ellen 37, 60–61, 62, 105, 197, 206, 287
Burton, Richard 25, 32, 39, 55, 99, 109, 112, 133, 151, 158, 159, **160**, 193, 208–209
Bus Stop 255, **256**
Busey, Gary 28, 141
Butch Cassidy and the Sundance Kid 172, 268
BUtterfield 8 158, 159
Butterflies Are Free 102, 113
Buttons, Red **102**, 233, 252, 277
"Buttons and Bows" 282
Bye Bye Birdie 9

Caan, James 91, 111, 202, 217, 228
Cabaret 1, 91, 111, 134
Cactus Flower 276
Caesar, Adolph 146
Cage, Nicholas 30, 125
Caged 216
Cagney, James 16, 119, 149, 192–193, 248, 252
Caine, Michael 76, 84, 87, 92, 132–134, 135, **135**, 242, 269–270, 288
The Caine Mutiny 152, 190, 191
Cal 24
Calamity Jane 248
Calhern, Louis 255
California Suite 9, 133, 134, **135**, 135–136, 276
Camelot 199
Cameron, James 59
Camille (1926 movie) 12
Camille (1937 movie) 12, 42, 83, 279
Campbell, Glen 274
Campion, Jane 22, 28
The Candidate 268
Candy, John 239
Cannon, Dyan 135, 275–276
Cannon, Vince 275, 276
Cape Fear (1962 movie) 118, 141
Cape Fear (1991 movie) 30, 118, 140, 141
Capote 17, 18
Capote, Truman 17, 18
Capra, Frank 8, 124, 128, 129, 161, 183, 186, 215
Captain Blood 121
Captain Newman, M.D. 91, 118
Captain Phillips 128
Captains Courageous 85, 96, 123, 152, 154, 155, 258

Index 295

Cardiff, Jack 54
The Cardinal 265, 266
Carefree 228, 231
Carey, Harry 215
"Carioca" 231
Carlin, Lynn 206, 276
Carmen Jones 71, 237
Carney, Art 61, 111, 175
Carol 138, 139
Caron, Leslie 53, 54, 115, 197, 222, 247
Carpenter, John 64
Carrie 61, 62, 103, 217
Carroll, Diahann 237
Carson, Jack 37
Carter, Ben 223
Carter, Rubin "Hurricane" 146, 147–148, 202
Casablanca 151, 168, 187, **190**, 190, 191, 215
Casino 22
Cassavetes, John 206, 276
Cassel, Seymour 206, 276
Cast Away 126, 128
Cat Ballou 142, 196, 209, 238
Cat on a Hot Tin Roof (movie) 51, 72, 73, 158, 159, 170, 171, 213
Cat on a Hot Tin Roof (television) 138
Catch Me If You Can 59, 214
Catherine of Valois 97
Cavalcade 123, 177
Chakiris, George 26, 241
The Champ 123
Champion 6, 212, 213
Chan, Jackie 234
Chandlee, Harry 265
"Change Partners" 228
Changeling 66, 67
Channing, Carol 199
Channing, Stockard 244
Chaplin 204
Chaplin, Charles 75, 92, 130, 232, 233, 234, 253, 262–264, **263**, 279
Chapter Two 217
Charade 116
Chariots of Fire 35
Charlie and the Chocolate Factor 243
Charlie Wilson's War 17, 18
Charles, Ray 284
Charles VIII 189
Charlotte (monarch) 24
Charly 14, 109, 163
The Chase 268
Chatterton, Ruth 71, 141, 257
Chekhov, Michael 117
Cher 1, 28, 197, 211
Chevalier, Maurice 185, 252, 280–281
Chicago 22, 45, 203, 204
Child, Julia 180
Children of a Lesser God 29, 31, 62
The Children's Hour 116, 194
The China Syndrome 142, 143, 148, **150**, 261

Chinatown 111, 144, 174, 175, 197, 206
Chocolat 89, 90, 243
Christie, Agatha 6, 88, 214
Christie, Julie 33–35, **34**, 45, 56, 89, 105, 199, 287
Church, Thomas Hayden 43–44
The Cider House Rules 132, 133, 242
Cimarron 211, 212
Cimino, Michael 64
Cinderella 199
Cinderella Liberty 37, 216, 217
The Circus 262, 279
The Citadel 129, 222
Citizen Kane 216, 260, 264
City Lights 262
City Slickers 13, 200, 201
A Civil Action 91
Clarke, Mae 193
Claudia 46
Claudine 237
Clayburgh, Jill 113, 143, 251
Clément, René 277
Cleopatra (1934 movie) 186
Cleopatra (1963 movie) 159, 255
The Client 13, 47, 48, 138
Clifford, Graeme 137
Clift, Montgomery 39, 124, 159, 174, 187, 240–241
Cline, Patsy 136, 137
Clooney, George 64, 130–132, **131**, 273, 288
Close, Glenn 16, 28, 31, 55, 103, 210–211, 215
Closer 43, 208
Coal Miner's Daughter 13, 61, 62
Cobb, Irving S. 186
Cobb, Lee J. 195
Coburn, Charles 186–187, 283
Coburn, James 218
Coen, Joel 19
Coen Brothers 19, 206, 274
Coffee and Cigarettes 139
Cohan, George M. 16, 192, 193
Cohan, Jerry 15
Colbert, Claudette 46, 58, 83, 166, 183, 185–186, 230, **230**
Cold Mountain 22, 125, 203, 204
Collateral 242, 284
The Collector 33
Collette, Toni 66
Collinge, Patricia 184
Colman, Ronald 8–9, 81, 101, 118, 259, 287
The Color of Money 170, 172, 242
The Color Purple (book) 270
The Color Purple (movie) 113, 237, 270
Colson, Christian 270
Coltrane, Ellar 275
Come and Get It 76, 156
Come Back, Little Sheba 39
Come Fill the Cup 88, 196
Come to the Stable 188

Coming Home 32, 66, 113, 141, 142, 143
Compson, Betty 71
Condemned 8
Conlon, Gerry 163, 164
Connelly, Jennifer 24, 136, 204
Connery, Sean 43, 133, 147
Conquest 42, 221
Conroy, Pat 258
The Constant Gardener 214, 220
The Constant Nymph 46, 168, 185
The Contender 63, 64
Conti, Tom 92
"The Continental" 227, 231
The Conversation 17, 91, 120, 214, 250
Cool Hand Luke 119, 170, 171, 196
Cooper, Annie Lee 271
Cooper, Bradley 29, 76, 271, 274–275
Cooper, Chris 218
Cooper, Gary 7, 41, 52, 92, 106, 116, 117, 129, 146, 151, 156, 157, **157**, 160–163, **162**, 184, 224, 225, 226, 245, 279, 288
Coppola, Francis Ford 91, 92, 113, 140, 250
Coquette 70, 71
The Corn Is Green 187
Cortese, Valentina 170
Cosell, Howard 32, 33, 285
Cota, Norman 247
Cotillard, Marion 34, 35
Cotton, Joseph 264
Coulouris, George 264
Country 62, 94, 136, 137
The Country Girl 38, 116, 152, 191, 192, 198, 226
Courtenay, Tom 33, 92, 214
The Courtship of Eddie's Father 234
Cover Girl 254
Cox, Joel 272
Crain, Jeanne 12
Crash 176
Craven, Wes 181
Crawford, Broderick 118
Crawford, Joan 49, 74, **167**, 188–189, 201, 222
Crazy Heart 63, 64, 131
Crichton, Charles 106, 108
Crimes and Misdemeanors 147, 201, 269
Crimes of the Heart 61, 62, **63**
Crimson Tide 148
Crisp, Donald 186
Cromwell, James 77, 218
Cronauer, Adrian 16
Cronyn, Hume 36
Crosby, Bing 51, 139, 152, 191–192, 221, 226, 284
Crossfire 188, 246
The Crossing Guard 125
Crowe, Russell 77, 125, 128, 202, 206, 218
The Crucible 164
Cruise, Tom 18, 21, 22, 23, 43, 133, 163, 203, 204, 242, 284

Cruz, Penélope 24, 204, 205, 206
Cry Freedom 43, 146
A Cry in the Dark 180, 181
Cukor, George 5, 129, 178, 259, 269
Curie, Marie 92, 93
The Curious Case of Benjamin Button 125–126, 205, 272, 273
Curtis, Tony 71, 72, 149, 259
Curtiz, Michael 191, 215
Cusack, Joan 250
Custer, George 144
Cyrano de Bergerac 155, 189

Daddy Long Legs 280
Daily Variety 156
Dallas Buyers Club 274
Damages 211
Damon, Matt 17, 273–274
Damsel in Distress 236
"The Dance of the Sea" 234
Dancing Lady 228
Dancing Pirate 254
Dandridge, Dorothy 71, 237
Dangerous 165, 166, 177
Dangerous Liaisons 103, 211
The Dark Angel 8
The Dark Knight 18, 207
Dark Passage 228
Dark Victory 42, 80, 165, 166
Darling 33, 199
Dassin, Jules 88
Davalos, Richard 244
Davey, Bruce 239
David Copperfield 253–254, 258
Davis, Bette 42, 50, 58, 70, 79, 80, 93, 95, 118, 152, 156, 157, 165–167, **167**, 168, 177, 179, 184, 189, 194, 227, 241, 255, 288
Davis, Geena 32, 47, 48, 103, 104, 285
Davis, Judy 95
Davis, Sammy, Jr. 82
Davis, Viola 22, 205, 207–208, 214
Day, Doris 193, **248**, 248–249
A Day at the Races 236
Day for Night 170
The Day of the Locust 113
Day-Lewis, Daniel 14, 15, 43, 59, 127, 131, 158, 163–165, **164**, 203, 205, 242, 274, 288
Days of Thunder 22
Days of Wine and Roses 39, 148, 149
The Dead 200
Dead End 192
Dead Man Walking 47, 48, **48**, 49, 65, 124, 125, 261, 262
Dead Poets Society 16, **17**, 43, 164
Dean, James 7, 159, 226, 243–244
Dear Heart 113
Death and the Maiden 211
Death of a Salesman (movie) 88, 123, 124, 213
Death of a Salesman (theater) 124, 213

Death of a Snow Queen 37
Death on the Nile 6, 89
Deconstructing Harry 269
The Deer Hunter 32, 140, 141, 179, 180
The Defiant Ones 71, 72, 232
Degeneres, Ellen 108
de Havilland, Olivia 37, 38, 55, 79, **80**, 121–122, 185, 212, 240, 288
De Laurentiis, Dino 137
Deliverance 32, 250–251
Delpy, Julie 275
Del Toro, Benicio 64, 214
De Luca, Michael 272
Demarest, William 283
DeMille, Cecil B. 69
Demme, Jonathan 127
Dench, Judi 24, 65, 89–91, **90**, 136, 138–139, 203, 288
Deneuve, Catherine 97
De Niro, Robert 13, 15, 17, 30, 32, 64, 76, 92, 103, 136, 140–142, **141**, 228, 238, 288
Dennis, Sandy 149
The Departed 59, 273
Depp, Johnny 26, 58, 125, 242–243
The Descendants 130, 131, **131**, 132
De Sica, Vittorio 74, 277
Designing Woman 118, 228
Destry Rides Again 245
Detective Story 6, 10, 11
The Devil and Daniel Webster (movie) 15
"The Devil and Daniel Webster" (story) 15
The Devil and Miss Jones 15, 186
The Devil Wears Prada 24, 180, 181
deWilde, Brandon 86, 201
Dial M for Murder 226
Diary of a Mad Housewife 105
The Diary of Anne Frank 100, 101
DiCaprio, Leonardo 23, 36, 58–60, **59**, 87, 243, 287
Dick Tracy 110, 111, 203, 267
Dickens, Charles 8, 108, 253–254
"Did I Remember?" 252
Dietrich, Marlene 161, 245
Dinesen, Isak 180
Dinner at Eight 252
The Dirty Dozen 276
Dirty Harry 271
Disney, Walt 232
Disraeli 8, 279, 280
Disraeli, Benjamin 8, 279
The Divine Lady 71, 257
Divorce Italian Style 39, 118
The Divorcee (1919 movie) 12
The Divorcee (1930 movie) 12, 42, 56, 57
Dix, Richard 212
Django Unchained 13, 15, 60, 76, 142, 285
Dmytryk, Edward 159
Do Not Go Gentle into That Good Night 85
Do the Right Thing 147

Dr. Ehrlich's Magic Bullet 235, 259–260, 265
Dr. Jekyll and Mr. Hyde 123
Dr. Strangelove 27
Doctor Zhivago 33, 107
Dodsworth 15, 52
Dog Day Afternoon 47, 110, 175
Don King 150
Donat, Robert 93, 96, 110, 129, 173, 184
Donehue, Vincent J. 9
Donen, Stanley 225
Donlevy, Brian 50, 99, 161
Double Indemnity 40, 41, 236
A Double Life 8, 101, 118, 259
Doubt 18, 67, 180, 181, 205, 207, 214
Douglas, Kirk 6–7, **7**, 213, 261, 287
Douglas, Melvyn 76, 85–86, 91, 92, 96, 119, 287
Douglas, Michael 16, 19, 66, 260–261
Dourif, Brad 19
Down and Out in America 11
Downey, Robert, Jr. 204, 242
Downhill Racer 119
Downton Abbey 136
Dragon Seed 216
Drake, Tom 187
Dreamgirls 15, 285
The Dresser 92, 213, 214
Dressler, Marie 81, 89, 245
Drew, Giorgiana 12
Dreyfuss, Richard 135, 209, 217
Driving Miss Daisy 43, 147, 164
Drums Along the Mohawk 186
A Dry White Season 147, 151, 152
Duck Soup 236
Duel in the Sun 46, 47, 117, 226, 227
Dujardin, Jean 132
Dukakis, Olympia 21
Duke, Patty 6, 94
Dumbo 232
Dumont, Margaret 236
Dunaway, Faye 62, 119, 197, 206, 249
Duncan, Isadora 55, 56
Duncan, Michael Clarke 133
Dunn, James 246
Dunne, Irene 38, 80, 83, 85, 211–212, 221, 279
Durbin, Deanna 96
Durning, Charles 251
Duvall, Robert 91–92, 111, 119, 133, 250, 288
Dylan, Bob 138, 139, 243

Eagels, Jeanne 71, 166
Earthquake 70, 247
East of Eden 243, 244
Eastwood, Clint 44, 67, 70, 79, 125, 130, 219, 239, 268, 271–272, 274
Easy Rider 174, 175
Ebert, Roger 176, 234
Eckhart, Aaron 22
Ed Wood 201, 202, 243

Educating Rita 92, 132, 133
Edward, My Son 54, 154
Edward Scissorhands 14, 84, 243
Edwards, Blake 149
Edzard, Christine 108
The Effect of Gamma Rays on Man-in-the-Moon Marigolds 37
The Egg and I 186, 188
Eggar, Samantha 33
El Cid 70
Eleanor of Aquitaine 177, 179
The Elephant Man 30
Elizabeth 23, 90, 138, 139
Elizabeth I (monarch) 24, 89, 90, 138, 139
Elizabeth I (television) 24
Elizabeth II 24
Elizabeth: The Golden Age 138, 139
Elliott, Denholm 163
Elmer Gantry 38, 39, 40, 149, 213
Emma 81
The Emperor Jones 146
Empire of the Sun 207
The End of the Affair 44, 45
Enders, Robert 106
Enemies, a Love Story 200
The English Patient 23, 229
The Entertainer 172, 174, 213
Ephron, Nora 181, 270
Equus 209
Erin Brockovich 20, 21, 213, 214
Escapade 83
E.T. The Extraterrestial 12
Eternal Sunshine of the Spotless Mind 64, 65
Etting, Ruth
Evans, Edith 91
"Evergreen" 98, 258
Every Day's a Holiday 253
Executive Suite 41, 198
Exit the King 23
Exodus 172
The Exorcist 37, 60, 61, 105
Eyes Wide Shut 22

Faces 206, 276
The Facts of Life 282
Fairbanks, Douglas, Jr. 174
Fairbanks, Douglas, Sr. 70, 71
Falk, Peter 88
"Falling in Love Again" 245
Fanny 221, 222
Fantastic Voyage 213
Far and Away 22
Far from Heaven 22, 44, 45, 204
Farewell, My Lovely 247
A Farewell to Arms (1932 movie) 161
A Farewell to Arms (1957 movie) 277
Fargo 19
Farmer, Frances 136, 137
The Farmer's Daughter 12, 222

Farnsworth, Richard 77
Farrow, Mia 259, 276
Fast Times at Ridgemont High 125
Fatal Attraction 28, 211
Father Goose 224
Father of the Bride 152, 154, 155, 159
Fellini, Federico 99
Fences 22, 146, 148, 207, 208
Ferber, Edna 123, 156, 212
Ferrer, José 61, 155, 189–190
Feury, Joseph 11
A Few Good Men 120, 175, 242
Field, Sally **20**, 21, 62, 94–95, 141, 143, 208, 288
Field, Todd 62, 65, 204
Field of Dreams 39
Fielding, Helen 204
Fielding, Henry 213
Fields, W.C. 253, 253–254
Fiennes, Ralph 13, 23, 26
Fight Club 273
The Fighter 207, 214
Film Stars & Their Awards 1
Finch, Peter 105, 141, 143, 198
Finding Neverland 65, 242, 243
Finian's Rainbow 228
Finkel, Abem 265
Finney, Albert 72, 92, 213–214, 249
The Firm 27, 28, 218, 242
Firth, Colin 45, 64
A Fish Called Wanda 108, 201
Fishburne, Laurence 127, 148
Fisher, Carrie 229
Fisher, Eddie 159, 229
The Fisher King 16, 17, 30
Fitzgerald, Barry 137, 191, 215, 283–284
Fitzgerald, Geraldine 264
Five Easy Pieces 9, 174, 175
Five Star Final 235
The Fixer 14
Flanagan, Father 152, 154
Flesh and the Devil 42
Fletcher, Louise 105, 176, 261
Flight 146, 148, 274
The Flight of the Phoenix 130
Florence Foster Jenkins 180
Flower Drum Song 234
Flying Down to Rio 231
The Flying Nun 94
Flynn, Errol 121
Foch, Nina 41, 198
Follow the Boys 254
Fonda, Henry 35, 39, 74–75, 85, 129, 142, 143, 149, 164, 171, 179, 287
Fonda, Jane 32, 35, 50, 56, 66, 75, 105, 113, 134, 142–143, **150**, 197, 268, 288
Fonda, Peter 175
The Fondas 15
Fontaine, Joan 46, 55, 93, 121, 122, 166, 168, 173, 185, 224, 232

Fontanne, Lynn 81
Foote, Horton 113, 114
For Me and My Gal 225
For Whom the Bell Tolls 46, 160, 162, 167, 168
Forbidden Games 277
Ford, Harrison 13, 31, 33, 249–250
Ford, John 75, 122, 192, 225, 239, 255, 284
Foreign Correspondent 157
Foreman, Miloš 193
Forrest Gump 43, 95, 126, 127–128, **127**
The Fortune Cookie 196, 197
42nd Street 231
Fosse, Bob 53, 137, 144
Fossey, Dian 285
Foster, Jodie 48, 103–104, **104**, 137, 211, 217, 285, 288
The Four Horsemen of the Apocalypse 251
Four in the Morning 89
Fox, Vivica 237
Foxx, Jamie **44**, 59, 242, 284–285
Frances 136, 137
Franciosa, Anthony 107
Frank, Anne 101
Frank, Melvin 105
Frank, Otto 101
Frankel, David 181
Frankenheimer, John 6
Frankie and Johnny at the Clair de Lune 203
Franklin, Carl 181
Franklin, Sidney 123
Frears, Stephen 200, 219
A Free Soul 12, 56, 57, 123, 183, 257
Freed, Arthur 282
Freeman, Morgan 43–44, **44**, 148, 164, 262, 272, 284, 287
The French Connection 119, **120**, 249
The French Lieutenant's Woman 180, 181
Fresh Prince of Bel-Air 244
Fricker, Brenda 200
Fried Green Tomatoes 203
Friedkin, William 119
From Here to Eternity 38, 39, 54, 67, 68, 116, 201, 210, 240, 247
Froman, Jane 50, 51
Frozen River 67
The Fugitive (movie) 13, 58, 250
The Fugitive (television) 250
Fuller, Samuel 210
"Fun House" 236
Funny Face 116
Funny Girl 98, 179, 258
Funny Lady 259

Gable, Clark 96, 129, 154, 183–184, **184**, 194, 226, 246, 247, 248
Game Change 45
Gandhi 25, 125, 163, 172, 233
Gandhi, Mahatma 25
Gangs of New York 59, 163, 164

Garbo, Greta 12, 41–43, 80, 83, 85, 92, 221, 279, 287
The Garden of the Finzi Continis 277
Gardenia, Vincent 140
Gardens of the World with Audrey Hepburn 117
Gardner, Ava 54, 115–116, 247
Gardner, Dede 270, 272
Garfield, John 8, 31
Gargan, William 157, 246
Garland, Judy 38, 96, 116, 135, 223, 241
Garner, James 31, 33, 249, 250
Garr, Teri 137
Garson, Greer 46, 74, 81, 92–94, 99, 117, 166, 168, 169, 184, 216, 288
Gaslight 5, 6, 41, 46, 167, 168, 191, 221
Gassman, Vittorio 101
Gauguin, Paul 99, 100
The Gay Divorcee 227, 231
Gaynor, Janet 83, 135, 279
Gazzo, Michael V. 140
Gehrig, Eleanor 184
Gehrig, Lou 160, 162, 184
The General 234
The General Died at Dawn 156, 161
Genet, Jean 11
Genn, Leo 88
Gentleman's Agreement 8, 117, 118, 124, 187, 188
Gentlemen Prefer Blondes 186
George, Chief Dan 144
George, Gladys 231
George VI 23
George Wallace 66
Georgia 77
Georgy Girl 197
Ghost 219
Ghostley, Alice 134
Gia 66
Giannini, Giancarlo 141
Giant 7, 159, 160, 243, 244
Gibson, Mel 239–240
Gidget 94
Gigi (movie) 195, 280
Gigi (theater) 115
Gilbert, Lewis 133
Gilda 254
Gilliam, Terry 272
Gingold, Hermione 195
Girl, Interrupted 66
Les Girls 225
Gish, Dorothy 227
Gish, Lillian 47, 68, 86, 226–227
Gladiator 128, 202, 206, 218
Gladney, Edna Kahly 92, 93
Gleason, Jackie 26
Gleason, James 215
Glengarry Glen Ross 14, 110, 112
The Glenn Miller Story 130

Gloria 61, 62, 206, 276
Glory 146, 147, 148, 201
Goddard, Paulette 80, 186
The Godfather 1, 35, 36, 64, 91, 110, 111, 133, 140, 151, 152, **153**, 251
The Godfather Part II 64, 91, 110, 111, 140, 144, 175, 228
Gods and Monsters 203
Goeth, Amon 13, 26
Going My Way 191, 215, 221, 283, 284
Goldberg, Whoopi 113, 219, 237, 270
Goldman, Emma 9, 10
Gone with the Wind 42, 47, 50, 71, 79, 80, **80**, 81, 93, 96, 121, 129, 173, 183, 184, 185, 199, 231
The Good Doctor 217
The Good Earth 42, 52, 82, 83, 166, 279
Good Morning, Vietnam 16
Good Night, and Good Luck 130
The Good, the Bad, and the Ugly 271
Good Will Hunting 16, 251, 273
The Goodbye Girl 35, 135, 209, 216, 217
"Goodbye Little Yellow Bird" 5
Goodbye, Mr. Chips (1939 movie) 81, 92, 93, 96, 129, 173, 184
Goodbye, Mr. Chips (1969 movie) 32, 108, 110
Goodfellas 112, 140, 141
Gooding, Cuba, Jr. 204, 242
Gordon, Ruth 259–260, 268
The Gorgeous Hussy 85, 128, 188, 208
Gorillas in the Mist 103, 285
Gosford Park 24, 134, 136
Gould, Elliott 276
The Graduate 49, 50, 143, 144, 171, 196, 197
Graham, Barbara 50, 51
Grahame, Gloria 69, 188
Grand Hotel 9, 42, 123, 188, 257
Grant, Cary 8, 12, 68, 119, 129, 169, 174, 178, **178**, 191, 223–224, 230, 253, 276
Grant, Lee 6, 10–11, 12, 103, 195, 217, 267, 287
Granville, Bonita 156
The Grapes of Wrath 74, 75, 129
Grayson, Kathryn 67
Graziano, Rocky 170
The Great Dictator 75, 157, 262
The Great Escape 249
Great Expectations 106
The Great Gatsby (1974 movie) 268
The Great Gatsby (2013 movie) 60
The Great Lie 184
The Great Race 149
The Great Santini 91, 92
The Great Waltz 83
The Great White Hope 105, 217
The Great Ziegfeld 82, 83, 237
The Greatest Show on Earth 69, 130, 192
The Greatest Story Ever Told 190, 201
Green, Guy 101
The Green Goddess 279, 280

The Green Mile 133
The Green Years 186, 187
Greene, Graham 45
Grey, Brad 273
Grey, Joel 91, 111
Grey Gardens 138
Griffith, Corrine 71
Griffith, D.W. 227
Griffith, Hugh 26, 122
Griffith, Melanie 250, 285
Griffiths, Trevor 266
The Grifters 200, 219
The Guardsman 81
Guess Who's Coming to Dinner 50, 73, 153, 154, 155, 171, 177, 179, 196, 197
Guffey, Burnett 267
Guinness, Alec 30, 87, 106–108, **107**, 198, 214, 288
Guinness Book of World Records 144
Gunfight at O.K. Corral 39
The Guns of Navarone 118
Guys and Dolls 68
Gwenn, Edmund 239
Gyllenhaal, Jake 220
Gypsy 241

Hackman, Gene 17, 78, 86, 91, 102, 112, 118–121, **120**, 136, 144, 145, 214, **263**, 272, 288
Hacksaw Ridge 239
Hagen, Jean 229
Haley, Jackie Earle 15
Hall, Grayson 247
Halliday, John **178**
Hallström, Lasse 58
Hamlet (1948 movie) 12, 172, **173**, 174, 192, 240
Hamlet (1990 movie) 89, 239
Hamlisch, Marvin 258
Hammerstein, Oscar, II 212
Hammett, Dashiell 86, 87, 108
The Hangover 274
Hanks, Tom 30, 87, 126–128, **127**, 145, 147, 164, 202, 288
Hannah and her Sisters 76, 84, 132, 133, 136, 269, 270
Hans Christian Andersen 282
Happy Days 126
Hard Eight 18
Harden, Marcia Gay 19
Hardy, Oliver 234–235
Harling, Robert 20
Harlow (1965 movie/Baker) 252
Harlow (1965 movie/Lynley) 232, 252
Harlow, Jean 231, 232, 252, 253
Harrelson, Woody 23, 76
Harris, Ed 77, 218
Harris, Richard 105
Harrison, Rex 100, 109
Harry and Tonto 61, 111, 175

Index

Hartman, Elizabeth 33, 73
Harvey 128, 129, 188
Harvey, Laurence 6, 69
The Harvey Girls 223
Hathaway, Anne 67, 95
Hauptmann, Bruno 30
Hawke, Ethan 275
Hawkins, Sally 269
Hawks, Howard 41, 76, 156, 161
Hawn, Goldie 61, 62, 68, 270, 276
Hayes, Helen 9, 77, 78, 81–82, 112, 116, 136, 150, 287
Hayward, Susan 50–51, 53, 55, 233, 287
Hayworth, Rita 254
Hearst, William Randolph 264
The Heart Is a Lonely Hunter 14
Heaven Can Wait 32, 34, 135, 266, 267, 275, 276
Heaven Knows, Mr. Allison 36, 54, 246, 265
Heavenly Creatures 65
Hecht, Ben 82
Hecht, Harold 39
Heckart, Eileen 102, 113
Hedda 104, 105
Heflin, Van 9
The Heiress 121, 122, 240
Held, Anna 82, 83
Helfgott, David 22, 23
Hell or High Water 63
Hellman, Lillian 56, 86, 87, 142, 143
Hello, Dolly! 226, 259
Hell's Angels 252
The Help 207
Hemingway, Ernest 161, 162, 277
Henley, Beth 62
Henried, Paul 166, *190*
Henry, Buck 32, 266
Henry II 30, 108, 109
Henry V (1946 movie) 117, 124, 172, 173, 174
Henry V (1989 movie) 89, 97, 164, 207
Henry VIII 193, 194, 209
Henson, Taraji P. 205
Hepburn, Audrey 14, 20, 54, 67, 73, 89, 114–117, *115*, 118, 121, 195, 198, 199, 244, 247, 288
Hepburn, Katharine 30, 35, 37, 39, 47, 50, 80, 81, 86, 87, 91, 101, 104, 105, 109, 117, 128, 129, 138, 139, 154, 155, 158, 165, 167, 169, 177–179, *178*, 180, 194, 197, 231, 232, 252, 258, 259, 269, 270, 288
Herald, Heinz 265
Here Comes Mr. Jordan 215
Here Comes the Groom 191–192
Here Comes the Navy 193
Herrick, Margaret 166
Hershey, Barbara 22
Hersholt, Jean 118, 232
Heslov, Grant 130, 132
Heston, Charlton 69–70, 133, 149, 236, 287
The High and the Mighty 192

"High Hopes" 68
High Noon 7, 69, 106, 151, 160, 162, 225, 226, 279
High Sierra 265
Hill, Gladys 265
Hill, James 39
Hiller, Wendy 194–195, 254
Hilton, James 8
His Girl Friday 222
A History of Violence 31, 32
Hitchcock, Alfred 12, 53, 128, 129, 140, 173, 185, 215, 248
Hitler, Adolf 30, 262
Hoffman, Dustin 22, 25, 32, 91, 111, 119, 120, 126, 143–146, *145*, 163, 171, 172, 174, 196, 242, 288
Hoffman, Joanna 65
Hoffman, Philip Seymour 15, 17–18, 76, 141, 207, 287
Holbrook, Hal 125
Hold Back the Dawn 121, 122
Holden, William 39, 47, 103, 116, 151, 198, 226, 240
Holiday, Billie 237
Holiday Inn 192
Holliday, Judy 198, 264
The Hollywood Review of 1929 234, 235, 257
Holm, Celeste 187, 188
Holt, Tom 216
Hondo 112, 113
Hook 21
Hooper 251
Hope, Bob 3, 96, 192, 254, *281*, 281–282
Hopkins, Anthony 29–30, 97, 104, *104*, 127, 141, 205, 287
Hopkins, Miriam 80
Hopper, Dennis 175
Hopper, Hedda 232, 255
Horn, Lena 237
Horovitz, Rachael 272
Horse Feathers 236
The Horse's Mouth 106, 107
The Hospital 26, 27
Hot Millions 88
The Hours 21, 22, 45, 204, 218
The House I Live In 67
The House of Rothschild 280
House of Sand and Fog 25, 26, 125, 204
Houseman, John 260
"How Do You Keep the Music Playing?" 251
How Green Was My Valley 186, 239, 255, 284
How the West Was Won 130, 158, 216, 224
How to Get Away with Murder 208
Howard, Leslie 165, 173, 195
Howard, Ron 126
Howards End 48, 55, 56, 97, 285
Hoyt, Judie G. 271
Hud 53, 72, 85, 86, 92, 170, 171, 241

Hudson, Jennifer 285
Hudson, Kate 19
Hudson, Rock 7, 38, 133, 159, 160, 243, *248*, 248, 249, 253
Hughes, Howard 58, 59, 86, 87, 252
Hugo, Victor 23
Hull, Josephine 188
The Human Comedy 95, 96, 194, 247
The Hunchback of Notre Dame 239
The Hundred-Foot Journey 25
The Hunger Games 28, 29
Hunnicutt, Arthur 7, 99
Hunt, Helen 34, 89, 95, 176
Hunt, Linda 139, 239
Hunter, Holly 27–28, 97, 242, 284, 287
Hunter, Kim 11
The Hurricane 77, 146, 147–148, 202
Hurt, John 30
Hurt, William 27, 31–32, 33, *114*, 250, 287
Husbands and Wives 269
Hush … Hush, Sweet Charlotte 216
Hussey, Ruth *178*
The Hustler 26, 73, 170, 171, *171*, 172
Huston, Anjelica *114*, 200, 214, 271
Huston, John 16, 174, 191, 200, 265, 265–266, 271
Huston, Tony 200
Huston, Walter 15–16, 52, 64, 189, 200, 266, 287
The Hustons 200
Hutton, Betty 69
Hutton, Timothy 59

I Am a Fugitive from a Chain Gang 51, 52
I Am Legend 244
I Am Sam 124, 125
"I Fall in Love Too Easily" 68
"I Finally Found Someone" 258
I Never Sang for My Father 85, 86, 119
I Remember Mama 38, 192, 211, 212
I Want to Live! 50, 51, 53, 55
The Ice Storm 285
The Ides of March 130, 132
If I Were King 8
I'll Cry Tomorrow 50, 51
"I'll Walk Alone" 254
I'm No Angel 253
I'm Not There 45, 138, 139
Imitation of Life 186
In Old Chicago 192
In the Bedroom 61, 62, 125, 204
"In the Cool, Cool, Cool of the Evening" 191
In the Heat of the Night 11, 73, 144, 171, 195, 196
In the Name of the Father 97, 127, 163, 164
In the Valley of Elah 13
Inception 60
Independence Day 244
The Indian Runner 125

Indiana Jones movies 31, 250
Indochine 97
Infernal Affairs 273
The Informer 52
Inge, William 267
Inglourious Basterds 75, 76, 77, 274
Inherit the Wind 153, 155, 226
Inside Daisy Clover 241, 259, 268
The Insider 77, 202
Interiors 9, 112, 113, 268
Intermezzo 168
Interstellar 274
Interview with the Vampire 273
Into the Wild 125
Into the Woods 180, 243
Intolerance 227
Invictus 43, 44, 273, 274
Iris 26, 64, 65, 89, 90, 275
Irma La Douce 52, 53, 149
The Iron Lady 180, 181, 207
Irons, Jeremy 181
Ironweed 175, 180, 181
Isadora 55, 56
It Happened One Night 58, 166, 183, 185–186, 261
It's a Great Feeling (movie) 282
"It's a Great Feeling" (song) 282
It's a Mad, Mad, Mad, Mad World 234, 238
It's a Wonderful Life 117, 124, 128, 129, 258
"It's Great Not to Be Nominated" 7
Ivanhoe 185
Ives, Burl 118, 196, 213
Ivory, James 37, 97

Jackie 208
Jackman, Hugh 274
Jackson, Glenda 37, 56, 61, 104–106, 217, 288
Jackson, Rachel 85
Jacobs, Michael 267
Jacqueline Susann's Once is Not Enough 7
James, Henry 22
Jandl, Ivan 240
Jane Eyre 185
Jannings, Emil 278
Jaws: The Revenge 133
The Jazz Singer 237
Jenkins, Florence Foster 180
Jerry Maguire 23, 203–204, 242
Jewison, Norman 77, 147
Jezebel 58, 75, 80, 165, 166, 194, 265
JFK 13
Joan of Arc 38, 168, 189, 212
Johnny Belinda 37, 38, 41, 122, 212, 216
Johnson, Ben 60, 64, *263*
Johnson, Mark 266
The Joker Is Wild 68
Jolie, Angelina 66–67, 287
The Jolson Story 117, 124
Jones, Gemma *98*

Jones, James Earl 217
Jones, Jennifer 46–47, 117, 168, 187, 198, 227, 230, 287
Jones, Shirley 39, **40**, 214
Jones, Tommy Lee 13–14, 15, 58, 76, 84, 142, 250, 287
Jordan, Neil 45
Joy 28, 29
Juarez 215, 265
The Judge 91
Judgment at Nuremberg 39, 153, 155, 170, 198, 199, 223, 240, 241, 245
Julia 35, 55, 56, 86, 87, 108, 133, 135, 142, 143, 180, 198, 199
Juliá, Raúl 31
Julie & Julia 180, 181
Julius Caesar 39, 151, 260
Junebug 214
Just Around the Corner 229
Justice, Milton 11

Kanin, Garson 259
The Karate Kid 78
Karsch, Andrew 258
Katagas, Anthony 272
Kaufman, George S. 123
Kaye, Danny 235, 282–283
Kazan, Elia 12, 118, 241, 269
Keaton, Buster 233, 234, 253
Keaton, Diane 19, 35–36, 50, 59, **63**, 113, 139, 143, 176, 279, 287
Keaton, Michael 274
Kedrova, Lila 100, 216
Keener, Catherine 66
Keitel, Harvey 25–26
Kellaway, Cecil 64
Kelly, Gene 67, 71, 225–226, 229, 254
Kelly, Grace 38, 116, 198, 223, 226
Kelly, Nancy 43, 100
Kennedy, Arthur 149, 212–213
Kennedy, George 119
Kennedy, Jackie 208
Kentucky 156
Kern, Jerome 212
Kern and Hammerstein 212
Kerr, Deborah 36, 51, 54–55, 65, 116, 212, 246, 247, 287
Key Largo 192, 228, 236
The Keys of the Kingdom 117, 187, 255
Kidman, Nicole 21–22, 29, 45, 204, 287
The Kids Are All Right 45, 208, 219
The Killers 39, 247, 265
The Killing Fields 234
King, Alan 82
King, Graham 273
King, Henry 46
King, Martin Luther, Jr. 118
King, Stephen 62, 203
The King and I 7, 54, 212, 244

King Kong 136–137
The King of Comedy 238
Kings Row 187, 215
The King's Speech 23
Kingsley, Ben 25–26, 28, 125, 163, 172, 233, 287
Kinsella, W.P. 270
Kirkland, Sally 227
Kiss of the Spider Woman 31, 33, 250
Kitty Foyle 231, 232
Kleiner, Jeremy 270, 272
Kline, Kevin 108, 201
Klute 56, 105, 142, 143
Knox, Alexander 191
Koch, Howard 265
Korjus, Miliza 83
Koskoff, Emma Tillinger 58
Koster, Henry 209
Kotch 150, 196, 197
Kovic, Ron 163, 242
Krainin, Julian 267
Kramer, Larry 105
Kramer, Stanley 72, 155, 198
Kramer vs. Kramer 25, 111, 144, 145, **145**, 180, 181, 217, 218
Kranz, Gene 218
Krause, Nick **131**
Krizan, Kim 275
Kruschen, Jack 88
Kubrick, Stanley 22, 88

L.A. Confidential 202
Ladd, Alan, Jr. 239
Lady for a Day 177
The Lady from Dubuque 136
Lady Gaga 200
Lady L 88
Lady Sings the Blues 237
Lahti, Christine 270
LaMotta, Jake 92
Lancaster, Burt 7, 38–39, **40**, 47, 55, 74, 93, 149, 287
Lanchester, Elsa 188, 194
Landau, Arthur 252
Landau, Martin 147, 201–202, 243, 269
The Landlord 10, 11
Lange, Hope 213
Lange, Jessica 13, 62, **63**, 78, 94, 113, 136, 136–138, 139, 288
Lange, Robert "Mutt" 258
Langtry, Lilly 157
Lansbury, Angela 1, 5–6, 88, 160, 187, 287
Lansky, Meyer 25
Larson, Brie 23
Lassie Come Home 158, 255
The Last Angry Man 51, 52, 69
The Last Command 278
The Last Detail 174, 175
The Last Emperor 207

The Last King of Scotland 110, 244
The Last Picture Show (book) 63
The Last Picture Show (movie) 60, 63, 64
The Last Samurai 242, 262
The Last Station 24, 25, 76
Last Tango in Paris 132, 151, 152
Laughton, Charles 58, 107, 177, 183, 193–194, 227, 239, 279
Laurel, Stan 234–235
Laurel and Hardy 234–235
Laurie, Piper 62, 73, 103, 217
The Lavender Hill Mob 106, 115
Law, Jude 18, 22, 125, 133, 273
Lawrence, Gertrude 199
Lawrence, Jennifer 28–29, 287
Lawrence, T.E. 108, 109
Lawrence of Arabia 39, 107, 108–109, **109**, 118, 122, 190, 213, 215
Lazar, Andrew 271, 274
Leachman, Cloris 60, **263**
A League of Their Own 126
Lean, David 33, 106, 107, 108, 178, 247
Leaving Las Vegas 30, 49, 125
Ledger, Heath 18, 143, 207, 220
Lee, Ang 131
Lee, Harper 118
Lee, Philomena 89, 90
Lee, Spike 147
Lee Daniel's The Butler 271
Leeds, Andrea 231
Le Gallienne, Eva 61
Leigh, Vivien 42, 77, 79–81, **80**, 93, 95, 101, 166, 173, 178, 183, 205, 212, 287
Leisen, Mitchell 122, 210
Lemmon, Jack 25, 39, 53, 62, 69, 78, 82, 111, 136, 148–150, **150**, 172, 175, 181, 196, 197, 236, 256, 263, 268, 282, 288
Lenny 144
Lenya, Lotte 267
Leo, Melissa 67, 214
Leone, Sergio 271
Lerner, Michael 19
LeRoy, Mervyn 52, 67, 88
Leto, Jared 108, 130, 274
The Letter (1929 movie) 71, 166
The Letter (1940 movie) 157, 165, 166
A Letter to Three Wives 6, 188, 210
Letters from Iwo Jima 271
Letts, Tracy 21
Levinson, Barry 16, 266
Lewis, C.S. 30
Lewis, Jerry 238
Lewis, Sinclair 15, 39
Libeled Lady 154, 231, 237, 252
Lieberman in Love (movie) 270
"Lieberman in Love" (story) 270
The Life and Death of Peter Sellers 23
The Life Aquatic with Steve Zissou 139
Life Is Beautiful 74

The Life of Emile Zola 51, 52
Life with Father 8
Li'l Abner 238
Lili 54, 115, 247
Lilies of the Field 71, 72, 171, 232
Lilith 119
Limelight 234, 262, 263, 264
Lincoln 13, 15, 76, 94, 142, 163, 164, **164**, 165, 208, 274
Lincoln, Abraham 13, 75, 163, 164
Lincoln, Mary Todd 94, 95, 259
The Lindbergh Kidnapping Case 30
Linklater, Richard 275
Lion 21, 22
The Lion in Winter (movie) 14, 30, 32, 108, 109, 177, 179, 258
The Lion in Winter (television) 211
Lithgow, John 16
Little Big Man 144
Little Caesar 235
Little Children 15, 24, 65
The Little Colonel 229
Little Dorrit 106, 108
The Little Foxes 165, 166, 184
Little Man Tate 104
Little Miss Sunshine 14
Little Voice 133
Little Women (1949 movie) 159
Little Women (1994 movie) 207
Littlefeather, Sacheen 143, 152
The Littlest Rebel 229
Litvak, Anatole 41, 212
The Lives of a Bengal Lancer 161
Lloyd, Frank 71, 257
Lloyd, Harold 232–233, 253
Lloyd, Phyllida 181
Loggia, Robert 126
Logue, Lionel 23
Lolita 101, 247
Lombard, Carole 245–246
The Lonely Passion of Judith Hearne 136
Lonelyhearts 9
Long Day's Journey into Night (movie) 86, 177, 179
Long Day's Journey into Night (theater) 138
The Long, Hot Summer 36, 170
The Long Voyage Home 224, 284
The Longest Day 224, 247, 255
The Longest Yard 251
Looking for Mr. Goodbar 35
The Lord of the Rings movies 139
The Lord of the Rings: The Fellowship of the Ring 139
Loren, Sophia 73–74, 88, 113, 205, 241, 277, 287
Lorenz, Robert 271, 274
Lorenzo's Oil 47, 48, 97
Lorring, Joan 187
Lost Horizon 8

Lost in Translation 125
The Lost Weekend 37, 50
Louis XVI 58
Love, Bessie 71
Love Actually 98
Love Affair 80, 211, 212, 221
Love Field 97
Love in the Afternoon 116
Love Is a Many-Splendored Thing (movie) 46, 47, 198
"Love Is a Many-Splendored Thing" (song) 280
Love Letters 46
Love Me or Leave Me 192, 193, 248
The Love Parade 252, 280
Love Story 13, 105
Love with the Proper Stranger 241, 249
"Lovely to Look At" 227
The Loves of Carmen 254
Lowe, Chad 79
Loy, Myrna 83, 236–237, 239
Lubitsch, Ernst 246, 252
Lucas, George 250
The Luck of the Irish 64
Luft, Joseph "Joey" 223
Lugosi, Bela 201, 202
Luhrmann, Baz 59
Lumet, Sidney 75, 143, 169, 179, 195, 197
Lust for Life 6, 7, 96, 99, 100, 260
Lynley, Carol 149, 197, 232, 252
Lynn, Doolittle 13
Lynn, Loretta 61, 62
Lyon, Sue 197

MacArthur, Charles 82
MacGraw, Ali 105
MacLaine, Shirley 21, 33, 35, 50, 51, 52 54, 149, 218, 267, 287
MacMurray, Fred 41, 177, 236
MacPherson, Jeanie 70
Mad Max 239
Madame Curie 46, 92, 93, 168
Madame X 71, 122, 257
Madden, John 89
Maddow, Ben 265
The Madness of King George 24
Madonna 125
Madsen, Virginia 208
Magic 30
"Magic Act" 235
Magnani, Anna 36, 39
The Magnificent Ambersons 216, 264
Magnificent Obsession 37, 38, 216
The Magnificent Seven 249
Magnolia 18, 133, 242
Maguire, Dorothy 12
Mahin, John Lee 265
The Maids 11
Main, Marjorie 186, 188, 223

"Make a Little Magic" 1
Mako 197
Malcolm X 146, 147
Malden, Karl 88, 118, 195
Malick, Terrence 130
Malle, Louis 47
Malone, Dorothy 228
The Maltese Falcon 16, 191, 265, 266
Mamet, David 137
A Man for All Seasons 55, 56, 116, 133, 193, 195, 197, 209
The Man in the Glass Booth 198, 199
"The Man That Got Away" 223
The Man Who Cried 139
The Man Who Knew Too Much 248
The Man Who Shot Liberty Valance 130
The Man Who Would Be King 133, 265
The Man with the Golden Arm 67, 68
Manchester by the Sea 220, 273
The Manchurian Candidate 5, 6
Mandela, Nelson 43, 44
Mangano, Joy 28
Manhattan 268
Manhattan Melodrama 237
Mankiewicz, Herman J. 264
Mann, Delbert 55
Mantell, Joe 149
Marathon Man 87, 145, 172, 174
March, Fredric **57**, 117, 122–124, 237, 288
Marie Antoinette 56, 58
Marjorie Morningstar 226, 241
The Mark 199
Marooned 118, 119
Marriage Italian Style 73, 74, 277
Marricone, Ennio 271
Marshall, E.G. 9
Marshall, Penny 126, 141
Marshall, Rob 205
The Martian 273, 274
Martin, Dean 238
Marty 39, 68, 116, 149, 155, 195, 226, 244
Marvin, Lee **34**, 142, 196, 209, 238
Marvin's Room 35, 36, 59
Marx, Chico 236
Marx, Groucho 236
Marx, Harpo 236
The Marx Brothers 236
Mary Poppins 6, 49, 199
Mary, Queen of Scots 55, 56
*M*A*S*H* 91
Mason, James 152, 197
Mason, Marsha 35, 37, 216–217
Masry, Ed 213
Massey, Raymond 15, 75, 259
The Master 18, 76, 95, 141, 214, 274
Mastroianni, Marcello 39, 74, 118
Match Point 269
The Mating Season 210
Matlin, Marlee 29, 62

Matthau, Walter 150, 196–197
May, Elaine 266
Mayer, Louis B. 83, 123
McCabe & Mrs. Miller 33
McCarey, Leo 235, 284
McCarthy, Frank 27
McCarthy, Joseph 130, 233
McCarthy, Kevin 88, 213
McCrea, Joel 186, 231
McCullers, Carson 14
McDaniel, Hattie 71, **80**, 121, 194, 231
McDonnell, Mary 97
McDormand, Frances 19–20, 287
McDowall, Roddy 5, 158, 159, 254–255, 284
McFarland, Joey 58
McGrath, Douglas 269
McGuire, Dorothy 46
McLaglen, Victor 52, 99
McMurtry, Larry 63
McNamara, Maggie 54, 116, 198, 247
McNichol, Kristy 217
McQueen, Steve (actor) 197, 249
McQueen, Steve (director) 272, 273
Me and the Colonel 282
Mean Streets 140
Meet Me in St. Louis 223
Melvin and Howard 59, 86, 87
Memel, Jana Sue 270
Men in Black 244
Mendes, Sam 59
Mercouri, Melina 73, 205
Meredith, Burgess 87, 113
The Messenger 76
Meteor 201
Michael, Paul 1
Michael Clayton 130, 131
Michael Collins 21
Midler, Bette 94
Midnight Cowboy 32, 144
Midnight in Paris 203, 269
A Midsummer Night's Dream 95–96, 121, 193
Mighty Aphrodite 65, 269
A Mighty Heart 66
Mildred Pierce 74, 187, 188, 222
Miles, Sarah 105, 247
Miles, Sylvia 247
Milk 124, 125, 126
Milk, Harvey 124, 126
Milland, Ray 37, 50, 226
Miller, Amara **131**
Miller, Arthur 86, 124, 212, 256
Million Dollar Baby 43, 44, 65, 78, 79, 219, 271, 272, 284
Mills, Hayley 230
Mills, John 119
Mills, Juliet 105
Min and Bill 245
Mineo, Sal 88, 149
Minnelli, Liza 134

Minnelli, Vincente 7, 154, 225
Miracle on 34th Street 210, 239, 241
The Miracle Worker 6, 49, 113, 179, 189
Mirren, Helen 24–25, 65, 136, 205, 287
The Mirror Has Two Faces 228, 258, 259
Les Misérables (1935 movie) 193
Les Misérables (1998 movie) 23
Les Misérables (2012 movie) 95, 274
Misery 21, 37, 202, 203, 228
The Misfits 256
Miss Sadie Thompson 254
Missing 25, 61, 62, 148, 172
Mission: Impossible 201
Mississippi Burning 19, 119, 120, 145
Mr. & Mrs. Bridge 36, 37
Mr. Deeds Goes to Town 52, 129, 160, 161, **162**
Mister Roberts 75, 148, 149, 193
Mr. Saturday Night 238
Mr. Skeffington 93, 165, 166, 215
Mr. Smith Goes to Washington 75, 96, 128, 129, 215
Mitchell, Joni 98–99
Mitchell, Margaret 79
Mitchell, Thomas 194, 215, 224
Mitchum, Robert 227, 246–247
Modern Times 262
Modine, Matthew 45
Mogambo 54, 116, 226, 247
Moneyball 272, 273
Mo'Nique 6
Monkey Business 236
Monroe, Marilyn 20, 53, 117, 149, 186, 219, 220, 244, 255–256, **256**, 266
Monsieur Verdoux 262, 263
Monster 36, 73
Monster's Ball 73, 204, 237
Moody, Ron 14
The Moon Is Blue 54, 116, 198
Moonstruck 28, 211
Moore, Chris 273
Moore, Grace 58
Moore, Julianne 22, 44–46, 204, 218, 285, 287
Moore, Mary Tyler 61, 62
Moore, Roger 1
Moorehead, Agnes 12, 216, 264
More, Lady Alice 195
More, Sir Thomas 195
The More the Merrier 46, 168, 186, 187
Moreno, Rita 223, 241
Morgan! 55, 56
Morgan, Peter 271, 274
Morita, Noriyuki "Pat" 78
Mork and Mindy 16
Morley, Robert 58
The Morning After 142, 143
Morning Glory 177
Morocco 161, 245
Mortensen, Viggo 32

Morton, Samantha 66
The Mosquito Coast 250
Mother 229
Mother Courage and Her Children 49
Moulin Rouge (1952 movie) 189, 265, 266
Moulin Rouge! (2001 movie) 21, 22
Mourning Becomes Electra 8, 222
Mrs. Brown 89
Mrs. Doubtfire 17
Mrs. Henderson Presents 89, 90
Mrs. Miniver 92, 93, 137, 184
Mrs. Parkington 92, 93, 216
Mulligan, Robert 241
Muni, Paul 15, 51–52, 69, 83, 154, 161, 287
Murder on the Orient Express 168, 169, **169**, 195, 213, 214, 228
Murdoch, Iris 64, 65, 89, 90
Murphy, Eddie 14, 238
Murphy's Romance 31, 33, 95, 250
Murray, Bill 125
Murray, Don 255
Murrow, Edward R. 130
Music Box 136, 137
"The Music Box" 235
Music of the Heart 180, 181
Mussolini, Benito 157
Mutiny on the Bounty (1935 movie) 52, 183, **184**, 193, 194, 239
Mutiny on the Bounty (1962 movie) 152
My Beautiful Laundrette 163
My Best Friend's Wedding 21
My Cousin Rachel 99, 122, 208, 209
My Cousin Vinny 97, 204
My Fair Lady 49, 100, 109, 116, 195, 199
My Favorite Year 25, 108, 110, 172
My Foolish Heart (movie) 50, 51
"My Foolish Heart" (song) 233
My Friend Flicka 255
My Gal Sal 254
My Left Foot 43, 127, 163, 200, 242
My Little Chickadee 253
My Man Godfrey 52, 245, 246
My Sister Eileen 222
My Week with Marilyn 219, 220, 252
Mystic Pizza 20
Mystic River 26, 124, 125, 261, 262, 271, 272

Nagel, Conrad 123
Nash, J. Carrol 246
Nash, John 202
Nashville 11
National Velvet 5, 96, 159, 160, 187
The Natural 211
Natwick, Mildred 268
Neal, Patricia 53, 86, 241
Neame, Ronald 107, 134
Neeson, Liam 55, 127, 239
Nell 103, 104, 137
Nelson, Barry 247

Nelson, Harmon Oscar 166
Nelson, Willie 243
Nero 87, 88
Network 62, 87, 90, 103, 141, 197, 198, 218
Never on Sunday 73
Newman, Paul 18, 25, 36, 37, 72, 86, 91, 139, 159, 170–172, **171**, 196, 205, 242, 249, 268, 288
The Next Karate Kid 78
Ngor, Haing S. 234
Nichols, Mike 181, 250
Nicholson, Jack 31, 33, 76, 77, 78, 85, 111, 120, 124, 125, 133, 136, 144, 158, 164, 165, 167, 174–177, **176**, 197, 200, 242, 250, 261, 273, 288
A Night at the Opera 236
'night, Mother 202
Night Moves 120
Night Must Fall 222
The Night of the Hunter 194, 227
The Night of the Iguana 247
Nine 22, 205
Ninotchka 42, 81, 85
Nissen, Greta 252
Niven, David 55, 72, 179, 254
Nixon 30, 208, 218
Nixon, Richard 30
No Country for Old Men 13, 18, 205, 206
No Man of Her Own 246
Nobody's Fool 18, 170, 172
Nolte, Nick 30, 141
None But the Lonely Heart 11, 12, 191, 223, 224, 284
Norma Rae 94, 143
Normand, Mabel 204
North by Northwest 201
North Country 19
Not as a Stranger 68
Notes on a Scandal 24, 89, 90, 138, 139
Notorious 215
Novarro, Ramón 69
"Now I Know" 282
Now, Voyager 165, 166, 215
Nozik, Michael 267
Number One 275, 276
Nunn, Trevor 105
The Nun's Story 115, 116
The Nutty Professor (1963 movie) 238
The Nutty Professor (1996 movie) 238
Nyong'o, Lupita 29

O Brother, Where Art Thou? 130
Oakie, Jack 157
Obama, Michelle 176
O'Brien, Edmond 101, 195, 247, 260
O'Brien, Margaret 103
O'Brien, Pat 193
O'Brien, Virginia 223
O'Connell, Arthur 26, 149, 198, 264

O'Connor, Donald 116, 229
The Odd Couple 149
Odets, Clifford 86, 224
Of Human Bondage 95, 165
Of Human Hearts 15, 128, 186
O'Hara, Maureen 238–239, 255
O'Herlihy, Dan 152
The Old Man and the Sea 72, 152, 155
"Old Time Rock and Roll" 242
Olin, Lena 200
Oliver! 14, 37
Oliver, Edna May 186
Olivier, Laurence 7, 30, 75, 81, 87, 91, 92, 96, 97, 117, 124, 129, 133, 134, 141, 145, 167, 172–174, **173**, 205, 209, 213, 214, 239, 240, 252, 288
The Omen 118
On Golden Pond 35, 39, 47, 74, 75, 142, 143, 164, 171, 177, 179
"On the Atchison, Topeka, and the Santa Fe" 223
On the Riviera 282
On the Town 68, 225
On the Waterfront 68, 151, 152, 191, 192, 195
Ondine 116
One Flew Over the Cuckoo's Nest (movie) 104, 105, 111, 116, 174, 175, 176, **176**, 197, 260, 261
One Flew Over the Cuckoo's Nest (theater) 261
One Foot in Heaven 196
One Hour Photo 17
One Hour with You 280
One Night of Love 58
One True Thing 180, 181, 203
One, Two, Three 193
O'Neal, Ryan 13, 279
O'Neill, Eugene 86, 146, 174, 176, 179
O'Neill, Oona **263**
Only Angels Have Wings 254
Only the Lonely 239
Only When I Laugh 217
Ordinary People 59, 61, 62, 267, 268
Orlean, Susan 180, 181
Osment, Haley Joel 66, 133
Othello 8, 134, 146, 172, 174
The Other Half of the Sky: A China Memoir 52, 53
O'Toole, Peter 14, 25, 32, 39, 55, 108–110, **109**, 112, 118, 139, 172, 209, 214, 288
Ouspenskaya, Maria 221
Out of Africa 113, 180, 181, 268
The Out-of-Towners 149
"Over the Rainbow" 223
Owen, Clive 43–44
The Ox-Bow Incident 99

Pacino, Al 18, 28, 91, 110–112, 119, 139, 144, 147, **153**, 175, 284, 288

Page, Geraldine 50, 73, 112–114, **114**, 181, 288
Paint Your Wagon 271
Pakula, Alan J. 181, 251
Pal Joey 254
Palance, Jack 13, 99, 189, 200–201, 204
The Paleface 282
Palin, Sarah 45
Palminteri, Chazz 269
Paltrow, Gwyneth 138
Panic in the Streets 200
The Paper Chase 260
Papillon 249
Paquin, Anna 98
The Paradine Case 11, 12, 118, 188
The Parent Trap 239
Parenthood 84
Parker, Alan 19
Parker, Bonnie 197
Parker, Eleanor 6
Parks, Larry 117, 124
Parsons, Estelle 267
Parsons, Louella 255
Parton, Dolly 133
A Passage to India 95, 113, 270
Passion Fish 97
The Passion of the Christ 240
Pasteur, Louis 51, 52
Pat and Mike 259
A Patch of Blue 6, 33, 73, 100, 101, 134, 259
Paterson, Patricia 222
The Patriot 278
Patton 26, 27, 68
Patton, George S. 26, 27
The Pawnbroker 195
Peck, Gregory 8, 39, 74, 93, 109, **115**, 116, 117–118, 124, 187, 188, 228, 255, 288
Peckinpah, Sam 87
Peggy Sue Got Married 62
Peirce, Gareth 97
Penn, Sean 26, **48**, 66, 77, 124–126, 130, 262, 269, 272, 288
Pennies from Heaven (movie) 191
"Pennies from Heaven" (song) 191
Penny Serenade 223, 224
Pentimento 56
The People vs. Larry Flynt 23
The Perfect Storm 130
Period of Adjustment 142
Pesci, Joe 112, 204
Pete 'n' Tillie 112, 113
Peyton Place 36, 212, 213
Pfeiffer, Michelle 97, 203
Philadelphia 30, 126, 127, 147, 164
The Philadelphia Story 75, 128, 129, 173, 177, 178, **178**, 224, 232
Philomena 89, 90, **90**
Phoenix, Joaquin 84, 274
The Pianist 164
The Piano 27, 28, 98

Pickford, Mary 70–71, 287
Pickup on South Street 210
Picnic 149, 198
The Picture of Dorian Gray 5, 187
Pidgeon, Walter 93, 255
The Pied Piper 255, 280
Pienaar, Jacobus Francois 273, 274
Pikser, Jeremy 266
Pillow Talk 210, **248**, 248, 249
Pinkett, Jada 237
Pinky 11, 12, 71
Pinter, Harold 49, 86
The Pirate 225
Pirates of the Caribbean: The Curse of the Black Pearl 26, 125, 242, 243
Pitt, Brad 77, 126, 272–273
A Place in the Sun 100, 101, 124, 159, 187, 240
Places in the Heart 62, 94, 218
Planet of the Apes 70, 255
Platoon 243
Play It Again, Sam 35
The Player 261
Playhouse 90 198
Plaza Suite 9
The Pleasure of His Company 228
Plimpton, Martha 84
Plummer, Christopher 76
Poitier, Sidney 11, 49, 71–73, **72**, 86, 148, 171, 232, 287
Pollack, Sydney **114**, 137
Pollard, Michael J. 119
Pollock 19, 218
Pollock, Jackson 218
Pollyanna 230
Ponti, Carlo 74
The Pope of Greenwich Village 112, 113
Popeye 16
Portman, Natalie 22, 29, 208, 219
The Portrait of a Lady 22
Portrait of Jennie 227
The Poseidon Adventure 1, 101, 102, **102**, 120, 255
Possessed 188, 189
Postcards from the Edge 180, 181
The Postman Always Rings Twice (1946 movie) 31, 137
The Postman Always Rings Twice (1981 movie) 137, 200
Powell, Dick 7
Powell, William 8, 52, 149, 237, 246
The Preacher's Wife 148
Precious 6
Prejean, Helen 47, 48
Preminger, Otto 68, 71, 129, 266
Pretty Woman 20, 21, 203
The Pride of the Yankees 156, 160, 162, 184
Primary Colors 202, 203
The Prime of Miss Jean Brodie 134, 136, 143
Primrose Path 232

The Prince and the Showgirl 256
The Prince of Tides 30, 258
Princess O'Rourke 37
The Prisoner of Zenda 8
Private Benjamin 61, 62
A Private Function 136
The Private Life of Henry VIII 193, 194
Private Worlds 185, 186
Prizzi's Honor 31, 33, 175, 176, 200, 250, 265, 271
The Producers 88
The Professionals 201
The Public Enemy 193, 252
The Pumpkin Eater 49
The Purple Rose of Cairo 84, 269
The Pursuit of Happyness 244
Pygmalion 194, 195
Pyle, Ernie 246

Quartet 136
"Que Sera, Sera" 248
The Queen 24, 65, 205
The Quiet American 132, 133
The Quiet Man 69, 99, 122, 224, 225, 239, 284
Quills 23
Quinn, Anthony 76, 96, 99–100, 107, **109**, 209, 233, 260, 288
Quiz Show 267
Quo Vadis 87, 88

Rabbit Hole 21, 22
Rachel Getting Married 67
Rachel, Rachel 36, 37, 170, 171
The Racket 235
Radio Days 84, 269
Rafelson, Bob 137
Raging Bull 92, 140, 141
Ragtime 193
Rain Man 120, 125, 126, 144, 145, 163, 242
Rainer, Luise 29, 42, 77, 79, 82–83, 87, 95, 128, 154, 156, 166, 179, 212, 279, 287
The Rainmaker 39, 177, 179
Rains, Claude 168, 187, 215, 283
Raintree County 36, 158, 159, 216, 241
Rambeau, Marjorie 232
Randolph, John 85
Random Harvest 8
Rasch, Raymond 262
Rathbone, Basil 8
Ray 59, 284
The Reader 65, 66, 67, 205
Reagan, Ronald 103
The Real Thing 211
Rear Window 130, 226
Rebecca 75, 129, 172, 173, 185, 232
Rebecca of Sunnybrook Farm 229
Rebel Without a Cause 149, 241, 243, 244
Red River 158, 240

Redford, Robert 60, 145, 149, 181, 267–268
Redgrave, Lynn 55, 121, 203
Redgrave, Michael 8, 55
Redgrave, Vanessa 55–56, 63, 65, 66, 94–95, 97, 105, 121, 287
The Redgraves 15
Redman, Joyce 134, 249
Redmayne, Eddie 274
Reds 2, 9, 10, 35, 120, 174, 176, 219, 266, 267
Reed, Donna 68, 210
Reed, John "Jack" 266
Reed, Rex 249
Reeve, Christopher 43
Reiner, Rob 203
Reinhardt, Max 121
Reisz, Karel 56
The Reivers 249
The Remains of the Day 29, 30, 97, 127
Remick, Lee 149
Requiem for a Dream 60, 61
Resurrection 60, 61, 62
Reuben, Reuben 92
The Revenant 58, 59, 60
Revere, Anne 5, 187, 188
Revolutionary Road 59, 66
Reynolds, Burt 17, 94, 250–251
Reynolds, Debbie 68, 203, 229
Rhames, Ving 150
Richard the Lionhearted 30
Richard III 7, 172, 174
Richardson, Ralph 122
Richardson, Tony 137, 213
The Right Stuff 218
Risky Business 242
Rita Hayworth and the Shawshank Redemption 254
Ritter, Thelma 55, 65, 188, 210, 215
The River 61, 62, 94
A River Runs Through It 272
Roach, Hal 235
Road to Hong Kong 192
Road to Perdition 170, 172
Road to Singapore 192
Rob Roy 77
Robards, Jason, Jr. 59, 76, 82, 86–87, 108, 128, 133, 135, 199, 287
Robbins, Tim 48, 261–262, 272
The Robe 39, 151, 209
Roberta 227, 231
Roberts, Eric 21
Roberts, Julia 20–21, **20**, 23, 28, 203, 214, 287
Roberts, Rachel 53, 105
Robertson, Cliff 14, 109
Robinson, Bill "Bo Jangles" 229
Robinson, Edward G. 156, 192, 235–236, 259
Robson, May 177
Rocky 87
The Rocky Horror Picture Show 47
Rodgers, Richard 82

Rodgers and Hammerstein 234
Rogers, Ginger 122, 231–232
The Rogue Song 235, 257
Roman Holiday 54, 68, 114, **115**, 115–116, 118, 247
The Roman Spring of Mrs. Stone 267
Romance 41, 42
Romancing the Stone 261
Romeo and Juliet 56, 58, 173
Room at the Top 69, 116, 159
A Room with a View 89, 134, 136, 163
Rooney, Mickey 95–97, 100, 129, 154, 194, 223, 288
Roosevelt, Eleanor 92, 93
The Rose 94
Rose, Reginald 74
The Rose Tattoo 39
Rosemary's Baby 259, 276
Rosenberg, Tom 271
Ross, Diana 237
Ross, Herbert 20, 35, 135
Ross, Shirley 254, 282
Rossellini, Roberto 54, 169
Rossen, Robert 73
Roth, Lillian 50, 51
Roth, Tim 77
Rourke, Mickey 126
Rowlands, Gena 61, 62, 206, 276
The Royal Family of Broadway 122, 123
The Royal Tenenbaums 120, 121
Rozsa, Miklos 259
Ruddy, Albert S. 271
Rudin, Scott 146
Rudolph, Alan 34
Ruehl, Mercedes 82
Ruffalo, Mark 45
Ruggles, Wesley 212
Ruggles of Red Gap 193
The Ruling Class 108, 110
Runaway Train 21, 31, 32, 33, 250
Rush, Geoffrey 21, 22–23, 28, 287
Russell, David O. 29
Russell, Harold 215, 230, 283
Russell, Ken 105
Russell, Larry 262
Russell, Rosalind 3, 51, 67, 68, 82, 222, 280, 281
The Russians Are Coming! The Russians Are Coming! 14
Rutherford, Margaret 134, 159
Ryan, Meg 126
Ryan's Daughter 105, 119, 247
Ryder, Winona 207

Sabrina (1954 movie) 114, 116, 198
Sabrina (1995 movie) 250
Sade, Marquis de 23
Sadie Thompson 257
Safety Last 233

The Saga of Gösta Berling 42
Saint, Eva Marie 68, 88, 192, 214
Same Time, Next Year 60, 61
San Francisco 52, 152, 154, 155
The Sand Pebbles 197, 249
Sande, Walter **155**
The Sandpiper 159
Sands of Iwo Jima 224
Sarah and Son 141
Sarandon, Chris 47
Sarandon, Susan 13, 47–49, **48**, 65, 97, 103, 104, 138, 261, 262, 287
Saturday Night and Sunday Morning 213
Save the Tiger 111, 148, 149, 175, 268
Saving Mr. Banks 99
Saving Private Ryan 126, 128, 273
Sayonara 151, 152, 233, 234, 277
Scarecrow 111, 119
The Scarlet Letter 227
Scent of a Woman 18, 110, 112, 147
Schary, Dore 88, 222
Schatzberg, Jerry 43
Schell, Maria 199
Schell, Maximilian 87, 170, 198–199
Schindler's List 13, 26, 127
Schlesinger, John 32, 33, 105, 163
Scofield, Paul 133, 209
Scorsese, Martin 43, 58, 60, 140, 141, 164, 172, 238, 247, 269
Scott, George C. 26–27, 28, 68, 86, 144, 146, **171**, 175, 287
The Scoundrel 82
The Sea Wolf 235–236
The Search 174, 240
"Secret Love" 248
Segal, George 105, **160**, 197
Sellers, Peter 23, 111
Selma 270, 271
Selznick, David O. 46, 80, 81, 168
Sennett, Mack 245
Sense and Sensibility 64, 65, 97, 98, **98**
Separate Tables 39, 51, 54, 55, 72, 194, 195, 254
September 84
Sergeant York 156, 160, 161, 196, 224, 265
Serpico 110, 111
Serving in Silence 211
The Sessions 95
Se7en 272
Seven Beauties 141
Seven Days in May 39, 247, 260
The Seven Year Itch 255
The Seventh Cross 154, 216
7th Heaven 279
Sevigny, Chloë 66
Sexy Beast 25, 26
"The Shadow of Your Smile" 159
Shadowlands 30
Shadows 276

Shaffer, Anthony 133
Shakespeare, William 58, 81, 85, 124, 146, 151, 173, 174, 239
Shakespeare in Love 22, 23, 89, 90, 138, 139, 203
Shall We Dance 228, 231
Shampoo 10, 11, 34, 266, 267
Shane 200, 201
Shanghai Express 245
Shannon, Michael 59
Sharif, Omar 33
Shaw, Clay (AKA Clay Bertrand) 13
Shaw, George Bernard 195
Shaw, Robert 193, 197
The Shawshank Redemption 43, 254, 262
She Done Him Wrong 224, 253
Shearer, Norma 12, 42, 56–58, **57**, 80, 93, 123, 173, 183, 193, 287
The Sheik 251
Sheldon, Sidney 230
Sheridan, Jim 97, 163, 164
Shine 22, 23
Ship of Fools 33, 190
The Shipping News 139
Shirley, Anne 231
Shoeshine 277
Short Cuts 19, 45
Show Boat (1936 movie) 212
Show Boat (1951 movie) 247
Shue, Elisabeth 49
Sideways 43, 79, 208
Siegel, Benjamin "Bugsy" 266
Signoret, Simone 33, 116, 159
The Silence of the Lambs 29, 30, 48, 103, 104, **104**, 127, 141, 205
Silkwood 180, 181
Silkwood, Karen 180, 181
The Silver Chalice 201
Silver Linings Playbook 13, 28, 29, 76, 95, 140, 274
Simmons, Jean 39, 107, 192
Simon, Neil 135, 136, 197, 217
The Sin of Madelon Claudet 81, 82, 122
Sinatra, Frank 67–69, 201, 287
Since You Went Away 46, 185, 186, 216, 230, 258
Singer, Bryan 77
Singin' in the Rain 225, 229
A Single Man 45, 64
The Singular Life of Albert Nobbs 211
Siodmak, Robert 12, 247
Sirk, Douglas 38
Siskel, Gene 176
Sister Kenny 222
Sitting Pretty 174, 239
Six Degrees of Separation 244
The Sixth Sense 66, 133
Sjöström, Victor 227
Sleepless in Seattle 127

312 Index

Sleuth 132, 133, 172, 174
Sling Blade 23
Smash-Up—The Story of a Woman 50, 51
Smilin' Through 123
The Smiling Lieutenant 185, 280
Smith, Jaden 244
Smith, Liz 249
Smith, Maggie 9, 78, 87, 133, 134–136, **135**, 143, 276, 288
Smith, Stevie 106
Smith, Will 125, 148, 244, 285
Smokey and the Bandit 94, 251
The Snake Pit 38, 121, 122, 212
Snodgrass, Carrie 105
So Proudly We Hail! 186
S.O.B. 199
A Soldier's Play 146
A Soldier's Story 146
Solitary Man 261
Some Came Running 51, 52, 53, 212, 213
Some Like It Hot 69, 148, 149, 256
Somebody Up There Likes Me 170, 249
Something's Gotta Give (movie) 19, 35, 36
"Something's Gotta Give" (song) 280
Sometimes a Great Notion 75
The Song of Bernadette 46, 168, 187
Song of the South 232
Sonny and Cher 1
Sons and Lovers 195
Sophie's Choice 137, 164, 180, 181
Sorry, Wrong Number 38, 39, 40, 41, 212
Sorvino, Mira 65
Soubirous, Bernadette 46
The Sound of Music 33, 199, 200
Sounder 237
Soylent Green 236
Spacek, Sissy 13, 61–62, **63**, 94, 203, 204, 287
Spacey, Kevin 77–78, 82, 86, 136, 148, 150, 202, 218, 229, 287
Spark, Muriel 134
Spartacus 7, 87, 88, 194
Speedy 233
Spellbound 117
Spielberg, Steven 214, 270, 271, 273
The Spiral Staircase 11, 12
Splash 126
Splendor in the Grass 73, 241, 267
Springsteen, Bruce 127
The Spy Who Came In from the Cold 209
Stage Door 231
Stagecoach 192, 215, 224
Stalag 17 39, 151, 198, 240
Stallone, Sylvester 133, 139
Stamp, Terence 86, 88
Stanwyck, Barbara 38, 39, 40–41, 83, 161, 212, 231, 279, 287
Stapleton, Maureen 9–10, **10**, 12, 82, 136, 287
Star! 199
The Star 165, 167, 241

A Star Is Born (1937 movie) 51, 83, 123, 279
A Star Is Born (1954 movie) 38, 116, 152, 223
A Star Is Born (1976 movie) 98, 258
Star Wars 87, 106, 107, **107**, 108, 250
Star Wars movies 250
Starman 63, 64
Starting Over 251
Steel Magnolias 20–21, **20**, 95
Steenburgen, Mary 136
Steiger, Rod 11, 144, 151, 171, 195–196
Steinbeck, John 75
Stella Dallas (1925 movie) 8
Stella Dallas (1937 movie) 40, 41, 83, 231, 279
Stephenson, James 157
Sterling, Jan 192
Stern, Itzhak 26
Steve Jobs 65
Stevens, George 38, 101, 159, 212
Stevens, Stella 87, 238
Stevens, Thaddeus 13, 76
Stevie 106
Steward, Kimberly 273
Stewart, James 69, 75, 96, 117, 124, 126, 128–130, 161, 162–163, 173, 178, **178**, 226, 258, 288
Stewart, Paul 264
Still Alice 45, 46, 285
The Sting 60, 149, 172, 267, 268
Stone, Irving 7
Stone, Sharon 22
The Story of G.I. Joe 246
The Story of Louis Pasteur 15, 51, 52, 154, 161
La Strada 99, 100
Straight, Beatrice 90, 103, 218
The Straight Story 77
Strasberg, Lee 140
The Stratton Story 216
The Strawberry Blonde 254
Streep, Meryl 18, 21, 24, 36, 49, 59, 67, 78, 110, 113, 114, 136, 137, 139, **145**, 148, 149, 158, 164, 167, 179–182, **182**, 203, 207, 218, 272, 288
Street Angel 279
Street Smart 43
A Streetcar Named Desire (movie) 11, 73, 79, 81, 88, 99, 101, 124, 151, 178, 191, 240, 269
A Streetcar Named Desire (television) 138
A Streetcar Named Desire (theater) 99, 200–201
Streisand, Barbra 37, 98, 105, 169, 179, 228, 258–259, 268
Stromboli 169
Stroud, Robert 38
Stuart, Gloria 59, 65
The Stunt Man 108, 110
The Subject Was Roses 68
Sudden Fear 99, 188, 189, 200, 201
Suddenly, Last Summer 73, 116, 158, 159, 177, 179, 241

Sugar Babies 96
Sullivan, Annie 49
Sullivan, Barry 7
Summer and Smoke 73, 112, 113
Summer Wishes, Winter Dreams 36, 37
Summertime 177, 178, 179
Sunday Bloody Sunday 104, 105, 163
The Sundowners 54, 55, 88, 246–247
Sunrise 279
Sunrise at Campobello 92, 93
Sunset Boulevard (movie) 155, 198, 234, 240
Sunset Boulevard (theater) 211
The Sunshine Boys 196, 197
Superman 120
Suspicion 93, 121, 166, 185, 224
Suzman, Janet 56, 105
Suzy 252
Swan Lake 208
Swank, Hilary **44**, 45, 65, 66, 76, 78–79, 95, 219, 272, 287
Swanson, Gloria 254, 257
The Swarm 122
Sweeney Todd: The Demon Barber of Fleet Street 243
Sweet and Lowdown 66, 77, 124, 125
Sweet Bird of Youth (movie) 112, 113, 171
Sweet Bird of Youth (theater) 113
Sweet Charity 53
Sweet Dreams 113, 136, 137, 218
"Sweet Leilani" 99, 191
Swing Shift 218, 270
Swing Time 227
Sybil 94
Syriana 130, 131, 273

A Tale of Two Cities 8
The Talented Mr. Ripley 18, 133, 139, 273
The Talk of the Town 8
Tamblyn, Russ 213
Tamiroff, Akim 156, 161
Tandy, Jessica 81, 203
Taps 125
Taradash, Daniel 27
Tarantino, Quentin 76, 85, 285
Taxi Driver 17, 103, 140, 141, 217
Taylor, Elizabeth 5, 36, **40**, 49, 51, 53, 55, 56, 116, 158–160, **160**, 179, 187, 209, 229, 240–241, 243, 288
Taylor, Rod 134
Teacher's Pet 196, 248
Teena, Brandon 78, 79
Temple, Shirley 96, 103, 186, 229–230, **230**
10 199
The Ten Commandments 69, 236
Tender Mercies 91, 92, 133
The Tender Trap (movie) 68
"The Tender Trap" (song) 68
The Tenth Man 30
Terms of Endearment 53, 77, 175, 176, 218

Test Pilot 237, 258
Testament 217, 218
Thalberg, Irving 3, 57
Thank God He Met Lizzie 138
"Thanks for the Memory" 254, 282
Thatcher, Margaret 180, 181
Their Own Desire 56, 57
Thelma & Louise 47, 48, 103, 272
Theodora Goes Wild 85, 211, 212
The Theory of Everything 274
There Will Be Blood 131, 163, 164, 165
Theron, Charlize 36, 73, 284
These Three 156
"They Can't Take That Away from Me" 228
They Knew What They Wanted 157, 246
They Shoot Horses, Don't They? 134, 142, 143, 175, 196
The Thin Man 237
The Thin Red Line 130
The Third Man 264
Thirteen 27, 28
Thirteen Conversations About One Thing 14
Thirty Seconds Over Tokyo 246
This Property Is Condemned 268
This Sporting Life 105
The Thomas Crown Affair 197, 249
Thompson, Emma 45, 48, 56, 65, 97–99, **98**, 285, 288
Thompson, J. Lee 141
Thornton, Billy Bob 23
Thoroughly Modern Millie 199
A Thousand Clowns 87
The Three Faces of Eve 36, 54
Three Little Words 228
The Three Musketeers 226
3 Women 62
Thunderbolt and Lightfoot 63, 64, 272
Tibbett, Lawrence 235, 257
Tilly, Jennifer 84
"Tit for Tat" 235
Titanic (1953 movie) 41
Titanic (1997 movie) 59, 64, 65, 89, 203
To Be or Not to Be (1942 movie) 246
To Be or Not to Be (1983 movie) 190
To Catch a Thief 224
To Die For 22
To Each His Own 38, 121, 122
To Have and Have Not 228
To Kill a Mockingbird 39, 91, 109, 117, 118
To Sir, with Love 73
Todd, Mike 159
Tolstoy, Leo 25
Tolstoy, Sofya 24, 25
Tom Jones 72, 213, 249
Tomei, Marisa 62, 97, 204, 205
Tomlin, Lily 11
Tommy 105
Tomorrow Is Forever 241
Tone, Franchot 183, 194

Index

Tonight and Every Night 254
Tootsie 25, 136, 137, 144, 145, 172
Top Gun 242, 261
Top Hat 227
Topkapi 88
Topper 224
Tortilla Flat 154
A Touch of Class 37, 61, 104, 105
Toulouse-Lautrec, Alphonse Charles de 189
Toulouse-Lautrec, Henri de 189, 266
The Towering Inferno 47, 64, 172, 197, 198, 227, 228, 249
Towne, Robert 266
Toy Story 128
Toys in the Attic 113
Tracy, Spencer 52, 72, 85, 87, 91, 96, 123, 124, 128, 146, 152–155, **155**, 156, 159, 171, 178, 179, 196, 199, 202, 221, 245, 259, 288
Traffic 64, 214, 261
Training Day 125, 146, 148, 202, 244, 275
Travels with My Aunt 134
Travers, P.L. 99
The Treasure of the Sierra Madre 15, 16, 174, 189, 191, 200, 265, 266
A Tree Grown in Brooklyn 246
The Tree of Life 273
Treves, Frederick 30
Trevor, Claire 192, 228, 236
Trial 149, 212, 213
Tribute 148
The Trip to Bountiful 112, 113–114, 181
"The Trolley Song" 223
Tropic Thunder 242
The Trouble with Harry 53
Troy 273
True Grit (1969 movie) 32, 91, 144, 209, 224, **225**
True Grit (2010 movie) 63, 64, 274
The Truman Show 218
Tucker, Sophie 253
Tucker: The Man and His Dream 201
Turner, Ike 127
Turner, Kathleen 31, 62
Turner, Lana 7, 31, 36, 137
Turner, Tina 237
The Turning Point 35, 49, 50, 53
12 Angry Men 74, 75, 150
12 Monkeys 77, 272, 273
Twelve O'Clock High 117, 118
12 Years a Slave 29, 272, 273
Twister 18
Two-Faced Woman 42
Two Women 73, 74, 113, 241, 277
Tyson, Cicely 237

Ullmann, Liv 1
Umeki, Miyoshi 233–234
Under the Volcano 213–214
Under the Yum Yum Tree 149

Unforgiven 112, 119, 120, 271, 272
Union Pacific 99
An Unmarried Woman 113, 143
The Unsinkable Molly Brown 229
The Untouchables 43, 147
Up in Arms 282
Up in the Air 64, 130, 131
Ure, Mary 195
Ustinov, Peter **40**, 76, 87–89, 279, 288
The Usual Suspects 77, 218

Vaccaro, Brenda 7
Valentino, Rudolph 119, 221, 251–252
The Valiant 51
Valiant Is the World for Carrie 231
The Valley of Decision 92, 93, 117
Van Dyke, Dick 9
Van Fleet, Jo 244
Van Gogh, Vincent 6, 7
Venus 108, 110
The Verdict 25, 170, 171–172
Verdon, Gwen 36
Verrill, Virginia 252
Vertigo 130
Vicky Cristina Barcelona 204, 205
Victor Victoria 199, 200
Victoria (monarch) 89
Vidor, Charles 277
Vidor, King 227
La Vie en Rose 34
The Vikings 7
The V.I.P.s 134, 159
Viva Zapata! 99, 151, 209
Voight, Jon 31, 32–33, 66, 141, 144, 250, 285, 287
Volver 205
von Sternberg, Josef 161, 278
Voyage of the Damned 10, 11, 103, 190, 195, 199, 217

Wag the Dog 144
Wahlberg, Mark 273
Waikiki Wedding 99, 191
Wait Until Dark 14, 115, 116
Walburn, Raymond **162**
Walk on the Wild Side 142
Walken, Christopher 59, 214
Walker, Alice 270
The Wall of Malapage 277
Wall Street 16, 260, 261
Wallace, Cornelia 66
Wallace, Sir William 239
Wallach, Ira 88
Walsh, Kevin J. 273
Walsingham, Francis 23
Walters, Barbara 228
Walters, Julie 133
Waltz, Christoph 13–14, 15, 75–77, 85, 142, 274, 285, 287

War and Peace 116
War of the Worlds (radio) 260, 264
Washbourne, Mona 106
Washington, Denzel 43, 77, 78, 125, 136, 146–148, **147**, 201, 202, 208, 244, 274, 275, 288
The Washington Post 87
Watanabe, Ken 242, 262
Waters, Ethel 12, 71
The Way of All Flesh 278
The Way We Were 37, 105, 258, 268
"The Way You Look Tonight" 227
Wayne, John 32, 64, 92, 110, 113, 144, 162, 209, 224–225, **225**, 238, 240
Weaver, Jacki 95
Weaver, Sigourney 45, 103, 112, 133, 250, 285
Webb, Clifton 174, 283
Wedding Crashers 274
Weingarten, Lawrence 179
Weir, Peter 250
Weisz, Rachel 214, 220
Weld, Tuesday 35, 197
Welles, Orson 68, 92, 130, 216, 241, 260, 264–265
Wertmüller, Lina 141
West, Mae 224, 253
West Side Story 26, 73, 223, 241
The Westerner 76, 156, 157, **157**, 161
The Whales of August 227
What Ever Happened to Baby Jane? 93, 165, 167, **167**, 179, 189
What's Eating Gilbert Grape 58, 243
What's Love Got to Do with It 127, 237
What's the Matter with Helen? 216
Whitaker, Forest 110, 244
White Banners 194
White Christmas (movie) 192
"White Christmas" (song) 192
White Heat 193
White Nights 113
Whitty, Dame May 137
Who's Afraid of Virginia Woolf? 49, 133, 158, 159, **160**, 197, 209
Wiest, Dianne 24, 76, 77, 84–85, 102, 136, 287
Wigand, Jeffrey 202
Wild Is the Wind 36, 99
Wild, Wild West 216
Wilde, Ted 233
Wilder, Billy 53, 149, 240
Wilkinson, Tom 62, 125, 204
William Shakespeare's Romeo + Juliet 59
Williams, Michelle 29, 219–220
Williams, Paul 98, 258
Williams, Robin 16–17, **17**, 30, 43, 141, 163, 251, 287
Williams, Tennessee 73, 112, 113, 159, 268
Willimon, Beau 130
Wills, Chill 88
Wilson 187, 191

Wilson, Woodrow 191
Winchester '73 130
Winfrey, Oprah 270–271
Winger, Debra 30, 53
Wings 161
The Wings of the Dove 89
Winningham, Mare 77
Winslet, Kate 24, 59, 64–66, 67, 89, 90, **98**, 205, 287
Winters, Jonathan 88
Winters, Shelley 6, **34**, 73, 76, 85, 100–103, **102**, 134, 159, 259, 288
Winter's Bone 28, 29
Wise, Robert 51, 199, 249
With a Song in My Heart (movie) 50, 210
"With a Song in My Heart" (song) 233
Witness 31, 33, 249, 250
Witness for the Prosecution 193, 194, 245
The Wizard of Oz 223
The Wolf of Wall Street 58, 60
Woman of the Year 154, 177, 178, 194
A Woman Under the Influence 206, 276
Women in Love 104, 105, 217
Wonder Boys 19, 261
Wonder Man 282
Wood, Natalie 53, 73, 149, 197, 239, 241, 249, 259, 267, 268
Wood, Sam 215
Woodard, Alfre 270
Woodley, Shailene **131**
Woodward, Joanne 36–37, 54, 171, 205, 287
Woolf, Virginia 21, 22
Woolley, Monty 255, 280
Working Girl 103, 250, 285
The World According to Garp 16, 210, 211
Wray, Fay 136
The Wrestler 126, 204, 205
Wright, Teresa 137, 156, 184–185
Written on the Wind 228
Wuornos, Aileen 36
Wuthering Heights 96, 129, 172, 173
Wyler, William 6, 69, 76, 124, 156, 157, 194, 240, 269, 270, 283
Wyman, Jane 37–38, 41, 122, 212, 216, 241, 287
Wynyard, Diana 177

X-Men: Days of Future Past 29, 237

Yankee Doodle Dandy 15, 16, 192, 193
The Year of Living Dangerously 139, 239
The Yearling 37, 38, 117, 124
Yentl 258
Yesterday, Today and Tomorrow 277
York, Alvin 160, 161
You Can't Take It with You 129, 257
"You Take My Breath Away" 242, 261
You'll Never Get Rich 254
Young, Gig 82, 88, 175, 196, 248

Young, Loretta 12, 222
Young, Neil 127
Young Frankenstein 120
Young Mr. Lincoln 15, 74
You're a Big Boy Now 112, 113

Zaentz, Saul 260, 261
Zapata, Emiliano 99, 151

Zapata, Eufemio 99
Zellweger, Renée 22, 45, 203–204
Zeta-Jones, Catherine 203
Ziegfeld, Florenz 83
Zindel, Paul 37
Zinnemann, Fred 56, 68, 269
Zola, Emile 51
Zorba the Greek 99, 100, 216